Pension Rights and Free Movement of Persons

Anna Tsetoura

Pension Rights and Free Movement of Persons

Springer

Anna Tsetoura
Social Sciences Faculty
Hellenic Open University
Patras, Greece

ISBN 978-3-031-91126-2 ISBN 978-3-031-91127-9 (eBook)
https://doi.org/10.1007/978-3-031-91127-9

This Springer imprint is published by the registered company Springer Nature Switzerland AG
The registered company address is: Gewerbestrasse 11, 6330 Cham, Switzerland

Competing Interests The author has no competing interests to declare that are relevant to the content of this manuscript.

Contents

Chapter 1
Introduction

Pensions are an issue for citizens who want adequate retirement benefits, for employers seeking cost-effective retirement benefits for their employees and for governments who throughout the Union are facing ageing populations.[1] Thus, the potential benefits of better cross-border pension provision are substantial.[2] One in four EU citizens depend on their pension income.[3] Citizens who work or reside in a state other than their state of origin represent a considerable size, as around 5.1 million European citizens aged 15 years and over reside in a Member State other than their Member State of origin.[4] Thus, the purpose of EU Regulations, in particular in the area of social security, has been, already since 1958, to circumvent, even partially, the implementation of the territorial sovereignty principle in order to achieve genuine free movement.[5]

In that a citizen of the European Union must be granted in all Member States the same treatment in law as that accorded to the national of those Member States who find themselves in the same situation, it would be incompatible with the right of freedom of movement were a citizen, in the Member State of which he is a national, to receive treatment less favourable than he would enjoy if he had not availed himself of the opportunities offered by the Treaty in relation to freedom of movement.[6] In exercising their competences Member States must also comply with

[1] Commission of the European Communities (2001), Communication from the Commission to the Council, the European Parliament and the Economic and Social Committee, The elimination of tax obstacles to the cross-border provision of occupational pensions, Brussels, 19.4.2001 COM(2001) 214, p. 3.

[2] Commission of the European Communities (2001), Communication from the Commission to the Council, the European Parliament and the Economic and Social Committee, The elimination of tax obstacles to the cross-border provision of occupational pensions, Brussels, 19.4.2001 COM(2001) 214, p. 3.

[3] Eatock (2015), p. 1.

[4] Eurostat New Cronos Database, domain: Labour Force Study (2001), p. 3.

[5] Cornelissen (1996), pp. 439–471.

A. Tsetoura, *Pension Rights and Free Movement of Persons*,
https://doi.org/10.1007/978-3-031-91127-9_1

Community law, in particular with the TFEU provisions giving every citizen of the Union the right to move and reside freely within the territory of the Member States.[7] Thus, as the Court has stated on many occasions, the Coordination Regulation has not set up a common scheme of social security, but allows different national schemes to exist and its sole objective is to coordinate those national schemes and laws,[8] each of which determines the conditions for affiliation to the various security schemes.[9]

Of course, the interaction between EU law and national social security law directly affects the evolution of national law in Member States. Indeed, the establishment of some regulations on an EU level, as well as the interpretation of the Regulations by the Court can prompt Member States to amend their national law so as to extend or limit the rights of both their nationals as well as of foreigners.[10] Coordination is a way of communication between national laws[11]that adjust their social security systems with regard to one another.[12]

1.1 The EU Regulation on Coordination of Social Security Systems

Since 1959, the Union has had a European system for coordinating Member States' social security systems that protects the rights of people moving within the Union. This means that the social protection of a significant number of people depends, in whole or in part, on the proper functioning of the coordination system.[13] The fundamental principle of the free movement of persons, services and capital (Articles 45–66 TFEU), as well as the prohibition of discrimination and Union citizenship (Articles 18–25 TFEU) are among the objectives to be fulfilled by EU. At the level of social security, the legal basis of the above principles, in application of which the Coordination Regulations have been established, lies in particular in articles 45–48

[6]Judgments of 11.07.2002, C-224/98, D'Hoop, European Court Reports, p. I-6191, paragraph 30; of 29.04.2004, C-224/02, Pusa, European Court Reports 2004, p. I-05763, paragraph 18.

[7]Judgment of 26.10.2006, C-192/05, Tas-Hagen and R. A. Tas, European Court Reports 2006, p. I-10451, paragraph 22.

[8]Judgment of 15.07.1988, Case 21/87, Borowitz, European Court Reports 1988 p. 03715, paragraph 23; Judgment of 12.06.1980, Case 733/79, Laterza, European Court Reports 1980 p. 1915, paragraph 8; Judgment of 09.07.1980, Case 807/79, Gravina, European Court Reports 1980 p. 2205, paragraph 7.

[9]Judgment of 12.07.1979, Case 266/78, Brunori, European Court Reports 1979 p. 02705, paragraph 5.

[10]Runft (1991), p. 9.

[11]Stergiou (1997), p. 9.

[12]Pennings (2003), p. 6.

[13]Commission of the European Communities (1997) Communication from the Commission, COM (97), p. 4.

(free movement of workers) in combination with article 21 (citizen's right Union to move and reside freely in the territory of member states) of the TFEU.

Beyond any doubt, the EU Coordination Regulation is the most important coordination tool in Europe and its rules are constantly being developed by the legislature and the Court, making it the most comprehensive and complex legal creation in the word.[14]The new basic Regulation No 883/04[15] came into force only in 2010 (01.05.2010) with the Implementing Regulation No 987/09[16] replacing the previous basic Regulation No 1408/71[17] and its Implementing Regulation No 574/72[18] respectively. The Regulations were adopted on the legal basis of free movement of workers as provided for in Article 48 TFEU relied on the idea that the coordination of national social security systems would benefit the free movement of workers.[19] Some of the decisions of the CJEU on coordination and the free movement of persons brought about a certain form of harmonization (negative integration).[20] The advantage of coordination though is that each member state can design and retain the social security system it can afford and that fits its labour market and cultural values.[21]

1.2 Objectives and Structure of the Book

Pension protection covers all phases of a person's life. Pension rights are related with the type of a pension system, the differences between the systems of the states under the application of which a moving person might fall and the benefits to which a moving pensioner is entitled. Pension benefits are a key aspect of social protection in the European Union.[22] For people with a European “pension CV”, there is no single European pension, but partial pensions paid in full to the beneficiary by the Member States involved, even if the beneficiary resides in another Member State (cross border pensions).[23] There is therefore an Europeanization of the Member States' obligation to grant and pay the pension due by them.[24]

The main objective of this book is to investigate the protection of pensions rights of the persons moving across EU. Coordination Regulation applies to pensioners

[14] Strban (2009), p. 86.

[15] Regulation (EC) No 883/2004, OJ L 166 of 30.4.2004, p. 1.

[16] Regulation (EC) No 987/2009, OJ L 284 of 30.10.2009, p. 1.

[17] Regulation (EEC) No 1408/71, OJ L 149, 5.7.1971, p. 2.

[18] Regulation (EEC) No 574/72, OJ L 74, 27.3.72, p. 138.

[19] Stevens (2022, 2024), p. 13.

[20] Pennings (2022), p. 7.

[21] Pennings and Vonk (2023), p. 442.

[22] Commission of the European Communities (1997), COM (97) 102.

[23] Schuler (2015), p. 337.

[24] Ibid.

who find themselves in cross-borders situations as European citizens. Our book consists of three parts. Part I includes Chaps. 2 and 3, Part II Chaps. 4 and 5, Part III Chaps. 6 and 7. The questions we have to answer are to which pension systems and pension benefits the coordination mechanism applies and what a pensioner has to "lose" while receiving more benefits from different member states. The key concepts for our purpose are: pension systems through which a person might move (Part I), pension benefits to which a person will be entitled at retirement (Part II) and pension loss which the pensioner might face in view of the receipt of more benefits (Part III).

In **Chap. 2** of the book, attempting to illustrate pension protection, we begin with presenting the pension systems, as there are various pension schemes and their classification is important in order to place a scheme under Coordination Regulation (or not). The classification includes public main and supplementary pension schemes which are differentiated from private pension schemes. Specifically, the new Regulation 883/2004 on coordination of social security systems does not provide a definition of the term 'social security systems' despite the title of this legal instrument. The key concepts to be analysed are social security system, statutory pension scheme, main and supplementary pension protection. The analysis of the said concepts is considered necessary in order to point out the importance of placing a scheme under Coordination Regulation. In parallel, the social role of supplementary pension rights is highlighted. Coordination Regulation tends to provide a broad protection of pension rights. However, it is the member states that will decide if they bring their supplementary pension schemes under Coordination Regulation utilizing the possibility provided i.e. the right to declarations. The example of French supplementary schemes is referred as schemes placed under Coordination Regulation aiming at their protection from competition law. In this vein, the relationship between Coordination Regulation and the Directive on supplementary pension rights is analysed, as well as the concept of the portability of pension rights. In **Chap. 3**, the case-law of the Court of Justice of the European Union is presented so as to bring into the light which pension systems are considered as social security systems according to the jurisprudence's interpretation. The case-law provides for significant interpretative approaches of the characteristics of a pension system pertaining to social security with an emphasis on the concepts of 'social solidarity', 'legislation', 'mandatory or optional affiliation to a scheme'. The element of the public authority intervention in terms of an official recognition of a pension scheme seems to be determinant for Coordination Regulation. At the same time, a part of literature considers certain characteristics crucial in order to conclude if the EU social security law or competition law will be applied on a pension scheme. Afterwards, we conclude which pension systems fall under the scope of Coordination Regulation.

Further, in **Chap. 4**, we examine which pension benefits are regarded as social security benefits to be distinguished from social assistance benefits and special non-contributory benefits. This is because Coordination Regulation applies to those pension benefits which can be considered as social security benefits, while social assistance is excluded from its scope of application. Special non-contributory benefits consist a special category of pension benefits which can be excluded from the basic provisions of Coordination Regulation (exportability) depending on their features and the member states' registrations in the respective Annex of Coordination Regulation. Moreover, in view of the importance of the residence criterion, the concept of residence is examined. Hence, the aim of the chapter is to point out which are the pensions to be coordinated. In **Chap. 5**, we illustrate the complications that have come up due to the new provisions of Coordination Regulation concerning funded schemes which fall under its scope of application and the way that the pension of a moving pensioner is calculated. Funded pension systems differ radically from pay-as-you-go pension systems. However, the whole mechanism of coordination had been built up on the latter, since the systems of the most member states were pay-as-you-go during the previous decades. The pro-rata rule (apportionment method) is suitable for the pay-as-you-go systems where time of insurance is crucial, taking into account all the periods of insurance across the member states and calculating the pension proportionally. Nevertheless, we doubt that the pro-rata rule is suitable for the funded schemes. Hence, there is the need to efficiently coordinate these two types of pension systems, as the persons move from one country to another and from one pension system to another. In view of the arisen issues, we present some ideas which can improve the mobility of pension rights so that the pension protection is not downgraded.

Finally, in Chaps. 6 and 7, we deal with the anti-overlapping rules, namely the rules of Coordination Regulation that apply when a pensioner is entitled to more benefits from different member states. Specifically, in **Chap. 6** we analyse the concept of overlapping and anti-overlapping rules through the case law in order to clarify their meaning and their practical impact which is becoming more complicated taking into account the amendment of the relevant provisions of the Regulation. We present cases before the Court referring to certain pension benefits to which the applicants were entitled in parallel with other benefits. At this point we highlight how a certain interpretative direction of the Court led the rules at issue to become more complicated. Specifically, the Petroni principle, the principle of favourability and the equal treatment between migrant and non-migrant pensioners are analysed. In **Chap. 7**, we explain the new anti-overlapping rules of the Regulation providing examples for each rule and we suggest an interpretation on the basis of our working hypothesis so that the application of the rules would be simpler and fairer. The benefits of the same kind and the benefits of the different kind are presented through the case-law. On the one hand, the practical effects of the anti-overlapping rules are examined in view of the existing interpretative approach; there is a significant pension loss due to the application of the anti-overlapping rules following a certain direction. On the other hand, the practical effects of the anti-overlapping rules are presented in view of our approach following a different direction. Making mathematic calculations to prove that pension loss would be limited following our suggestion, we insist on the importance of this application of anti-overlapping rules for ensuring the pension rights of the European citizens.

References

Commission of the European Communities (1997) Communication from the Commission. Modernising and improving social protection in the European Union. COM (97), Brussels

Cornelissen R (1996) The principle of territoriality and the Community Regulations on social security (Regulations 1408/71 and 574/72). Common Mark Law Rev 33:439–471. In: Cornelissen R, 50 years of European social security coordination. Eur J Soc Secur 11:9–45

Eatock D (2015) European Union pension systems Adequate and sustainable? In: Briefing, European Parliament Think Tank. Available at https://www.europarl.europa.eu/RegData/etudes/BRIE/2015/571327/EPRS_BRI(2015)571327_EN.pdf. Accessed 25 Nov 2024

Commission of the European Communities (2001) Communication from the Commission to the Council, the European Parliament and the Economic and Social Committee. The elimination of tax obstacles to the cross-border provision of occupational pensions. COM (2001) 214 final, Brussels 19.4.2001

Regulation (EC) No 883/2004 of the European Parliament and of the Council of 29 April 2004 on the coordination of social security systems, OJ L 166 of 30.4.2004, p.1

Regulation (EC) No 987/2009 of the European Parliament and of the Council of 16 September 2009 laying down the procedure for implementing Regulation (EC) No 883/2004 on the coordination of social security systems, OJ L 284 of 30.10.2009, p.1

Regulation (EEC) No 1408/71 of the Council of 14 June 1971 on the application of social security schemes to employed persons and their families moving within the Community, OJ L 149, 5.7.1971, p.2

Regulation (EEC) No 574/72 of the Council of 21 March 1971 fixing the procedure for implementing Regulation (EEC) No 1408/71 on the application of social security schemes to employed persons and their families moving within the Community, OJ L 74, 27.3.1972, p. 138

Eurostat New Cronos database (2001) domain: Labour Force Study, in Commission of the European Communities (2001) Communication from the Commission to the Council, the European Parliament and the Economic and Social Committee, The elimination of tax obstacles to the cross-border provision of occupational pensions. COM, Brussels

Pennings F (2003) Introduction to European social security law, 4th edn. Intersentia, Antwerp-Oxford-New York

Pennings F (2022) European social security law, 7th edn. Intersentia, Antwerp – Oxford-New York, p 7

Pennings F, Vonk G (2023) The future of European social security law. In: Pennings F, Vonk G (eds) Research handbook on European social security law, 2nd edn. Edward Elgar Publishing, UK-USA, p 442

Runft H (1991) Unification of Europe and social security of repatriates - the limits of community and national social security law. Ant. N. Sakkoulas Publishing, Athens-Komotini

Schuler R (2015) Regulation (EC) No 883/04-Overview. In: Fuchs M, Cornelissen R (eds) EU social security law- a commentary on EU Regulations 883/2004 and 987/2009. C.H. Beck-Hart- Nomos, Baden-Baden, p 337

Stergiou A (1997) The Community Judicature and the coordination of the social security systems. Sakkoulas Publications, Thessaloniki

Stevens Y (2022) EU pension law. Edward Elgar Publishing, UK-USA

Stevens Y (2024) EU pension law. Edward Elgar Publishing, UK-USA

Strban G (2009) The existing bilateral and multicultural social security instruments binding EU states and non-EU states. In: Pieters D, Schouckens P (eds) The social security co-ordination between the EU and non-EU countries. Intersentia, Antwerp-Oxford-Portland, p 86

Part I
Pension Systems

Chapter 2
Main and Supplementary Pension Protection

2.1 Conceptual Framework

When studying pensions from a legal angle, one realises quickly that pensions are truly a highly technical, fragmented and detailed topic.[1] Most analysts agree that even if social security is perceived as a public good, it is neither entirely public nor entirely private, thus making it easy for a given social security system to be subject to a mixed governance structure, a characteristic common to most public services.[2]

As the Social Protection Committee has pointed out, the classification followed by the multi-pillar system has not been incorporated into EU legislation, as the concept of pillars has not been included in the defined scope of the EU institutions, while the boundaries between the three pillars are not clearly distinguishable, resulting in different views on the pillar to which a pension system belongs.[3] However, the European Commission has used the pillar model extensively in its communications to describe European systems by placing them in a common framework.[4]

In particular, the **Commission** refers to the **three-pillar model**:[5] "The **first pillar** consists of statutory schemes, in which participation is generally compulsory for the entire employed or resident population. These schemes are usually financed on a **pay-as-you-go basis**, where current contributions are used directly to finance pension payments to retired people. These pension benefits are guaranteed by the State and the scheme is usually managed by a public body. **Second pillar** schemes may be set up unilaterally by an employer or as a result of a collective agreement or a

[1] Stevens (2022), p. 2.

[2] Vonk (2010), pp. 2–15.

[3] The Social Protection Committee (2008), pp. 6–7.

[4] Commission of the European Communities (2001), The elimination of tax obstacles to the cross-border provision of occupational pensions, Brussels, 19.4.2001 COM (2001) 214 final, p. 5.

[5] Ibid.

A. Tsetoura, *Pension Rights and Free Movement of Persons*,
https://doi.org/10.1007/978-3-031-91127-9_2

contract agreed individually or collectively between the employer(s) and the employee(s) or their respective representatives. In general, under the second pillar **employers and/or employees pay contributions to a pension institution, which invests them**. The assets held by the pension institution are used to pay retirement benefits to the members of the scheme. The **third pillar** consists of **individual schemes**, which generally take the form of contracts taken out by individuals, in their personal capacity, with life assurance companies or other financial institutions, although some Member States have personal pension schemes to which both employer and employees contribute".

Thus, in many EU countries, the budgetary provision for old age has traditionally been based on the three proposed pillars: a state system (usually a **pay-as-you-go** system) under public management with compulsory membership and a limited objective of alleviating poverty in the elderly (first pillar), a **funded** occupational system under private management but also with compulsory membership (second pillar) and finally, private pension plans/savings (third pillar).[6] Moreover, social security systems are financed in two broad ways, by **contributions** (regular payments made by insured persons and/or employers either flat-rate or a percentage of earnings) or by **taxes** (all types of financing from the state budget, including income taxes, consumption taxes, etc.).[7]

Further, as it is argued, what differentiates one type of pension system from another is the set of rules governing the calculation of benefits when the insured retires.[8] There are three different calculation methods in the European Union countries: defined-contribution, defined-benefit and notional defined-contribution.[9] In a **defined contribution (DC)** pension plan, employees accumulate money in individual accounts managed by the plan sponsor, while their contributions are deducted directly from their pay-checks and the employer's portion of these contributions is often matched by that of the employer.[10] The pension benefit accumulated during the employee's working career will depend on the contributions paid while working and the investment returns generated by the balance in the plan.[11] The **defined benefit (DB)** plan, in contrast, calculates the benefit in relation to factors such as the final salary, length of pensionable service and age of the members, and not to the value of the fund's assets.[12] Of course, if the state guarantees, as is often the case, a minimum level of benefits in an otherwise defined contribution system, the system de facto provides defined benefits up to a certain level.[13] In any case, most studies conclude that participants bear the brunt of the risk in DC systems, while employers assume

[6]OECD (2005), p. 22; Deutsche Bank (2003), p. 20.

[7]MISSOC (2024); European Commission (2014a).

[8]Blake (1998), p. 265.

[9]Saritas (2019), p. 3.

[10]Broadbent et al. (2006), p. 7.

[11]Ibid.

[12]Blake (1998), p. 265.

[13]European Commission (2001a), p. 8.

most of the risks in traditional DB systems.[14] In particular, the distribution of risks regarding future levels of pension benefits is different in funded DC schemes, compared to DB or unfunded schemes, given that the final outcome in funded DC schemes is generally unknown, since it depends on future levels of rates of return, and not only on "pension accruals".[15] As to the **defined-contribution schemes (NDC)**, according to World Bank:[16] "Notional accounts are designed to mimic a defined contribution plan, where the pension depends on contributions and investment returns. (For this reason, they are sometimes called 'notional, defined-contribution' schemes). Pension contributions are tracked in accounts which earn a rate of return. However, in notional accounts, the return that contributions earn is a notional one, set by the government, not the product of investment returns in the markets. Pension accounts in this system are called 'notional' because there is no pot of pension fund money, just a series of individual claims on the future public budget. When the individual reaches pension age, accumulated contributions and notional returns—termed notional capital—are converted to an annuity. By adjusting the annuity rate, the government can adjust the pension value to take account of life expectancy".

Finally, there are also pension unit systems, in which employees earn pension points/pension units based on their earnings and years of contribution and upon retirement, the sum of the pension units is multiplied by a pension unit value to convert them into a regular pension payment.[17]

To begin with, despite its new title "Regulation on the coordination of social security systems", the Regulation contains no definition of social security or a social security system. In the absence of a generally accepted definition of social security and the relevant definition of a social security system, the issue shifts to the field of pensions, where it is crucial to determine which pension system is subject to the Regulation. Moreover, the Regulation does not establish a general criterion for a precise distinction between social security and social assistance, given the fact that the old conceptual categories tend to lose their clarity.[18] These issues are crucial in order to determine whether and how the Regulation applies to the coordination of the various pension systems that establish cross-border movement, which pension benefits are coordinated and how the pension of a migrant person is ultimately calculated. However, where a social security system and consequently a pension

---

[14] OECD (2011), p. 10; European Parliament (2011), Directorate General for Internal Policies-Policy Department A: Economic and Scientific Policy, "Pension systems in the EU – contingent liabilities and assets in the public and private sector", p. 33.

[15] The Social Protection Committee (2008), p. 4.

[16] World Bank Pension Reform Primer, "Notional accounts -Notional defined contribution plans as a pension reform strategy", p. 1 https://www.worldbank.org/ext/en/home.

[17] OECD (2005); OECD (2015), p. 124. Such systems (pension points systems), where employees earn pension points based on their individual earnings for each year of contribution, have been identified in France and specifically in occupational schemes and in the public systems of Estonia, Germany and Slovakia.

[18] Tsantilas (1996), p. 35.

scheme fall under the Regulation, it does not mean that all benefits potentially provided under this system shall also be covered. After all, the Court itself examines any disputed benefit in order to determine whether it constitutes a social security benefit and is therefore subject to the Regulation or whether it constitutes social assistance which is excluded from the material scope of the Regulation.

The key criterion for the application of the Regulation is the affiliation with a social security system, even against a single risk.[19] Taking into account the general provisions, in order to determine whether a pension system is subject to the material scope of Regulation, according to Article 3 of Regulation No 883/04 (Article 4 of Regulation No 1408/71), it should first be decided whether it is based on the legislation within the meaning of Article 1 (l) of Regulation No 883/04—previously Article 1 (j) of Regulation No 1408/71.

2.2 Statutory Pension Scheme

Subject to the provision of Article 3 (1) of Regulation No 883/04, this Regulation applies to the *legislations* that concern social security branches relating to the social risks listed in the same Article. It should therefore be examined whether a pension system is statutory. Of course, the distinction between the schemes for which the application of the coordination regulations is most suitable and those that should be regulated by other legal instruments is not always easy.[20] As a result, the Commission did not proceed with its initial 1998 proposal for Regulation No 883/04 to also include non-statutory pension schemes.[21] The frequently used term "pension fund" refers to pension schemes using a particular financing method.[22] Stevens claims that Coordination Regulation 883/2004 only applies to statutory pension schemes and the coordination provided for in the Regulation does not extend to supplementary or occupational schemes.[23]

However, in order to determine the content of the term "legislation" as contained in Article 3 (1) of Regulation No 883/04 regarding the material scope of the Regulation, reference should be made to the relevant article of the Regulation containing the definition of legislation.

It is worth noting that **as long as collective agreements and supplementary pension schemes meet the above conditions, they can fall within the scope of the Regulation.** This is expressly noted by the Court, according to which, when old-age benefits have been mentioned in a declaration under Article 9 of Regulation No

[19] Mavridis (2004), p. 810.

[20] Leppik (2006), pp. 47–51.

[21] Verschueren (2009), p. 146.

[22] Commission of the European Communities (1991), Communication from the Commission to the Council, SEC (91) 1332, p. 1, footnote 1.

[23] Stevens (2022, 2024), pp. 13–14.

883/2004, they fall within the scope of that regulation.[24] The Court has ruled that Article 5(a) of Regulation No 883/2004 must be interpreted as meaning that (in circumstances such as those at issue in the main proceedings of the Knauer case) old-age benefits provided under an occupational pension scheme of one Member State and those provided under a statutory pension scheme of another Member State—both schemes being within the scope of that regulation—are equivalent benefits within the meaning of that provision, where both categories of benefits have the same aim of ensuring that their recipients maintain a standard of living commensurate with that which they enjoyed prior to retirement.[25]

2.3 The Right to Declarations

Although in some countries collective agreements regulate an important part of social security and have been declared binding, they do not fall within the scope of the Regulation; this is due to the conditions laid down by the provisions mentioned above, provided that Member States have not availed themselves of the right provided by them.[26] France is an exception: with the relevant declarations,[27] France integrated its collective agreements on unemployment benefits in the Regulation scope,[28] while with its declaration on 29 March 1999,[29] France included its supplementary pensions schemes ARRCO and AGIRC in the scope of the Regulation.[30]

It is worth noting, that in a recent case the Court held that the principle of sincere cooperation, laid down in Article 4(3) TEU, that every Member State, for the purposes of the declarations covered by Article 5 of Regulation No 1408/71 and Article 9(1) of Regulation No 883/2004, must carry out a proper assessment of its own social security regimes and, if necessary, following that assessment, declare them as falling within the scope of those regulations;[31] it also follows from this

[24] Judgment of the Court of 21.01.2016, Case C-453/14, Knauer, Digital reports (Court Reports - general) ECLI:EU:C:2016:37, paragraph 23, invoking also judgments Mora Romero, C-131/96, EU:C:1997:317, paragraph 25, as well as Pérez García etc., C-225/10, EU:C:2011:678, paragraph 36.

[25] Judgment of the Court of 21.01.2016, Case C-453/14, Knauer, Digital Reports (Court Reports - general) ECLI:EU:C:2016:37, paragraph 38.

[26] Pennings (2012), p. 54.

[27] Official Journal of the EU L 90 of 2 April 1987; Lyon-Caen and Lyon-Caen (1993), p. 226.

[28] Pennings (1990), p. 189.

[29] OJ C 215/1 of 28.07. 1999.

[30] Pennings (2003), p. 60; Pennings (2012), p. 54.

[31] By analogy, judgments of 10.02.2000, Case C-202/97, Fitzwilliam (FTS), European Court Reports 2000 p. I-00883, EU:C:2000:75, paragraph 51, and Judgment of 26.01.2006, Case C-2/05, Herbosch Kiere, European Court Reports 2006 p. I-01079, EU:C:2006:69, paragraph 22.

principle that the other Member States are entitled to expect that the Member State concerned had fulfilled those obligations.[32]

Thus, those declarations create a presumption that the national laws in a declaration under Article 5 of Regulation No 1408/71 or Article 9 of Regulation No 883/2004 fall within the material scope of those regulations and bind, in principle, the other Member States. Conversely, where a Member State has refrained from declaring a national law under those regulations, the other Member States can, generally, infer from it that that law does not fall within the material scope of those regulations.[33]

Moreover, as long as the declarations of a Member State are not amended or withdrawn, the other Member States must take them into account. It is incumbent on the Member State which issued the relevant declaration to reconsider its merits and, possibly, amend it in case where another Member State expresses doubts regarding the accuracy of the declaration.[34] In the first place, if a declaration raises questions and if the Member States cannot reach agreement, in particular regarding the classification of laws or schemes within the scope of Regulations No 1408/71 and No 883/2004, they may turn to the Administrative Commission, mentioned in Articles 80 and 81 of Regulation No 1408/71 and in Articles 71 and 72 of Regulation No 883/2004.[35] In the second place, if the Commission does not succeed in reconciling the points of view of the Member States on the question of the legislation applicable in the case in point, it is, where appropriate, for the Member State doubting the correctness of a declaration by another Member State to tell the Commission or, as a last resort, bring proceedings under Article 259 TFUE in order for the Court to examine, in the context of those proceedings, the question of applicable legislation.[36,37]

However, beyond such exemptions for the French supplementary pension schemes, it is argued that collective agreements do not fall within the scope of the Regulation; as a result, periods of insurance completed abroad cannot be used to complete qualifying periods (vesting periods) in the supplementary pension schemes.[38] To put it otherwise, collective or private agreements that cover social security risks, such as occupational pension schemes that do not correspond to the

---

[32] Judgment of the Court of 03.03.2016, Case C-12/14, European Commission v Republic of Malta, Digital reports (Court Reports - general) ECLI:EU:C:2016:135, paragraph 37.

[33] European Commission v Republic of Malta, paragraph 38.

[34] To that effect, judgment of 30.03.2000, Case C-178/97, Barry Banks, European Court Reports 2000 I-02005, EU:C:2000:169, paragraph 43.

[35] Judgment of the Court of 03.03.2016, Case C-12/14, European Commission v Republic of Malta, Digital reports (Court Reports - general) ECLI:EU:C:2016:135, paragraph 41.

[36] Along the same lines, judgment of 30.03.2000, Case C-178/97, European Court Reports 2000 page I-02005, EU:C:2000:169, paragraph 44.

[37] Judgment of the Court of 03.03.2016, Case C-12/14, European Commission v Republic of Malta, Digital reports (Court Reports - general) ECLI:EU:C:2016:135, paragraph 41.

[38] Pennings (2012), p. 54.

express conditions above, are deemed excluded from the scope.[39] As will be demonstrated, supplementary pension schemes may fall within the scope of the Regulations based on the criteria adopted by the Regulation. In fact, the supplementary pension schemes of some Member States that have made a declaration in Annex VIII, part 2 regarding the application of Article 52 (5) of Regulation No 883/04 already fall within that scope.

2.4 Supplementary and Occupational Insurance

What the national systems in the EU do have in common is that they are based on three pillars.[40] There are, however, major differences in the weighting and the financing of the various pillars (subsistence protection versus protection of living standards). The first pillar of pension provision is financed either from taxes or on a pay-as-you-go basis; the latter means that pension rights are acquired while the person entitled to a pension is still working through payment of the pensions of the current generation of pensioners.[41] The first pillar, the compulsory state pension scheme, has been joined by a second, company pensions, and a third, private provision very largely based on the funding system.[42] According to Stevens, although this model has become quasi-archetypical throughout the world, legally speaking, it cannot be said to exist, as the enormous technical and legal differences between countries are just too great and wide to be covered by this model.[43]

As to the supplementary pension protection, it has to be noted that various synonym terms are often used to denote supplementary pensions. Thus, such pensions are sometimes referred to as supplementary, other times as ancillary and sometimes as occupational. As Stevens observes, the three-pillar model, in which ‘statutory pension’ represent the first pillar, ‘supplementary pensions’ the second pillar and ‘personal pensions’ the third pillar, has become a common starting point when analysing the pension systems in the EU.[44] From his legal perspective though, models or typologies of pension schemes do not exist because of the immense

[39] Verschueren (2011), slide 26.

[40] Committee on Economic and Monetary Affairs (1999), Draft Report on the communication from the Commission ‘Towards a single market for supplementary pensions – results of the consultations on the Green Paper on supplementary pensions in the single market’ (COM(1999)134 – C5-0135/1999 – 1999/2131(COS)), Rapporteur: Wilfried Kuckelkorn, PR\384894.en.doc, p. 11.

[41] Ibid.

[42] Ibid.

[43] Stevens (2022), p. 1.

[44] Ibid.

technical and legal differences,[45] while he also considers the relevance of categorising pension systems highly questionable in legal terms.[46]

Other scholars note that, **the terms "ancillary insurance", "supplementary insurance" and "occupational insurance" can be considered as synonymous.**[47]

Indeed, the Commission itself noted in a relevant communication that **as far as pension schemes are concerned, the words "supplementary" and "occupational" are synonymous,**[48] as pensions are normally related to income from work and hence to a professional occupation, while all these schemes have in common that they originated from initiatives of the private sector.[49]

Specifically, **the Commission considers said pension schemes to be part of a national social security system, provided** that they are intended to supplement the benefits provided by statutory social security schemes or to replace them, with reference to Article 2 of Directive No 86/378/EEC,[50,51] which then continues "whether membership of such schemes is compulsory or optional" (Article 2 (1) of Directive No 86/378/EEC). It is also argued however that, although the terms supplementary and occupational are considered synonymous, their use may be ambiguous,[52] as they refer to a different aspect: the first term emphasizes that these systems, at least in the private sector, supplement the benefits provided by the national social security schemes, while the second term highlights the nature of their origins as the result of the initiative by employers and organizations.[53] As otherwise noted, Community law defines the concept of "occupational insurance" sometimes in a narrow way and other times more broadly, depending on the applicable Community law provisions, as it is a widely used term.[54,55]

According to the Committee on Legal Affairs and Citizens' Rights, the Green Paper and the political context suggest that the Commission is focusing its attention above all on the situation as regards pension funds for groups of people ***determined***

[45] As above, p. 3.

[46] Stevens (2022), p. 4.

[47] Paparrigopoulou-Pehlivanidi (2013), p. 33, footnote 79; Anagnostou-Dedouli (2005), p. 35.

[48] Similarly, Anagnostou-Dedouli (2005), p. 35.

[49] Commission of the European Communities (1991), Communication from the Commission to the Council, SEC (91) 1332, p. 1, footnote 1.

[50] European Economic Community (1986), Council Directive No 86/378/EEC of 24 July 1986 on the implementation of the principle of equal treatment for men and women in occupational security schemes, OJ L 225 of 12/08/1986 p. 0040-0042.

[51] Commission of the European Communities (1991) Communication from the Commission to the Council, SEC (91) 1332, p. 1, footnote 1.

[52] ApRoberts (1993), pp. 51–66.

[53] Andrietti (2000), p. 6.

[54] European Economic Community (1977) Council Directive 77/187 EU of 14-2-77, as amended with Directive 95/50/EEC of the Council of 29 June 1998 (EE L. 201/17.7.1998).

[55] Paparrigopoulou-Pehlivanidi, COMMENT on the ECJ judgment C-559/07 Commission of the European Communities v Hellenic Republic, pp. 3–4.

according to their occupation, exercise of a given profession or a similar kind of relationship (that is to say, pillar 2 pension funds) and the workings of competition between these funds and pillar 3 benefit schemes.[56] Contributions paid into pillar 2 pension funds are normally ***managed*** along the lines of funded schemes and ***invested*** on the international capital markets by professional investors who in most cases are not the same persons as the fund managers.[57]

Pillar 2 schemes are administered by private institutions, and benefits are not guaranteed by the state, while contributions are set by reference to income, and payment of contributions is generally shared by employers and employees.[58] These schemes are linked to an employment relationship and are generally funded,[59] with contributions accumulated and invested in order to provide benefits in the future, rather than to pay benefits to those who have already retired.[60] It is thus noted that the more general term "supplementary pension schemes" covers the entire second pillar field; the terminology differs from state to state: for example in occupational schemes "pensions professionnelles", "occupational pensions" in the United Kingdom and in Ireland, while in France the adverb "complémentaire" (complementary) is used and not "additionnel" (supplementary).[61] It is however noted by scholars that the second pillar funded pension schemes, being occupational or for special groups/categories, are based on a pension promise originating from an employment relationship or from belonging to a professional category, with emphasis on that category's group solidarity (DB type schemes) or the collective or individual responsibility (DC type schemes).[62]

Migrant workers' rights to a basic pension, i.e. the rights arising from first pillar insurance schemes, were guaranteed with Regulation No 1408/71; however, no such care was given to the workers' rights from supplementary-occupational schemes (second pillar insurance schemes), which created obstacles in seeking employment in other Member States.[63]

---

[56] Commission of the European Communities (1997b), Committee on Legal Affairs and Citizens' Rights, Rapporteur Enrico Ferri, Report on the Commission Green Paper entitled "Supplementary Pensions in the Single Market" Explanatory Statement, point 4.

[57] Commission of the European Communities (1997b), Committee on Legal Affairs and Citizens' Rights, Rapporteur Enrico Ferri, Report on the Commission Green Paper entitled "Supplementary Pensions in the Single Market" Explanatory Statement, point 4.

[58] Commission of the European Communities (1997a), COM(97)283 final, Green Paper, p. 3.

[59] Eatock (2015).

[60] Commission of the European Communities (1997a), Green Paper COM (97) 283 final, p. 3.

[61] Anagnostou-Dedouli (2005), p. 35.

[62] Eatock (2015).

[63] Bakavou (2015), p. 66.

2.5 Occupational and Private Pension Schemes

As regards the distinction of occupational from supplementary private pensions, the decisive factor is that in the case of supplementary private pensions, the insurance policy is a fully individual decision taken by the insured person, while an occupational pension is based on an agreement or contract between employers and employees.[64] While **occupational and private pension schemes are usually fully funded,** the degree of their funding relative to the pension promises may differ, due to the fact that future pension benefits can be related either to salary and career length (defined-benefit system) or to paid contributions (defined-contribution system).[65]

In private (individual) pension schemes, the insured persons have the ownership of pension assets;[66] access to such a scheme does not require an employment relationship, even though in some cases the contribution may be set on the basis of the wage.[67] The insurance contract specifies a schedule of contribution in exchange of which benefits will be paid when the members reach a specific retirement age. The scheme provider administers the scheme by managing the pension assets through a separate account on behalf of its members.[68] Recently, the regulation introducing a Pan-European Pension Product was introduced.[69] It has been argued that even this is about a product in the third-pillar, it could potentially be used as a complement to second-pillar arrangements for mobile workers with a view of removing some of the barriers faced by this group.[70]

The exclusion of third-pillar private pensions from the material scope of the Regulation has been suggested, treating them as the only pension schemes that may be excluded from its scope on the basis of the wording of the Regulation, as they are not based on legal provisions within the meaning of Article 1, sub-paragraph l, of Regulation No 883/04.[71] In line with the above point of view, it is also suggested that the decisive method for finding a way to define the schemes' limits, which is also useful for coordination, is the method that takes into account the method of the schemes' establishment, which in a way determines their legal form and their financing method.[72] However, the introduction of a legal provision is

[64] European Commission (2005), Directorate-General for Economic and Financial Affairs, p. 98.

[65] European Commission (2009a), Directorate-General for Economic and Financial Affairs, p. 30.

[66] This means that the owner enjoys the rewards and bears the risksregarding the value of the assets.

[67] European Commission (2014b), The 2015 Ageing Report, p. 107; European Commission, Directorate-General for Economic and Financial Affairs, p. 112.

[68] European Commission (2014b), The 2015 Ageing Report, p. 107; European Commission, Directorate-General for Economic and Financial Affairs, p. 107.

[69] Regulation 2019/1238 of the European Parliament and of the Council of 20 June 2019 on a Pan-European Pension Product (PEPP) [2019] OJ L 198/1 (PEPP Regulation).

[70] Schmidt (2023), p. 296.

[71] Schuler (2015), p. 237.

[72] Perrin (1990), p. 112; Anagnostou-Dedouli (2005), pp. 36–37.

possible for specific schemes, making them mandatory following their establishment and operation.

More specifically, for the most part, private (individual) pension schemes (based on individual insurance policies) are non-mandatory, without however excluding the possibility of them being statutory; in the latter case, they are close to social security schemes.[73] Mandatory private pension schemes are therefore similar to public schemes.[74] Non-mandatory private pensions are based on individual insurance contracts between the individual and the private pension scheme provider, usually an insurance company or a pension fund.[75]

As it is thus apparent from the information on private pension schemes, these schemes can become mandatory.[76] In that case, they must be provided for in the law and thus become statutory. Moreover, the binding-law imposition of a minimum social solidarity participation is attributed to their mandatory character.[77] Mandatory private schemes may, therefore, fall within the scope of Regulation No 883/04 as statutory schemes. It is also possible, however, for non-mandatory private schemes to fall within its scope, if they are provided by law. The intervention of public authorities seems to override the strictly individual decision and the private basis upon which the conclusion of a contract between private parties is based, by conferring them a collective character, i.e. a social element that is embedded in social security.

Moreover, occupational pension schemes, which sometimes are based on the solidarity of a professional category (DB type schemes) and sometimes on the collective or individual responsibility (DC type schemes).[78] More specifically, pensions provided by occupational schemes are those that, rather than being statutory by law, are linked to an employment relationship with the scheme provider. They are based on contractual agreements between employers and employees, either at the company level or their organizations at the union level.[79] These schemes are run by private sector pension funds, insurance companies or the sponsoring companies themselves (in balance sheets).[80] Some countries, such as the United Kingdom, have occupational pension schemes where the employer happens to be the government.[81]

---

[73] European Commission (2005), Directorate-General for Economic and Financial Affairs, p. 112; European Commission (2014b), The 2015 Ageing Report, p. 107.

[74] European Commission (2014b), The 2015 Ageing Report, p. 107.

[75] European Commission (2014b), The 2015 Ageing Report, p. 107.

[76] European Commission (2005), Directorate-General for Economic and Financial Affairs, p. 112; European Commission (2014b) The 2015 Ageing Report, p. 107.

[77] Aggelopoulou (2003), pp. 55–56.

[78] Eatock (2015).

[79] European Commission (2014b), The 2015 Ageing Report, p. 106.

[80] European Commission (2014b), The 2015 Ageing Report, p. 106.

[81] European Commission (2014b), The 2015 Ageing Report, p. 107.

It is crucial that these schemes can be quasi-mandatory, in the sense that, on the basis of a nation—or industry-wide bargaining agreement, the employers are obliged to provide an occupational pension scheme to their employees, while at the same time, the participation of an individual remains voluntary.[82] Besides, occupational schemes can be equivalent to statutory earnings-related pension schemes or complementary to them.[83]

2.6 The Relationship Between the Coordination Regulation and the Directive on Supplementary Pension Rights

In its Communication of July 1991,[84] the Commission started a discussion at Community level, on the role of supplementary pension schemes and their impact on free movement.[85] As a follow up to this communication, the Commission services have explored on several occasions, in conjunction with the representatives of Member States, Social Partners and pension funds, how to remove obstacles to cross-border mobility of employed and self-employed persons in the European Union in the field of supplementary pensions.[86] The Commission anticipated growth in supplementary pensions and there has been a desire to facilitate labour mobility, as well as to buttress retirement provision through the EU' internal market in the face of population ageing and strained public systems.[87]

The importance of the social function attributed to supplementary pensions has been recognised by the Community legislature's adoption of Council Directive 98/49/EC of 29 June 1998, on safeguarding the supplementary pension rights of employed and self-employed persons moving within the Community, which does not differentiate between the pensions of employed persons and those of self-employed persons.[88]

[82] European Commission (2014b), The 2015 Ageing Report, p. 107.

[83] Ibid.

[84] Commission of the European Communities (1991) Communication from the Commission to the Council, SEC (91) 1332.

[85] The improvement of the possibility of transferring rights from supplementary schemes with the open coordination method has been examined, but this method has been called into question as to its adequate contribution in this area. See Stevens (2003), p. 22.

[86] Commission of the European Communities (1997a) Green Paper, COM (97) 283 final, p. 25.

[87] Schmidt (2023), p. 287.

[88] Judgment of the Court of 12.09.2000, Joined cases C-180/98 to C-184/98, Pavlov and others, European Court Reports 2000 I-06451, paragraph 66; of 21.09.1999, Case C-67/96, Albany International BV, European Court Reports 1999 p. I-05751, paragraph 106.

Council Directive 98/49/EC[89] was the first specific measure aiming to improve the exercise of the right to freedom of movement of workers in terms of the supplementary pension schemes. The Court itself has held that the importance of the social function attributed to supplementary pensions has been recognized by the Community legislature's adoption of Council Directive 98/49/EC on safeguarding the supplementary pension rights of employed and self-employed persons moving within the Community.[90] It is noted however that, as a rule, in order to acquire supplementary occupational pension entitlements, the employment relationship must have existed for a minimum period or contributions in respect of the employee must have been paid into an occupational pension scheme for a minimum period, because only when such minimum periods have been completed is there a guarantee that the employee's pension rights will not be "forfeited" wholly or partially upon his departure from the scheme or simply upon termination of his employment contract.[91] The term "qualifying periods" has come into use to describe such minimum periods.[92]

It has, of course, been noted that this Directive is only a means for facilitating the freedom of movement of persons and cannot fulfil any other requirements beyond that, since it only refers to a vested right to a pension.[93] It therefore does not guarantee all the rights of migrant workers arising from a supplementary insurance scheme, as it does not provide for a "genuine portability", i.e. the comprehensive possibility for migrant workers to acquire and retain occupational pension entitlements.[94] Thus, it has been argued that there is no guarantee for the right of the worker that acquires pension rights, possibly even for employment periods shorter than those defined in the scheme as a "minimum vested entitlement" or at the beginning of their career (e.g. not all Member States recognise pension rights for internship periods), to maintain and transfer those rights to a new scheme.[95]

Admittedly, resorting to the Treaty provisions has sometimes been proved to be effective for safeguarding workers.[96] Thus, in Maurits Casteels v British Airways[97] (BA), the Court held that (paragraph 36): Article 45 TFEU must be interpreted as

[89] Council Directive 98/49/EC, of 29 June 1998, on safeguarding the supplementary pension rights of employed and self-employed persons moving within the Community, OJ L 209 of 25.7.1998, p. 46.

[90] Judgment of the Court of 21.09.1999, Case C-67/96, Albany International BV, European Court Reports 1999 p. I-05751, paragraph 106.

[91] Opinion of the Advocate General Juliane Kokott of 11 November 2010, Case C-379/09, Maurits Casteels v British Airways plc, paragraph 2.

[92] Opinion of the Advocate General Juliane Kokott of 11 November 2010, Case C-379/09, Maurits Casteels v British Airways plc, paragraph 2.

[93] Fuchs (2000), p. 67.

[94] Bakavou (2015), p. 68.

[95] Bakavou (2015), p. 68.

[96] Ravelli (2012), p. 63.

[97] Judgment of the Court of 10.03.2011, Case C-379/09, Maurits Casteels v British Airways plc, European Court Reports 2011 I-01379.

precluding, in the context of the mandatory application of a collective labour agreement:

- for the determination of the period for the acquisition of definitive entitlements to supplementary pension benefits in a Member State, the non-inclusion of the years of service completed by a worker for the same employer in establishments of that employer situated in different Member States and pursuant to the same coordinating contract of employment; and
- a worker who has been transferred from an establishment of his employer in one Member State to an establishment of the same employer in another Member State from being regarded as having left the employer of his own free will.

Said case concerned a BA employee, who at all times worked for the company in the territory of various Member States, but could not acquire entitlement to supplementary pension benefits for the period of work completed in Germany on the ground that Mr Casteels voluntarily left the Düsseldorf establishment without serving the minimum period required for the acquisition of definitive supplementary pension rights under the scheme in force in that establishment. According to the Arbeidshof te Brussel, under the German legislation in force during the period in question, Mr Casteels was entitled only to repayment of his own contributions, to the exclusion of those paid by his employer. Therefore, as regards entitlement to supplementary pension benefits, Mr Casteels was, by reason of the fact that he had worked in different Member States (Belgium, Germany, France) for the same employer (BA), in a less favourable position than if he had always worked in Belgium for that employer.

By contrast, as noted by the Court, workers employed in the Düsseldorf establishment who have a length of service with BA equal to that of Mr Casteels but who have not exercised their right to free movement are able to claim an uninterrupted length of service for purposes of verifying completion of the period required, pursuant to the provisions of the Collective Agreement, for acquisition of definitive entitlement to supplementary pension benefits under the scheme in force at that establishment (paragraph 26). Those workers benefit from continuity in the acquisition of their rights to a supplementary pension, whereas the period during which Mr Casteels acquired rights under the scheme in force at that establishment was unable to reach the minimum threshold required by Clause 7 of the Collective Agreement on the ground that the acquisition of length of service with BA had, with regard to Mr Casteels, been interrupted by virtue of the fact that it resulted from periods of service completed in establishments of that same employer in different Member States (paragraph 26).

Thus, by making no provision for account to be taken of years of service completed by a BA employee in a BA establishment in another Member State, and by treating the consensual transfer of a BA employee to a BA establishment in another Member State as a voluntary departure from BA, the Collective Agreement thus places workers who exercise their right to free movement at a disadvantage inasmuch as they suffer financial losses as well as an adverse effect on their supplementary pension rights (paragraph 29). The prospect of such a disadvantage is liable to dissuade workers, such as Mr Casteels, from leaving their employer's establishment in one Member State in order to take up a position with an establishment of that same employer in another Member State[98] (paragraph 29).

As highlighted in the context of the above case, therefore, the absence of a provision on the minimum required period of service is particularly striking.[99] This is also the reason for which the German legislation can still apply relatively long waiting periods as a condition for acquiring pension entitlements.[100]

2.7 The "Portability" of Pension Rights

The term "portability" refers to the possibility of acquiring and keeping or transferring pension entitlements in the event of professional mobility, while **the term "transferability" refers to one specific way of achieving portability,** namely by transferring a capital representing the acquired pension entitlements from one scheme to another.[101]

According to the relevant theory, "pension portability" can be defined as the capacity of workers covered by an occupational pension plan to preserve the actuarially fair value of their accrued rights over time, while moving to a different employer and possibly to a different pension scheme.[102] Initial Directive's proposal in 2005 (COM/2005/0507 final—COD 2005/0214) targeted portability, but in 2007, Commission amended its proposal (COM/2007/0603 final—COD 2005/0214) so that it left out portability rules and shifted the focus on minimum requirements for enhancing worker mobility by improving the acquisition and preservation of supplementary pension rights. When a migrant in not entitled to full preservation of the real value of their accrued rights over time, either in the old or in the new scheme, pension portability is not guaranteed and a portability loss is expected to arise, i.e. a shortfall of actual retirement benefits from those that would have been paid if there had been no movement and change in scheme membership.[103]

The issues regarding the acquisition of pension entitlements and the concentration of large volumes of retirement benefits have been highlighted as general portability issues.[104] In addition to them, there are particular cross-border issues: tax systems' conflicts, cross-border transfer of the capitalised value of pension rights and

---

98 Regarding this, see judgment of 01.04.2008, C-212/06, Gouvernement de la Communauté française and Gouvernement wallon, European Court Reports 2008, p. I-1683, paragraph 48.

99 Bollen-Vandenboorn and Stevens (2012), p. 78.

100 Bollen-Vandenboorn and Stevens (2012), p. 78.

101 European Commission (2002).

102 Andrietti (2000), p. 2.

103 Andrietti (2000), p. 2.

104 Jacob (2003), p. 25.

cross-border participation of pension schemes.[105] It is of course argued that in defined-contribution occupational schemes, after a short vesting period, the worker assumes ownership of their pension account, which ensures the portability of accrued pension rights.[106] Occupational pension schemes usually define a maturity/vesting period representing the minimum length of service to be completed for someone to obtain pension entitlements; thus, workers "leaving the system" before the completion of the required vesting period forfeit their pension rights.[107]

2.8 The New Directive 2014/50/EU on Supplementary Pension Rights

Since supplementary retirement provision is becoming increasingly important in many Member States as a means to secure people's standard of living in old age, the need for improving the conditions for acquiring and preserving pension rights, in order to reduce obstacles to worker's freedom of movement between Member States[108] translated in the adoption of Directive 2014/50/EU.[109] The relevant definitions on supplementary pension and the supplementary pension scheme contained in the new **Directive 2014/50/EU**[110] are much shorter in comparison to those in the Directive 98/49.[111] Council Directive 98/49/EC was a first specific measure, aiming to improve the exercise of the right to free movement of workers in relation to supplementary pension schemes. According to Article 3(a) of Directive 98/49/EC: "'supplementary pension scheme' means any occupational pension scheme established in conformity with national legislation and practice such as a group insurance contract or pay-as-you-go scheme agreed by one or more branches or sectors, funded scheme or pension promise backed by book reserves, or any collective or other comparable arrangement intended to provide a supplementary pension for employed or self-employed persons;" (Article 3, point (b), Directive 98/49/EC).

According to Article 3, sub-paragraph a), Directive 2014/50/EU "supplementary pension" means a retirement pension provided for by the rules of a supplementary

[105] Jacob (2003), p. 25.

[106] Andrietti (2000), p. 2.

[107] Andrietti (2001), p. 3.

[108] Directive 2014/50/EU, Preamble, recital 16.

[109] Directive 2014/50/EU of the European Parliament and of the Council of 16 April 2014 on minimum requirements for enhancing worker mobility between Member States by improving the acquisition and preservation of supplementary pension rights, OJ L 128, 30.4.2014, p. 2.

[110] Directive 2014/50/EU was also adopted by the EEA Joint Committee, Decision No 188/2014 of 25 September 2014 See DECISION OF THE EEA JOINT COMMITTEE No 188/2014 of 25 September 2014 amending Annex VI (Social security) to the EEA Agreement [2015/1256].

[111] Council Directive 98/49/EC of 29 June 1998 on safeguarding the supplementary pension rights of employed and self-employed persons moving within the Community OJ L 209, 25.7.1998 pp. 46–49.

pension scheme established in accordance with national law and practice; **"supplementary pension scheme" means any occupational retirement pension scheme** established in accordance with national law and practice and linked to an employment relationship, intended to provide a supplementary pension for employed persons (article 3, sub-paragraph b), Directive 2014/50/EU).

The above definition, although seemingly simpler than the definition of the older relevant Directive 98/49/EU raises doubts due to its generality. Thus, despite stating that **Directive 2014/50/EU applies** to "any occupational pension scheme", it seems appropriate to make a reference to the Preamble of the Directive. Therefore, as stated in the preamble/recitals, paragraph/ recital 11, this Directive should apply to all supplementary pension schemes established in accordance with national law and practice that offer supplementary pensions for workers, such as **group insurance contracts, pay-as-you-go schemes agreed by one or more branches or sectors, funded schemes or pension promises** backed by book reserves, or any collective or other comparable agreement. The new Directive guarantees workers' pension rights before their vesting stage, i.e. rights created for the worker in the supplementary insurance scheme to which they are affiliated to; these rights, however, have not become due at the time of leaving, in the sense that the worker is entitled to a refund of their paid contributions, in contrast with the former situation, where the worker that left the scheme before establishing entitlement to a pension right forfeited the contributions already paid.[112]

According to recital 19 of the Preamble of Directive 2014/50/EU, **where an employment relationship is terminated before an outgoing worker has accrued vested pension rights and when the scheme or the employer bears the investment risk,** in particular in **defined contribution** schemes, the scheme should always **refund the pension contributions** of the outgoing worker. Where an employment relationship is terminated before an outgoing worker has accrued vested pension rights and **when the outgoing worker bears the investment risk,** in particular in **defined contribution** schemes, the scheme may **refund the value of the investments** derived from those contributions. The investment value may be more or less than the contributions paid by the outgoing worker. Alternatively, the scheme may reimburse the sum of the contributions (preamble/recitals, paragraph/ recital 19).

More specifically, as stated in recital 17 of the Preamble of Directive 2014/50/EU, the fact that in some supplementary pension schemes, pension rights can be forfeited if a worker's employment relationship ends before he or she has completed **a minimum period of scheme membership *("vesting period")*** or before he or she has reached the **minimum age *("vesting age")*** can prevent workers who move between Member States from acquiring adequate pension rights. The requirement of a lengthy waiting period before a worker can become a member of a pension scheme can have a similar effect. Such conditions therefore represent obstacles to workers'

[112] Bakavou (2015), p. 71.

freedom of movement. By contrast, minimum age requirements for membership do not constitute an obstacle to freedom of movement, and are therefore not addressed by this Directive (preamble/recitals, paragraph/ recital 17).

In addition, this Directive introduces the concept of dormant rights in the supplementary pension scheme to which the worker is subject.[113] Outgoing workers have the right to leave their vested pension rights as dormant pension rights in the supplementary pension scheme in which their entitlement was established.[114] As regards the preservation of dormant pension rights, the level of protection may be considered equivalent where, particularly in the context of a defined contribution scheme, the outgoing workers are afforded **the possibility of having the value of their vested pension rights discharged to a supplementary pension scheme which meets the conditions laid out in this Directive** (preamble/recitals, paragraph/ recital 20). The value of those rights at the time when the member leaves the scheme should be established in accordance with national law and practice. Where the value of those rights is adjusted, account should be taken of the particular nature of the scheme, the interests of the deferred beneficiaries, the interests of the remaining active scheme members and the interests of retired beneficiaries (preamble/recitals, paragraph/ recital 21).

As expressly clarified in recital 22 of the Preamble of Directive 2014/50/EU, **this Directive does not create any obligation to establish more favourable conditions for dormant pension rights** than for the rights of active scheme members. Moreover, it should be highlighted that this Directive **does not provide for the transfer of vested pension rights** (preamble/recitals, paragraph/ recital 24). According to Article 5 (3), Directive 2014/50/EU, Member States may **allow supplementary pension schemes not to retain the vested rights of an outgoing worker but to pay,** with the worker's informed consent, including as regards applicable charges, **a capital sum equivalent to the value of the vested pension rights,** as long as the value of the vested pension rights does not exceed a threshold established by the Member State concerned. The Member State shall inform the Commission of the threshold applied.

It should also be noted that the implementation of the Directive as well as the Regulation requires a cross-border element, the movement between two or more states. Indeed, this Directive is not applicable to the acquisition and preservation of supplementary pension rights of workers moving within a single Member State (preamble/recitals, paragraph/ recital 6).

From the above, **it can be concluded that the same kind of supplementary pensions may fall under Regulation No 883/04 or Directive** 2014/50/EU **solely on the basis of the choice of Member States regarding their declarations.** This has been included in Directive 2014/50/EU itself (Preamble, recital 3).

[113] Bakavou (2015), p. 71.

[114] Recital 20 and Article 5 Directive 2014/50/EU.

2.9 Placing a Scheme Under Regulation 883/04 or Directive 2014/50

The above remark is important as the possibility of placing a supplementary/occupational insurance scheme under Regulation No 883/04 or Directive 2014/50 is relevant as to whether it will also fall under the **Directive 2016/2341**[115] on the Institutions for Occupational Retirement Provision (**IORP II Directive**). Although the previous relevant Directive **2003/41/EC** on the supervision of institutions for occupational retirement provision (**Directive IORP**)[116] has been replaced by the recast Directive 2016/2341/EU (IORP II Directive), Directive 2003/41/EC (Directive IORP) is mentioned here for the purposes of theoretical discussion. More specifically, Directive 2003/41/EC excludes from its scope institutions managing social-security schemes, which are already coordinated at Community level, while it takes into account the specificity of institutions which, in a single Member State, manage both social-security schemes and occupational pension schemes (Preamble, Directive 2003/41/EC, recital 11).

As however noted in Directive 2003/41, since social security schemes are coming under increasing pressure, occupational retirement pensions will increasingly be relied on as a complement in the future (Preamble, Directive 2003/41/EC, recital 5). Moreover, the ageing population presents a major challenge to pension systems in all Member States.[117] Occupational retirement pensions should therefore be developed, without, however, calling into question the importance of social security pension systems in terms of secure, durable and effective social protection, which should guarantee a decent standard of living in old age and should therefore be at the centre of the objective of strengthening the European social model (Preamble, Directive 2003/41/EU, recital 5).

The central importance of pensions for Europe's social and economic success and the increased risk for cross-border spill-overs from national pension policies mean that pensions are increasingly becoming a matter of common concern in the EU.[118]

[115]Directive (EU) 2016/2341 of the European Parliament and the Council of 14 December 2016 on the activities and supervision of institutions for occupational retirement provision (IORPs) (recast), L 354/37, 23.12.2016, OJ L 354, 23.12.2016, pp. 37–85 Current consolidated version: 09/01/2024.

[116]Directive 2003/41/EC of the European Parliament and of the Council of 3 June 2003 on the activities and supervision of institutions for occupational retirement provision, Official Journal of the European Union, 23.9.2003, L 235/10. Commission Implementing Regulation (EU) No 643/2014 of 16 June 2014 laying down implementing technical standards with regard to the reporting of national provisions of prudential nature relevant to the field of occupational pension schemes according to Directive 2003/41/EC of the European Parliament and of the Council.

[117]European Commission (2012) White Paper, COM (2012) 55 final, p. 2. See Commission Staff Working Document (2008) (SWD) [SEC (2008) 2911] and also European Commission and Economic Policy Committee (2009) 2009 Ageing Report.

[118]European Commission (2012) White Paper, COM (2012) 55 final, p. 3.

Ensuring an adequate and sustainable retirement income for EU citizens now and in the future is a priority for the European Union.[119] Indeed, the success of retirement reforms in the Member States is a major determining factor for the smooth functioning of the Economic and Monetary Union and will affect the EU's ability to achieve two of the five targets of the Europe 2020 Strategy—raising the employment rate to 75% and reducing the number of people at risk of poverty by at least 20 million.[120] It is also worth noting that pension funds are an integral part of financial markets and their design can promote or inhibit the free movement of labour or capital.[121]

Directive 2003/41/EC or the IORP Directive represents thus a first step for an internal market for occupational retirement provision organised at a European scale. Although, the Directive defines its scope through negative wording and not explicitly, given that Article 2 on the scope sets out the cases where the Directive does not apply, it is noted that this Directive was adopted for the non-mandatory second pillar schemes, while its scope excludes all first pillar public bodies established by law.[122] The Directive applies mainly to schemes established following an agreement between employees and employers (Article 2); it thus applies to IORPs that are contractual, non-mandatory and operating as funded schemes.[123]

By setting the "prudent person" rule as the underlying principle for capital investment and making it possible for institutions to operate across borders, the redirection of savings into the sector of occupational retirement provision is encouraged, thus contributing to economic and social progress (Preamble, Directive 2003/41/EC, recital 6).[124] The prudential rules laid down in this Directive are intended both to guarantee a high degree of security for future pensioners through the imposition of stringent supervisory standards, and to clear the way for the efficient management of occupational pension schemes (Preamble, Directive 2003/41/EU, recital 7).

According to the European Parliament and the Council, **institutions which are completely separated from any sponsoring undertaking and which operate on a funded basis** for the sole purpose of providing retirement benefits should have freedom to provide services and freedom of investment, subject only to coordinated prudential requirements, regardless of whether these institutions are considered as legal entities (Preamble, Directive 2003/41/EC, recital 8).

As clarified by the Economic and Social Committee in its opinion on this Directive, the Directive applies exclusively to institutions for retirement provisions which are separate from the sponsoring undertaking, which are not responsible for

[119] European Commission (2010) Green Paper COM (2010) 365 final, p. 2.

[120] European Commission (2012) White Paper, COM (2012) 55 final, p. 3.

[121] European Commission (2010) Green Paper COM (2010) 365 final, p. 3.

[122] Stergiou (2015), p. 190.

[123] Nikolakopoulou-Stefanou (2004), p. 66; Stergiou (2015), p. 190.

[124] See also European Commission (2009b) Report from the Commission COM (2009) 203 final.

statutory social security schemes and which operate on a funded basis.[125] Other institutions for retirement provision do not have to comply with the provisions of the directive.[126] In practice, this Directive will have an impact wherever funded pension schemes exist alongside the pay-as-you-go and balance sheet pension provision systems.[127] However, as set out in Article 3 ("application to institutions operating social-security schemes"), Directive 2003/41, **institutions for occupational retirement provision which also operate compulsory employment-related pension schemes which are considered to be social security schemes covered by Regulations (EEC) No 1408/71 and (EEC) No 574/72 shall be covered by this Directive in respect of their non-compulsory occupational retirement provision business.** In that case, the liabilities and the corresponding assets shall be ring-fenced and it shall not be possible to transfer them to the compulsory pension schemes which are considered as social security schemes or vice versa.

As evident from the IORP Directive, European Union is interested in mobility and free movement of persons, services and capital, as well as the application of uniform rules of supervision, control and transparency of supplementary insurance bodies.[128] However, in particular for companies which establish book reserves in order to provide retirement benefits to their employees and only to the extent that they wish to have cross-border activities, the International Accounting Standards (IAS) are relevant.[129] This is interesting as the defined-benefit supplementary occupational insurance schemes must provide a guarantee for covering their obligations (benefits), i.e. a reserves guarantee, in case they exercise cross-border activities.[130]

On 27 March 2014, the European Commission adopted a proposal for reviewing the above Directive and establishing new rules on institutions for occupational retirement provision (IORP II) aiming to improve the governance and transparency of these institutions in Europe, as well as the promotion of cross-border activity and long-term investments.[131] According to the Commission's estimates, pension systems across the European Union (EU) have to adapt in order to ensure adequate, safe

---

[125] European Economic and Social Committee (2001) Opinion on the "Proposal for a Directive of the European Parliament and of the Council on the activities of institutions for occupational retirement provision" (2001/C 155/07)52001AE0403, Official Journal C 155 of 29/05/2001 p. 0026 – 0031, paragraph 3.4.

[126] European Economic and Social Committee (2001) Opinion on the "Proposal for a Directive of the European Parliament and of the Council on the activities of institutions for occupational retirement provision" (2001/C 155/07)52001AE0403, Official Journal C 155 of 29/05/2001 p. 0026 – 0031, paragraph 3.4.1.

[127] European Economic and Social Committee (2001) Opinion on the "Proposal for a Directive of the European Parliament and of the Council on the activities of institutions for occupational retirement provision" (2001/C 155/07)52001AE0403, Official Journal C 155 of 29/05/2001 p. 0026 – 0031, paragraph 3.4.1.

[128] Nikolakopoulou-Stefanou (2004), p. 69.

[129] Nikolakopoulou-Stefanou (2004), p. 69.

[130] Nikolakopoulou-Stefanou (2004), p. 70.

[131] See also Pensions Europe (2024) Input for the Impact Assessment on pillar II and III requirements of the IORP II Directive (update) 18 July 2013, www.pensionsEurope.eu.

and sustainable pensions, while the single market can also contribute decisively to this goal, given that institutions for occupational retirement provision (IORP) are, like other financial institutions, an integral part of the Single market.[132] Moreover, completing the internal market for pension products has a direct impact on the EU's growth potential and therefore directly contributes towards meeting the Europe 2020 objectives.[133] The goal of the **Directive 2016/2341**[134] on the Institutions for Occupational Retirement Provision (**IORP II Directive**) is to facilitate the development of occupational retirement savings and to provide sustainable and adequate occupational pensions to European citizens.[135] The IORP II Directive sets common standards ensuring the soundness of occupational pensions and adequately protecting pension scheme members and beneficiaries. The 2016 review of the Directive significantly increased these minimum harmonisation standards, introducing, among others: (I) new governance requirements; (II) new rules on IORPs' own risk assessment; (III) new information requirements, including the introduction of an annual Pension Benefit Statement; (IV) enhanced powers for supervisors.[136] The Commission started preliminary work on the IORPII directive review but will issue its proposal during the 2024–2029 EC mandate.

Further, **questions arise from considering supplementary pension funds as undertakings in terms of their potential association** to Directive 2014/51/EU[137] amending Directives 2003/71/EC and **2009/138/EC (Solvency II)**[138] and Regula-

---

[132] European Commission (2014c) Commission Staff Working Document, SWD (2014) 102 final, p. 1.

[133] European Commission (2010) Green Paper COM (2010) 365 final, p. 4.

[134] Directive (EU) 2016/2341 of the European Parliament and the Council of 14 December 2016 on the activities and supervision of institutions for occupational retirement provision (IORPs) (recast), L 354/37, 23.12.2016, OJ L 354, 23.12.2016, pp. 37–85 Current consolidated version: 09/01/2024.

[135] Pensions Europe (2024).

[136] Ibid.

[137] Directive 2014/51/EU of the European Parliament and of the Council of 16 April 2014 amending Directives 2003/71/EC and 2009/138/EC and Regulations (EC) No 1060/2009, (EU) No 1094/2010 and (EU) No 1095/2010 in respect of the powers of the European Supervisory Authority (European Insurance and Occupational Pensions Authority) and the European Supervisory Authority (European Securities and Markets Authority), Official Journal of the European Union, L 153/1, 22.5.2014.

[138] Directive 2009/138/EC of the European Parliament and of the Council, of 25 November 2009 on the taking-up and pursuit of the business of Insurance and Reinsurance (Solvency II), Official Journal of the European Union L 335/1, 17.12.2009, with Commission Implementing Regulation (EU) 2016/165 of 5 February 2016 laying down technical information for the calculation of technical provisions and basic own funds for reporting with reference dates from 1 January until 30 March 2016, in accordance with Directive 2009/138/EC of the European Parliament and of the Council (Solvency II).Official Journal of the European Union L 32/31, 9.2.2016.

tions (EC) No 1060/2009,[139] (EU) No 1094/2010[140] and (EU) No 1095/2010,[141] in respect of the powers of the European Supervisory Authority (European Insurance and Occupational Pensions Authority) and the European Supervisory Authority (European Securities and Markets Authority). Besides, the Commission has long held the position that pension and life insurance funds and the managers of these funds must be subject to prudential supervision,[142] obviously treating supplementary pension funds as of comparable size to insurance companies. Consumers (i.e. future pensioners) must be protected in an area where they have little knowledge, so supervision must ensure that fund managers execute their fiduciary duties correctly.[143] Acknowledging that in some cases, these funds are covered by regulations specific to them, while in others, they are regulated on the same footing as life insurance companies, the Commission had already reached the conclusion that these funds are subject to the same minimum solvency requirements, rules as to technical provisions and investments restrictions and other provisions as life insurance companies.[144]

Therefore, the idea formed is that **it is up to each Member State's discretion whether it will place its supplementary/occupational pension schemes under the Coordination Regulation No 883/04 or under Directive 2014/50/EU and by extension under Directive 2003/41/EC and Implementing Regulation No 648/2014/EU**. It is worth noting that integrating French ARRGO and AGIRC supplementary schemes into the scope of Regulation No 1408/71 was considered the best way to protect them from the application of EU competition law.[145]

It becomes clear that the result is an inconsistent and non-uniform approach to schemes of the same form, which is, however, a consequence of preserving national sovereignty in the field of social policies and the power of States to freely organise their social security systems. Moreover, according to settled case-law, the organisation of the national social security schemes remains an exclusive competence of the Member States.[146] As is well known, social security is governed by mandatory rules and is based on the principle of territoriality,[147] which is derived by the legal requirement that State power is exercised only within the limits of its own territory; Community law overrides that territoriality, however, to the extent that it ensures continuity of the insurance relationship in space and time.[148]

---

[139] Regulation (EC) No 1060/2009.

[140] Regulation (EU) No 1094/2010.

[141] Regulation (EU) No 1095/2010.

[142] Commission of the European Communities (1997a) Green Paper, p. 10.

[143] Commission of the European Communities (1997a) Green Paper, p. 10.

[144] Commission of the European Communities, Green Paper, p. 10.

[145] Ghailani et al. (2011), p. 138.

[146] Katrougalos (2006), p. 251. See also Kremalis (1996); Mousi (2002).

[147] Cornelissen (1998), p. 689.

[148] Mavridis (2004), p. 804.

The problem that will, of course, arise in the future is how to calculate the pension of a person that has insurance periods both in a supplementary/occupational scheme under the Coordination Regulation and in a supplementary/occupational scheme not covered by the Regulation; in such case, the aforementioned Directives can be applied simultaneously with the Coordination Regulation. The question is not just about the calculation itself; there are questions as to which principles should apply in such a case in view of the principles developed in the context of the Regulation and the case-law interpretations given based on the central axis of the Regulations, i.e. the Treaty provisions on free movement. The importance of the necessity to adjust the Coordination Regulation can be highlighted, taking into account the integration of the French supplementary pension schemes into the scope of the Regulation, which constituted the best way to protect them from the application of European competition law.[149]

2.10 The Social Role of Supplementary Pensions

It should be noted that protecting the administration of pension funds by establishing investment and prudential rules, aiming to safeguard the rights of the retired persons affiliated to them is one matter; their connection with the removal of obstacles to investment and in general the Capital Markets Union, which was promoted within EU in 2015 is a different matter altogether.[150] This would entail treating supplementary pension funds and undertakings as absolutely identical; such an approach is untenable, in view of the social function attributed to supplementary pension funds, even in situations where not all solidarity indicators referred to in theory and case-law are present. This view has been accepted by the Court and is reflected in the Directive on supplementary pensions. Moreover, as already stated, a different legal instrument already exists for pension funds, providing prudential rules specifically for the institutions for occupational retirement provision that are based on social partners' agreements (IORP II Directive, Implementing Regulation No 2014/643/EU).

Indeed, the Commission has previously made the connection between retirement reforms in Member States with the functioning of the Economic and Monetary Union, as well as the pension funds which are considered an integral part of financial markets and the free movement of capital.[151] Moreover, in the context of the Green Paper on supplementary pensions, the Commission had asked whether the prudential rules which apply to life assurance schemes should apply to pension funds. In the

[149] OSE (2011), p. 138.

[150] See European Commission (2010) Action Plan on building a Capital Markets Union.

[151] See European Commission (2010) Green Paper SEC (2010) 830, COM (2010) 365 final, p. 3; European Commission (2001b) Communication from the Commission COM (2001) 286 final, p. 8.

requested relevant opinion, it was held that now that pension funds and insurance companies are increasingly operating in each other's territory as far as some products are concerned, they should be offering the same products to the same customers under the same market conditions, because this is the only way to achieve a "level playing field".[152] Of course, it was held that opinions are still divided as to whether collective social agreements concluded by employers' and employees' organisations are covered by the rules on competition in Articles 85 and 86, EC Treaty, given that neither the wording of the Treaty articles nor the case-law of the Court of Justice of the European Communities provided a clear answer; the Green Paper makes no relevant reference either.[153] However, the various Directives adopted regarding supplementary pensions and undertakings indicate *a contrario* that pension funds are distinct from undertakings. In this way, the EU legislator seems to indirectly recognise a presumed superiority of their social nature over the business/economic activities that they may develop.

The above connection of pensions with the full liberalisation of investments and capital markets would therefore be inappropriate and dysfunctional, as it seems to overlook or, in any event, fail to recognise the importance of the social mission of the Union and of pensions themselves, the specific Directives, as well as the Coordination Regulation as a legislative instrument incorporating the Union's social objectives.[154]

In addition, the above opinion rightly acknowledges that the main function of pensions is social.[155] Attention should therefore be drawn to the adoption of EU instruments that cumulatively aim at distinct objectives of a different nature. In view of the complexity of the pensions schemes and the functioning of the Union, it is essential for uniformity not to be detrimental to the substance and the social identity of pensions, through convergence tendencies between sectors (social and economic-monetary) with characteristics intended to be regulated in parallel and not uniformly.[156] Moreover, a change in the structure of pension systems is a long-term process, where there will always be a need for a "policy mix" between pay-as-you-go on the one hand and funded schemes on the other hand. In most Member States, mandatory state pensions will continue to account for a large proportion of pension benefits, with the emphasis on solidarity between and within generations.[157]

These concerns are not devoid of purpose, especially in view of the review of the Directive on Institutions for Occupational Retirement Provision, as they highlight the fragile social context currently maintained by the European legislature regarding supplementary pensions. From a financial point of view, it can be argued that both IORPs and insurance companies are financial service providers (of a retirement

---

152 Boogert-Quaak (1998).

153 Ibid.

154 For more details, see Tsetoura (2015), p. 283 et seq.

155 Boogert-Quaak (1998), p. 22.

156 See also Tsetoura (2015), p. 283 et seq.

157 Boogert-Quaak (1998).

insurance product), which includes an obligation to secure pension arrangements—promises to the insured persons (recital 20, Directive 2003/41 and the proposal for its amendment).[158] **However, the existence of a common financial aspect cannot entail their absolute assimilation.** This assimilation effort actually tends to promote the prevalence of the business nature to the detriment of the social parameters of pension funds, while it could, for example, accentuate the elements of corporate social governance.

It is noted that in the proposal (of 27.3.2014) for amending Directive 2003/41-EC-IOPRP I, otherwise known as IORP II,[159] the Commission followed the regulatory framework of Directive Solvency II,[160] while, as it is also noted, the European Insurance and Occupational Pensions Authority[161] (EIOPA)[162] also recommended to the Commission to apply the governance framework of Directive Solvency II on IORPs.[163,164]

This proposal was criticised by the European pension sector stating that IORPs function as social institutions[165] with no commercial purpose and are managed by representatives of the employers and the employees or by worker's associations, while their governance is incorporated into the regulatory framework of the applicable national social labour law.[166] The above criticisms are based on the view that the interests of the members are better served on this basis than if the IORPs operated on a purely commercial basis.[167] Technically, within this context, the Council introduced a new wording in the recitals of the IORP II proposal, indicating that "IORPs are pension institutions with a social purpose", which seems to exclude occupational retirement benefits institutions that choose to operate (also) with a commercial purpose (recital 20 IORP II Proposal recast).[168]

---

[158] Borsjé and van Meerten (2015), p. 390.

[159] Proposal for a Directive/* COM/2014/0167 final - 2014/0091 (COD) * See also Revision of the IORP Directive.

[160] Directive 2009/138/EC, with Commission Implementing Regulation (EU) 2016/165 of 5 February 2016 laying down technical information for the calculation of technical provisions and basic own funds for reporting with reference dates from 1 January until 30 March 2016, in accordance with Directive 2009/138/EC of the European Parliament and of the Council (Solvency II). Official Journal of the European Union, L 32/31, 9.2.2016.

[161] European Insurance and Occupational Pensions Authority (2024).

[162] European Insurance and Occupational Pensions Authority (2011).

[163] European Insurance and Occupational Pensions Authority (2011). See also European Insurance and Occupational Pensions Authority (2012).

[164] Borsjé and van Meerten (2015), p. 390.

[165] Statement on IORP II by PensionsEurope (umbrella organization of pension funds) on the IORP II Proposal: "IORPS are first and foremost social institutions". www.pensionseurope.eu. The Netherlands Pension Federation (umbrella organization of Dutch pension funds) uses exactly the same words in its Position Paper on the IOPR II Proposal www.pensioenfederatie.nl.

[166] Borsjé and van Meerten (2015), p. 391.

[167] Borsjé and van Meerten (2015), p. 391.

[168] Borsjé and van Meerten (2015), p. 391, footnote 18.

The importance of continuing to treat supplementary pension institutions as a distinct legal arrangement, and certainly not as any other undertaking, lies in securing state supervision, as well as professional solidarity, i.e. the criteria to which case-law also refers to as distinct characteristics of their social function. What power would the States have to organise their social security systems and decide the regulating legal regime, if, for capital market purposes and pursuant to the Directives, supplementary pension institutions were to be treated as operating solely as undertakings? Besides, in many states, the second pillar is so widespread that it has taken the characteristics of a general system, since it covers almost obligatorily[169] the active population system, while at the same time it is regulated by the state.[170] Moreover, in view of public-private partnerships, the new schemes that are quasi-private under the supervision of a public body have transcended the earlier definitions that regarded as public only the pensions that were granted directly by the State.[171,172]

In any case the difficulties posed by the different terminology, the diversity[173] and the differences of the insurance schemes within the European Union,[174] just like the difficulties of accurately defining the pillars, cannot result in ambiguity up to the point of indirectly removing the social elements of pensions and in this particular case of supplementary pensions. The Directives on supplementary pensions are also of particular importance in the context of the Regulation provisions on funded schemes.

References

Aggelopoulou O (2003) The obligatory character as a characteristic element of social insurance, Dissertation, EKPA (National and Kapodistrian University of Athens), Ant. N. Sakkoulas Publishing, Athens

Anagnostou-Dedouli A (2005) Social security by legal persons governed by public or private law. Ant. N. Sakkoulas Publishing, Athens-Komotini

Andrietti V (2000) Portability of Supplementary Pension Rights in the European Union, IRISS Working Paper Series 2000-01, IRISS at CEPS/INSTEAD. Available at https://liser.elsevierpure.com/ws/portalfiles/portal/11792098/Working%20Paper%20n_2000-01. Accessed 25 Nov 2024

Andrietti V (2001) Occupational pensions and interfirm job mobility in the European Union. Evidence from The ECHP Survey May 14, CeRP Working Papers 05, Center for Research on Pensions and Welfare Policies, Turin, p 3

[169] Féraud (1975), p. 6.

[170] Anagnostou-Dedouli (2005), p. 34.

[171] Esping-Andersen (1990).

[172] Stergiou (2009), p. 20.

[173] Michas Bequerie (1996), pp. 519, 525.

[174] Anagnostou-Dedouli (2005), p. 35.

ApRoberts L (1993) Complementary retirement pensions: towards a definition of terms. Int Soc Secur Rev 46(4):51–66, also published in International Social Security Association (ed) (1994) Complementary Pensions: European Perspectives, Geneva

Bakavou M (2015) Employee social security - supplementary forms. Nomiki Bibliothiki, Athens

Blake D (1998) Pension schemes as options on pension fund assets implications for pension fund management, Insurance: Mathematics and Economics 23. http://pensions-institute.org. Accessed 28 Dec 2024

Bollen-Vandenboorn A, Stevens Y (2012) *Mauris Casteels v British Airways*: limitation of length of service with one employer in the context of the acquisition of pension rights not EU proof. Eur J Soc Law:78

Boogert-Quaak J (1998) Opinion (Rule 147) for the Committee on Legal Affairs and Citizens' Rights, Committee on Employment and Social Affairs. In: Commission of the European Communities (1998) Green Paper entitled "Supplementary Pensions in the Single Market" (COM(97)0283 - C4-0392/97

Borsjé P, van Meerten H (2015) A European pensions union: towards a strengthening of the European pension systems. In: Pennings F, Vonk G (eds) Research handbook on European social security law. Edward Elgar publishing, UK-USA, p 390

Broadbent J, Palumbo M, Woodman E (2006) The shift from defined benefit to defined contribution pension plans -implications for asset allocation and risk management, Prepared for a Working Group on Institutional Investors, Global Savings and Asset Allocation established by the Committee on the Global Financial System, December http://www.bis.org/publ/wgpapers/cgfs27broadbent3.pdf. Accessed 28 Dec 2024

Commission of the European Communities (1991) Communication from the Commission to the Council, Supplementary social security schemes: the role of occupational pension schemes in the social protection of workers and their implications for freedom of movement, SEC p 1, footnote 1

Commission of the European Communities (1997a) Supplementary pensions in the Single Market: A Green Paper. COM (97) 283 final, Brussels

Commission of the European Communities (1997b) Committee on Legal Affairs and Citizens' Rights, Rapporteur Enrico Ferri, Report on the Commission Green Paper entitled "Supplementary Pensions in the Single Market" Explanatory Statement

Commission of the European Communities (2001) Communication from the Commission to the Council, the European Parliament and the Economic and Social Committee, The elimination of tax obstacles to the cross-border provision of occupational pensions, Brussels, 19.4.2001 COM (2001) 214 final

Commission Staff Working Document (2008) (SWD) "Demography Report 2008 – Meeting social needs in an ageing society" [SEC(2008) 2911]

Cornelissen R (1998) The principle of territoriality and the Community regulations on social security. EDKA (Social Security Law Review):689

Council Directive 98/49/EC, of 29 June 1998, on safeguarding the supplementary pension rights of employed and self-employed persons moving within the Community, OJ L 209 of 25.7.1998

Deutsche Bank Research (2003) EU Monitor Pension reforms in the EU, Economics, November https://www.dbresearch.com. Accessed 28 Dec 2024

Directive 2003/41/EC of the European Parliament and of the Council of 3 June 2003 on the activities and supervision of institutions for occupational retirement provision, Official Journal of the European Union, 23.9.2003, L 235/10

Directive 2009/138/EC of the European Parliament and of the Council, of 25 November 2009 on the taking-up and pursuit of the business of Insurance and Reinsurance (Solvency II), Official Journal of the European Union L 335/1, 17.12.2009, with Commission Implementing Regulation (EU) 2016/165 of 5 February 2016 laying down technical information for the calculation of technical provisions and basic own funds for reporting with reference dates from 1 January until 30 March 2016, in accordance with Directive 2009/138/EC of the European Parliament and of the Council (Solvency II).Official Journal of the European Union L 32/31, 9.2.2016

Directive 2014/50/EU of the European Parliament and of the Council of 16 April 2014 on minimum requirements for enhancing worker mobility
Directive 2014/51/EU of the European Parliament and of the Council of 16 April 2014 amending Directives 2003/71/EC and 2009/138/EC and Regulations (EC) No 1060/2009, (EU) No 1094/2010 and (EU) No 1095/2010 in respect of the powers of the European Supervisory Authority (European Insurance and Occupational Pensions Authority) and the European Supervisory Authority (European Securities and Markets Authority), Official Journal of the European Union, L 153/1, 22.5.2014
Eatock D (2015) European Union pension systems Adequate and sustainable? In: Briefing, European Parliament Think Tank. Available at https://www.europarl.europa.eu/RegData/etudes/BRIE/2015/571327/EPRS_BRI(2015)571327_EN.pdf. Accessed 25 Nov 2024
Esping-Andersen G (1990) The three worlds of welfare capitalism. Princeton University Press, Princeton, New Jersey
European Commission (2001a) Directorate-General for Economic and Financial Affairs, Economic paper Number 149, A Case for Partial Funding of Pensions with an Application to the EU Candidate Countries by Heikki Oksanen, March http://ec.europa.eu/economy_finance/publications/publication11052_en.pdf. Accessed 28 Dec 2024
European Commission (2001b) Communication from the Commission to the European Parliament and the Council Financial Services Political Challenges, June 2001, Fourth Progress, Brussels, 01.06.2001 COM (2001)286 final, p 8
European Commission (2002) Press release database, Pensions: Commission decides to attack obstacles to job mobility in pension schemes, IP/02/846 Brussels. https://europa.eu/rapid/press-release_IP-02-846_en.htm. Accessed 25 Nov 2024
European Commission (2005) Special Report No 4/2005, "The 2005 projections of age-related expenditure (2004–50) for the EU-25 Member States: underlying assumptions and projection methodologies" by the Economic Policy Committee and the European Commission (Economic and Financial Affairs DG)
European Commission (2009a) Pension schemes and Pension Projections in the EU-27 Member States 2008-2060 Volume I – Report EUROPEAN ECONOMY Occasional Papers No. 56
European Commission (2009b) Report from the Commission on some key aspects concerning Directive 2003/41/EC on the activities and supervision of institutions for occupational retirement provision (IORP Directive), Brussels, 30.4.2009 COM 203 final
European Commission (2010) Green Paper towards adequate, sustainable and safe European pension systems SEC (2010)830 Brussels, 7.7.2010 COM 365 final
European Commission (2012) White Paper, An Agenda for Adequate, Safe and Sustainable Pensions, Brussels, 16.2.2012 COM 55 final
European Commission (2014a) Social Europe-EU Employment and Social Situation - Quarterly Review Special Supplement 'Towards tax reforms that reconcile efficiency with equity concerns' prepared by G. Lejeune, J. Lüttge, and V. Maestri from the Employment Analysis and Social Analysis Units in DG EMPL, Luxembourg: Publications Office of the European Union
European Commission (2014b) The 2015 Ageing Report- Underlying Assumptions and Projection Methodologies, EUROPEAN ECONOMY 8/2014
European Commission (2014c) Commission Staff Working Document, Executive Summary of the Impact Assessment, accompanying the document Proposal for a Directive of the European Parliament and of the Council amending Directive 2003/41/EC on the activities and supervision of institutions for occupational retirement provision IORP II, Brussels, 27.3.2014 SWD(2014) 102 final, p 1
European Commission and Economic Policy Committee (2009) "2009 Ageing Report: Economic and budgetary projections for the EU-27 Member States (2008-2060)", European Economy, volume 2
European Economic and Social Committee (2001) Opinion on the "Proposal for a Directive of the European Parliament and of the Council on the activities of institutions for occupational

retirement provision" (2001/C 155/07)52001AE0403, Official Journal C 155 of 29/05/2001 p 0026 – 0031, paragraph 3.4
European Economic Community (1977) Council Directive 77/187 of 14-2-77, as amended with Directive 95/50/EEC of the Council of 29 June 1998 (EE L. 201/17.7.1998)
European Economic Community (1986) Council Directive No 86/378/EEC of 24 July 1986 on the implementation of the principle of equal treatment for men and women in occupational security schemes, OJ L 225 of 12/08/1986
European Insurance and Occupational Pensions Authority (2011) EIOPA-CP-11/001, 8 July 2011. EMF reply Consultation EIOPA-CP-11/001 8 July 2011 Comments Template on EIOPACP11/001 Draft response to Call for Advice on the review of Directive 2003/41/EC Scope, cross border activity, prudential regulation and governance. https://register.eiopa.europa.eu/Publications/Comments/IORP-CfA-Response_EMF-FEM.pdf. Accessed 25 Nov 2024
European Insurance and Occupational Pensions Authority (2012) EIOPA-BOS-12/015 15 February 2012 EIOPA's Advice to the European Commission on the review of the IORP Directive 2003/41/EC. https://register.eiopa.europa.eu/Publications/Consultations/EIOPA-BOS-12-015_EIOPA_s_Advice_to_the_European_Commission_on_the_review_of_the_IORP_Directive.pdf. Accessed 25 Nov 2024
European Insurance and Occupational Pensions Authority (2024). https://eiopa.europa.eu. Accessed 25 Nov 2024
European Insurance and Occupational Pensions Authority (EIOPA). https://eiopa.europa.eu/about-eiopa. Accessed 25 Nov 2024
European Parliament (2011) Directorate General for Internal Policies-Policy Department A: Economic and Scientific Policy, Pension systems in the EU – contingent liabilities and assets in the public and private sector
European Parliament, Committee on Economic and Monetary Affairs (1999) Draft Report on the communication from the Commission 'Towards a single market for supplementary pensions – results of the consultations on the Green Paper on supplementary pensions in the single market' (COM(1999)134 – C5-0135/1999 – 1999/2131(COS)), Rapporteur: Wilfried Kuckelkorn, PR\384894.en.doc
Féraud L (1975) Les pensions complémentaires, Essai d'analyse comparée, AISS Etudes et Recherches 7:6
Fuchs M (Hrsg) (2000) Nomoskommentar, Europäisches Sozialrecht, 4. Auflage, Nomos Verlagsgesellschaft, Baden Baden
Ghailani D, Guardiancich I, Natali D, Ferrera M, Jessula M (2011) Scope of the coordination system in the pension field- Final report, Tender VT/2010/104, 15 September 2011, Replies and Interviews to National Experts, French Ministry of Health and Solidarities, France, p 138
Jacob R (2003) Portability of supplementary pensions in the EU. In: Mortensen J, Sauto R (eds) Cross-border portability of pension rights: an important condition for an integrated market of pension provision – Exploratory Workshop. Centre for European Policy Studies, Brussels, p 25
Katrougalos G (2006) The impact of Community law on social security law. EDKA (Social Security Law Review):251
Kremalis K (1996) International and European social security law. Ant. N. Sakkoulas Publishing, Athens-Komotini
Leppik L (2006) Coordination of pensions in the European Union: the case of mandatory defined-contribution schemes in the Central and Eastern European Countries. Eur J Soc Secur:47–51
Lyon-Caen A, Lyon-Caen G (1993) Droit social international et européen. Dalloz, Paris
Mavridis P (2004) The freedom of movement of persons, employees and services as a fundamental principle of European integration: their employment and social security. EDKA (Social Security Law Review):810
Michas Bequerie S (1996) Régimes privés de retraites complémentaires. Essai de comparaison des systèmes allemande, anglais et français dans une perspective Communautaire. Droit social, pp 519, 525

MISSOC (2024) Glossary F- Financing principle. https://www.missoc.org/glossary/financing-principle/. Accessed 28 Dec 2024

Mousi N (2002) The social policy of the European Union. Papazisi, Athens

Nikolakopoulou-Stefanou I (2004) Developing Community and Greek occupational insurance scheme law. In: Amitsis G, Lixouriotis I, Petroglou P (eds) Occupational insurance schemes and labour law issues regarding private group insurance. Ant. N. Sakkoulas Publishing, Athens-Komotini, p 66

OECD (2005) Pensions at a glance – public policies across OECD countries. OECD Publishing. http://www.oecd-ilibrary.org/docserver/download/8105021e.pdf?expires=1456218934&id=id&accname=guest&checksum=69FE983F61075039C83EBE4E37CEEDC3. Accessed 28 Dec 2024

OECD (2011) Pension markets in focus, Issue 8, OECD Publishing (July). https://web-archive.oecd.org/2012-06-14/93527-48438405.pdf. Accessed 28 Dec 2024

OECD (2015) Pensions at a Glance 2015: OECD and G20 indicators. OECD Publishing, Paris. https://doi.org/10.1787/pension_glance-2015-en. Accessed 26 Jan 2025

OSE (2011) European social observatory deliverable - Authors: D. Ghailani, I. Guardiancich, D. Natali, M. Ferrera and M. Jessula, Scope of the coordination system in the pension field - Final report, Tender VT/2010/104, 15 September 2011 www.ose.be

Paparrigopoulou-Pehlivanidi P (2013) Social security law. Nomiki Bibliothiki, Athens

Pennings F (1990) Benefits of doubt. a comparative study of the legal aspects of employment and unemployment schemes in Great Britain, Germany, France and the Netherlands. Tilburg Law Rev 3(1):90–92

Pennings F (2003) Introduction to European social security law, 4th edn. Antwerp-Oxford-New York, Intersentia

Pennings F (2012) European social security law. Wolters Kluwer Law & Business, Netherlands

Pensions Europe (2024) Input for the Impact Assessment on pillar II and III requirements of the IORP II Directive (update) 18 July 2013. https://pensionseurope.eu/policy-priorities/iorp-ii-directive/. Accessed 25 Nov 2024

Perrin G (1990) Réflexions préalables à la coordination des régimes Complémentaires privés de Sécurité Sociale dans la Communauté Économique Européenne. Annuaire European Institute of Social Security, Les protections complémentaires en matière de sécurité sociale, p 112

Proposal for a Directive of the European Parliament and of the Council on the activities and supervision of institutions for occupational retirement provision (recast) /* COM/2014/0167 final - 2014/0091 (COD) * See also Revision of the IORP Directive

Ravelli F (2012) The ECJ and supplementary pensions discrimination in EU law. Eur J Soc Law:63

Regulation 2019/1238 of the European Parliament and of the Council of 20 June 2019 on a Pan-European Pension Product (PEPP) [2019] OJ L 198/1 (PEPP Regulation)

Regulation (EC) No 1060/2009 of the European Parliament and of the Council of 16 September 2009 on credit rating agencies, Official Journal of the European Union, L 302/1, 17.11.2009

Regulation (EU) 1094/2010 of the European Parliament and of the Council of 24 November 2010 establishing a European Supervisory Authority (European Insurance and Occupational Pensions Authority), amending Decision No 716/2009/EC and repealing Commission Decision 2009/79/EC, OJ L 331, 15.10.2010, p. 48–83

Regulation (EU) No 1095/2010 Action Plan on building 2010 establishing a European Supervisory Authority (European Securities and Markets Authority), amending Decision No 716/2009/EC and repealing Commission Decision 2009/77/EC, Official Journal of the European Union, L 331/84, 15.12.2010

Saritas S (2019) "How does financialised pension provision exacerbate the impact of the crisis in Europe?" https://www.hetecon.net/wp-content/uploads/2019/12/Saritas_406-637-1-RV.pdf. Accessed 28 Dec 2024

Schmidt E (2023) Occupational pensions and the protection of mobile persons. In: Pennings F, Vonk G (eds) Research handbook on European social security law, 2nd edn. Edward Elgar Publishing, UK-USA, p 296

Schuler R (2015) Regulation (EC) No 883/2004-Overview. In: Fuchs M, Cornelissen R (eds) EU social security law – a commentary on EU Regulations 883/2004 and 987/2009. C. H. BECK-Hart- Nomos, Baden-Baden, p 237

Stergiou A (2009) Public Private Partnership in public pension schemes (Market infiltration into the State). Reprinted from the Labour Law Review 68:20

Stergiou A (2015) Constitutional issues of Mandatory Occupational Insurance Funds – Opinion. DEN (Labour Law Report): 190

Stevens Y (2003) The improvement of the legal framework concerning pension portability: is open coordination an option? In: Mortensen J, Sauto R (eds) Cross-border portability of pension rights: an important condition for an integrated market of pension provision – Exploratory Workshop. Centre for European Policy Studies, Brussels

Stevens Y (2022) EU pension law. Edward Elgar Publishing, UK-USA

Stevens Y (2024) EU pension law. Edward Elgar Publishing, UK-USA

The Social Protection Committee (2008) Privately managed funded pension provision and their contribution to adequate and sustainable pensions adopted, pp 4–7

Tsantilas P (1996) Issues in defining social security in European Community Law (the case-law of the Court of Justice of the European Communities). In: Kremalis K (scientific coordinator) Issues in defining the limits of private and social security, possibilities for private insurance complementing or partially substituting social security. Ant. N. Sakkoulas Publishing, Athens-Komotini, p 35

Tsetoura A (2015) The role of fundamental social rights against financial policies in the European architecture: the impact on domestic developments. EDKA (Social Security Law Review):283 et seq

Verschueren H (2009) Regulation 883/2004 and invalidity and old-age pensions. Eur J Soc Secur 1–2:146

Verschueren H (2011) The scope of the EU social security coordination. Available at https://www.coe.int/t/dg3/sscssr/Source/VERSCHUERENMAV_EU.pdf. Accessed 25 Nov 2024

Vonk G (2010) Social security as a public interest: a multidisciplinary inquiry into the foundations of the regulatory welfare state. Eur J Soc Secur 12(1):2–15

World Bank Pension Reform Primer, "Notional accounts -Notional defined contribution plans as a pension reform strategy" https://www.worldbank.org/ext/en/home. Accessed 26 Jan 2025

Chapter 3
Coordination of Pension Systems

3.1 "Public Investiture" as a Distinct Characteristic of a Pension Scheme

As put forth in the Regulation, its scope includes all social security (pension) systems that are statutory or, more accurately, that are provided for in "legislation" (within the meaning of Article 1, sub-paragraph l, Regulation No 883/04) and fulfil the conditions of Article 1 (sub-paragraphs l and w) and Article 3, Regulation No 883/04. Member States' social security systems should thus be treated in the same way when applying the Coordination Regulation, regardless of whether the system is based on employment or residence.[1] The correlation between inputs (income from any kind of financing) and outputs (benefits), i.e. how they are regulated, is crucial, as evident by their particular legal characteristics.

Thus, it would be **inconsistent** to exclude from the Regulation the main mandatory funded schemes, when, at the same time, supplementary pension schemes can be included simply with Member States taking advantage of their ability to make the necessary decisions and declarations. Along the same lines, it would be inconsistent to consider as falling outside the Regulation's scope the optional supplementary funded pension schemes established by law (see analysis below of Judgment Fédération française des sociétés d'assurance/FFSA), when the schemes in question which are established by collective agreements and are included in the relevant declarations of Member States may fall within the scope of Regulation No 883/04. In addition, it would not be acceptable that workers who depend heavily on supplementary social security provision are prevented from exercising their right to free movement for fear of losing an adequate level of social security cover.[2] As already noted, these systems could not continue indefinitely be undefined: not social security schemes falling under the coordination regime, nor systems with no social security

[1] Sakslin (2000), p. 179.

[2] Commission of the European Communities (1993), Green Paper, COM (93) 551, p. 61.

A. Tsetoura, *Pension Rights and Free Movement of Persons*,
https://doi.org/10.1007/978-3-031-91127-9_3

character subject to competition.[3] Provided that a supplementary pension scheme has been established by a collective agreement within a framework laid down by law and affiliation to that scheme has been made compulsory by the public authorities, it constitutes an element of the system of social protection and the sectoral pension fund responsible for the management of it must be regarded as contributing to the management of the public social security service.[4]

Moreover, the question of treating occupational supplementary pensions as social security pensions is also relevant. Given that occupational pensions are pensions provided on the basis of occupational activity and on the basis of a collective agreement or a contract agreed between the social partners or at the company level between the firms and the employees, the decisive distinction with a social security pension is that it is not statutory but based on an agreement.[5] The schemes can be quasi-mandatory in the sense that, on the basis of a nation- or industry-wide bargaining agreement, the employers are obliged to provide an occupational pension scheme to their employees while the participation for an individual remains voluntary.[6] The schemes are run by private sector pension funds, insurance companies or the sponsoring companies themselves (in balance sheets). Occupational schemes can be equivalent to statutory earnings-related pension schemes or complementary to them; they are schemes that play an equivalent role to social security schemes in the pension provision.[7]

As argued by Winderstein, there is a strong *prima facie* argument to say that health and pension insurance covering (almost) the entire population are universal services, the provision of which may justify or require special monopoly rights, i.e. compulsory affiliation.[8] Affiliation to a supplementary pension scheme can become mandatory, in view of the social function of supplementary pension schemes and the margin of appreciation enjoyed, according to settled case-law, by the Member States in organising their social security systems.[9] Moreover, as already proven, the hypothesis that is the base of the distinction between basic and supplementary pension schemes, i.e. the presumption that the former are public and the

[3]Lyon-Caen and Lyon-Caen (1994), p. 227; Commission of the European Communities (1997).

[4]Judgment of the Court of 21.09.1999, Case C-67/96, Albany International BV, European Court Reports 1999 p. I-05751, paragraph 73.

[5]European Commission (2005), Directorate-General for Economic and Financial Affairs, p. 98.

[6]European Commission (2005), p. 111.

[7]European Commission (2005), p. 111.

[8]Winterstein (1999), p. 9.

[9]Judgments of 7.02.1984, Case 238/82, Duphar and others, European Court Reports 1984, p. 523, paragraph 16; judgment of 17.02.1993, joined cases C-159/91 and C-160/91, Poucet and Pistre, European Court Reports 1993 p. I-00637, paragraph 6; and of 17.06.1997, Case C-70/95, Sodemare and others, European Court Reports 1997, p. I-3395, paragraph 27. Judgment of 21.09.1999, Case C-219/97, Maatschappij, European Court Reports 1999 I-06121 ECLI:EU:C:1999:437, paragraph 112; Judgment—21/09/1999—Brentjens' Case C-117/97 (joined cases C-115/97, C-116/97, C-117/97) ECLI:EU:C:1999:434, paragraph 122.

latter are private, is not true.[10] More specifically, the State as an employer can provide supplementary pensions, while it is possible to find supplementary schemes that, even if privately set up and administered, are designed and/or regulated in such a way that makes them substantially very close to public schemes.[11] Indeed, a very important element to consider in a classic analysis of pension schemes' public/private nature is the extent of government intervention in their establishment and regulation.[12]

In both the first and the second pillars, retirement provision is largely collective and the freedom of individual workers not to become a member of some pension scheme is very limited, even if the employer may be free not to establish a scheme or not to offer membership in it to some of the employees.[13] Retirement provision is largely compulsory for individual workers whose personal initiative is usually limited to the third pillar, i.e. additional personal savings, life assurance contracts and the acquisition of real property.[14] The fact that retirement provision in the first two pillars—which represent by far the most important sources of income during retirement—is largely compulsory for workers, can be explained by the observed tendency of individuals not to make sufficient provision by themselves.[15]

It is incumbent on each Member State to consider whether, in view of the particular features of its national pension system, the laying down of minimum requirements would still enable it to endure the level of pension which it seeks to guarantee in a sector by compulsory affiliation to a pension fund; public authorities are not therefore precluded from conferring on a pension fund the exclusive right to manage a supplementary pension scheme in a given sector.[16]

Moreover, according to settled case-law, in allowing derogations from the general rules of the Treaty on certain conditions, Article 90 (2) seeks to reconcile the Member States' interest in using certain undertakings, in particular in the public sector, as an instrument of economic or social policy with the Community's interest in ensuring compliance with the rules on competition and the preservation of the

---

[10] ApRoberts (1993), pp. 51–66.

[11] Andrietti (2000), p. 5.

[12] Andrietti (2000), p. 5.

[13] Commission of the European Communities (1991), Communication from the Commission to the Council, SEC (91) 1332 final, p. 6.

[14] Commission of the European Communities (1991), Communication from the Commission to the Council, SEC (91) 1332 final, p. 6.

[15] Commission of the European Communities (1991), Communication from the Commission to the Council, SEC (91) 1332 final, p. 6.

[16] Judgment of the Court of 21 September 1999, Case C-219/97, Maatschappij, European Court Reports 1999 I-06121 ECLI:EU:C:1999:437, paragraphs 112–113; judgment—21/09/1999—Brentjens' Case C-117/97 (joined cases C-115/97, C-116/97, C-117/97) ECLI:EU:C:1999:434, paragraphs 122–123; judgment of 21.09.1999, Case C-67/96, Albany International BV, European Court Reports 1999 p. I-05751, paragraphs 122–123.

unity of the Common Market.[17] Thus, Member States cannot be precluded, when defining the services of general economic interest which they entrust to certain undertakings, from taking into account of objectives pertaining to their national policy or from endeavouring to attain them by means of obligations and constraints which the impose on such undertakings.[18]

If the exclusive right of the fund to manage the supplementary pension scheme for all workers in a given sector were removed, undertakings with young employees in good health engaged in non-dangerous activities would seek more advantageous insurance terms from private insurers. The progressive departure of "good" risks would leave the sectoral pension fund with responsibility for an increasing share of "bad" risks, thereby increasing the cost of pensions for workers, particularly those in small and medium-sized undertakings with older employees engaged in dangerous activities, to which the fund could no longer offer pensions at an acceptable cost.[19] Such a situation would arise particularly in a case where the supplementary pension scheme managed displays a high level of solidarity resulting, in particular, from the fact that contributions do not reflect the risk, from the obligation to accept all workers without a prior medical examination, the continuing accrual of pension rights despite exemption from the payment of contributions in the event of incapacity for work, the discharge by the Fund of arrears of contributions due from an employer in the event of insolvency and the indexing of the amount of pensions in order to maintain their value.[20]

It is therefore concluded that the first phrase of Article 1 (l) of Regulation No 883/04 includes all systems provided for in legislation, whether public or private, mandatory or not and, obviously, regardless of the way they regulate their inputs and outputs (pay-as-you-go, funded, mixed, defined contributions, defined benefits, notional defined contributions or NDC, unit-linked pension programs). The fact that insurance may be provided in whole or in part by a private insurer based on a private contract is therefore irrelevant, since the conclusion of such contract is directly related to the application of social security legislation, as the cover of the coordination regulations depends solely on the statutory source, i.e. the legal basis of the relevant schemes, which should be objectively assessed and not just on the basis of the Member States' declarations.[21]

---

[17] Judgments of 19.03.1991, Case C-202/88, French Republic v Commission of the European Communities, European Court Reports 1991, p. I-1223, paragraph 12; of 23.10.1997, Case C-157/94, Commission of the European Communities v Kingdom of the Netherlands, European Court Reports 1997, p. I-5699, paragraph 39; of 21.09.1999, Case C-67/96, Albany International BV, European Court Reports 1999 p. I-05751, paragraph 103.

[18] Judgment of 23.10.1997, Case C-157/94, Commission of the European Communities v Kingdom of the Netherlands, European Court Reports 1997, p. I-5699, paragraph 40; of 21.09.1999, Case C-67/96, Albany International BV, European Court Reports 1999 p. I-05751, paragraph 104.

[19] Albany International BV, paragraph 108.

[20] Albany International BV, paragraph 109.

[21] Verschueren (2009), p. 147.

It seems that, indirectly, the legislator has taken into account the distinction of the schemes on the basis of their establishment method. Thus, on the one hand, there are affiliated schemes that are established as a manifestation—responsibility of state power and schemes established as a manifestation of private initiative in the first phrase of Article 1 (l) of Regulation No 883/04. On the other hand, there are affiliated schemes established as a manifestation of collective autonomy in the second sub-paragraph of Article 1 (l) of Regulation No 883/04. Of course, even collective autonomy entails a private initiative; for this reason, it is also possible for occupational/supplementary schemes to be characterised as private.[22] However, it is still for the Member States to decide whether to include or not a supplementary scheme in its declaration regarding affiliation to the Regulation.

In order to ensure the level of pensions they intend to guarantee in a professional sector, many Member States have made affiliation to occupational insurance funds mandatory.[23] The legal technique is the following: Social partners' representatives agree to establish an occupational insurance fund; then, the Administration acquires by law the ability to make affiliation to that fund mandatory for the parties that signed its founding agreement and its members.[24] The occupational scheme that is established in this way may have a contractual basis but the same compulsory character as a statutory scheme.[25] The Court has held that if the social partners' agreement or the decision of self-employed workers to establish an occupational insurance fund is not contrary to competition rules, the State's decision to make affiliation to that fund compulsory, cannot be considered as contrary to competition rules.[26] As aptly observed by **Leppik in the examination of the relation between Regulation No 1408/71 and Directive 98/49, the categories of "statutory" and "supplementary" do not constitute a logical pair; the logical pairs of respective concepts would be statutory—non-statutory and basic—supplementary.**[27] The typology of pension schemes in the EU legislation has assumed that only basic pension schemes are governed by legislation, while supplementary pension schemes are non-statutory.[28]

However, some additional remarks are necessary. While public authority intervention does not necessarily entail assigning to a scheme a mandatory character (it may simply extend its scope), the compulsory nature of a system means, in any event, that the State intervenes by exercising public authority. Thus, while public statutory schemes may be voluntary, private mandatory schemes, although based on the private element (which may refer to both the method of their establishment and

---

[22] European Commission (2014), The 2015 Ageing Report, pp. 106–107.

[23] Petroglou (2004), p. 93.

[24] Petroglou (2004), p. 93.

[25] Tandaroudas (2004), p. 93.

[26] Judgment of the Court of 21.09.1999, joined cases C-115/97 to C-117/97, Brentjens', European Court Reports 1999 I-06025 ECLI:EU:C:1999:434, paragraphs 65–69.

[27] Leppik (2006), p. 47.

[28] Ibid.

their administration) are regulated by private law, they may be regulated by public law to the extent they become mandatory as schemes regulating social security rights for which public authorities intervene with a decision. It is argued that social security law is part of public law, regulating relations between states and not between individuals.[29] However, with a simple legislative choice on EU level, i.e. Regulation No 883/04, the spheres of influence of both branches of law, public and private, are being expanded resulting in a restriction for the purposes of social security. Moreover, it is argued that even if social security is perceived as a public interest, it is neither totally public nor totally private, thus making it easier for the social security system in question to be subject to a mixed governance structure, a common feature for most public services.[30]

As can be observed in conclusion, the sole criterion set out in the Regulation for a pension system, and the pension granted as a result, to fall within its scope is the regulatory or public character/element (direct by law or indirect through its complementary role to a statutory obligation or through a decision by public authorities) which is evident in the method of establishing a system. In this way the participation of members in a scheme is protected, in the sense that this participation is statutory when based on legislation or public authority decisions. Thus, the two common features that should be detected in all the schemes covered by the Regulation is the regulation of social security rights with coverage of the relevant traditional social risks (Article 3 (1), Regulation No 883/04) and the existence of a public element. The public element can be a statutory provision or a public authority decision. It could be argued that the Regulation assumes from this "public investiture" a social mission. Otherwise said, it assumes that the presence of state/public authority guarantees a circle of solidarity for the protection of which public authorities intervene.

3.2 The Court's Jurisprudence

As already demonstrated, the Regulation's wording seems to adopt a formal or organic criterion for an organisation and a scheme to fall within its scope, in the sense of it being provided solely by law (or a decision by a public authority), without making references to its operation and the purpose of the institutions of a social security system.

The Court holds a different position from the Regulation: it treats mandatory affiliation to a scheme as serving exclusively the principle of solidarity, which is the primary structural component of a social security scheme, according to the Court's approach. Even in the Gauman-Cerri judgment, which is examined below, the conclusion of a contract with the private insurance body and consequently the

[29] Pennings (2003), p. 5.
[30] Vonk (2010), pp. 2–15.

affiliation to the relevant scheme was mandatory. According to CJEU, the concept of a social security institution arises in a functional way, regardless of the legal status, i.e. as long as a social objective is served in the operation of a public service.[31] However, a general reference to the social objectives of the Fund is not enough; they should result from concrete measures, from a series of solidarity indicators.[32]

In that regard, the Court has held that reference must be made to the components of each social security benefit and in particular to the objectives pursued by such benefit and the conditions for granting it.[33] According to the Court, it is possible that certain laws, because of the classes of persons to which they apply, their objectives, and the detailed rules for their application, may simultaneously contain elements belonging to both the categories of social security and social assistance.[34] Similarly, in a more recent case,[35] the Court held that the concept of a "social assistance system" must be defined by reference to the objective pursued and not by reference to formal criteria—depending on whether it is provided on the basis of objective criteria or exclusively based on the state of need of the interested party.[36] It seems therefore that the case-law interpretation focuses on the objective of a benefit, of a scheme and of a social security body/institution.

CJEU has been participating in the conversation on the compatibility of a social security institution with competition rules.[37] In principle, as CJEU has consistently accepted, the assignment of a specific economic activity to a public body does not in itself preclude it from being characterised as economic.[38] However, irrespective of whether a body falls within the concept of an undertaking or not, if it operates primarily on the basis of the principle of solidarity and has no profit-making purpose, then the CJEU excludes it from the application of the Regulation's rules.[39] However, it should be noted that in a recent judgment, CJEU insists on the objective component, but from a different perspective. It seems therefore to take into account a rationale of proportional protection, which may be provided regardless of a mandatory or optional basis. More specifically, it focuses more on the objective pursued by the benefits provided under a scheme and in particular on ensuring that their recipients maintain a standard of living commensurate with what they enjoyed prior to retirement.[40]

---

[31] Stergiou (2014), p. 35.

[32] Ibid.

[33] Tsantilas (1996), p. 36.

[34] Judgment of 22.06.1972, Case 1/72, Frilli, European Court Reports *1972 p. 00457*, paragraph 13.

[35] Judgment of the Court of 19.09.2013, Case C-140/12, Brey, Digital reports (Court Reports—general) ECLI:EU:C:2013:565.

[36] Stergiou (2014), p. 42.

[37] Paparrigopoulou-Pehlivanidi (2002).

[38] Stergiou (2015), p. 190.

[39] Ibid.

[40] Judgment of the Court of 21.01.2016, Case C-453/14, Knauer, Digital Reports (Court Reports—general) ECLI:EU:C:2016:37, paragraph 38.

3.2.1 The Principle of Solidarity: Mandatory vs. Optional Affiliation

The principle of solidarity as a feature of a social security scheme emerges from the case law of the Court, which also indicates the importance of the kind of the affiliation to the system.

3.2.1.1 Poucet and Pistre

The Court had already referred to the principle of solidarity as an integral part of social security schemes in the joined cases **Poucet and Pistre.**[41] In this case, the questions were raised in proceedings brought by Poucet and Pistre respectively against Caisse Mutuelle Régionale du Languedoc-Roussillon (Camulrac), which manages the sickness and maternity insurance scheme for self-employed persons in non-agricultural occupations, and the company which acts as its agent, Assurances Générales de France (AGF) and against Caisse Autonome Nationale de Compensation de l'Assurance Vieillesse des Artisans de Clermont-Ferrand (Cancava). In those proceedings, Mr Poucet and Mr Pistre sought the annulment of orders served on them to pay social security contributions to the two funds mentioned above. Without challenging the principle of compulsory affiliation to a social security scheme, they considered that, for such purposes, they should be free to approach any private insurance company established within the territory of the Community and not have to be subject to the conditions laid down unilaterally by the abovementioned organisations, which hold a dominant position, contrary to the rules on freedom of competition laid down in the Treaty.

Under the social security system at issue in the main proceedings, self-employed persons in non-agricultural occupations were the subject of compulsory social protection, including that provided by autonomous statutory schemes, in particular the sickness and maternity insurance scheme, which was applicable to all self-employed persons in non-agricultural occupations and the old-age insurance scheme for the craft occupations concerned. As the Court noted, those schemes pursued a social objective and embodied the principle of solidarity. Indeed, those schemes are intended to provide cover for all the persons to whom they apply, against the risks of sickness, old age, death and invalidity, regardless of their financial status and their state of health at the time of affiliation (Poucet and Pistre, paragraph 9).

In the old-age insurance scheme, solidarity is embodied in the fact that the contributions paid by active workers serve to finance the pensions of retired workers (Poucet and Pistre, paragraph 11). It is also reflected by the grant of pension rights where no contributions have been made and of pension rights that are not proportional to the contributions paid (Poucet and Pistre, paragraph 11). Finally, there is

[41] Judgment of 17.02.1993, joined cases C-159/91 and C-160/91, Poucet and Pistre, European Court Reports1993, p. I-00637.

solidarity between the various social security schemes, in that those in surplus contribute to the financing of those with structural financial difficulties (Poucet and Pistre, paragraph 12). From the above, it follows that the social security schemes are based on a **system of compulsory contribution, which is indispensable for application of the principles of solidarity and the financial equilibrium of those schemes** (paragraph 13).

As follows from the general Court case-law, in the context of competition law, the concept of an undertaking encompasses every entity engaged in an economic activity, regardless of the legal status of the entity and the way in which it is financed.[42] However, **sickness funds and the organisations involved in the management of the public social security system fulfil an exclusively social function. That activity is based on the principle of national solidarity and is entirely non-profit** (Poucet and Pistre, paragraph 18). The benefits paid are statutory benefits bearing no relation to the amount of the contributions. Accordingly, that activity is not an economic activity and, therefore, **the organizations to which it is entrusted are not undertakings** within the meaning of Articles 85 and 96 of the Treaty (Poucet and Pistre, paragraph 19). As a result, according to the Court, the concept of an undertaking within the meaning of Articles 85 and 86 of the Treaty does not encompass organisations charged with the management of social security schemes of the kind referred to in the judgments of the national court (Poucet and Pistre, paragraph 20).

3.2.1.2 Garcia

Similarly, in **Garcia,**[43] the question was raised in various proceedings challenging final orders to settle unpaid contributions, served on the plaintiffs in the main proceedings by a number of social security organisations. The social security schemes involved covered health and maternity insurance for the self-employed in non-agricultural trades, old-age insurance for those in skilled manual trades and old-age insurance for those in industrial and commercial trades. According to the main proceedings' plaintiffs, the monopoly established by French legislation in the field of social insurance is incompatible with Community rules, specifically with Directive 92/49/EEC. The national tribunal noted that under Article 2(2) of Directive 92/49/EEC that directive is to apply "neither to the types of insurance or operations, nor to undertakings or institutions to which Directive 73/239/EEC does not apply, nor to the bodies referred to in Article 4 of that Directive". The First Council Directive of 24 July 1973 on the coordination of laws, regulations and administrative provisions relating to the taking-up and pursuit of the business of direct insurance

---

[42] See mainly, Judgment of 23.04.1991, Case C-41/90, Höfner and Eiser, European Court Reports 1991, p. 1-1979, paragraph 21; judgment of 17.02.1993, joined cases C-159/91 and C-160/91, Poucet and Pistre, European Court Reports 1993 p. I-00637, paragraph 17.

[43] Judgment of 26.03.1996, Case C-238/94, García, European Court Reports 1996 p. I-01673.

other than life assurance (OJ 1973 L 228, p. 3) does not apply, under Article 2(1) (d) thereof, to "insurance forming part of a statutory system of social security".

The national tribunal wondered none the less whether, in the light of certain recitals in the preamble to Directive 92/49/EEC, Article 2(2) thereof should not be interpreted as referring solely to the structures of social security schemes, whereas the content of those schemes—cover against the risks concerned (old-age, sickness and invalidity)—still falls within the scope of the directive and is thus excluded from the monopoly enshrined in the French legislation. As the Court stressed in its judgment of 17 February 1993 in joined cases Poucet and Pistre (Garcia, paragraph 13), social security schemes such as **those at issue in the main proceedings which are based on the principle of solidarity, require compulsory contributions in order to ensure that the principle of solidarity is applied** and that their financial equilibrium is maintained (Garcia, paragraph 14). If Article 2(2) of Directive 92/49/EEC were to be interpreted in the manner contemplated by the national tribunal, the obligation to contribute would be removed and the schemes in question would thus be unable to survive (Garcia, paragraph 14). At this stage, the observations of the Commission regarding supplementary schemes should be highlighted; the Commission notes that in both the first and the second pillars, the freedom of individual workers not to become a member of some pension scheme is very limited.[44] The fact that retirement provision in the first two pillars—which represent by far the most important sources of income during retirement—is largely compulsory for workers, can be explained by the observed tendency of individuals not to make sufficient provision by themselves.[45] By making retirement provision compulsory for individuals and by pooling risks, first- and second- pillar pension schemes reduce the risk of poverty during old age and the likelihood of an individual having to claim social assistance after retiring from work.[46]

3.2.1.3 Cisal di Battistello

Along the same lines, in **Cisal di Battistello,**[47] the Court held that a social security body is not an undertaking and its activity is not an economic activity, when that body fulfils a social function.[48] However, the application of the principle of solidarity (for example, where the amount of contributions is not proportional to the insured

[44] Commission of the European Communities (1991), Communication from the Commission to the Council, SEC (91) 1332 final, p. 6.

[45] Commission of the European Communities (1991), Communication from the Commission to the Council, SEC (91) 1332 final, p. 6.

[46] Commission of the European Communities (1991), Communication from the Commission to the Council, SEC (91) 1332 final, p. 7.

[47] Judgment of the Court of 22.02.2002, Case C-218/00, Cisal di Battistello, European Court Reports 2002 I-00691, ECLI:EU:C:2002:36.

[48] Stergiou (2014), p. 35.

risk) as well as state supervision are required.[49] This was the first case, where the Court explored the possibility of a public social security scheme falling under the rules of competition, otherwise said, of treating a statutory scheme as an undertaking.[50]

The crucial issue which the Court had to address was whether such a scheme, despite its statutory character, could display characteristics similar to those found in private insurance schemes and if, as a result, could fall within the scope of the rules of competition; the Court had also to address the reverse scenario, i.e. whether the differences between public and private insurance schemes are that fundamental as to totally exclude public social security schemes from being considered as an undertaking.[51] This judgment helped clarify that the pursuit of a social and not an economic purpose (since assigning a specific economic activity does not render such an activity non-economic) is not enough to exclude an insurance fund from qualifying as an undertaking; it should also operate on the basis of the principle of solidarity.[52]

3.2.1.4 Kattner

The Court followed a similar reasoning in **Kattner,**[53] where it examined the case of an occupational insurance fund with a non-profit status, to which affiliation was compulsory (Kattner, paragraph 5). The Court noted that insurance funds as the one in question, as public law bodies, are involved in the management of the German social security system and in this respect they fulfil a social function, which is entirely non-profit making (Kattner, paragraph 35). This judgment follows the Poucet and Pistre and Cisal judgments, where the Court's goal was to determine whether the social security bodies concerned in each case could be classified as undertakings, and therefore have the protective competition rules apply to them, as set out in Articles 81 and 82 EC.[54]

In Kattner, however, the Court examined the compulsory affiliation to a statutory insurance body not in the light of competition, rather than the freedom to provide services, according to the relevant theory, by introducing the element of economic equilibrium and applying the principle of proportionality.[55] This case was of great scientific interest; CJEU examined the issue of bodies providing social security from

[49] Ibid.

[50] Bakavou (2015), p. 96.

[51] Ibid.

[52] Bakavou (2015), p. 96.

[53] Judgment of the Court of 5.03.2009, Case C-350/07, Kattner, European Court Reports 2009 I-01513 ECLI:EU:C:2009:127.

[54] Gkritsi (2012), p. 40.

[55] Gkritsi (2012), p. 40.

the perspective of Articles 49 and 50 TEC[56] (now 56 and 57 TFEU), in order to determine whether compulsory affiliation to a statutory occupational insurance fund is a hindrance to the freedom to provide services.[57] More specifically, it is crucial to determine each time if the social purpose of the body is realised, i.e. if it meets a minimum coverage threshold and does not exceed what is necessary to achieve the objective pursued, thereby leaving other (private bodies) to offer their services in the context of e.g. supplementary contracts to cover further or more specific risks.[58]

However, as in the previous Poucet and Pistre and Cisal cases, the crucial elements for the Court were the application of the principle of solidarity (Kattner, paragraphs 44–59) and state supervision (Kattner, paragraphs 60–68). The Court, therefore, noted that according to the German legislation (Article 176, SGB VII), employers' liability insurance associations are under an obligation to apportion any excess costs amongst themselves where the expenditure of one association significantly exceeds the average expenditure of all the associations (Kattner, paragraph 48). It follows that the principle of solidarity is thus also applied amongst all branches of industry at the level of the country as a whole, with different employers' liability insurance associations being grouped together in a risk community, which enables them to effect an equalisation of costs and risks between them (Kattner, paragraph 48).[59] In addition, the Court upheld its judgment in Cisal (paragraph 40), according to which the value of the benefits paid by employers' liability insurance associations is not necessarily proportionate to the insured person's earnings (Kattner, paragraph 55). The absence, however, of any direct link between the contributions paid and the benefits granted thus entails solidarity between better paid workers and those who, given their low earnings, would be deprived of proper social cover if such a link existed (Kattner, paragraph 59).[60]

Furthermore, the fact that employer's liability insurance associations are given a degree of latitude, within the framework of a system of self-management, in order to lay down the factors that determine the amount of contribution and benefits cannot as such as such change the nature of those associations' activity (Kattner, paragraph 61).[61] Consequently, according to the Court, Articles 81 EC and 82 EC are to be interpreted to the effect that a body such as the employer's liability insurance association to which undertakings in a particular branch of industry and a particular territory must be affiliated is not an undertaking within the meaning of those provisions, but fulfils an exclusively social function, where such a body operates

[56] Giesen (2009), p. 311; Tsotsorou and Sklikas (2012), pp. 41 et seq.

[57] Bakavou (2015), p. 97.

[58] Gkritsi (2012), p. 40.

[59] See by analogy, judgment of 17.02.1993, C-159/91 and C-160/91, Poucet and Pistre, European Court Reports 1993, p. I-637, paragraph 12; Judgment of 16/03/2004—AOK Bundesverband and Others Case C-355/01 (joined cases C-264/01, C-306/01, C-354/01, C-355/01) ECLI:EU:C:2004:150, paragraph 53.

[60] Cisal judgment, paragraph 42, cited above.

[61] See, AOK Bundesverband and others judgment, cited above, paragraph 56.

within the framework of a scheme which applies the principle of solidarity and is subject to State supervision, which it is for the referring court to verify (Kattner, paragraph 68). Following this judgment, it was argued that in the absence of a common social policy consensus at a European level, the Court left a wide margin of appreciation to the Court of each State as the sole formally and substantially competent body to make the distinction between the element of solidarity, state supervision and a minimum social security coverage by public bodies, so that private bodies are not effectively excluded.[62]

At the same time, however, it has been pointed out that for the purpose of establishing the principle of solidarity, the Court is focusing its investigation on certain indications, such as the lack of for-profit purpose, the compulsive affiliation,[63] the lack of total correspondence between contributions and benefits and the calculation of contributions in relation to income from work.[64] Compulsory affiliation as an indication of social purpose is necessary for maintaining the financial stability of the Fund.[65] The financial system for covering costs largely depends on whether the insurance scheme was established as a compulsory statutory scheme or based on a contract as an optional scheme.[66]

3.2.1.5 Fédération française des sociétés d'assurance/FFSA

The Court followed an **opposite approach** in **Fédération Française des Sociétés d'Assurance/FFSA**[67] on the **optional supplementary old-age insurance scheme** for self-employed farmers, established pursuant to Article 1122-7 of the Code Rural (JORF of 27 November 1990, p. 14581, hereinafter: decree 90-1051). **Decree 90-1051 laid down the organisation and detailed rules for operation of the supplementary old-age insurance scheme for self-employed farmers** financed by voluntary contributions deductible from taxable earnings, which **was created by Law No 88-1202** of 30 December 1988 on the adaptation of farming to its economic and social environment.

In accordance with the second paragraph of Article 1 of Decree 90-1051, the new supplementary scheme is managed by the Caisse Nationale d'Assurance Vieillesse Mutuelle Agricole (CNAVMA) with the assistance of the agricultural social insurance funds for individual departments or for areas covering more than one

---

[62] Gkritsi (2012), p. 40.

[63] Paparrigopoulou-Pehlivanidi (2013), p. 142.

[64] Stergiou (2015), p. 191.

[65] Ibid.

[66] Paparrigopoulou-Pehlivanidi (2013), p. 143, where the author noted that there is no optional pay-as-you-go scheme, especially in the form of solidarity between generations, because it is not universal and therefore the financing of benefits is not secured.

[67] Judgment of 16.11.1995, Case C-244/94, Fédération française des sociétés d'assurance, European Court Reports 1995 p. I-04013.

department (the local funds-MSA). The applicants in the main proceedings have argued before the Conseil d'Etat that the grant of a monopoly of management of the scheme in question to the CNAVMA, assisted by the local funds (MSA), and the tax deductibility of contributions paid to the CNAVMA, placed the latter in a position to eliminate competing insurance companies from the market in life assurance and in capitalization and retirement savings schemes. Since it had doubts as to the interpretation of Community law, the Conseil d'Etat decided to stay the proceedings and ask the Court "whether a **non-profit-making organization which manages an old-age insurance scheme intended to supplement a basic compulsory scheme, established by law as an optional scheme and operating according to the principle of capitalisation** in keeping with the rules laid down by the authorities in particular with regard to conditions for membership, contributions and benefits, is to be regarded as an undertaking for the purposes of Article 85 et seq. of the Treaty".

In the submission of the French Government, the CNAVMA, which has been merged since 1 January 1994 with the other two central agricultural benevolent funds to form a single organization, the Caisse Centrale de la Mutualité Sociale Agricole (the CCMSA), is not an undertaking within the meaning of Article 85 et seq. of the Treaty. In support of its argument, the French Government refers to the various characteristics of the supplementary retirement scheme for self-employed farmers, known as "Coreva", and of the body managing it (FFSA, paragraph 7).

Although the Court ruled that the Coreva scheme pursues a social purpose (it was created to protect against various risks a population whose income is lower and whose average age is higher than those of other socio-economic categories, and whose basic old-age insurance scheme is not sufficient), it concluded that in this case the principle of solidarity does not apply. More specifically, **the fact that the Coreva scheme operates in accordance with the capitalisation method rather than on a redistributive basis, because management by the latter method is possible only in the case of compulsory schemes which implement the principle of solidarity between several individual, which is not the case here** (FFSA, paragraph 8). Besides, taking into account that in the context of competition law, the concept of an undertaking encompasses every entity engaged in an economic activity, regardless of the legal status of the entity and the way in which it is financed,[68] the Court referred to the Poucet and Pistre judgment, where it held that said concept does not encompass bodies entrusted with the management of certain compulsory social security schemes based on the principle of solidarity. **Such solidarity necessarily required** the various schemes to be managed by a single body and **membership of those schemes to be compulsory** (FFSA, paragraph 15).

At this point, it should be emphasized that capitalization seems to be perceived by the Court to be of a different nature depending on the system in which it operates. By

[68] See amongst others, judgment of 23.04.1991, Case C-41/90, Höfner and Eiser, European Court Reports 1991, p. I-1979, paragraph 21 and judgment of 17.02.1993, joined cases C-159/91 and C-160/91 Poucet and Pistre, paragraph 17.

contrast, we can thus conclude from the previous judgment that in case of capitalisation in a compulsory scheme context, the principle of solidarity applies. Of course, this contradicts the choice of the Regulation to include in its scope, under the conditions examined, supplementary pension schemes, not only when they have become mandatory, but also when their scope has been extended (Article 1 (l), second sub-paragraph, Regulation No 883/04). Unless it should also be concluded that schemes whose scope is extended by decisions of public authorities should also be mandatory, by analogy with systems made mandatory by decisions of public authorities. This, however, cannot be concluded from the relevant provisions of the Regulation.

In that regard, the Court noted that membership of the Coreva scheme is **optional**, that the scheme operates in accordance with **the principle of capitalisation** and that the benefits to which it confers entitlement depend solely on the *amount* of contributions paid by the recipients and the financial results of the investments made by the managing organisation. The CCMSA therefore carries on an economic activity in competition with life assurance companies (FFSA, paragraph 17). As the Commission has rightly observed, a farmer wishing to supplement his basic pension will opt, as between the CCMSA and an insurance company, for the solution which guarantees the better investment.

The principle of solidarity is reflected in this case by the fact that contributions are not linked to the risks incurred, by the placing of resources corresponding to the contributions paid at the disposal of the scheme in the event of the premature death of a member, by a mechanism for granting exemption from payment of contributions in the event of illness, and by the temporary suspension of payment of contributions for reasons connected with the economic situation of the holding (FFSA, paragraph 19). Such provisions already exist in certain group life assurance policies, or may be included therein. **In any event, the principle of solidarity is extremely limited in scope, which follows from the optional nature of the scheme. In those circumstances, it cannot deprive the activity carried on by the body managing the scheme of its economic character** (FFSA, paragraph 19). However, the pursuit of a social purpose is also a limitation that cannot prevent the activity in question from being characterised as economic in nature.

The Court concluded, as a result, that a non-profit-making organisation which manages an old-age insurance scheme intended to supplement a basic compulsory scheme, established by law as an optional scheme and operating according to the principle of capitalisation in keeping with the rules laid down by the authorities in particular with regard to conditions for membership, contributions and benefits, is an undertaking within the meaning of Article 85 et seq. of the Treaty (FFSA, paragraph 22).

At this point, it should be noted that the aforementioned Court's judgment in FFSA raises a new question, whether statutory schemes who meet the legal requirements as set out in the Regulation, but which do not have the necessary solidarity indications due to the combination of two elements, i.e. the capitalisation and the optional character, fall within the scope of the Regulation or not. The peculiarity of the case is that the supplementary pension scheme in question is not based on contractual provisions, but on regulatory provisions, i.e. in law.

3.2.1.6 Gaumain-Cerri

In addition, taking also into account the **Gaumain-Cerri judgment,** contradictions can be identified in the case-law. As it has been noted, the affiliation of a scheme to the scope of the Regulation is not affected by **whether insurance is provided in whole or partially by a private insurance body.**[69] This conclusion in confirmed by the Court's judgment in joined cases **Gaumain-Cerri**[70] where the affiliation of the scheme to the Regulation was examined in cases where **conclusion of a private care insurance policy is compulsory and where its conditions are determined by law.**[71]

The questions were raised in proceedings between Ms Gaumain-Cerri and the KKH care fund and Ms Barth and the Landesversicherungsanstalt Rheinprovinz respectively with regard to decisions adopted by those two bodies refusing to pay pension insurance contributions to which they claim to be entitled as third parties providing assistance to reliant persons in receipt of benefits under German social insurance against the risk of reliance on care (care insurance). In the relevant judgment part where the national legal framework is described, it is noted that in Germany, care insurance was introduced, from 1 January 1995, by the Pflegeversicherungsgesetz (Care Insurance Law), contained in Volume XI of the Sozialgesetzbuch (German Code of Social Law, "the SGB"). Care insurance gives entitlement, first, to benefits designed to cover the costs incurred for care provided in the home by a third person. Among others, care insurance will pay old age and invalidity insurance contributions, as well as accident insurance, for the third party assisting the insured person. It is such payment of old age insurance contributions which has given rise to the two disputes in the main proceedings.

Ms S. Gaumain-Cerri, of German nationality, and her spouse, who is French, reside in France and practise their profession on a part-time basis as frontier workers in an undertaking established in Germany. By virtue of that employment, both are covered by German care insurance. Their son, who lives with them, is handicapped and, as a dependant of his parents, is in receipt of care insurance benefits, namely the care allowance. The parents themselves, at home and on a voluntary basis, are in the role of carers providing assistance to a reliant person. However, the KKH care fund, the body providing insurance against the risk of reliance on care in this case, refuses to pay the old age insurance contributions of Ms S. Gaumain-Cerri and of her husband in respect of their activity as carers for a reliant person on the ground that

---

[69] Verschueren (2009), p. 147.

[70] Judgment of the Court of 8.07.2004, joined cases C-502/01 and C-31/02, Gaumain-Cerri, European Court Reports 2004 p. I-06483.

[71] Gaumain-Cerri, paragraph 10.

they are not resident within Germany. For her part, Ms M. Barth, who is of German nationality, is resident in Belgium, near the German border, and looks after a retired civil servant in Germany. She receives from the latter EUR 400 per month. The assistance provided by Ms M. Barth was also regarded as non-professional.

The reliant person whom she assists is in receipt of care insurance benefits from two bodies, the Landesamt für Besoldung und Versorgung Nordrhein-Westfalen, as the basic social insurance provider for retired civil servants, and the PAX Familienfürsorge Krankenversicherung (PAX), as an additional insurer **under a compulsory private care insurance policy the conditions of which are required by law** to be identical to those applicable to the basic social insurance. For reasons similar to those put forward in respect of Ms S. Guamain-Cerri, regarding the fact that she is resident out of Germany, the Landesversicherungsanstalt Rheinprovinz discontinued payment of the contributions enabling Ms M. Barth to acquire pension rights.

More specifically, the question raised was whether the fact that the benefit in question is provided by a **private-law institution** acting under the same conditions as PAX in respect of the person cared for by Ms M. Barth is of any relevance. As noted by the Court, care insurance gives entitlement to full or partial direct payment of certain expenditure entailed by the insured person's reliance on care such as the payment of monthly financial aid allowing the insured to choose the method of assistance they prefer and, for example, to remunerate in one form or another the third party assisting them. The care insurance scheme provides cover, furthermore, against the risks of accident, old age and invalidity for some of those third parties (paragraph 23). Accordingly, benefits of that type are essentially intended to supplement sickness insurance benefits to which they are, moreover, linked at the organizational level, in order to improve the state of health and the quality of life of persons reliant on care (paragraph 24).

As the Court stressed, the fact that a third party assisting the person reliant on care is personally in receipt of such a benefit is of no consequence on account of the fact that the person whose reliance on care justifies the grant of the whole of the benefit is thereby benefiting from a scheme designed to help him to receive, in the most favourable conditions possible, the care which his condition *requires*. That benefit is thus fully covered by that branch of sickness insurance (paragraph 21). The same may be said, moreover, with regard to the care allowance proper when it is used in whole or in part to remunerate the third party assisting the person reliant on care (paragraph 21). According to the Court's judgment, the fact that care insurance is at times provided **in whole or in part by a private insurer on the basis of a private insurance contract cannot put it outside the scope of Regulation No 1408/71, since the conclusion of such a contract follows directly from the application of the social security legislation in issue** (paragraph 22). In that regard, the obligation in question does not arise from provisions of industrial agreements as mentioned in the second paragraph of Article 1(j) of Regulation No 1408/71, which are in principle excluded from the scope of that Regulation (paragraph 22).

3.2.1.7 Knauer

Furthermore, in **Knauer,**[72] the Court followed a different line of thought regarding the approach of a social security pension system falling within the Regulation's scope. Mr A. Knauer and Mr R. Mathis reside in Austria and, in their capacity as recipients of an Austrian pension, are insured under the health insurance scheme in accordance with the General Social Security Law. On account of their previous employment in Switzerland and in Liechtenstein, they receive old-age pensions provided by a pension fund under the Liechtenstein occupational pension scheme (the Liechtenstein pension fund). The Health Insurance Fund has, since October 2011, required Mr A. Knauer and Mr R. Mathis to pay contributions to the health insurance scheme in respect of the monthly pension benefits paid to them by the Liechtenstein pension fund. By two decisions of 10 December 2013, the Landeshauptmann von Vorarlberg reduced the amount of the contributions payable by Mr A. Knauer and Mr R. Mathis to the health insurance scheme on the ground that only a portion of the occupational pension scheme, namely that corresponding to the minimum statutory benefits, was within the scope of Regulation No 883/2004 and was thus covered by the obligation laid down in Paragraph 73a of the General Social Security Law to pay contributions. By contrast, the supplementary portion provided for by the Law on Occupational Benefits, corresponding to the benefits paid at a higher level than the minimum payments, was considered not to be within the scope of the regulation. The same was held to be true of the portion from the Liechtenstein pension fund corresponding to the benefits paid in respect of contributions made before the entry into force of the Law on Occupational Benefits, that is to say, before 1 January 1989.It was held that that portion had to be treated in the same way as the supplementary portion. The Health Insurance Fund brought an appeal before the referring court against both those decisions and Mr A. Knauer appealed against the decision concerning him. According to the Health Insurance Fund, the contributions payable must be calculated on the basis of the whole of the monthly pension payments made by the Liechtenstein pension fund to Mr A. Knauer and Mr R. Mathis, whilst, in Mr A. Knauer's submission, no contribution is due on those pension payments.

According to the referring court, a comparison of the statutory conditions for the provision of old-age pensions granted, on the one hand, under the General Social Security Law and, on the other, under the Law on Occupational Benefits tends to suggest that the benefits concerned are equivalent benefits within the meaning of Article 5(a) of Regulation No 883/2004. The referring court considers that those pensions come within the scope of that regulation. More specifically, said pensions are based on the legislation of the State in question which relates to the branch or system of social security for old-age benefits and, in addition, the Law on Occupational Benefits was notified by the Principality of Liechtenstein as falling in its

[72] Judgment of the Court of 21.01.2016, Case C-453/14, Knauer, Digital Reports (Court Reports-general) ECLI:EU:C:2016:37.

entirety within the material scope of Regulation No 883/2004 (Knauer, paragraph 20).

However, the referring court considers that it is possible that the Liechtenstein occupational pension scheme—regardless of the fact that it falls within the category of coordinated pension schemes as is confirmed by the above mentioned notification—cannot be regarded as equivalent within the meaning of Article 5 of Regulation No 883/2004, in view of the possibility it affords persons insured under it of freely arranging their own pension scheme and that the inclusion of benefits from that scheme in their entirety in the contribution basis of the Austrian health insurance scheme has to be regarded, from the perspective of EU law, as an unlawful measure in that it represents an obstacle to the exercise of the freedom of movement enshrined in Article 45 TFEU (Knauer, paragraph 21). In those circumstances the Verwaltungsgerichtshof decided to stay the proceedings and to refer the following question to the Court of Justice for a preliminary ruling.

According to the CJEU, it is undisputed that the occupational pension scheme at issue in the main proceedings was covered, in its entirety, by a declaration made under Article 9 of Regulation No 883/2004 by the Principality of Liechtenstein, which must be treated in the same way as a Member State for the purposes of applying that regulation. The old-age benefits under that scheme must therefore be regarded as falling within the scope of the regulation (Knauer, paragraph 24). Second, although the question refers to Article 5 of Regulation No 883/2004 in general, it in fact concerns the interpretation of the concept of "equivalent benefits" as referred to in point (a) of Article 5 (Knauer, paragraph 25). In those circumstances, the question raised by the referring court must be understood as asking whether Article 5(a) of Regulation No 883/2004 is to be interpreted as meaning that, in circumstances such as those at issue in the main proceedings, old-age benefits provided under an occupational pension scheme of one Member State and those provided under a statutory pension scheme of another Member State—both schemes being within the scope of that regulation—are equivalent benefits within the meaning of that provision (Knauer, paragraph 26).

The wording of that provision does not give any indication of the way in which the words "equivalent benefits" should be interpreted. However, as the Advocate General has argued in point 54 of his Opinion and contrary to what is suggested by the Commission, the concept of "equivalent benefits" within the meaning of Article 5(a) of Regulation No 883/2004 does not necessarily have the same meaning as the concept of "benefits of the same kind", to which Article 53 of the regulation refers. Indeed, if the EU legislature had intended to apply the criteria developed by the case-law for interpreting the concept of "benefits of the same kind" in the context of the application of the rules to prevent overlapping, it would have used the same terms in connection with the application of the principle of equal treatment (Knauer, paragraph 28). As regards the context of Article 5(a) of Regulation No 883/2004, it is true, as the Austrian Government asserts, that other provisions, such as Article 30 of Regulation No 883/2004 and Article 30 of Regulation No 987/2009, are to govern the conditions in which the institution of a Member State may, in circumstances such as those at issue in the main proceedings, request and recover contributions for sickness benefits. However, that fact does not, of itself, prevent Article 5(a) from also governing those conditions (Knauer, paragraph 29).

Moreover, it is clear from Article 30 of Regulation No 883/2004 and Article 30 of Regulation No 987/2009 that those articles place certain specific restrictions on the right of Member States to request and recover contributions for, inter alia, sickness benefits. Thus, those articles are not intended to regulate such requesting and recovery in such a way that, under the introductory sentence of Article 5 of Regulation No 883/2004, that requesting and recovery are excluded from the field of application of Article 5(a) (Knauer, paragraph 30). In this context, it should first be stated that two old-age benefits cannot be regarded as being equivalent within the meaning of Article 5(a) of Regulation No 883/2004 merely because they are both within the scope of that regulation. More specifically, apart from the fact that the Court's case-law does not support an interpretation to that effect, such an interpretation would render nugatory the requirement for equal treatment, laid down in Article 5(a) and intended by the EU legislature, given that that provision is, in any event, intended to apply only to benefits falling within the scope of the regulation (Knauer, paragraph 32).

Next, as regards more particularly old-age benefits such as those at issue in the main proceedings the concept of "equivalent benefits" within the meaning of Article 5(a) of Regulation No 883/04 must be interpreted as referring, in essence, to two old-age benefits that are comparable[73] (Knauer, paragraph 33). As regards the comparability of such old-age benefits, account must be taken of the aim pursued by those benefits and by the legislation which established them[74] (Knauer, paragraph 34).

So far as the case before the referring court is concerned, it is clear from the actual wording of the question that the aim of both the old-age benefits paid under the Liechtenstein occupational pension scheme and those paid under the Austrian statutory pension scheme is to ensure that the recipients of the benefits maintain a standard of living commensurate with that which they enjoyed prior to retirement (Knauer, paragraph 35). It follows that old-age benefits such as those at issue in the main proceedings must be regarded as being comparable. In that regard, as the Advocate General has observed in point 60 of his Opinion, the fact that there are differences relating, inter alia, to the way in which the rights to those benefits have been acquired, or to the fact that it is possible for the insured to obtain voluntary supplementary benefits, does not give grounds for reaching a different conclusion (Knauer, paragraph 36).

Finally, according to the Court, there does not appear to be any objective justification for applying differential treatment, in circumstances such as those at issue in the main proceedings, to the old-age benefits in question. There might in

[73] To this end, judgment of 21.02.2008, Case C-507/06, Klöppel, European Court Reports 2008 I-00943 ECLI:EU:C:2008:110, paragraph 19.

[74] By analogy, judgment of 01.10.2015, Case C-432/14, O v Bio Philippe Auguste SARL, Digital Reports (Court Reports—general) ECLI:EU:C:2015:643, paragraph 33.

some circumstances be such justification if, as the EFTA Surveillance Authority has rightly pointed out, contributions for sickness benefits were levied in Austria on the old-age benefits provided under the Liechtenstein occupational pension scheme, even though such contributions had already been levied in Liechtenstein. However, it does not appear from the documents before the Court that that was the situation in the case before the referring court (Knauer, paragraph 37). Consequently, the answer to the question referred is that Article 5(a) of Regulation No 883/2004 must be interpreted as meaning that, in circumstances such as those at issue in the main proceedings, **old-age benefits provided under an occupational pension scheme of another Member State**—both schemes being within the scope of that regulation—**are equivalent benefits** within the meaning of that provisions, **where both categories of benefits have the same aim of ensuring that their recipients maintain a standard of living commensurate with that which they enjoyed prior to retirement** (Knauer, paragraph 38). Therefore, in view of the recent developments in the case-law, it could be argued that a new dimension is being assigned to the objective of maintaining a similar standard of living before and after retirement.

3.2.2 The Broad Interpretation of the Term "Legislation"

As the Court has held in **Bozzone**, in joined cases **Laborero and Sabato,** as well as in the more recent **de Ruyter**, this definition of the term "legislation" is remarkable for its breadth, including as it does all provisions laid down by law, regulation and administrative action by the Member States and must be taken to cover all the national measures applicable in the specific sector and case.[75] That interpretation is also borne out by the objective pursued by Regulation No 1408/71 and by the principles on which that regulation is based.[76] In addition, in joined cases **Laborero and Sabato**, the Belgian Government contended that the voluntary insurance scheme established by the Law of 17 July 1963 does not come under "a social security scheme of a Member State for employed or self-employed persons", since it is an independent scheme, unconnected with the general Belgian scheme of social security and covering persons totally different from those covered by that general scheme.[77] The Court held that that argument could not be upheld, recalling that according to Article 4 (2) of Regulation No 1408/71, the regulation applies to all general and special social security schemes. A voluntary insurance scheme

[75] Judgment of the Court of 31.03.1977, Case 87/76, Bozzone, European Court Reports 1977 00687, paragraph 10; judgment of 9.07.1987, joined cases 82 and 103/86, Laborero and Sabato, European Court Reports 1987 03401, paragraph 23; judgment of 26.02.2015, Case C-623/13, de Ruyter, Digital reports (Court Reports—general) ECLI:EU:C:2015:123, paragraph 32.

[76] Judgment of the Court of 26.02.2015, Case C-623/13, de Ruyter, Digital reports (Court Reports—general) ECLI:EU:C:2015:123, paragraph 33.

[77] Judgment of the Court of 9.07.1987, joined cases 82 and 103/86, Laborero and Sabato, European Court Reports 1987 03401, paragraph 16.

governing matters which fall unquestionably within those covered by the regulation, as defined in Article 4 (1), cannot thus be removed from the ambit of the regulation merely because it is independent of a general scheme or because employed persons must fulfil special conditions in order to join the scheme.[78]

Indeed, the purpose of the provisions on continued optional insurance is the completion, preservation or increase of the insurance period required for sickness and maternity benefits in kind and in cash, as well as for pensions;[79] it is thus a social purpose. According to a prevailing insurance law principle and in the absence of an express provision to the contrary, optional insurance is governed by all the rules applying to compulsory insurance.[80] At a national level, an optional insurance period is recognized as a regular insurance period (and not as notional).[81] Indeed, the Court has ruled that national social security rules which apply to persons who pursue or who have pursued activities either wholly or partly outside the Community must be regarded as "legislation" within the meaning of Article 2 of Regulation No 1408/71.[82]

In order to ensure free movement of workers within the European Union, while upholding the principle of equal treatment of those persons under the various measures of national legislation, Title II of Regulation No 1408/71 has established a system of coordination concerning, inter alia, the determination of the legislation applicable to persons who make use, under various circumstances, of their right to freedom of movement.[83] Besides, according to settled case-law, the existence of an employment relationship is irrelevant for the purposes of the application of Regulation No 1408/71, as the determining factor in this regard is the fact that a person is insured, compulsorily or on an optional basis, for one or more of the contingencies covered by a general or special social security scheme mentioned in Article 1(a) of that regulation.[84]

The above positions regarding the scope of the Regulation are also in line with the former Court approach, which was clearly formulated early on, under the first Coordination Regulation No 3/58; its point of reference was the definition of legislation, which was actually very similar with the relevant definition in the current

[78] Laborero and Sabato, paragraph 17.

[79] Psilos (2007), p. 818.

[80] Sarmas (1994), p. 403.

[81] Stergiou (2014), p. 514.

[82] Judgment of the Court of 23.10.1986, Case 300/84, van Roosmalen, European Court Reports 1986 03097 ECLI:EU:C:1986:402, paragraph 31.

[83] See, to that effect, judgments Derouin, C-103/06, EU:C:2008:185, paragraph 20; Tomaszewska, C-440/09, EU:C:2011:114, paragraphs 25 and 28; de Ruyter, paragraph 34.

[84] Judgment de Ruyter, paragraph 31; see, to that effect, judgments of 12.05.1998, Case C-85/96, Martínez Sala, European Court Reports 1998 I-02691 ECLI:EU:C:1998:217, paragraph 36; of 10.03.2011, Case C-516/09, Borger, European Court Reports 2011 I-01493 ECLI:EU:C:2011:136, paragraphs 26 and 28.

form of Regulation No 883/04. Thus, as noted in **Vaassen-Göbbels,**[85] pursuant to Article 1 (b) of Regulation No 3, "the term 'legislation' shall mean all laws, regulations and other enforceable provisions ... of each Member State relating to the social security schemes and branches of social security set out in Article 2(1) and (2) of this Regulation".[86] Thus according to the Court, the expression "enforceable provisions" is clearly **intended to cover social security schemes and branches of social security which are managed by institutions other than the public authorities and which have a certain freedom of action in relation to the latter.**[87] Moreover, according to Article 1 (e) of Regulation No 3, "the term 'institution' shall mean ... the agency or authority responsible for enforcing all or part of the legislation".

Furthermore, as the Court noted, the juxtaposition of the terms "agency" and "authority" makes it clear that Regulation No 3 also applies to enforceable provisions governing the functioning of institutions established under private law, all the more so as these are not expressly excluded by any provisions of Regulation No 3.[88] **The concept of "enforceable provisions" thus applies to rules which, while being drawn up and applied in the form of private law and by bodies constituted under private law, are integrated into a Member State's social security scheme,** by reason of the fact that they are designed to supplement, or be a substitute for, laws and regulations relating to social security.[89] It was apparent for the Court that there is in **Regulation No 3 a manifest concern not to exclude from the benefit of its provisions schemes managed otherwise than by the State,** and which, at least in several Member States, cover a large proportion of the social security arrangements.[90]

It should be stressed that based on the Court's position in the above mentioned FFSA case, it may seem that optional capitalization schemes which do not fulfil the CJEU required solidarity requirements should be excluded from the scope of the Regulation. However, the Court's attitude cannot be considered clear in all cases. On the one hand, the Court (Poucet and Pistre, Garcia, Cisal di Battistello) considers that the basic social protection schemes do not fall under the competition rules and that social security institutions are not undertakings; however, the concept of a "scheme" and of the "principle of solidarity", which are used to justify this solution, are not clear.[91] On the other hand, the Court has held (FFSA) that where these institutions

---

[85] Judgment of the Court of 30.06.1966, Case 61/65, Widow G. Vaassen-Göbbels, European Court Reports 1966 00377.

[86] Vaassen-Göbbels, p. 343 of the Greek version of the judgment.

[87] Vaassen-Göbbels, as above.

[88] Judgment of the Court of 30.06.1966, Case 61/65, Widow G. Vaassen-Göbbels, European Court Reports 1966 00377, p. 343 of the Greek version of the judgment.

[89] Judgment of the Court of 30.06.1966, Case 61/65, Widow G. Vaassen-Göbbels, European Court Reports 1966 00377, p. 344 of the Greek version of the judgment.

[90] Vaassen-Göbbels, as above.

[91] Mavridis (1998a), p. 771.

(or similar ones) operate in the context of managing an optional supplementary insurance scheme, which is based on the principle of capitalization, they must be treated as undertakings within the meaning of the Treaty provisions in the field of competition.[92] It has also been argued that the case-law following the FFSA judgment offsets the existence of exclusive rights by satisfying the general interest; the State acquires a responsibility under the Treaty when it grants exclusivity to an undertaking: the responsibility of the efficient operation of a public service, in order to ensure user satisfaction.[93,94] In general, the nature of the activity pursued is crucial for characterizing some institutions as undertakings.[95]

Furthermore, in a series of similar cases Albany,[96] Brentjens,[97] Maatschappij,[98] the Court held that sectoral pension funds are undertakings and that the compulsory affiliation to them is compatible with the rules of competition, while in the joined cases Van Schijndel and van Veen,[99] the Court did not rule on the matter, despite the Opinion of the Advocate General arguing that it was a social security institution.[100] The abovementioned judgments are discussed in detail below, taking also into account the relevant opinions formulated by academics.

In addition, in the most recent Hoogstad,[101] the Court recalled that, according to the first paragraph of Article 1(j) of Regulation No 1408/71, the term 'legislation' means, in respect of each Member State, statutes, regulations and other provisions and all other implementing measures, present or future, relating to the branches and schemes of social security covered by Article 4(1) and (2) (para. 24). However, in accordance with the second subparagraph of Article 1(j), the term 'legislation' excludes provisions of existing or future industrial agreements, whether or not they have been the subject of a decision by the authorities rendering them compulsory or extending their scope (para. 25). Mr Hoogstad, who has Netherlands nationality, worked, in the period from 1 November 1996 to 31 December 2004, for a Belgian employer that built up two supplementary pension funds for him. After completing his professional career, Mr Hoogstad settled, in 2007, in Ireland with his

92 Mavridis (1998a), p. 771.

93 Dewost (1995), p. 153.

94 Mavridis (1998a), p. 776.

95 Judgment of 19.01.1994, Case C-374/92, Eurocontrol, European Court Reports 1994, p. I-43; judgment of 18.03.1997, case C-349/95, Call; Mavridis (1998a), p. 771.

96 Judgment of the Court of 21.09.1999, Case C-67/96, Albany International BV, European Court Reports 1999 p. I-05751.

97 Judgment—21/09/1999—Brentjens' Caw C-117/97 (joined cases C-115/97, C-116/97, C-117/97) ECLI:EU:C:1999:434.

98 Judgment of the Court of 21.09.1999, Case C-219/97, Maatschappij, European Court Reports 1999 I-06121 ECLI:EU:C:1999:437.

99 Judgment of the Court of 14.12.1995, joined cases C-430/93 and C-431/93, van Schijndel and van Veen, European Court Reports 1995 I-04705 ECLI:EU:C:1995:441.

100 Van Schijndel and Van Veen Opinion of Advocate General F.G. Jacobs of 15 June 1995, paragraph 62.

101 Judgement of 26.10.2016, Hoogstad, case C-269/15, ECLI:EU:C:2016:802.

wife who is a national of that Member State. When Mr Hoogstad reached the age of 60, in February 2008, the lump sum payments were paid to him from the two supplementary pensions. In Belgium, the lump sum payments concerned were the object of two deductions. Mr Hoogstad sought the repayment of the sums that had been withheld from him on the ground that he was not, at the time of the payment of those lump sums, subject to the Belgian social security legislation. By judgment of Labour Tribunal, Brussels, the National Institute for Health and Disability Insurance and NPO were ordered to repay the amounts withheld. After its appeal was also unsuccessful before the Labour Court, Brussels, the NPO lodged an appeal in cassation. The NPO submits that the lump sum payments of the supplementary pension to Mr Hoogstad were made pursuant to schemes that are not to be regarded as 'legislation' within the meaning of the first subparagraph of Article 1(j) of Regulation No 1408/71 and that those lump sums are not therefore within the material scope of application of that regulation. Consequently, the deductions made to the supplementary pensions are not incompatible with Article 13(1) of that regulation. As the Court pointed out, while it is clear from the very formulation of the question referred that the payments from supplementary pension schemes which Mr Hoogstad had benefitted from in the main proceedings 'are not legislation within the meaning of the first subparagraph of Article 1(j) of Regulation No 1408/71', it remains the case that the contribution levied on those supplementary pension schemes is capable of falling within the scope of that regulation (para. 26).

The Court reiterated that the concept of 'legislation' is broad, including all the types of legislative, regulatory and administrative measures adopted by the Member States, and must be taken to cover all the national measures applicable in the matter[102](para. 27). Furthermore, the Court has held that levies which are not imposed on employment income and substitute income of workers but which are imposed on income from assets, are liable to fall within the scope of the regulation where it is found that the proceeds of those levies are allocated specifically and directly to the financing of certain branches of social security in the Member State in question[103] (para. 30). The same conclusion must follow with regard to levies, such as those at issue in the main proceedings, that are imposed on supplementary pension schemes, since the proceeds of those contributions are allocated specifically and directly to the financing of certain branches of social security in the Member State in question (para. 31).

The Court concluded that Article 13(1) of Regulation No 1408/71 precludes a national law, such as that at issue in the main proceedings, which imposes levies of contributions that have a direct and sufficiently relevant link with the legislation governing the branches of social security listed in Article 4 of that regulation on payments made under supplementary pension schemes even though the beneficiary of that supplementary pension scheme does not reside in that Member State and is

[102] Judgment of 26 February 2015, *de Ruyter*, C-623/13, EU:C:2015:123, paragraph 32.

[103] Judgment of 26 February 2015, *de Ruyter*, C-623/13, EU:C:2015:123, paragraph 28.

subject, in accordance with Article 13(2)(f) of that regulation, to the social security legislation of the Member State in which he resides.

3.3 Divergent Interpretative Approaches

According to the Committee on Legal Affairs and Citizen's Rights, pension funds could serve to reduce the proportion accounted for by State welfare benefits as a whole, help maintain income levels after retirement and enable the Welfare State to continue on a sustainable footing without decreasing pensioner's income.[104] On the other hand, the institutions offering retirement provision rank alongside the biggest financial institutions in the EU, bearing in mind that pension fund assets already amount to the equivalent of 20% of EU GDP.[105]

In general, the CJEU has held that sometimes social security bodies are not covered by competition rules and sometimes, while they are covered by them, they are exempted on the basis of Article 86 (2) EEC[106] (and currently Article 106 (2) TFEU).[107] Competition law generally applies to undertakings within the Community, unless the existence of a public service can be established, delimiting the compatibility of general interest services with the Treaty rules.[108] Although the main social security bodies were not considered as undertakings, the nature of an undertaking within the meaning of Article 86 was still associated with supplementary funds.[109]

The Court's mixed interpretative approaches are evident in the judgments analyzed below. The case-law is particularly circumstantial and variable regarding occupational insurance funds in the so-called "second pillar".[110] On 2.9.1999, the

[104] Commission of the European Communities (1997) Committee on Legal Affairs and Citizens' Rights, point 4.

[105] Commission of the European Communities (1997) Committee on Legal Affairs and Citizens' Rights, point 4.

[106] Stergiou (2015), p. 190.

[107] "Undertakings entrusted with the operation of services of general economic interest or having the character of a revenue-producing monopoly shall be subject to the rules contained in the Treaties, in particular to the rules on competition, in so far as the application of such rules does not obstruct the performance, in law or in fact, of the particular tasks assigned to them. The development of trade must not be affected to such an extent as would be contrary to the interests of the Union".

[108] Mavridis (1996), p. 1086; Mavridis (1998b), p. 773.

[109] Stergiou (2015), p. 190.

[110] Katrougalos (2006), p. 255; Synodinos (2000), pp. 882 et seq.; Paparrigopoulou-Pehlivanidi (2002); Dupeyroux (2000), p. 409.

Court issued Albany,[111] Brentjens,[112] Maatschappij,[113] three similar judgments, which caused, as noted, severe uncertainty and insecurity of law in the competition law legal circles.[114] In these judgments, the Court was asked to rule on whether the actions of the Netherlands' State to make insurance in certain supplementary insurance funds compulsory is compatible with Community competition law, i.e. whether that compulsory affiliation was justified in the context of Community law as a whole.[115]

According to the Court's settled case-law, competition law provisions have been applied as mandatory law in all economic sectors and activities,[116] despite the existence of other specific provisions.[117] However, in the above judgments, it is argued that the Court accepts a slight derogation in its firm position on collective labour agreements, following, in this respect, the Opinion of Advocate General Jacobs, who offers a comparative analysis of Member States' law and U.S.A. law and takes into particular account the fact that the conclusion of collective labour agreements is encouraged by primary Community law itself.[118]

To follow the evolution of the definition of "legislation" from the former to the new Regulation, in connection with the issue of the schemes falling within the Regulation's scope, it would be useful to examine in detail the Court's rulings in **Albany International BV.**[119] In that case, the Court decided on the **declassification of compulsory affiliation as a social element in a supplementary funded pension scheme.**

The questions were raised in an action brought by Albany International BV (hereinafter "Albany") against the Textile Industry Trade Fund (hereinafter "the Fund") concerning Albany's refusal to pay to the Fund contributions for 1989 on the ground that compulsory affiliation to the Fund by virtue of which such contributions are claimed from it is contrary to Article 3(g) of the EC Treaty (currently, after amendment, Article 3(1)(g) EC) and Articles 85, 86 and 90 of the Treaty. Paragraphs 3–7 of the judgment describe the Dutch pension system.[120]

---

[111] Judgment of the Court of 21.09.1999, Case C-67/96, Albany International BV, European Court Reports 1999 p. I-05751.

[112] Judgment—21/09/1999—Brentjens' Case C-117/97 (joined cases C-115/97, C-116/97, C-117/97) ECLI:EU:C:1999:434.

[113] Judgment of the Court of 21.09.1999, Case C-219/97, Maatschappij, European Court Reports 1999 I-06121 ECLI:EU:C:1999:437.

[114] Synodinos (2000), p. 882.

[115] Synodinos (2000), p. 882.

[116] Goldman and Lyon-Caen (1983), pp. 490, 504, 506, 524.

[117] Kotsiris (1986), p. 223.

[118] Synodinos (2000), p. 882.

[119] Judgment of 21.09.1999, Case C-67/96, Albany International BV, European Court Reports 1999 p. I-05751.

[120] The pension system in the Netherlands is based on three pillars. The first is a statutory basic pension, granted by the State. That compulsory statutory scheme entitles the whole population to receive a pension of a limited amount, regardless of the wage which they actually received

Affiliation to the Fund was made compulsory by an order of the Minister for Social Affairs and Employment of 4 December 1975 (hereinafter **"the order making affiliation compulsory"**). Albany was operating a textile business which had been affiliated to the Fund since 1975. Until 1989 the Fund's pension scheme paid a flat-rate benefit. The pension awarded to workers was not proportional to their wage but was a fixed amount for each worker. Albany decided that the scheme was insufficiently generous and in 1981 concluded arrangements with an insurance company for a supplementary pension for its workers so that the total pension to which they would be entitled after 40 years' employment amounts to 70% of their last salary. Subsequently, however, the Fund modified its pension scheme, with effect from 1 January 1989. Since then its scheme awards workers an amount which likewise represents 70% of their final salary. Following the change to the Fund's pension scheme, Albany asked to be exempted from affiliation.

In the present case, it was noted that **like the category of agreements referred to above which derive from social dialogue, the agreement at issue in the main proceedings was concluded in the form of a collective agreement and is the outcome of collective negotiations between organisations representing employers and workers** (Albany, paragraph 62). On the other hand, as far as its purpose is concerned, that agreement establishes, in a given sector, a supplementary pension scheme managed by a pension fund to which affiliation may be made compulsory. Such a scheme seeks generally to guarantee a certain level of pension for all workers in that sector and therefore contributes directly to improving one of their working conditions, namely their remuneration (Albany, paragraph 63). Therefore, since the agreement at issue in the main proceedings does not fall within the scope of Article 85 (1) of the Treaty, Member States are free to make it compulsory for persons not bound by it. Consequently, the answer to the second questions was that **Articles 3 (g), 5 and 85 of the Treaty do not prohibit a decision by the public authorities to make affiliation to a sectoral pension fund compulsory** at the request of organisations representing employers and workers in a given sector (Albany, paragraph 70).

First, compulsory affiliation of all workers in a given sector to a supplementary pension scheme pursues an essential social function within the pension system applicable in the Netherlands because of the extremely limited amount of the statutory pension calculated on the basis of the minimum statutory wage (Albany, paragraph 73). **Second, the sectoral pension fund is non-profit making.**

previously, calculated by reference to the statutory minimum wage. The second pillar comprises supplementary pensions provided in the context of employment or self-employed activity, which serve in most cases to top up the basic pension. Such supplementary pensions are normally managed by collective schemes covering a sector of the economy, a profession or the employees of an undertaking by funds affiliation to which has been made compulsory, as in the case in the main proceedings, by the Law of 17 March 1949 on compulsory affiliation to a sectoral pension fund, (hereinafter the "BPW").The third pillar comprises individual pension or life assurance policies which may be concluded on a voluntary basis. The Wages Tax Law provides that pension contributions are deductible only if the pension does not exceed a "reasonable" level.

It is managed jointly by both sides of the industry, who are equally represented on its management committee, while the sectoral pension fund collects an average contribution fixed by that committee which strikes a balance, collectively, between the amount of the premiums, the value of the benefits and the extent of the risks (Albany, paragraph 74). **Third, operation of the sectoral fund is based on the principle of solidarity.** Such solidarity is reflected by the obligation to accept all workers without a prior medical examination, the continuing accrual of pension rights despite exemption from contributions in the event of incapacity for work, the discharge by the fund of arrears of contributions due from an employer in the event of the latter's insolvency and by the indexing of the amount of the pensions in order to maintain their value (Albany, paragraph 75). **Such solidarity makes compulsory affiliation to the supplementary pension scheme essential. Otherwise, if "good' risks" left the scheme, the ensuing downward spiral would jeopardise its financial equilibrium** (Albany, paragraph 75).

Consequently, **such a fund must be regarded as an undertaking occupying a dominant position** within the meaning of Article 90 (1) of the Treaty (Albany, paragraph 92). According to settled case-law an undertaking which has a legal monopoly in a substantial part of the common market may be regarded as occupying a dominant position within the meaning of Article 86 of the Treaty.[121]

3.4 Critical Remarks on the Court's Case-Law

As can be concluded by the above rulings, the Court recognises the power of Member States to make affiliation to a supplementary pension scheme established via a collective agreement compulsory, with a decision by the public authorities. It also acknowledges that sectoral pension funds pursue a social purpose and demonstrate elements of solidarity, as well as a lack of a profit-making purpose. At the same time, however, the Court considers such funds as undertakings. Although admitting that an undertaking can be not-for-profit can entail some inconsistencies, the Court uses as a basis for this classification the competitiveness of the sectoral pension fund, which **engages in an economic activity in competition with insurance companies** (Albany, paragraph 84). At the same time, however, it accepts that the supplementary pension scheme at issue in the main proceedings **fulfils an essential social function within the Netherlands pensions system by reason of the limited amount of the statutory pension, which is calculated on the basis of the minimum statutory wage** (Albany, paragraph 105). It also accepts, that the supplementary pension scheme managed exclusively by the Fund displays a **high level of**

[121] Judgments of 10.12.1991, Case C-179/90, Merci convenzionali porto di Genova, European Court Reports 1991, p. 1-5889, paragraph 14; judgment of 13.12.1991, Case C-18/88, GB-Inno-BM, European Court Reports 1991, p. 1-5941, paragraph 17; judgment of 21.09.1999, Case C-67/96, Albany International BV, European Court Reports 1999 p. I-05751, paragraph 91.

solidarity resulting, in particular from *the fact that contributions do not reflect the risk, from the obligation to accept all workers without a prior medical examination, the continuing accrual of pension rights despite exemption from the payment of contributions in the event of incapacity for work, the discharge by the Fund of arrears of contributions due from an employer in the event of insolvency and the indexing of the amount of pensions in order to maintain their value* (Albany, paragraph 109). More specifically, such constraints which render **the service provided by the Fund less competitive than a comparable service provided by insurance companies** go towards justifying the exclusive right of the Fund to manage the supplementary pension scheme (Albany, paragraph 110), while the removal of the exclusive right conferred on the Fund might make it impossible for it to perform the tasks of **general economic interest** entrusted to it under economically acceptable conditions and threaten its financial equilibrium (Albany, paragraph 111).

The Court appears to be confused as it considers the fund in question both as a competing undertaking and, on the other hand, as a service with a social function and a high level of solidarity that makes it less competitive than a comparable service provided by insurance companies. Social security bodies, however, engage in both economic and social activities, so that many times border on the limits of the concept of an "undertaking".[122] As noted in the present case, the sectoral pension fund itself determines the amount of the contributions and benefits and the Fund operates in accordance with the principle of capitalisation (Albany, paragraph 81). Accordingly, by contrast with the benefits provided by organisations charged with the management of compulsory social security schemes of the kind referred to in Poucet and Pistre, cited above, the amount of the benefits provided by the Fund depends on the financial results of the investments made by it, in respect of which it is subject, like an insurance company, to supervisions by the Insurance Board (Albany, paragraph 82).

Thus, according to the relevant academic theory, agreements concluded following collective negotiations between social partners may[123] be exempted from the scope of Article 81 (1) EC Treaty, but only following an in concreto analysis of the nature and scope of each collective agreement in question as well as an examination of whether it pursues an economic purpose; as a result only the agreements that pursued exclusively social purposes can be exempted.[124] As it is thus pointed out, a body must pursue a social purpose and operate in accordance with the principle of solidarity; this applies to bodies not being classified as undertakings and to bodies classified as undertakings but subsequently exempted from competition rules.[125]

[122] Kessler (1996), p. 421.

[123] Albany, paragraph 60; Brentjens', paragraph 57; Maatschappij, paragraph 47.

[124] Synodinos (2000), p. 882.

[125] Stergiou (2015), p. 190.

More specifically, the Court seeks to offset in concreto the data of each system with a set of indications,[126] such as the basic or supplementary nature of social security, compulsory or optional affiliation, the principle of solidarity or the principle of capitalisation, whether the amount of benefits paid depends solely on the amount of the contributions paid or from the results of the investments made by the fund in question, in order to determine judicially which element prevails, the economic element or the solidarity one.[127] This process is not easy nor completely predictable.[128]

This is probably the reason for which the Poucet and Pistre judgment was used by the aforementioned Advocate General in joined cases Schijndel and van Veen[129] to reach a different conclusion. More specifically, as highlighted by the Advocate General,[130] the position in relation to social security schemes is more complex, as pension schemes take a variety of forms, ranging from State social security schemes at one end of the spectrum to private individual schemes operated by commercial insurers at the other. Although the potential for competition exists even between those schemes (as demonstrated by the fact that in the United Kingdom private pension arrangements may partly replace the state social security system), it seems clear that the Community competition rules were not intended to apply to State social security schemes. The difficulty lies in classifying intermediate categories of schemes.[131]

In its initiatives in the sphere of pensions, the Commission, in pursuing its three goals of cross-border pension fund management, removal of restrictions on investment of pension fund assets and cross-border membership of schemes,[132] has recognised the broad range of schemes and also the need to respect the choices made by Member States regarding pension arrangements. The Commission's Amended Proposal of 26 May 1993 recognises in its preamble that further work is necessary on the question of cross-border membership of pension funds in order to take account of the different types of institutions and so as not to call in question the functioning of institutions with compulsory membership (see last recital).

---

[126] Stergiou (2014), p. 35; Stergiou (2015), p. 191.

[127] Synodinos (2000), p. 893.

[128] Synodinos (2000), p. 893.

[129] Judgment of the Court of 14.12.1995, joined cases C-430/93 and C-431/93, van Schijndel and van Veen, European Court Reports 1995 I-04705 ECLI:EU:C:1995:441.

[130] Van Schijndel and Van Veen Opinion of Advocate General F.G. Jacobs of 15 June 1995, paragraph 57.

[131] Van Schijndel and Van Veen Opinion of Advocate General F.G. Jacobs, as above, paragraph 57.

[132] See Commission's working document of 23 October 1990 on completion of the internal market for private retirement provisions in the sphere of private pensions, annexed to the Commission's observations in Case C-244/94. See also Proposal of 21 October 1991 for a Council Directive relating to the freedom of management and investment of funds held by institutions for retirement provision (91/C 312/04, OJ 1991 C 312, p. 3), as amended on 26 May 1993 (93/C 171/11, OJ C 171, p. 13).

He notes that the Court has already had occasion to consider the scope of the Treaty rules on competition in relation to certain schemes falling in the intermediate category and which were subject to control by public authorities in Poucet and Pistre.[133] In those cases, the Court concluded that the administration of the systems consisted of a purely social function and not of a pursuit of economic activity and that those systems were not covered by the definition of an "undertaking" given in Höfner and Eiser.[134] In his opinion, the pension fund in question there, although different in certain respects from those at issue in Poucet and Pistre, it does have the essential characteristics which led the Court to its conclusion in those cases.[135] The Fund unquestionably performs a purely social function. It was set up by the physiotherapists' profession and compulsory membership of it was provided for at the request of the profession by a ministerial decree issued under the Pensions Law. The aims of that Law are to ensure that retirement incomes reflect the rising general level of incomes, to allow younger colleagues to contribute to the higher cost of providing pensions for older colleagues and to provide for pension rights in respect of years prior to the entry into force of the schemes. The Fund is non-profit making. Its board of directors, who do not receive remuneration but merely expenses (Article 7 of the Fund's Statutes), is made up exclusively of members of the Fund (Article 5 of the Statutes).

Furthermore, it appears from the Fund's written observations that the scheme operated by it entails a substantial degree of solidarity between members which goes beyond that which would normally be expected of commercial arrangements.[136] A standard contribution is levied and a standard pension is paid regardless of the age at which an individual member entered the profession and regardless of his state of health on joining; moreover, pension rights are granted retrospectively for those members who were already engaged in the profession when the scheme entered into force.[137] In the light of the foregoing, the Fund more closely resembles a social security institution than a commercial insurer, and the scheme itself is more akin to a social security scheme than to commercial pension arrangements, even those organized on a collective basis.[138] The members of the scheme are contributing to a common fund rather than receiving a commercial service.

Consequently, the Advocate General believes that the **Fund, in its relations with its members, does not act as an undertaking, but as a social institution** which the members of the profession have entrusted with responsibility for making their

[133]Van Schijndel and Van Veen Opinion of Advocate General F.G. Jacobs of 15 June 1995, paragraph 58.

[134]Judgment of 23.04.1991, Case C-41/90, Höfner and Elser, European Court Reports *1991 I-01979* ECLI:EU:C:1991:161.

[135]Van Schijndel and Van Veen Opinion of Advocate General F.G. Jacobs of 15 June 1995, paragraph 62.

[136]Ibid, paragraph 63.

[137]Ibid, paragraph 63.

[138]Van Schijndel and Van Veen Opinion of Advocate General F.G. Jacobs of 15 June 1995, paragraph 64.

pension arrangements and that, notwithstanding the fact that the scheme is funded, so that pensions are financed from reserves rather than from current contributions.[139] The Fund has convincingly argued that the establishment of substantial reserves is necessary if a scheme not financed from the State budget is to maintain the real value of pensions in times of severe inflation. **That pension funds are major investors on capital markets** certainly explains the Commission's initiatives with respect to cross-border fund management and investment, but **it is not a decisive factor in determining whether in its relations with its members a fund acts as an undertaking for the purposes of competition law.**[140]

The above remarks by the Advocate General are also the basis for Prodromos Mavridis to reach the conclusion, in his relevant analysis that competition law does not apply to conventional schemes, given that they relate to standard social security schemes.[141] He also notes that the exclusion of conventional supplementary schemes from Community coordination creates an issue of compatibility with Articles 48–51 of the Treaty, which prohibit the loss of advantages in case of mobility, as it cannot be denied that a sectoral (supplementary) pensions is a social security advantage.[142] According to him, a sectoral pension should be treated the same way as an old-age benefit within the meaning of Article 4 (1) (c) of Regulation No 1408/71.[143] It should also be noted that, for the purposes of ensuring a uniform application of the rules under Chapter 3, Title III of the Regulation, the CJEU has discussed in detail the classification of a series of benefits as retirement benefits "of the same kind", as well as the classification of national provisions as unlawfully against overlapping, following a thorough examination of the constituent elements of each benefit, of its purpose and the conditions for granting it, irrespective of the classification of that benefit legal provision or administrative practice by the national legislature.[144]

However, the change in the Advocate General's approach is quite impressive as evident in his shared opinion on the Albany,[145] Brentjens[146] and Maatschappij[147]

---

[139] Van Schijndel and Van Veen Opinion of Advocate General F.G. Jacobs of 15 June 1995, paragraph 65.

[140] Van Schijndel and Van Veen Opinion of Advocate General F.G. Jacobs of 15 June 1995, paragraph 65.

[141] Mavridis (1998a), p. 780.

[142] Mavridis (1998a), p. 782.

[143] Mavridis (1998a), p. 782.

[144] Tsotsorou (2007), p. 662.

[145] Judgment of the Court of 21.09.1999, Case C-67/96, Albany International BV, European Court Reports 1999 p. I-05751.

[146] Judgment—21/09/1999—Brentjens' Case C-117/97 (joined cases C-115/97, C-116/97, C-117/97) ECLI:EU:C:1999:434.

[147] Judgment of the Court of 21.09.1999, Case C-219/97, Maatschappij, European Court Reports 1999 I-06121 ECLI:EU:C:1999:437.

cases. As he, himself, states,[148] the decision-making mechanisms and the financial factors which influence the level of contributions and benefits are relevant. *On the one hand,* schemes in which the levels of benefits and contributions are fixed by the legislator are to be distinguished from schemes in which those levels are fixed by independent decision of the fund's management board. In that context, the principle underlying paragraph 21 of the judgment in FFSA and certain other judgments of the Court is relevant:[149] independent entities which are in a position to generate effects which the competition rules seek to prevent should be subject to those rules. *On the other hand,* schemes where the State guarantees a certain level of contributions or benefits are different from those where the State does not intervene. That feature was important for the Court's judgment in Poucet and Pistre where there was solidarity between the various social security institutions (paragraph 12), with those in surplus contributing to the financing of those with financial difficulties.[150] By contrast, in the present cases—as in FFSA—the level of benefits depends solely on the amount of contributions, the financial results of the investments made by the managing body and the costs generated by that body. Accordingly, in the present cases, too, the elements of solidarity are not strong enough to deprive the funds' activities of their economic nature.

Stevens argues that the Albany,[151] Brentjens[152] and Maatschappij[153] cases form a grand break-through in the field of social policy whereby employers are forbidden to opt out of the occupational system, even if this system is performing less than average; thus, via this prohibition, it stimulates solidarity.[154] The Court accepted the argument that the social impact should prevail on free competition.[155]

Accordingly, in **Pavlov,**[156] where the question on whether an occupational Fund is to be regarded as an "undertaking" within the rules on competition of the Treaty, the Advocate General noted that the questions referred and their legal and procedural

[148]Opinion of Jacobs—Case C-67/96, Joined Cases C-115/97, C-116/97 and C-117/97 and Case C-219/97 Opinion of Advocate General F.G. Jacobs of 28 January 1999, European Court Reports 1999 I-05751 ECLI:EU:C:1999:28, paragraphs 338–343.

[149]Judgments of 08.11.1983, 96/82 to 102/82, 104/82, 105/82,108/82 and 110/82, IAZ and others v Commission (European Court Reports 1983, p. 3369, paragraph 20); judgment of 17.12.1991, T-6/89, Enichem Anic v Commission, European Court Reports 1991, p. II-1623, paragraph 235.

[150]Reference to that feature was also made in the summary of that judgment in the FFSA and others judgment, paragraph 15.

[151]Judgment of the Court of 21.09.1999, Case C-67/96, Albany International BV, European Court Reports 1999 p. I-05751.

[152]Judgment—21/09/1999—Brentjens' Case C-117/97 (joined cases C-115/97, C-116/97, C-117/97) ECLI:EU:C:1999:434.

[153]Judgment of the Court of 21.09.1999, Case C-219/97, Maatschappij, European Court Reports 1999 I-06121 ECLI:EU:C:1999:437.

[154]Stevens (2001), p. 13.

[155]Stevens (2001), p. 13.

[156]Judgment of the Court of 12.09.2000, joined cases C-180/98 to C-184/98, Pavlov, European Court Reports 2000 I-06451 ECLI:EU:C:2000:428.

context are basically identical with the last three questions referred to the Court by the Hoge Raad in Van Schijndel and Van Veen,[157] but the Court did not have to consider the substantive questions of competition law.[158] He noted, however, that when drawing analogies, it must be kept in mind that those cases concerned sectoral pension funds which were set up on the basis of collective agreements between managements and labour and which provided supplementary pensions to employees in a certain sector of industry, whereas the present cases concern a pension fund set up by members of a profession which provides pensions to the members of that same profession.[159]

Thus, in Pavlov, the Advocate General examined whether the activities of the Fund are of an economic nature.[160] More specifically, he held that the Fund has three different functions within the medical specialists' pension scheme. "First, it is one potential provider of pension insurance services to the members of the scheme who have chosen to insure with the Fund; secondly, it supervises compliance with the affiliation requirement by members who have chosen to insure that part of the scheme with an insurance company; thirdly, with regard to the second part of the pension scheme (indexation, retroactive pension rights, invalidity regime, complementary survivors benefit) it acts as an insurer with an exclusive right" (paragraphs 167–171).

Ultimately, however, the Advocate General expressed the opinion that the Fund is to be classified as an undertaking on the basis of the following criteria: the risk elements in question (including the indexation mechanism) are financed according to the capitalisation principle; the Fund determines contributions and benefits autonomously and according to actuarial principles. Consequently, the amount of the benefits provided by the Fund depends on its administrative costs and the financial results of the investments made by it; a State guarantee against the risks flowing from bad investments does not seem to exist. Finally, the Fund is subject to the supervision of the Insurance Board which also controls insurance companies (paragraph 178).

According to the Advocate General, **the capitalisation principle and control by the insurance board are indicators that the insurance in question is at least potentially an activity in which a normal insurer might engage** (paragraph 179). The autonomy of the Fund and the risks connected to its investments entail the risk of conduct which the competition rules seek to prevent. Therefore the same rationale applies again: although the constraints of solidarity listed above might partly justify

---

[157] Judgment of the Court of 14.12.1995, joined cases C-430/93 and C-431/93, van Schijndel and van Veen, European Court Reports 1995 I-04705 ECLI:EU:C:1995:441.

[158] Opinion of Jacobs—Joined Cases C-180/98 to C-184/98 Opinion of Advocate General F.G. Jacobs of 23 March 2000 Pavlov and others, European Court Reports 2000 I-06451ECLI: EU:C:2000:151, paragraph 3.

[159] Opinion of Jacobs—Joined Cases C-180/98 to C-184/98 Opinion of Advocate General F.G. Jacobs of 23 March 2000 Pavlov and others, European Court Reports 2000 I-06451ECLI: EU:C:2000:151, paragraph 4.

[160] Opinion of Jacobs, as above, paragraphs 168–180.

the Fund's exclusive rights under Article 90(2) of the Treaty, they do not go so far as to prevent its activities from being regarded as economic activities (paragraph 179) and the Fund itself as an undertaking within the meaning of the competition rules of the Treaty (paragraph 180). **From the above wording, it can be observed that the defining criteria for supporting the economic nature of a scheme and diminish its social function is the principle of capitalisation, in particular, in combination with optional affiliation to it.**

Furthermore, it is worth noting the fact that the CJEU has accepted that **not excluding occupational funds from the scope of Article 82 EC Treaty would make impossible the realisation of their operations, given that if the exclusive right** of the pension fund to manage the supplementary pension scheme for all workers in a given sector were removed, undertakings with young employees in good health in non-dangerous activities would seek more advantageous insurance terms from private insurers.[161] The progressive departure of "good" risks would leave the sectoral pension fund with responsibility for an increasing share of "bad" risks, thereby increasing the cost of pensions for workers particularly those in small and medium-sized undertakings with older employees engaged in dangerous activities, to which the fund could no longer offer pensions at an acceptable cost.[162] Therefore, merely creating a dominant position by granting exclusive rights is not in itself incompatible with Article 86 EC Treaty, but a Member State is in violation of the Treaty's competition rules only when the undertaking in question is or may be in abuse of its dominant position, by exercising the exclusive rights conferred on it.[163]

Therefore, in Albany, Brentjens' and Maatschappij, the Court held that due to their purposes, but also given that the universal nature of these funds and the coverage of "good" risks, unlike private insurance companies, have an impact on their competitiveness, Articles 82, 86 and 90 EC Treaty do not prohibit public authorities from granting them a monopoly status and the exclusive right to regulate, in their area of competence, a supplementary pension scheme.[164] As noted, by accumulating heterogeneous criteria, said case-law creates issues regarding the predictability of the Court's judgments and legal certainty.[165] It should not be overlooked, however, that the case-law criteria may be unevenly formulated because they deal with the interpretation of non-uniform systems.

---

[161] Judgment of 21.09.1999, Case C-67/96, Albany International BV, European Court Reports 1999 p. I-05751, paragraph 108; Judgment—21/09/1999—Brentjens' Case C-117/97 (joined cases C-11 5/97, C-116/97, C-117/97) ECLI:EU:C:1999:434, paragraph 108; Judgment of the Court of 21.09.1999, Case C-219/97, Maatschappij, European Court Reports 1999 I-06121 ECLI:EU:C:1999:437, paragraph 98.

[162] Judgment of 21.09.1999, Case C-67/96, Albany International BV, European Court Reports 1999 p. I-05751, paragraph 108; judgment of the Court of 21.09.1999, Case C-219/97, Maatschappij, European Court Reports 1999 I-06121 ECLI:EU:C:1999:437, paragraph 98.

[163] Petroglou (2004), p. 94.

[164] Katrougalos (2006), p. 257.

[165] Synodinos (2000), p. 881. See also Hatzopoulos (2005), pp. 123–160.

Besides, the failure to find uniformity in the EU States, due to the great institutional differences between the supplementary insurance institutions and the state social security schemes has already been highlighted.[166] It is precisely because of the different structure of the national social security systems, that the Community legislature makes no distinction between basic and supplementary insurance.[167] The case-law preserves legal uncertainty, as the classification of a supplementary insurance organisation as a social security institution depends, on a case by case basis, on its specific characteristics.[168]

Moreover, the classification of social security schemes as occupational or statutory is a disputed legal issue,[169] meaning that the distinction between statutory and occupational (contractual) schemes has often emerged as a delicate process of misuse of power.[170] CJEU extended the concept of an occupational scheme, pushing it to the limits, in order to extend the application of gender equality; this extension put the emphasis on employment as the defining criterion for the classification of a scheme.[171] In this context and based on a number of cases the Court accepts as a decisive criterion for the classification of insurance schemes as occupational, the existence of a link between the employment relationship and the old-age pensions, while it also holds that the structural elements of a scheme for granting pensions are not of decisive importance.[172]

A connection between the case-law on the Coordination Regulation and the case-law on Directives 79/7/EEC[173] and 96/97/CE[174] would be interesting to make. The issue of defining the scope of Directive 79/7/EEC (statutory social security schemes) in relation to Article 141 EEC (previously Article 119), which established equal pay for men and women providing the same work and Directive 96/97/EC (occupational social security schemes) has repeatedly been presented before the Court, which accepts that the decisive criterion for a social security system to fall under 141 EEC is the payment of a retirement benefit on the basis of an employment relationship between the insured person and their former employer.[175]

Neither the method of financing nor the way in which the system is managed are the decisive criteria; accordingly, it is not decisive whether they were established via collective negotiations and agreements nor whether they are subject to Regulation

---

166 Kremalis (1996a), p. 40.

167 Tsotsorou (2007), p. 663.

168 Stergiou (2014), p. 35, footnote 100; see Paparrigopoulou-Pehlivanidi (2002), pp. 155 et seq.

169 Paparrigopoulou-Pehlivanidi (2007a), Comment on the Council of State judgment (Plenary Session) No 3088/2007, p. 3; Anagnostou-Dedouli (2005), p. 79; Petroglou (2004), p. 76.

170 Stergiou (2014), p. 281.

171 Stergiou (2014), p. 281.

172 Anagnostou-Dedouli (2005), p. 94.

173 European Economic Community (1979) Council Directive 79/7/EEC, p. 24.

174 Council Directive 96/97/EC, *p. 0020 – 0024.*

175 Paparrigopoulou-Pehlivanidi (2007a) Comment on the Council of State judgment (Plenary Session) No 3088/2007, p. 2.

No 1408/71.[176] National security law was also significantly affected, given that, as interpreted by the Court, the broad wording of Article 141 EC Treaty **also covers the retirement benefits of occupational insurance funds** where the insurance relation arises directly from the existence of an employment relationship.[177] According to the evolving case-law, this criterion applies where the pension relates to a particular category of workers and is provided on the basis of an employment relationship; its amount depends on the employment duration and the salary.[178] Thus, the regulatory scope of Article 141 also includes statutory schemes, mandatory or not, regardless of their structure in accordance with a funded or a pay-as-you-go scheme and regardless whether they insure persons employed in the private sector or civil servants.[179]

In any event, it is argued that it would be inconceivable to exclude contractual schemes from the Treaty rules, if, for example, they directly violate such rules or hinder the realisation of the objectives as set out in Articles 48–51 of the Treaty; such a conclusion is inevitable, following the Bosman[180] and Vougioukas[181] judgments.[182] In particular regarding the Vougioukas case, it is highlighted that, although Regulation No 1408/71 at the time expressly excluded from its scope the special schemes for civil servants,[183] this explicit exclusion did not prevent the Court from recognising that Article 51 of the Treaty provides to migrant workers, including civil

[176]Paparrigopoulou-Pehlivanidi (2007b) Comment on the ECJ judgment C-559/07 Commission of the European Communities v Hellenic Republic, p. 2, footnote 5; Paparrigopoulou-Pehlivanidi (2007a) Comment on the Council of State judgment (Plenary Session) No 3088/2007, p. 2 and the case-law cited therein: ECJ C-262/88, Barber, European Court Reports 1990, I-1889; C-7/93 Beune, European Court Reports. 1994, I-4471; C-366/99 Griesmar, European Court Reports 2001, I-9383; C-351/00 Niemi, European Court Reports. 2002, I-7007; C-109/01 Ten Oever, European Court Reports 1993, I-4879. Also compare, Kontizas (1996), pp. 529 et seq; Stergiou (1996), pp. 81 et seq; Tsampasi (2000), p. 3; Koukoulis-Spiliotopoulos (1993), pp. 156–159; Nikolakopoulou Stefanou (1992), pp. 85 et seq.; Anagnostou-Dedouli (2000), pp. 801 et seq.; Weatherill and Beaumont (1995), pp. 616–632.

[177]Tsapasi (1996), p. 328.

[178]Katrougalos (2006), p. 259 and the case-law cited therein.

[179]Katrougalos (2006), p. 259 and the case-law cited therein. See also ECJ, Case C-147/95 Evrenopoulos, European Court Reports 1997, p. I-2057 with a comment by Petroglou (1997), p. 270.

[180]Judgment of the Court of 15.12.1995, Case C-415/93, Union royale belge des sociétés de football association ASBL v Jean-Marc Bosman, Royal club liégeois SA v Jean-Marc Bosman and others and Union des associations européennes de football (UEFA) v Jean-Marc Bosman. European Court Reports 1995 I-04921 ECLI:EU:C:1995:463.

[181]Judgment of the Court of 22.11.1995, Case C-443/93, Vougioukas, European Court Reports 1995 I-04033 ECLI:EU:C:1995:394.

[182]Mavridis (1998a), pp. 782 and 787, where it is noted that already in the Court's judgment of 17.04.1997, Case C-147/95, Dimossia Epicheirissi Ilektrismou (DEI) v Efthimios Evrenopoulos, European Court Reports 1997 I-02057 ECLI:EU:C:1997:201 regarding men-women equality in the context of an occupational pension scheme the Treaty applies in such systems.

[183]Milionis (2007), p. 819; Mavridis (1998b), pp. 191–192.

servants, the right to aggregate insurance periods, a right that cannot be limited by Regulation No 1408/71.[184]

However, even before these judgments, the Court's case-law confirmed the application of Articles 48 and 59 in any actions by private law legal entities.[185] More specifically in Walrave,[186] the Court stressed that the prohibition of any discrimination in Articles 7, 48 and 59 does not only apply to the action of public authorities but extends likewise to rules of any other nature aimed at regulating in a collective manner gainful employment and the provision of services (Walrave, paragraphs 16–17). Indeed, the abolition between Member States of obstacles to freedom of movement for persons and to freedom to provide services, which are fundamental objectives of the Community contained in Article 3 (c) of the Treaty, would be compromised if the abolition of barriers of national origin could be neutralized by obstacles resulting from the exercise of their legal autonomy by associations or organizations which do not come under public law (Walrave, paragraph 18). Since, moreover, working conditions in the various Member States are governed sometimes by means of provisions laid down by law or regulation and sometimes by agreements and other acts concluded or adopted by private persons, to limit the prohibitions in question to acts of a public authority would risk creating inequality in their application (Walrave, paragraph 19).

Undoubtedly, contractual/supplementary schemes have been acquiring a role that becomes progressively more and more important; in addition, the system of collective agreements between social partners is one of the greatest acquis of the European social model.[187] In addition, it cannot be overlooked that in some domestic legal systems, supreme courts consider as part of the same set both statutory old-age insurance schemes and supplementary pension schemes.[188]

Indeed, it is generally accepted that said pension schemes tend to become schemes substituting social security: basic and supplementary schemes are subject to common rules and common principles.[189] Besides, as noted, following pressure from the European Parliament to extend the mechanism for the entitlement to and calculation of the benefit of the Regulation to the contractual second-pillar pension schemes, which public authorities have made mandatory or the scope of which they have extended, the Council has incorporated in the preamble of Regulation No 883/04 its sixth recital.[190] In the end, the long-running public debate regarding the

[184]Mavridis (1998a), p. 783.

[185]Mavridis (1998a), p. 782.

[186]Judgment of the Court of 12.12.1974, Case 36/74, B.N.O. Walrave, L.J.N. Koch v Association Union cycliste internationale, Koninklijke Nederlandsche Wielren Unie και Federación Española Ciclismo. European Court Reports 1974 01405 Greek 1974/00563 Portuguese 1974/00595 Spanish 1974/00571 Swedish II/00409 Finnish II/00415 ECLI:EU:C:1974:140.

[187]Mavridis (1998a), p. 778.

[188]Prétot (1997), p. 476; Kremalis (1996a, b); Stergiou (1997).

[189]Dupeyroux (1993), p. 777; Dupeyroux (1990), p. 741; Mavridis (1998a), p. 779.

[190]Tsotsorou (2007), pp. 663–664.

choice between funded or not or public v private has been abandoned in view of a combination of schemes designed to create an effective pension scheme able to include both state and occupational pensions.[191]

3.5 Conclusions as to the Schemes Subject to Coordination

As it can be concluded, the Court applies a functional criterion in order to determine whether a system constitutes social security: is the principle of solidarity being served? Thus, social security schemes are those that combine a social-nature component with a compulsory element that is interconnected with a specific form of the principle of solidarity (Poucet and Pistre). **The principle of solidarity assumes a broad universal scope due to the mandatory nature of the scheme as opposed to what applies for an optional scheme.** Thus, in FFSA, optional affiliation, application of the principle of capitalisation and the fact that benefits depended solely on the amount of the contributions paid by the beneficiaries and on the financial results of the investments made by the managing organisation implied that that organisation carried on an economic activity in competition with life assurance companies. Neither the social objective pursued, nor the fact that it was non-profit-making, nor the requirements of solidarity, nor the other rules concerning, in particular, the restrictions to which the managing organisation was subject in making investments changed the fact that the managing organisation was carrying on an economic activity.

Of course, it should be noted that the concepts of a social security scheme and of an undertaking are not mutually exclusive, since in Albany a pension scheme was regarded as social security operating on the basis of the principle of solidarity and, at the same time, as an undertaking. The question is which element prevails in the operation of a scheme, the economic or the social. Provided that social security institutions exercise both financial and social activities, the Court seeks each time to determine whether it is the economic element or the solidarity one that prevails.[192]

According to academic theory, when all the elements of solidarity and social character are present (lack of profit-making purpose, mandatory character, lack of absolute equivalence between contributions and benefits, calculation of benefits based on wages), the Court accepts that the fund in question fulfils a social character mission and is not therefore an undertaking within the meaning of Articles 101 and 102 TFEU, nor is it subject to rules of competition; when it is subject to such rules, it is excluded from their application,[193] for the purposes of fulfilling its specific mission as an undertaking of general economic interest.[194] In Albany, for example,

---

[191] Stevens (2001).

[192] Petroglou (2004), p. 86.

[193] Stergiou (2015), pp. 190–191.

[194] Petroglou (2004), p. 91.

the "social mission" was that all workers in the Netherlands after 40 years of employment should be entitled to a total pension amounting to 70% of their last salary.[195] Thus, the "immunity" granted to supplementary pension schemes is considered important in the sense that the social role of such schemes "legitimises certain practices", i.e. the exclusive rights granted to them.[196]

Where cases fall in between, the systems are evaluated depending on the prevailing features which may give rise or not to a social purpose.[197] It is further argued that the criteria used by the CJEU are simply the result of the statutory or contractual method of establishment of each scheme; there is thus a presumption, according to which, a statutory scheme is not an undertaking and is not governed by European business competition law, while a contractual scheme (of supplementary insurance) is treated by European law as an undertaking because it has all the conceptual features of private insurance.[198] The presumption, as noted, is refutable and is confirmed by the mandatory or optional nature of the scheme in question, the extent of social solidarity or reciprocity and the application of a pay-as-you-go or a funded scheme.[199]

Moreover, the Court had remarked in Albany that the request made to the public authorities by the organisations representing employers and workers to make affiliation to the sectoral pension fund set up by them compulsory is part of a regime established under a number of national laws, designed to exercise regulatory authority in the social sphere.[200] As a result, taking advantage of the possibility provided by the Regulation, pension schemes falling within the Regulation scope that are considered to be social security, are, at the same time, subject to competition rules, as they are regarded pursuant to CJEU case-law as undertakings. Additional confusion is caused by the fact that in other cases, such as in FFSA, a supplementary pension scheme was considered by the Court as an undertaking, unable to constitute social security due to its failure to apply the principle of solidarity due to the optional character of the scheme. However, said scheme was established by law. At the same time, the fact that the Court has regarded an additional insurer as social security under a compulsory private care insurance policy, the conditions of which are required by law, should not be overlooked.[201]

Regarding the case-law approach in FFSA, it has been argued that it facilitates the assessment of various elements (of a social and economic nature) that usually govern mixed insurance regimes in relation to the allowed regulatory interventions of the

[195] Mavridis (2004), p. 101.

[196] Mavridis (2004), p. 101.

[197] Stergiou (2015), p. 191.

[198] Paparrigopoulou-Pehlivanidi (2013), p. 144.

[199] Paparrigopoulou-Pehlivanidi (2013), p. 144.

[200] Judgment of the Court of 21.09.1999, Case C-67/96, Albany International BV, European Court Reports 1999 p. I-05751, paragraph 66.

[201] Judgment of the Court of 8.07.2004, joined cases C-502/01 and C-31/02, Gaumain-Cerri, European Court Reports 2004 p. I-06483.

legislator.[202] Thus, as long as the social elements (e.g. expense coverage based on a pay-as-you-go scheme or compulsory affiliation to a specific institution) prevail at the expense of economic elements, additional regulatory interventions for social solidarity are at the discretion of the national legislature; in contrast, if the economic elements prevail (e.g. expense coverage based on a funded scheme or optional affiliation to the insurance regime), legislative intervention is fairly limited, in accordance with Community competition rules (Article 85 et seq. EC Treaty), regardless whether there are constitutional or other restrictive national barriers.[203]

In addition, the Court has stated that the decisive factor for the application of Regulation No 1408/71 is that there must be a direct and sufficiently relevant link between the provision in question and the legislation governing the branches of social security listed in Article 4 of Regulation No 1408/71.[204] The question thus arises as to whether the Court's approach of social security schemes in a more general context matches the approach of social security schemes as per the Regulation's wording for the purposes of applying the coordination rules. Will the supplementary pension scheme in question established by law as a supplement to the basic mandatory scheme be subject to the Regulation as a statutory scheme or will it be excluded due to its optional character that, according to case-law, results in limited solidarity?

Although the CJEU case-law raises concerns regarding the application of the principle of solidarity, by attempting a literal interpretation of the Regulation provisions, the idea that optional statutory pension schemes can be excluded does not seem valid. Although, in FFSA the Court did not regard an optional statutory supplementary pension scheme as social security due to its "weak" solidarity, the scope of the Regulation seems to also include such schemes. Besides, according to settled case-law, the existence of an employment relationship is irrelevant for the purposes of the application of Regulation No 1408/71, the determining factor is the fact that a person is insured, compulsorily or on an optional basis, for one or more of the contingencies covered by a general or special social security scheme mentioned in Article 1 (a) of the Regulation.[205]

Moreover, as noted, **regarding the principle of solidarity and the social objective, it would be hasty to accept that capitalisation is incompatible with the concept of solidarity.**[206] The term "funded" refers to the method of financing a

---

[202] Kremalis (1996a), p. 64.

[203] Kremalis (1996a), p. 64.

[204] Judgment of the Court of 26.02.2015, Case C-623/13, de Ruyter, Digital reports (Court Reports—general) ECLI:EU:C:2015:123; Judgments of Rheinhold & Mahla, EU:C:1995:144, paragraph 23; Commission v France, EU:C:2000:84, paragraph 35; and Commission v France EU:C:2000:85, paragraph 33.

[205] Judgment of the Court of 26.02.2015, Case C-623/13, de Ruyter, Digital reports (Court Reports—general) ECLI:EU:C:2015:123, paragraph 31; judgments Martínez Sala, C-85/96, EU: C:1998:217, paragraph 36 and Borger, C-516/09, EU:C:2011:136, paragraph 26 and 28.

[206] Stergiou (2014), p. 31.

scheme and not to the method of distribution of resources.[207] Funded defined-benefit schemes, in particular, retain vestigial traces of solidarity, in that they allow for some redistribution of income among the members of the scheme.[208] Thus, it is stressed that even a fully-funded scheme can shift the balance from high-earners to low-wage earners, i.e. to have redistributive results, while at the same time it maintains full capitalization.[209] It is also noted that even in fully funded defined-benefit pension schemes, there is a state commitment in the form of a guarantee (for certain non-contributory periods or in case of low performance levels associated with excessive inflation).[210]

A funded scheme may also be run by the state as a pay-as-you-go scheme, it can be supported by the state budget, be equally mandatory and exclude competition and choice.[211] In addition, one could object to the Court's failure to also emphasise the insurance (redistributive) nature of social security institutions and in particular of pension schemes; the over-emphasising of the social nature can prove to be crushing for the amount of benefits and push them down to a minimum subsistence figure.[212] It is also interesting to examine the academic approaches, according to which, although the two opposite schemes, i.e. the pay-as-you-go and the funded one, seem to be different, should the essence of their operation be examined, their differences disappear.[213] More specifically, some academics argue that any pension scheme, be it a pay-as-you-go or a funded one or a combination of both, is a zero-sum game for all participating generations.[214]

The organic or formal criterion has the advantage of simplifying things as it focuses on the fact that a specific action comes from an administrative body which is embedded in the administrative hierarchy and which applies administrative (public) law.[215] On the other hand, the substantial or functional criterion often imposes delicate balances and evaluations, as it does not place significant importance on the organisation format of the competent institution, but rather in whether that particular action expresses sovereign will or exercises public authority.[216] Of course, the new dimension assigned to the purpose element in Knauer regarding the maintenance of a similar standard of living before and after retirement should not be overlooked. It is indisputable, however, that the organic criterion has a long tradition and deep roots, while the functional criterion appeared much later when the state

---

[207] Vourloumis (2005), p. 45.

[208] Commission of the European Communities (1997), p. 5.

[209] Barr and Diamond (2008), p. 36, footnote no. 2.

[210] MISSOC Glossary B—Benefit calculation rules.

[211] Spraos and Tinios (1998), p. 3.

[212] Stergiou (2014), p. 35, footnote 35.

[213] Spraos and Tinios (1998), p. 3.

[214] Sinn (1997), p. 6; Sinn (1998); Geanakopolos et al. (1998), pp. 14–15; Sinn (2000), p. 391; Wissenschaftlicher Beirat beim Bundesministerium für Wirtschaft (1998), pp. 19–20.

[215] Skouris (1996), p. 159.

[216] Skouris (1996), p. 159.

began to resort to private law organisational forms, in order to successfully cope with the multiple and varied tasks it undertook in new areas of activity.[217] Thus, pursuant to the provisions of Article 1 (l) and Article 3 (1) of Regulation No 883/04, it can be concluded that the scope of Regulation applies to all existing pension schemes which are based on law *lato sensu,* regardless of whether they are basic (principal) or supplementary, mandatory or optional, pay-as-you-go or funded (or mixed), of (pre)defined contributions or (pre)defined benefits (or notional predefined contributions), under public or private management. **The Regulation sets a single criterion which is perhaps the safest at this stage of development of the European schemes: the statutory criterion, i.e. their establishment by law or their formalisation with the institutional type of a public authority decision. There is therefore a requirement for regulatory intervention by the state.** Indeed, funded schemes are already integrated into the system of coordination rules.

References

ApRoberts L (1993) Complementary retirement pensions: towards a definition of terms. Int Soc Secur Rev 46(4):51–66, also published in International Social Security Association (ed) (1994) Complementary pensions: European perspectives, Geneva

Anagnostou-Dedouli A (2000) Implementation criteria of the equal treatment principle of Article 119 EEC Treaty in social security. EDKA (Social Security Law Review): 801 et seq

Anagnostou-Dedouli A (2005) Social security by legal persons governed by public law. Ant. N. Sakkoulas Publishing, Athens

Andrietti V (2000) Portability of supplementary pension rights in the European Union. IRISS working paper series 2000-01, IRISS at CEPS/INSTEAD. https://liser.elsevierpure.com/ws/portalfiles/portal/11792098/Working%20Paper%20n_2000-01. Accessed 25 Nov 2024

Bakavou M (2015) Employee social security - supplementary forms. Nomiki Bibliothiki, Athens

Barr N, Diamond P (2008) Reforming pensions, principles and policy choices. Oxford University Press, Oxford

Commission of the European Communities (1991) Communication from the Commission to the Council, Supplementary social security schemes: the role of occupational pension schemes in the social protection of workers and their implications for freedom of movement, SEC, p 6

Commission of the European Communities (1997), Supplementary pensions in the Single Market: A Green Paper, 10.06.1997, COM (97) 283 final

Commission of the European Communities (1997) Committee on Legal Affairs and Citizens' Rights, Rapporteur Enrico Ferri, Report on the Commission Green Paper entitled "Supplementary Pensions in the Single Market" Explanatory Statement, point 4

Dewost JL (1995) Service public et droit communautaire – Principes de base. Europe Concurrence et Service public, Masson

Dupeyroux J-J (1990) Les exigences de la solidarité. Droit social: 741

Dupeyroux J-J (1993) Droit de la Sécurité sociale, 12th edn. Dalloz, Paris

Dupeyroux J-J (2000) Sur les régimes complémentaires, bref rappel de quelques données de base. Droit Social: 409

[217] Skouris and Tachos (1984), pp. 11 et seq.

Commission's working document of 23 October 1990 on completion of the internal market for private retirement provisions in the sphere of private pensions, annexed to the Commission's observations in Case C-244/94

Proposal of 21 October 1991 for a Council Directive relating to the freedom of management and investment of funds held by institutions for retirement provision (91/C 312/04, OJ 1991 C 312, p. 3), as amended on 26 May 1993 (93/C 171/11, OJ C 171, p 13)

Commission of the European Communities (1993) Green paper - European Social Policy, COM (93) 551

Council Directive 96/97/EC of 20 December 1996 amending Directive 86/378/EEC on the implementation of the principle of equal treatment for men and women in occupational social security schemes, Official Journal No L 046 of 17/02/1997 p 0020 – 002

Commission of the European Communities (1997) Supplementary pensions in the single market: a green paper. 10.06.1997, COM (97) 283 final

European Commission (2005) Directorate-General for Economic and Financial Affairs, European economy, Special Report No 4/2005, "The 2005 projections of age-related expenditure (2004–50) for the EU-25 Member States: underlying assumptions and projection methodologies" by the Economic Policy Committee and the European Commission (Economic and Financial Affairs DG)

European Commission (2014) The 2015 ageing report - underlying assumptions and projection methodologies. European economy 8/2014

European Economic Community (1979) Council Directive 79/7/EEC of 19 December 1978 on the progressive implementation of the principle of equal treatment for men and women in matters of social security ?? L 6, 10.1.1979, p 24

Geanakopolos J, Mitchell OS, Zeldes SP (1998) Would a privatized social security system really pay a higher rate of return? NBER working paper 6713, pp 14–15

Giesen R (2009) Unfallversicherungsmonopol und EG-Vertrag. Zeitschrift, für europäisches Sozial- und Arbeitsrecht, Berlin

Gkritsi F (2012) Compulsory affiliation in statutory social security schemes from the perspective of Community law, CJEU judgment of 5.3.2009, Kattner Case. EDKA (Social Security Law Review): 40

Goldman B, Lyon-Caen A (1983) Droit européen de la concurrence. Dalloz, Paris

Hatzopoulos V (2005) Health law and policy: the impact of the EU. In: De Burca (ed) EU law and the welfare state: in search of solidarity. OUP/EUI, Oxford, pp 123–160

Katrougalos G (2006) The impact of community law on social security law. EDKA (Social Security Law Review): 255

Kessler F (1996) Droit de la concurrence et régimes de protection sociale: un bilan provisoire, in Service public et Communauté européenne entre l'intérêt général et le marché, Tome I, Colloque de Strasbourg du 17–19 octobre 1996, p 421

Kontizas D (1996) The application of the principle of equality between men and women in community social security law. EDKA (Social Security Law Review): 529 et seq

Kotsiris L (1986) Competition law. Sakkoulas Publishing, Thessaloniki

Koukoulis-Spiliotopoulos S (1993) Les sanctions non pécuniaires. In: L'accès à l' égalité entre femmes et hommes dans la Communauté Européenne. Presses Universitaires de Louvain, Louvain, pp 156–159

Kremalis K (1996a) Issues in defining the limits of private and social security, possibilities for private insurance complementing or partially substituting social security. Ant. N. Sakkoulas Publishing, Athens

Kremalis K (1996b) Social security clauses in collective employment agreements and social dialogue, EPIKAYP. Ant. N. Sakkoulas Publishing, Athens

Leppik L (2006) Coordination of pensions in the European Union: the case of mandatory defined-contribution schemes in the Central and Eastern European Countries. Eur J Soc Secur: 47

Lyon-Caen A, Lyon-Caen G (1994) Droit social international et européen. Dalloz, Paris

Mavridis P (1996) Le citoyen européen peut-il se faire soigner dans l'État de son choix? Droit social

Mavridis P (1998a) Supplementary pension schemes: European competition law or community social law - some unconventional thoughts. EDKA (Social Security Law Review): 783

Mavridis P (1998b) L'arrêt Vougioukas: Une revolution discrete? Cahiers du droit européen:191–192

Mavridis P (2004) The "acquis communautaire" on social security: three observations, one question and two proposals in: The Greek Ombudsman, European Commission, IKA, International conference - free movement of workers and coordination of social security systems, Athens, 20–21 June 2003. Sakkoulas Publications, Athens, p 101

Milionis N (2007) Interpretative issues from the implementation of regulation no 1408/71/EEC according to the case-law of the Court of Auditors. EDKA (Social Security Law Review): 819

Nikolakopoulou Stefanou I (1992) The convergence of social security systems in West Europe. I. Sideris Editions, Athens

Paparrigopoulou-Pehlivanidi P (2002) Supplementary social security in European community competition law. Ant. N. Sakkoulas Publishing, Athens

Paparrigopoulou-Pehlivanidi P (2007a) Comment on the Council of State judgment (Plenary Session) No 3088/2007, p 2. http://scholar.uoa.gr/paparigo/publications/%CF%83%CF%87%CF%8C%CE%BB%CE%B9%CE%BF-%CF%83%CF%84%CE%B7%CE%BD-%CE%B1%CF%80%CF%8C%CF%86%CE%B1%CF%83%CE%B7-%CF%83%CF%84%CE%B5-%CE%BF%CE%BB-30882007. Accessed 25 Nov 2024

Paparrigopoulou-Pehlivanidi P (2007b) COMMENT on the ECJ judgment C-559/07 Commission of the European Communities v Hellenic Republic, p 2, footnote 5. http://scholar.uoa.gr/paparigo/publications/%CF%83%CF%87%CE%BF%CE%BB%CE%B9%CE%BF-%CF%83%CF%84%CE%B7%CE%BD-%CE%B1%CF%80%CF%8C%CF%86%CE%B1%CF%83%CE%B7-%CE%B4%CE%B5%CE%BA-c-55907-%CE%B5%CF%80%CE%B9%CF%84%CF%81%CE%BF%CF%80%CE%AE-%CE%B5%CE%BA-%CE%BA%CE%B1%CF%84%CE%AC-%CE%B5%CE%BB%CE%BB%CE%B7%CE%BD%CE%B9%CE%BA%CE%AE%CF%82-%CE%B4%CE%B7%CE%BC%CE%BF%CE%BA%CF%81%CE%B1%CF%84%CE%AF%CE%B1%CF%82. Accessed 25 Nov 2024

Paparrigopoulou-Pehlivanidi P (2013) Social security law. Nomiki Bibliothiki, Athens

Pennings F (2003) Introduction to European social security law, 4th edn. Intersentia, Antwerp

Petroglou A (1997) Comment on ECJ, Case C-147/95 Evrenopoulos, European Court Reports 1997, p. ⍰-2057. EDKA (Social Security Law Review): 270

Petroglou A (2004) Occupational insurance funds and the Court of Justice of European Communities case-law. In: Amitsis G, Lixouriotis I, Petroglou P (eds) Occupational insurance schemes and labour law issues regarding private group insurance. Ant. N. Sakkoulas Publishing, Athens, p 93

Prétot X (1997) La conformité à la Constitution de la loi instituant les fonds de pensions. Droit social 476

Psilos G (2007) Optional insurance. DEN (Labour Law Report): 818

Sakslin M (2000) Social security co-ordination - adapting to change. Eur J Soc Secur 2:179

Sarmas I (1994) Constitutional and administrative case-law of the Council of State, evolutionary study of the major issues, 2nd edn. Ant. N. Sakkoulas Publishing, Athens

Sinn H-W (1997) The value of children and immigrants in a pay-as-you-go pension system: a proposal for a partial transition to a funded system. NBER working paper 6229, p 6

Sinn H-W (1998) Comment on Axel Börsch-Supan. In: Siebert H (ed) Redesigning social security. Mohr Siebeck, Tübingen

Sinn H-W (2000) Why a funded pension system is useful and why it is not useful. Int Tax Public Financ 7:391

Skouris V (1996) Administrative procedural law I, 2nd edn. Sakkoulas, Athens

Skouris V, Tachos A (1984) Special administrative law, Introduction. Sakkoulas, Thessaloniki

Spraos G, Tinios P (1998) Pay-as-you-go and funded schemes: impressions and substance. Econ Stat Bull National Bank of Greece 10:3

Stergiou A (1996) Equal treatment of men and women in community social security law. EDKA (Social Security Law Review): 81 et seq

Stergiou A (1997) Social security clauses and collective agreements, the Greek experience - social security supplementary schemes. OMED (Organisation for Mediation and Arbitration), 4–6 July 1997

Stergiou A (2014) Social security law, 2nd edn. Sakkoulas, Athens

Stergiou A (2015) Constitutional issues of mandatory occupational insurance funds. DEN (Labour Law Report): 190

Stevens Y (2001) The role of occupational pension schemes in Europe, elements and techniques of solidarity used within funded occupational pension schemes, p. 3, research funded by the Fund for scientific research of Katholieke Universiteit Leuven and the Federal Office for Scientific, Technical and Cultural Affairs (Research project SO/01/006: Invisible pensions in Belgium) and presented as a paper at the Ninth Annual Colloquium of Superannuation Researchers on the 9 and 10 of July 2001 at the University of New South Wales-School of Economics and Actuarial Studies in Sydney

Synodinos C (2000) The limits of applying community competition law in the social security sector. Ambivalence in CJEU case-law. Thoughts on the occasion of Albany, Brentjens' and Maatschappij judgments. EDKA (Social Security Law Review): 882

Tandaroudas C (2004) Legal protection of migrant workers in EEC. In: Petroglou A, Occupational insurance funds and the Court of Justice of European Communities case-law. In: Amitsis G, Lixouriotis I, Petroglou P (eds) Occupational insurance schemes and labour law issues regarding private group insurance. Ant. N. Sakkoulas Publishing, Athens

Tsampasi A (2000) Thoughts and remarks on community social security law. EDKA (Social Security Law Review): 3

Tsantilas T (1996) Issues in defining social security in European community law (the case-law of the Court of Justice of the European communities). In: Kremalis K (scientific coordinator) Issues in defining the limits of private and social security, possibilities for private insurance complementing or partially substituting social security. Ant. N. Sakkoulas Publishing, Athens, p 36

Tsapasi A (1996) Gender equality in social security under the constitution and community law. EDDD (Public & Administrative Law Review): 328

Tsotsorou T (2007) Loss of retirement rights due to the non-application of regulation (EEC) no 1408/71 on the statutory supplementary insurance systems. EDKA (Social Security Law Review): 662

Tsotsorou T, Sklikas N (2012) Is the monopoly of social security schemes compatible with European law? EDKA (Social Security Law Review): 41 et seq

Verschueren (2009) Regulation 883/2004 and invalidity and old-age pensions. Eur J Soc Secur (1–2):147

Vonk G (2010) Social security as a public interest: a multidisciplinary inquiry into the foundations of the regulatory welfare state. Eur J Soc Secur 12(1):2–15

Vourloumis P (2005) The social security scheme in simple words. Potamos, Athens

Weatherill S, Beaumont P (1995) EC law: the essential guide to the legal workings of the European community, 2nd edn. Penguin Books, London

Winterstein A (1999) Nailing the jellyfish: social security and competition law. Eur Competition Law Rev 20(6):9

Wissenschaftlicher Beirat beim Bundesministerium für Wirtschaft (1998) Grundlegende Reform der gesetzlichen Rentenversicherung. Bundesministerium für Wirtschaft, Studienreihe No. 99, Bonn

Part II
Pension Benefits

Chapter 4
Coordination of Pensions

4.1 Pension Benefits in the Coordination Regulation

Within the coordination framework, no specific definition is provided for the social risks covered by the scope of Regulation No 883/04, i.e. Article 3 of Regulation No 883/04 in combination with Article 1 (l) of Regulation No 883/04 on legislation.

The Coordination Regulation treats differently long-term benefits, such as invalidity, old-age or survivors' pensions in comparison with short-term benefits, such as unemployment and sickness benefits that are coordinated in accordance with the principle of integration (only a single benefit is granted to the migrant worker and is calculated in accordance with the law of a single Member State).[1,2] For the coordination of invalidity, old age or survivors' pensions, the partial pension method that is set out in Article 50 of Regulation No 883/04 applies.[3] A decisive criterion for the implementation of the Regulation is the affiliation to a social security system, even against a single risk, and not the actual exercise of an activity; the time of exercising an activity is equally unimportant.[4] This could mean that economically non-active persons may be entitled to a pension if a national legislation provides for a retirement benefit for such persons, such as a Scandinavian system based on residence.[5]

As noted, the Coordination Regulation does not define the nature of a social security benefit.[6] It is also argued that, taking into account the different national

---

The Sections 4.1, 4.2, 4.3, 4.4, 4.5 are also included in the article of mine Tsetoura (2023).

---

[1] Pennings (2012, 2022), p. 176.

[2] Pieter Van der Mei (2003), p. 247.

[3] Pennings (2012, 2022), p. 176.

[4] Mavridis (2004), p. 810.

[5] Mavridis (2004), p. 295; Fuchs (2015), p. 80.

[6] Mavridis (2004), p. 295; Fuchs (2015), p. 80.

A. Tsetoura, *Pension Rights and Free Movement of Persons*,
https://doi.org/10.1007/978-3-031-91127-9_4

systems of social benefits, such a definition would not be possible, nor useful.[7] For the purposes of the Coordination Regulation, a social security benefit is, as established by case-law, a benefit granted a) without any individual and discretionary assessment of personal needs, to recipients on the basis of a legally defined position and b) provided that it concerns one of the risks expressly listed in the Regulation scope (exhaustive list).[8]

Regulation No 883/04 provides a specific definition of "pension" for the purposes of its implementation. More specifically, under Article 1 (w) of Regulation No 883/04, the term "pensions" means not only pensions but also lump-sum benefits which can be substituted for them and payments in the form of reimbursement of contributions and, subject to the provisions of Title III, revaluation increases or supplementary allowances. The previous definition under Article 1 (t) of Regulation No 1408/71 was also similar.[9] According to Article 1 of Regulation No 1408/71, the Court has noted that the term "benefits" is to be understood as meaning, in the widest sense, all pensions, including increments, re-evaluation allowances or supplementary allowances.[10]

Additionally, the distinction between pre-retirement benefits and old-age benefits is crucial because the aggregation rule of Article 6 Regulation 883//2004 does not apply to pre-retirement benefits (Article 66 Regulation 883/2004). The Court seems to have adhered to the EU social security law perspective by closely scrutinising the characteristics of Poland's national social security benefits to determine whether the claimant's bridging pension ought to be classified as an old-age benefit or as a pre-retirement benefit in Czerwiński.[11] In Czerwiński, the Court reviewed the differences between pre-retirement benefits and old-age benefits, focussing on the characteristics of so-called 'bridging pensions' in Poland's social security system. The applicant Czerwiński had completed contribution and non-contribution periods in Poland as well as in both Germany and Norway for periods of work as a second engineer and a chief engineer on a boat, respectively. The Polish authorities, referring to Article 9 of Regulation No. 883/2004, claimed that bridging pensions fall within the scope of pre-retirement benefits, whereas the referring court concluded that such pensions should be classified as old-age benefits.

The description of the dispute mentions "contribution periods", which are compared with "insurance periods", which used to be the key determinant of a pension applicant's status. The concept of reciprocity applies in this regard between the type

[7] van Raepenbusch (2015), p. 80.

[8] Mavridis (2004), p. 811; Stergiou (2014), p. 42; Katrougalos (2006), p. 252.

[9] Judgment of the Court of 6.07.2000, Case C-73/99, Movrin, European Court Reports 2000 I-05625, paragraph 34.

[10] Judgment of the Court of 22.06.1972, Case 1/72, Frilli, European Court Reports 1972 00457 ECLI:EU:C:1972:56, paragraph 17.

[11] Judgement of the Court of 30 May 2018, Case C–517/16, Stefan Czerwiński v Zakład Ubezpieczeń Społecznych Oddział w Gdańsku, ECLI:EU:C:2018:350.

of pension the applicant is requesting and his or her contribution record (as opposed to his or her insurance record); it is not connected to the applicant's social security status or to the criterion of residence or employment. The key question is whether the applicant has contributed to a social security system (even if that system also provides for non-contribution periods).

By comparing old-age benefits with pre-retirement benefits, the Court concluded that the essential characteristic of an old-age benefit lies in the fact that it is intended to safeguard the subsistence of persons who, when reaching a certain age, leave employment and are no longer required to be available for work at their employment office[12] (para. 45). By contrast, a **pre-retirement benefit** (even if it bears certain similarities with an old-age benefit in terms of content and purpose, namely, amongst other things, to safeguard the subsistence of persons who have reached a certain age), differ notably from an old-age benefit insofar as it **pursues an objective that is connected with employment policy inasmuch as it helps to release posts held by workers who are close to retirement age for the benefit of younger unemployed persons, an objective that became quite apparent in the context of the economic crisis Europe was facing at the time**[13] (para. 46). It follows that pre-retirement benefits are more closely connected to financial crises in business, to restructuring, redundancies and rationalisation (para. 47).

The concept of 'pre-retirement benefit' is defined in Article 1(x) of the Regulation, and refers to all cash benefits other than unemployment benefits or early old-age benefits, which are provided to workers who have reached a certain age and who have reduced, ceased or suspended their remunerative activity until they qualify for an old-age pension or an early retirement pension, the receipt of which is not conditional upon the individual being available to the competent State's employment services (para. 48). Under this provision, 'pre-retirement benefits' differ from 'early old-age benefits' in that the latter is provided *before* the individual has reached the standard pension entitlement age and either continues to receive this benefit once he or she reaches that age or until that benefit is replaced with another old-age benefit (para. 49). Furthermore, to the extent that the national legislation at issue explicitly refers to the worker's age but makes no reference to the objective of releasing employment positions for younger unemployed workers, **the benefit at issue in the main proceedings appears to be more similar to an old-age benefit** (para. 53).

Finally, the Court stated that Article 4 of the **law on bridging pensions outlines the general conditions relating to age, length of service and evidence of long contribution and non-contribution periods, which, as a rule, are requirements**

[12] Judgement of 5 July 1983, *Valentini*, 171/82, EU:C:1983:189, paragraph 14.

[13] To that effect, see judgement of 5 July 1983, *Valentini*, 171/82, EU:C:1983:189, paragraphs 16 and 17.

that are connected with entitlement to old-age benefits, unlike the conditions generally laid down for entitlement to pre-retirement benefits (para. 55). Since the bridging pension continues to be provided once the standard age for old-age pension entitlement has been reached or is replaced by another old-age benefit (para. 56), the Court concluded that a benefit such as that at issue must be considered to be an 'old-age benefit' within the meaning of Article 3(1)(d) of Regulation 883/2004.

In ***Bocero Torrico***,[14] while the question referred for a preliminary ruling related explicitly to Article 48 TFEU, the referring court also mentioned the provisions of Regulation No 883/2004. Mr Bocero Torrico and Mr Bode applied to the INSS for an early retirement pension, having completed contribution periods in Spain and Germany. The pension applications were rejected on grounds that the amount payable was below the minimum monthly pension corresponding to the applicants' family situation on their 65th birthday. According to Spanish social security legislation, the amount of pension to be received must be higher than the minimum pension due to the respective person when he or she reaches the age of 65 and becomes eligible for an early retirement pension. The national courts reflected the intention of the Spanish legislation to avoid supplementing retirement pensions up to the statutory minimum of persons who have not yet reached the statutory retirement age, thus retaining them in the labour market.

In this regard, the Court pointed out that no provision in Title I of Regulation 883/2004, which comprises the general provisions of that Regulation, or in Title III, Chapter 5 of that Regulation, which covers the applicable special provisions, inter alia, old-age pensions, precludes such a rule (para. 26). However, the applicants in the main proceedings disputed the interpretation of the competent institutions and the Spanish courts to determine eligibility for an early retirement pension, namely that the concept of the amount of 'pension to be received' only refers to the pension payable by the Kingdom of Spain, and does not include pensions from other Member States that might be due to the respective person (para. 28).

As the Advocate General stated in point 45 of his Opinion, Article 5 of Regulation 883/2004 must be considered as being applicable to situations such as those at issue in the main proceedings. The 'receipt of social security benefits', according to the provision, refers to the pension the applicants in the main proceedings are entitled to (para. 31). On the other hand, the factual situations addressed in the main proceedings do not fall within the scope of Article 6 of Regulation 883/2004. Instead, the issue was whether the amount of pension due to the applicants in another Member State should be taken into account for the purpose of determining eligibility for an early retirement pension (para. 32).

As regards old-age pensions, the Court had previously interpreted the concept of 'equivalent benefits' in Article 5(a) as referring to two types of old-age benefits that

[14] Judgement of the Court of 5 December 2019, Joined Cases C-398/18 and C-428/18, Antonio Bocero Torrico (C-398/18), Jörg Paul Konrad Fritz Bode (C-428/18) V Instituto Nacional de la Seguridad Social, Tesorería General de la Seguridad Social, ECLI:EU:C:2019:1050.

are comparable in terms of their objective and the legislation that established them[15] (para. 36). The refusal of one Member State's competent authorities to take the pension benefits to which a worker who has exercised his or her right to free movement is entitled in another Member State into account to determine eligibility for an early retirement pension, is likely to put that worker in a less favourable position than a worker who has spent his or her entire career in only one Member State (para. 42).

As the Advocate General noted in point 49 of his Opinion, even if such considerations were to represent general interest objectives within the meaning of the case law, the arguments put forward by the INSS and the Spanish government do not justify discriminatory application of such a requirement to the detriment of workers who have exercised their right to freedom of movement (para. 45).

Thus, the Court concluded that Article 5(a) of Regulation 883/2004 must be interpreted as precluding the legislation of a Member State which requires that—as a condition for a worker to be eligible for an early retirement pension—the amount of pension to be received must be higher than the minimum pension that would be due to that worker upon reaching statutory retirement age under the respective legislation, where the term 'pension to be received' is interpreted as referring only to the pension from that particular Member State, and does not include the pension that worker might receive through equivalent benefits payable by one or several other Member States.

4.1.1 Pension Benefits as Social Security Benefits

The need for a uniform implementation of European law requires the identification of the characteristics of each benefit, in particular the objectives pursued and the conditions for granting them; what is of particular interest is the operation of the benefit, its purpose, defined in accordance with the conditions for granting and maintaining the benefit.[16] Thus, every time that the Court examines a benefit, it examines whether its particular characteristics reveal a benefit within the meaning of the Regulation, regardless of the classification assigned by the national legislature.[17]

According to settled case-law, a benefit may be regarded as a social security benefit in so far as it is granted to the recipients, without any individual and discretionary assessment of personal needs in the specific situation, on the basis of

[15] To that effect, see judgement of 21 January 2016, *Vorarlberger Gebietskrankenkasse and Knauer*, C-453/14, EU:C:2016:37, paragraphs 33 and 34.

[16] Mavridis (2004), p. 295.

[17] Mavridis (2004), p. 295.

a legally defined position and relates to one of the risks expressly listed in Article (3) (1) of Regulation No 883/2004.[18] According to a different wording, a benefit may be regarded as a social security benefit in so far as it is granted without any **individual and discretionary assessment of personal needs, to recipients** on the basis of a legally defined position and provided that it concerns one of the risks expressly listed in (at the time) Article 4 (1) of Regulation No 1408/71 (currently Article 3 (1) of Regulation No 883/04).[19]

Any case-law references to "law" should be understood as references to "legislation" within the meaning of Article 1 (l) of Regulation No 883/04. Moreover, the list of risks contained in Article 3 (1) of Regulation No 883/2004 is exhaustive and that, as a result, a branch of social security not mentioned in the list does not fall within that category, even it confers upon individuals a legally defined position entitling them to benefits.[20] Accordingly, in order to distinguish between different categories of social security benefits, the risk covered by each benefit must also be taken into consideration.[21] Of course, regarding the interpretation of these criteria in view of a benefit there is no doubt that, as regards the first conditions, the provisions concerning its grant confer on recipients a legally defined right.[22]

Thus, according to the relevant case-law interpretation, a crucial element for the classification of a benefit as a social security benefit and its resulting affiliation to the Coordination Regulation is its potential link with one of the traditional social risks set out in Article 3 (1) of Regulation No 883/04. For this classification, the case-law

[18] Judgment of the Court da Silva Martins, C-388/09, EE:C:2011:439, paragraph 38; Case 249/83, Hoeckx, European Court Reports 1985, p. 973, paragraphs 12 to 14; and on the other hand in case 122/84, Scrivner and Cole, European Court Reports 1985, p. 1027, paragraphs 19 to 21; as well as judgments of 20.06.1991, C-356/89, Newton, European Court Reports 1991, p. I-3017 and of 16.07.1992, C-78/91, Hughes, European Court Reports 1992, p. I-4839, paragraph 15.

[19] Judgments cited above: Hughes, paragraph 15; Hoever and Zachow, paragraph 18; Molenaar, paragraph 20; Commission v Luxembourg, paragraph 29; Celozzi, paragraph 17; Acciardi, paragraph 14; Meints, paragraph 24 and, in particular Judgment of 20.06.1991, Case C-356/89, Newton, European Court Reports 1991, p. 1-3017, paragraph 11; of 24.02.1987, joined cases 379/85 to 381/85 and 93/86, Giletti, European Court Reports 1987, p. 955, paragraphs 11 and 12; of 27.03.1985, Case 249/83, Hoeckx, European Court Reports 1985, p. 973, paragraphs 12 to 14; as well as of 08.03.2001, Case C-215/99, Jauch, European Court Reports 2001 p. I-01901, paragraph 25; of 21.02.2006, Case C-286/03, Hosse, European Court Reports 2006 p. I-01771, paragraph 37; of 21.07.2011, Case C-503/09, Lucy Stewart, paragraph 32, CJEU case-law, EDKA (Social Security Law Review) LII (2011), p. 929; of 18.12.2007, joined cases C-396/05 to C-419/05 and C-450/05, Habelt, European Court Reports 2007, p. I-11895, paragraph 63; of 11.09.2008, Case C-228/07, Petersen, European Court Reports 2008, p. I-6989, paragraph 19.

[20] Judgments cited above: Scrivner, paragraph 19; judgment of 11.07.1996, Case C-25/95, Otte, European Court Reports 1996, p. I-3745, paragraph 22; of 27.03.1985, Case 249/83, Hoeckx, European Court Reports 1985 p. 00973, paragraph 12.

[21] Judgment of 18.07.2006, Case C-406/04 De Cuyper, European Court Reports 2006, p. I-6947, paragraph 27.

[22] Judgment of 16.07.1992, Case C-78/91, Hughes, European Court Reports 1992 p. I-04839, paragraph 16; of 05.03.1998, Case C-160/96, Molenaar, European Court Reports 1998 p. I-00843, paragraph 21.

has established certain characteristics which a benefit must display in order to justify its classification as a social security benefit. More specifically, the Court has repeatedly held that the distinction between benefits excluded from the scope of Regulation No 1408/71 and those which fall within its scope is based essentially on the **constituent elements of each particular benefit, in particular its purposes and the conditions on which it is granted,** and not on whether a benefit is classified as a social security benefit by national legislation.[23]

4.2 Social Assistance

Pursuant to Article 3 (5) of the new Regulation No 883/04, which is also in accordance with Article 4(4) of the old Regulation No 1408/71, social assistance falls in principle outside the scope of the Regulation. National social security systems remain anchored on the principle of territoriality, especially regarding non-contributory benefits, such as social assistance benefits, the amount of which is determined by the cost of living in each Member State.[24]

However, despite the exclusion of social assistance from the material scope of the Regulation, it is not clear within that Regulation how social assistance is defined and where the dividing line between social security and social assistance should be set.[25] Although it may seem desirable, from the point of view of applying the regulation, to establish a clear distinction between legislative schemes which come within social security and those which come within assistance, it is possible that certain laws, because of the classes of persons to which they apply, their objectives, and the detailed rules for their application, may simultaneously contain elements belonging to both the categories mentioned and thus defy any general classification.[26] As it has been argued, the exclusion of social assistance includes the difficulties of distinguishing between social assistance and social security, taking also into account the fact that benefits are being modernised and becoming more complicated, as well as the fact that Community law also extends to those social benefits and services that

[23] Judgment of 16.07.1992, Case C-78/91, Hughes, European Court Reports 1992 p. I-04839, paragraph 14; of 10.10.1996, , joined cases C-245/94 and C-312/94, Hoever and Zachow, European Court Reports 1996 p. I-04895, paragraph 17; of 05.03.1998, Case C-160/96, Molenaar, European Court Reports 1998 p. I-00843, paragraph 19; of 01.04.2008, Case C-212/06, Government of Communauté française and Gouvernement wallon v Gouvernement flamand, European Court Reports 2008 p. I-01683, parahraph 16; of 10.03.1993, Case C-111/91, (Commission v Luxembourg) Commission of the European Communities v Grand Duchy of Luxembourg, European Court Reports 1993 p. I-00817, paragraph 28; of 18.01.2007, Case C-332/05, Celozzi, European Court Reports 2007 p. I-00563, paragraph 16; of 2.08.1993, Case C-66/92, Acciardi, European Court Reports 1993, p. I-4567, paragraph 13; and of 27.11.1997, Case C-57/96, Meints, European Court Reports 1997, p. I-6689, paragraph 23; of 27.03.1985, Case 122/84, Scrivner, European Court Reports 1985 p. 01027, paragraph 18.

[24] Verschueren (2007), p. 315.

[25] Paskalia (2009), p. 1185.

[26] Judgment of 22.06.1972, Case 1/72, Frilli, European Court Reports 1972 p. 00457, paragraph 13.

[27] Sakslin (2000), p. 173.

do not fall within the scope of the Coordination Regulation.[27] Given that the interpretation of Community law is primarily the responsibility of competent authorities, the lack of a precise definition of social security and social assistance leads directly to an uneven interpretation of the regulation in the various Member States.[28] The question of distinguishing social security benefits and assistance benefits has been present in the case-law since the early application of Regulation No 1408/71.

4.3 The Broad Case-Law Interpretation

Whenever the Court had to classify certain benefits that were not based on paid contributions,[29] it noted that despite the necessity for a distinction, it could not rule out the possibility that certain legislations contain at the same time elements of both social security and assistance, due to the kind of persons to which they apply, their purposes and the methods for the implementation.[30] Pursuant to the material scope of the Regulation (Article 4 (2a) of Regulation No 1408/71 and currently Article 3 (2) of Regulation No 883/04), contributions cannot be the fundamental difference between social insurance (security) and social assistance.[31] As noted, according to case-law social assistance benefits are those granted at discretion and/or guarantee a minimum income to the persons that do not fall within one of the social security benefits set out in the relevant Article of the Coordination Regulation (1408/71 and currently 883/04).[32]

In addition, it is noted that the decisive criteria that arise from the case-law regarding the classification of a benefit as social security or social assistance are the main purpose of the benefit and the method for its financing.[33] Thus the Court held that the German benefits in question in Habelt et al[34] were old-age and survivors' benefits due to their financing via social security contributions.[35] In view of the difficulty in determining whether a payment is a contribution, tax or a different type of payment, it is argued that the decisive criterion for treating a

[27] Sakslin (2000), p. 173.

[28] Sakslin (2000), p. 173.

[29] Judgment of 22.06.1972, Case 1/72, Frilli, European Court Reports 1972 p. 00457; of 28.05.1974, Case 187/73, Callemeyn, European Court Reports 1974 p. 00553; of 13.11.1974, Case 39/74, Costa, spouse Mazzier v Belgian State, European Court Reports 1974 01251 ECLI:EU:C:1974:122; of 05.05.1983, Case 139/82, Piscitello, European Court Reports 1983 p. 01427.

[30] Tsantilas (1996), pp. 35–36.

[31] Tsantilas (1996), p. 36.

[32] The Greek Ombudsman (2012), p. 844.

[33] Paskalia (2009), pp. 1187–1188, with reference to cases C-406/04 De Cuyper, C-228/07 Petersen.

[34] C-396/05, C-419/05, C-450/05 Habelt et al.

[35] Paskalia (2009), p. 1188.

payment as a social security contribution is whether it is paid for the funding of a social security scheme and not whether benefits are obtained in return on the basis of a specific payment.[36]

Furthermore, in Hoeckx,[37] the Court analysed the characteristics of the benefit in question focusing on the element of need and the criterion of destitution and held that the Belgian minimum subsistence allowance constitutes a social assistance benefit and as such it is excluded from the scope of the Regulation. More specifically, the Court remarked that the "minimex" is characterised on the one hand by the fact that it confers upon recipients a legally defined position and, on the other hand, by the fact that it is granted to any person who does not have adequate means and is unable to "obtain them either by his own efforts or in any other way" (Article 1 (1) of the Law of August 1974); it thus adopts **need** as an essential criterion for its application and does not make any stipulations as to periods of work, contribution or affiliation to any particular social security body covering a specific risk (Hoeckx, paragraph 13). A claimant need only show that "he is prepared to accept work" unless prevented by his state of health or compelling social reasons; furthermore, he is required to exercise his rights to social benefits or even any rights to maintenance if the public social welfare centre considers it necessary (Article 6, paragraphs 1 and 3 of the 1974 Law cited above) (Hoeckx, paragraph 13).

It follows that an allowance like the one at issue, being a general social benefit, cannot be classified under one of the branches of social security listed in Article 4 (1) of Regulation No 1408/71 and therefore does not constitute a social security benefit within the specific meaning of the regulation (Hoeckx, paragraph 14).Thus, the social benefit guaranteeing a minimum means of subsistence in a general manner such as that provided for by the Belgian Law of 7 August 1974 does not fall within the material scope of Regulation No 1408/71 as defined by Article 4 (1) and (2) of Regulation No 1408/71 (Hoeckx, paragraph 15).

However, if a social assistance benefit can be linked to one of the social risks, as listed in Article 3 (1) of Regulation No 883/04, it can fall within the material scope, provided that some additional criteria are met (case-law extension of the material scope to social assistance mutatis mutandis with "traditional social security").These criteria have been formulated by the Court taking into account the non precisely distinct limits between social security and social welfare benefits, in view of the mixed characteristics displayed by many social security schemes.

As clearly stated in Newton, although by virtue of certain of its characteristics, a legislation has much in common with social assistance, particularly since the grant of the benefit provided for is not dependent on the completion periods of employment, insurance or contribution, nevertheless in certain circumstances it is more similar to social security.[38] Thus, by virtue of certain of its features, national legislation on

[36]Paskalia (2009), p. 1188, with reference to case C-249/04, Allard, paragraph 16.

[37]Judgment of the Court of 27.03.1985, Case 249/83, Hoeckx, European Court Reports 1985 00973 ECLI:EU:C:1985:139.

[38]Judgment of the Court of 20.06.1991, Case C-356/89, Newton, European Court Reports 1991 p. I-03017, paragraph 13.

guaranteed income has certain affinities with social assistance—in particular where it prescribes need as an essential criterion for its application and does not stipulate any requirement as to period of employment, membership or contribution—nevertheless, it approximates to social security because it does not prescribe consideration of each individual case, which is a characteristic of assistance, and confers on recipients a legally defined position giving them the right to an analogous benefit.[39]

Taking into account the wide definition of the range of recipients, such legislation in fact fulfils a double function; it consists on the one hand in guaranteeing a subsistence level to persons wholly outside the social security system, and on the other hand in providing an income supplement for persons in receipt of inadequate social security benefits.[40] Thus, the Court had held in Frilli that the term "benefits" is to be understood as meaning, in the widest sense, all pensions, including all fractions thereof chargeable to public funds, increments, reevaluation allowances or supplementary allowances (paragraph 17). Thus as regards a wage-earner or assimilated worker who has completed periods of employment in a Member State, resides in that State and is entitled to a pension there, the legislative provisions giving all elderly residents a legally protected right to a minimum pension are provisions which, as regards these workers, come within the field of social security covered by Article 51 of the Treaty and within the regulations adopted in application of that article, even where such legislation might fall outside this classification as regards other categories of recipients (paragraph 18). As a result, a benefit such as the one of minimum guaranteed income which was at issue in Levatino[41] must be regarded as an "old-age benefit" within the meaning of the Regulation (paragraph 21).In this case, the beneficiary's rights must be determined in accordance with the provisions of Chapter 3 of Title III of the Regulation, that is to say, in particular, in accordance with the provisions of Article 46 and 51 of Regulation No 1408/71[42] (currently Articles 52–59 of Regulation No 883/04).

From the above, it can be concluded that a benefit that is a supplement to a pension linked to one of the risks of old age, invalidity or death, even if it guarantees a minimum or guaranteed income, it can be considered as a social retirement benefit. Moreover, Regulation No 883/04 in the definition of "pensions" refers to supplementary allowances understood as pensions, just as in Regulation No 1408/71.

Accordingly, the Court held that, in so far as a legislation confers a right to supplementary benefits designed to increase the amount of pensions paid by way of social security, without any assessment of individual needs or circumstances, which is a characteristic of assistance, it comes within the social security schemes within the meaning of Regulation No 1408/71.[43] As a result, Regulation No 1408/71 does not exclude from its scope *ratione materiae* a supplementary allowance paid by a

[39] Judgment of 22.06.1972, Case 1/72, Frilli, European Court Reports 1972 p. 00457, paragraph 14.

[40] Frilli, paragraph 15.

[41] Judgment of the Court of 22.04.1993, Case C-65/92, Levatino, European Court Reports 1993 I-02005 ECLI:EU:C:1993:149.

[42] Levatino, paragraph 21.

[43] Judgment of the Court of 24.02.1987, joined cases 379, 380, 381/85 and 93/86, Giletti, European Court Reports 1987 00955 ECLI:EU:C:1987:98, paragraph 11; of 17.12.1987, Case 147/87, Zaoui, European Court Reports 1987 05511 ECLI:EU:C:1987:576, paragraph 8.

national solidarity fund such as the Fonds national de solidarité and granted to recipients of old-age, survivors' or invalidity pensions with a view to providing them with a minimum means of subsistence, provided that the persons concerned have a legally protected right to grant such an allowance.[44]

In conclusion, the Court had quite early on accepted that whilst it may seem desirable from the point of view of applying this Regulation to establish a clear distinction between legislative schemes that fall respectively within social security and assistance, one cannot exclude the possibility that by reason of the persons covered, its objectives and its method of application, a legislation can come close to both these categories.[45] A legislation such as the one in question in the preliminary ruling in the joined Giletti cases, as well as in Newton, Frilli and Piscitello, fulfils a dual function, in so far as, in the first place, it guarantees a minimum means of subsistence to persons in need and, in the second place, it provides additional income for the recipients of social security benefits which are inadequate, having regard to the broad definition of the persons entitled to the benefit at issue.[46]

In particular, as stressed in Giletti,[47] **the fact that a single law may also provide for advantages which can be classified as assistance** cannot alter, for the purposes of Community Law, the intrinsic social security character of a benefit linked to an invalidity, old-age or survivor's pension to which it is an automatic supplement (Giletti, paragraph 11). Otherwise, legislation having ceased to concern itself with the assessment of need (means necessary) in the individual case—a characteristic feature with assistance—conferring on the persons entitled a legally defined status, it falls within the system of social security within the meaning of the Regulation.[48]

In that regard, it is worth noting that in **Piscitello** where a social pension was under examination, the Court held that a benefit such as **the social pension provided for in Article 26 of Italian Law No 153 of 30 April 1969**, which, in the first place, confers on recipients a legally defined status which is not conditional upon any discretionary individual assessment of their personal needs or circumstances, and,

---

[44] Judgment of the Court of 17.12.1987, Case 147/87, Zaoui, European Court Reports 1987 05511 ECLI:EU:C:1987:576, paragraph 9.

[45] Judgment of 09.10.1974, Case 24/74, Biason, European Court Reports 1974 999, paragraph 9; judgment of 24.02.1987, joined cases 379, 380, 381/85 and 93/86, Giletti, European Court Reports 1987 p. 00955, paragraph 9; of 20.06.1991, judgment C-356/89, Newton, European Court Reports 1991 p. I-03017, paragraph 12; of 27.03.1985, Case 249/83, Hoeckx, European Court Reports 1985 p. 00973, paragraph 12.

[46] Judgment of 24.02.1987, joined cases 379, 380, 381/85 and 93/86, Giletti, European Court Reports 1987 p. 00955, paragraph 10; of 20.06.1991, Case C-356/89, Newton, European Court Reports 1991 p. I-03017, paragraph 14; of 22.06.1972, Case 1/72, Frilli, European Court Reports 1972 p. 00457, paragraph 15; as well as of 28.05.1974, Case 187/73, Callemeyn, European Court Reports 1974 p. 00553, paragraph 8; of 05.05.1983, Case 139/82, Piscitello, European Court Reports 1983 p. 01427, paragraph 12.

[47] Judgment of 24.02.1987, joined cases 379, 380, 381/85 and 93/86, Giletti, European Court Reports 1987 p. 00955, paragraph 11.

[48] Judgment of 09.10.1974, Case 24/74, Biason, European Court Reports 1974 p. 00999, paragraph 10.

secondly, may be paid as a supplement to the income of recipients of social security benefits, in principle falls within the field of social security referred to in Article 51 of the EEC Treaty and is not excluded from the scope of Regulation No 1408/71 by the provisions of Article 4(4) thereof.[49] A benefit of that kind provided for in Article 26 of the abovementioned Italian law is paid in accordance with the conditions and on the basis of objective criteria laid down by that law to elderly nationals in order to provide them with minimum means of subsistence. Such a pension must therefore be assimilated to an old-age benefit within the meaning of Article 4(1) (c) of Regulation No 1408/71.[50]

It could be argued that this is a Court interpretation providing a negatively defined function (ancillary) to social security, in order to broaden the concept of social security as used and regulated in the Regulation. This interpretation came up with a broad definition of the regulated issues, mitigating at the same time the damaging consequences identified in the case-law from the exclusion of social assistance from its scope.

Thus, a social assistance benefit may fall within the scope of the Regulation only if it is guaranteed by the law and not granted following an individual assessment, i.e. if the relevant national legislation recognises (by law) a legally enforceable subjective right to this benefit.[51] Accordingly, the Regulation does not apply to general social assistance benefits, which are provided to the those in need as a minimum decent subsistence income without any link to a social risk listed as such (Article 3 (1) Regulation No 883/04), but only to special categories of benefits, such as where the legislature has provided for unemployment or pension assistance benefits and at the same time has acknowledged a subjective right to them.[52]

It follows, therefore, that a benefit that exhibits social assistance characteristics may fall within the scope of the Regulation as a social security benefit because it otherwise approximates social security. In this way, however, each case should be examined to determine whether it is a social security benefit with social assistance characteristics linked to one of the social risks of the material scope of the Regulation and, in this case old age, death or invalidity as social security benefits. It is, by extension, extremely difficult to distinguish these benefits as associated at the same time to both social security and social assistance from the special non-contributory cash benefits which are in between social security and social assistance but which are not treated as social security benefits for the purposes of the application of the Regulation.

[49] Judgment of the Court of 5.05.1983, Case 139/82, Paola Piscitello v Istituto nazionale della previdenza sociale (INPS), European Court Reports 1983 01427, Operative part 1.

[50] Piscitello, Operative part 2.

[51] Schouckens and Monserrez (2011), p. 18.

[52] Schouckens and Monserrez (2011), p. 18.

4.4 Special Non-contributory Cash Benefits[53] and the Residence Criterion

Special non-contributory benefits are one of the most difficult fields of coordination law.[54] As noted in academic theory, the criteria of Regulation No 1408/71 for the classification of benefits as special non-contributory are also preserved in Regulation No 883/04, i.e. the purpose of the benefit, its financing method and its inclusion to the relevant Annex.[55] A special benefit is defined by its purpose, while the non-contributory nature of the benefit is determined by its financing.[56] Special non-contributory benefits are benefits of a mixed kind. They are characterised by the fact that they are connected partly to social security, in that they benefit as of right persons who fulfil the conditions for the grant of the social security benefits to which they are linked, and partly to social assistance, in the sense that they are not dependent on periods of work or contributions and that they are intended to relieve a clear need.[57]

The scheme of Regulation No 1408/71 shows that the concept of "social security benefit" within the meaning of Article 4(1) of Regulation No 1408/71 (and currently Article 3(1) of Regulation No 883/04) and the concept of "special non-contributory benefit" within the meaning of Article 4 (2a) and (2b) of Regulation No 1408/71 on special non-contributory benefits (replaced with Article 3 (3) of Regulation No 883/04) are mutually exclusive.[58] A benefit which satisfies the conditions of a "social security benefit" within the meaning of Article 4 (1) of Regulation No 1408/71 and currently Article 3 (1) of Regulation No 883/04 therefore cannot be analysed as a "special non-contributory benefit".[59] It follows by contrast that if a benefit is regarded as a special non-contributory benefit, it does not constitute a social security benefit.

As the Court has pointed out, the Community legislature is entitled to adopt provisions which derogate from the principle that social security benefits are exportable.[60] Of course, as noted, such derogating provisions and, a fortiori, Article 4 (2b) of Regulation No 1408/71, which excludes certain specific benefits from the scope of that regulation, must be interpreted strictly. This means that that article can

---

[53] Article 3 (3) of Regulation No 883/04 combined with Article 70 of Regulation No 883/04 - Article 4 (2a) and (2b) of Regulation No 1408/71 combined with Article 10[a] of Regulation No 1408/71.

[54] Paskalia (2009), p. 1184.

[55] Paskalia (2009), p. 1184.

[56] Fuchs (2015), p. 419, invoking judgment of 6.07.2006, Case C-154/05, Kersbergen-Lap and Dams-Shipper, European Court Reports, p. I-6249, paragraph 30.

[57] Paskalia (2009), p. 1189, invoking judgment in Case C-160/02 Skalka, paragraph 22.

[58] Judgment of 21.02.2006, Case C-286/03, Hosse, European Court Reports 2006 p. I-01771, paragraph 36.

[59] Cited above, Hosse judgment, paragraph 36.

[60] Among others, judgment of 4.11.1997, Case C-20/96, Snares, European Court Reports 1997, p. I-6057, paragraph 41.

apply only to benefits which satisfy cumulatively the conditions it lays down, that is, benefits which are both special and non-contributory.[61]

According to the Court's wording, a special benefit within the meaning of Article 4 (2a) of Regulation No 1408/71 is defined by its purpose: it must either replace or supplement a social security benefit and be by its nature social assistance justified on economic and social grounds and fixed by legislation setting objective criteria.[62] Thus, in Skalka, the Austrian compensatory supplement that tops up a retirement pension or an invalidity pension was held as being by nature social assistance in so far as it is intended to ensure a minimum means of subsistence for its recipient where the pension is insufficient. Its grant is dependent on objective criteria defined by law and, consequently, it must be classified as a "special benefit" within the meaning of Regulation No 1408/71.[63]

The relevant determining criterion is how the benefit is actually financed.[64] The Court must consider whether that financing comes directly or indirectly from social contributions or from public resources.[65] In the case of the Austrian compensatory supplement, the costs are borne by a social institution which then receives reimbursement in full from the relevant Land, which in turn receives from the Federal budget the sums necessary to finance the benefit. At no time do the contributions of insured persons form part of this financing arrangement. Consequently, it is established that the Austrian compensatory supplement must be regarded as being non-contributory within the meaning of Article 4(2a) of Regulation No 1408/71.[66] As follows from this case-law, supplementary benefits provided to pensioners with income below a certain level are generally considered as special non-contributory benefits.[67]

It is clear that national legislation which places at a disadvantage certain of its nationals simply because they have exercised their freedom to move to another Member State amounts to a restriction on the freedoms conferred by Article 21 (1) TFEU on every citizen of the Union.[68] Such a restriction can be justified,

---

[61] Judgment of 21.02.2006, Case C-286/03, Hosse, European Court Reports 2006 p. I-01771, paragraph 25.

[62] Judgments of 04.11.1997, C-20/96, Snares, European Court Reports 1997, p. I-6057, paragraphs 33, 42 and 43; of 11.06.1998, C-297/96, Partridge, European Court Reports 1998, p. I-3467, paragraph 34; and of 31 May 2001, C-43/99, Leclère and Deaconescu, European Court Reports 2001, p. I-4265, paragraph 32; C-160/02 Skalka, paragraph 25.

[63] Judgment of the Court of 29.04.2004, Case C-160/02, Skalka, European Court Reports 2004 I-05613 ECLI:EU:C:2004:269, paragraphs 26–27.

[64] Jauch, paragraphs 32 and 33; Skalka, paragraph 28.

[65] Skalka, paragraph 28.

[66] Skalka, paragraphs 29–30.

[67] Paskalia (2009), p. 1195.

[68] Judgment of 11.07.2002, Case C-224/98, D'Hoop, European Court Reports 2002, p. I-06191, paragraph 35; of 29.04.2004, Case C-224/02, Pusa, European Court Reports 2004, p. I-05763, paragraph 20; of 18.07.2006, Case C-406/04, De Cuyper, European Court Reports 2006 p. I-06947, paragraph 39; of 23.04.2009, Case C-544/07, Rüffler, European Court Reports 2009 p. I-03389, paragraph 73.

with regard to Community law, only if it is based on objective considerations of public interest independent of the nationality of the persons concerned and proportionate to the legitimate objective of the national provisions.[69]

The residence criterion was considered in the EU legislative process as creating a genuine link, otherwise said a genuine connection between the interested applicant and the host Member State for the establishment of entitlement to the special non-contributory benefits of the relevant Annex of the Regulation.[70] Indeed, the Court has held that it is legitimate for the national legislature to wish to ensure that there is a real link between the applicant for a specific allowance and the relevant state,[71] as well as to ensure the financial balance of the social security system.[72] Therefore, in circumstances where acquisition of entitlement to a non-contributory benefit is not subject to conditions as regards contributions, it can be considered to be legitimate for a Member State to award such benefit only after it has been established that there was a genuine link between the claimant and the competent State.[73] The existence of such a link could effectively be established, in particular, by a finding that the person in question had been, for a reasonable period, actually present in that Member State.[74]

The question is whether the legal status of the special non-contributory benefits is precisely defined, taking into account the Court's judgments and thoughts in Hosse[75] and Jauch.[76] More specifically, in some instances the Court seemed to exclude the

[69] Judgment of 18.07.2006, Case C-406/04, De Cuyper, European Court Reports 2006 p. I-06947, paragraph 40; of 26.10.2006, Case C-192/05, K. Tas-Hagen and Tas, European Court Reports 2006 p. I-10451, paragraph 33; of 4.12.2008, Case C-221/07, Zablocka-Weyhermüller, European Court Reports 2008 p. I-09029, paragraphs 37; of 23.04.2009, Case C-544/07, Rüffler, European Court Reports 2009 p. I-03389, paragraphs 74; as well as of 22.05.2008, Case C-499/06, Nerkowska, European Court Reports 2008 p. I-03993, paragraph 34.

[70] Van Overmeiren et al. (2011), p. 15.

[71] Judgments of 11.07.2002, Case C-224/98, D' Hoop, European Court Reports 2002, p. I-6191, paragraph 38; of 23.03.2004, Case C-138/02, Collins, European Court Reports 2004, p. I-2703, paragraph 67.

[72] Judgments of 28.04.1998, Case C-158/96, Kohll, European Court Reports 1998, p. I-1931, paragraph 41; of 11.09.2008, Case C-228/07, Petersen, European Court Reports 2008, p. I-6989, paragraph 57.

[73] Judgment of 21.07.2011, Case C-503/09, Lucy Stewart, European Court Reports2011 p. I-06497, paragraph 92.

[74] Lucy Stewart, paragraph 93.

[75] Judgment of 21.02.2006, Case C-286/03, Hosse, European Court Reports 2006 p. I-01771, paragraph 36. According to paragraph 36 of the Hosse judgment: "The scheme of Regulation No 1408/71 shows that the concept of 'social security benefit' within the meaning of Article 4(1) and the concept of 'special non contributory benefit' within the meaning of Article 4(2a) and (2b) of the regulation are mutually exclusive. A benefit which satisfies the conditions of a 'social security benefit' within the meaning of Article 4(1) of Regulation No 1408/71 therefore cannot be analysed as a 'special non-contributory benefit'".

[76] Judgment of 08.03.2001, Case C-215/99, Jauch, European Court Reports 2001 p. I-01901, paragraph 18. According to paragraph 18 of the Jauch judgment: "Article 4(2a) of Regulation No 1408/71 concerns 'special non-contributory benefits' which are provided under legislation other

possibility of making a connection between special non-contributory benefits and the concept of social security benefits within the meaning of Article 4 (1) of Regulation No 1408/71 and currently Article 3 (1) of Regulation No 883/04 (Hosse, paragraph 36); in other instances, the Court, treating said benefits as social assistance, left the door open for them to be indirectly brought within the field of social security to which that Regulation applies, given that they are intended to provide supplementary, substitute or ancillary cover against the risks covered by the branches of social security referred to in the material scope of the Regulation (Jauch, paragraph 18).The extension of the latter's scope was guaranteed due to its link with traditional social security, keeping in mind the criteria examined above in the relevant section.

It is understandable therefore to wonder, if it is noted that a benefit cannot be classified as special non-contributory but as a social security benefit, i.e. concepts which are mutually exclusive (Hosse, paragraph 36)—case in point in Hosse a sickness benefit linked with the risk of sickness (Hosse, paragraph 46)—which criterion would it be possible to use in other cases to link a special non-contributory benefit with the traditional fields of social security as falling under social welfare (Jauch, paragraph 18), so as to result in the latter case, via the conditions applicable on social assistance, to be classified as a social security benefit. Otherwise, it should be classified either as a sickness benefit pursuant to Article 4 (1) of Regulation No 1408/71 as a social security benefit as such or as associated simultaneously with both categories of social security and social assistance or as a special non-contributory benefit pursuant Article 4 (2^a) of Regulation No 1408/71. Another issue is the purpose of special non-contributory benefits as supplementary, substitute or ancillary to social security benefits (Article 4 (2^a) of Regulation No 1408/71).

The above question lies in the fact that when a special non-contributory benefit cannot be regarded as falling within social security, then it cannot also be regarded as falling within the social assistance scope. On the contrary, it is worth noting that according to the wording of the law, said benefits exhibit characteristics of both social security law (pursuant to Article 4 (1) of Regulation No 1408/71) and social assistance law (Article 70 (1) of Regulation No 883/04).

There is no doubt that it is **not clear from the case-law when** a benefit may be considered as relating to both categories of social security and social assistance and therefore **be a social security benefit,** and when a benefit is considered as a **special non-contributory benefit** (although once again a connection exists with both social security and social assistance) and therefore is **not a social security benefit**.

In any event, regarding special non-contributory benefits, the Court has repeatedly stressed that the principle of exportability of social security benefits applies if

---

than that relating to the traditional branches of social security listed in Article 4(1) of that regulation, or even come under social and medical assistance expressly excluded from the scope of Regulation No 1408/71 by Article 4(4), but which may nevertheless be brought within the field of social security to which that regulation applies if they are intended to provide supplementary, substitute or ancillary cover against the risks covered by the branches of social security referred to in Article 4(1) of the regulation".

the Community legislature has not adopted provisions which derogate from that principle.[77] As held by the Court, in particular as regards special non-contributory benefits in Annex IIa to Regulation No 1408/71, it is open to the Community legislature when implementing Article 51 of the Treaty to adopt provisions which derogate from the principle of exportability of social security benefits. This means that **the condition of residence in the State of the competent institution may legitimately be required for the grant of benefits closely linked with the social environment**.[78] The justification for limiting the export of these benefits was mainly that they were not based on the payment of contributions by the beneficiary and that they were meant to guarantee a level of subsistence taking into account the cost of living and integration in a particular Member State.[79]

The Court must therefore examine for each benefit in question whether it is a special and non-contributory benefit, i.e. whether the benefit in question, listed in Annex IIa to Regulation No 1408/71 is of a special nature and is not based on contribution payment (cited above, Jauch judgment, paragraph 22).The aforementioned Court judgment regarding the examination of the special and non-contributory elements being satisfied was reiterated in the subsequent relevant judgments.[80] It should be noted that according to the Court's case-law, it follows that the special character of a benefit is defined by its purpose: it must either replace or supplement a social security benefit and display the characteristics of social assistance justified by economic and social reasons on the basis of a regulation providing for objective criteria.[81]

---

[77] Among others, judgment of 31.03.1977, Case 87/76, Bozzone, European Court Reports 1977, p. 191; of 5.05.1983, Case 139/82, Piscitello, European Court Reports 1983, p. 1427, paragraph 16; of 24.02.1987, joined cases 379/85, 380/85, 381/85 and 93/86, Giletti and others, European Court Reports 1987, p. 955, paragraph 16; and of 12.07.1990, Case C-236/88, Commission v France, European Court Reports, p. I-3163, paragraph 16.

[78] Judgment of 31.05.2001, Case C-43/99, Leclere and Deaconescu, European Court Reports 2001 p. I-04265, paragraph 32; of 27.09.1988, Case 313/86, Lenoir, European Court Reports 1988 p. 05391, paragraph 16; and of 04.11.1997, Case C-20/96, Snares, European Court Reports 1997 p. I-06057, paragraph 42.

[79] Coucheir et al. (2008), p. 11.

[80] Judgment of 16.01.2007, Case C-265/05, Perez Naranjo, European Court Reports 2007 p. I-00347, paragraph 31; of 6.07.2006, C-154/05, Kersbergen-Lap and Dams-Shipper, European Court Reports 2006, p. I-6249, paragraph 27; of 29.04.2004, Case C-160/02, Skalka, European Court Reports 2004 p. I-05613, paragraph 21.

[81] Judgment of 4.11.1997, Case C-20/96, Snares, European Court Reports 1997, p. I-6057, paragraphs 33, 42 and 43; of 11.06.1998, Case C-297/96, Partridge, European Court Reports 1998, p. I-3467, paragraph 34; of 05.05.2011, Case C-537/09, Bartlett, paragraph 26, EDKA (Social Security Law Review) LII (2011), p. 948; as well as judgments cited above: Leclère and Deaconescu, paragraph 32; Kersbergen-Lap and Dams-Shipper, paragraph 30; and Skalka, paragraph 25.

4.5 A Pension as a Social Security Benefit[82] or as a Special Non-contributory Benefit and Member States' Practice

To begin with, it should be noted that, in theory, a benefit that pursuant to the national legislation of a State Member is a pension benefit does not constitute a pension for the purposes of the application of the special part of the Coordination Regulation. That means that the pension should, according to the national legislation, be a social security benefit pursuant to the Regulation so that the pension rules thereof can apply. It could generally be observed that pensions associated with insurance periods (contributions on income) or with residence periods (usually relating to income tax for the purpose of funding social security), otherwise pensions associated with the participation in the funding of a social security scheme, are subject to pension rules with no problems. Problems mainly arise in pensions with "assistance characteristics" in particular given the broad definition of pensions in Article 1 of Regulation No 883/04.

As particularly noted, the special rules for calculating the old-age pensions of Title III of the Regulation do not apply to the special non-contributory old-age pensions.[83] Otherwise, old-age, invalidity and survivors' pensions that are provided for in national law and display characteristics of a special non-contributory cash benefit and that have been included for this reason in Annex XI of Regulation No 883/04 are treated by the Regulation as special non-contributory non-exportable cash benefits and not as pensions for the purposes of applying Articles 50–60 and 40–49 of Regulation No 883/04. This is also set out in Regulation No 883/04 itself and in particular Article 70 (3) of Regulation No 883/04, according to which Article 7 and the other chapters of Title 7 do not apply to special non-contributory cash benefits.

In addition, as has become clear, pensions falling under social assistance and provided for in the relevant national legislation regarding assistance benefits are excluded by the scope of the Regulation. The focus is therefore on those pension benefits that are associated to both categories of social security and social assistance. These benefits, in so far as they relate to one of the social risks of old age, invalidity or death fall within the scope of the Regulation and in particular the rules of Articles 50–60 and 40–49 of Regulation No 883/04. The complexity of this issue, which has probably been exacerbated by existing case-law is apparent from the declarations in the relevant Annexes X and XI of Regulation No 883/04.

---

[82] In itself or as relating to social security and social assistance.

[83] Verschueren (2009), pp. 225–226.

On the one hand, in Annex X of Regulation No 883/04 on special non-contributory cash benefits, there are many states that have listed as special non-contributory benefits social pensions of non-contributory nature (Ireland, Spain, Cyprus, Poland, Portugal, Slovenia, Slovakia). On the other hand, a national pension (which is not classified as contributory or non-contributory)[84] can also be found listed by Finland in Annex XI on special provisions for the application of the legislation of the Member States. As is well known, it is within Member States' power to organise their social security schemes. It is thus possible for non-contributory pensions to be included or excluded from the Regulation rules on retirement benefits, depending on their national characteristics. The question is, of course, whether, for example, the social non-contributory pensions of the States listed in Annex X share characteristics with the national Finnish pension. For example, the social security national pension of Finland also includes a residence requirement for a specific amount of time in its territory, in order for someone to be entitled to said benefit;[85] such a requirement is usually associated with special non-contributory benefits. Moreover, in accordance with Article 70 (3) of Regulation No 883/04, the provisions on waiving the residence rules (principle of exportability) of Article 7 of Regulation No 883/04 (former Article 10 of Regulation No 1408/71) do not apply to said benefits, nor do the provisions of the other chapters in Title III.

In view of this rough distinction of the categories in which the benefits in question can be classified, the aim is to find a tangible and clear criterion to enable the European coordination social security law to treat similar benefits in a uniform manner. Besides, the Regulation does not establish a general criterion for the precise distinction between social security and social assistance, taking also into account the fact that the old conceptual categories tend to lose their clarity.[86] Indeed, in many EU countries, the boundaries between social security and social assistance are blurred.[87]

It is worth noting that the Italian social pension (supplementary allowance) of the Italian Law No 153 of 30 April 1969 that was treated in Piscitello[88] as a social security benefit associated with both categories of social security and social

[84] National pensions and guarantee pensions are financed by the State, as set out in: European Commission (2013b), Your social security rights in Finland, July 2013, p. 6. See also European Commission (2024a), Your social security rights in Finland, MISSOC (2024), p. 26. In the 2024 update it is stated that the national Finnish pension is paid by Kela without indicating its financing method. National pensions are granted and paid by Kela (Kansaneläkelaitos), the Finnish national Social Insurance Institution. But see also MISSOC 2024 - Finland (1 January 2024), https://www.missoc.org/missoc-database/comparative-tables/results/, where it is mentioned that the finnish national pension is financed by taxation.

[85] European Commission (2024a), p. 26; MISSOC (2024).

[86] Tsantilas (1996), p. 35. See also Martinsen (2007).

[87] Jorens and Lherhoud (2011), p. 13.

[88] Judgment of the Court of 5.05.1983, Case 139/82, Piscitello, European Court Reports 1983 01427, See also above: The retirement benefit as a social security benefit distinct from social welfare.

assistance and in particular as an old-age retirement benefit under Regulation No 883/04 is registered in Annex X on special non-contributory benefits. More specifically, Italy has listed this benefit under point a), Annex X, Regulation No 883/04 so as to be considered as a special non-contributory benefit.

In this way, said benefit listed as special non-contributory is not exportable and not subject to the other provisions of the other chapters of Title III of the Regulation, i.e. the rules on pensions. This happens despite the contrary judgment of the Court in the relevant case, where it held that provided that Regulation No 1408/71 does not contain special provisions regarding these allowances, it must be accepted that the waiving of residence rules provided for in Article 10 (1) of Regulation No 1408/71 also applies to these benefits.[89,90] Accordingly, France's supplementary allowances, which in the Giletti and Zaoui cases examined above were considered as social security benefits, under the Regulation No 883/04 regime, they are listed as special non-contributory benefits in Annex X of Regulation No 883/04.

However, it should also be taken into account that it is not impossible for a benefit listed as a special non-contributory benefit under Regulation No 883/04, to be included in the context of the national scheme in social assistance which falls outside the scope of the Regulation, such as for example the social pension of Cyprus.[91]

It is clear therefore that at this stage the application of the provisions on pensions depends among others on how each national retirement benefit is defined by the relevant State in the context of the European coordination system. Of course, added confusion is caused by the fact that both in the case of retirement benefits that are considered social security benefits due to their association with both categories of social security and social assistance, as well as in the case of special non-contributory retirement benefits, it is possible to relate to non-contributory benefits intended to provide ancillary coverage and ensure a minimum income. The only element that arises from the case-law and that could maybe act as a dividing line is the dual function recognised for the former by the Court. Besides, the question arises whether such a classification can be presumed solely on the basis of listing a benefit under the relevant Annex. Regarding special non-contributory benefits, the Court initially followed this rationale treating the will and action of Member States on registrations as a decisive criterion; later, however, the Court started examining in detail the characteristics of each benefit from scratch.

---

[89] Piscitello, Operative part 2.

[90] Of course, the Piscitello case is prior to the adoption of Regulation No 1247/92 which sought to exclude the so-called special non-contributory benefits from the principle of exportability or, otherwise said, it sought to create a different coordination system that would differ in regards to these benefits (Explanatory Memorandum of Regulation No 1247/92, paragraph 6). The benefits considered to be special non-contributory following agreements between the legislative body and Member States were registered in Annex IIa which was integrated in Regulation No 1408/71 (currently Annex X of Regulation No 883/04). See also the general provisions, above in Chap. 2 on the material scope and special non-contributory cash benefits.

[91] European Commission (2024b) Annex X, Regulation No 883/04.

4.5.1 The Underlying Logic of Special Non-contributory Benefits

It is worth noting however that special non-contributory benefits are granted in the State of residence regardless of previous taxation of a person.[92] Besides, as set out in Article 70 (2) (b) of Regulation No 883.04, the financing of special non-contributory benefits derives from compulsory taxation intended to cover general public expenditure and *the conditions for providing and for calculating the benefits are not dependent on any contribution in respect of the beneficiary.* According to the same provision, special non-contributory benefits that are provided to supplement a contributory benefit shall not be considered to be contributory benefits for this reason alone. Therefore, it is decisive that special non-contributory benefits lack any contribution allocation and participation to the financing of a social security scheme.[93]

The rationale behind the method of financing could therefore be reflected in the case-law as an element of differentiation of benefits. In the case of special non-contributory benefits, although they can be financed by taxation, it is not necessary to establish the participation of persons in their financing. The provision of special non-contributory benefits is then associated with the conditions for granting them, which are limited to residence, which is used as a proof of a social link (with moral and material implications) with the State in question and does not refer to periods of insurance.

However, academics have expressed reservations regarding the ambiguity of the concept of residence in the Coordination Regulation, taking into account that the different concepts of residence in the Member States and the schemes based on residence introduce added complications.[94] Besides, there are different types of national residence conditions, while the concept of residence itself may be understood in a different way in the context of the national scheme of each Member State, resulting in the operation of several "concepts of residence".[95] Along the same lines, it is argued that it is up to each Member State's legislation to determine whether a person resides or not in its territory.[96]

It is argued, however, that any residence requirement in national law must be compatible with the residence requirement as it is to be understood in the context of the application of the Regulation.[97] A nationally defined residence concept could indeed lead to a situation where a person having lived all of their life in the EU is not

---

[92] O'Neill (2011), p. 3.

[93] Schouckens and Monserrez (2011) in: P. Schouckens, EU social security coordination law, Reading material, KU Leuven, p. 20 invoking the Jauch judgment, Case 215/99.

[94] Jorens et al. (2010), p. 43.

[95] Roberts and Bolderson (1999); Roberts (2001), p. 37; Coucheir et al. (2008), p. 2.

[96] Sakslin (2000), p. 179; Jorens et al. (2008), p. 11 invoking Court judgment of 20.05.2008, Case C-352/06, Bosmann, European Court Reports 2008 I-03827 ECLI:EU:C:2008:290.

[97] Coucheir et al. (2008), p. 15.

considered to be resident by the legislation of any Member State or where it satisfies the residence condition of several Member States' legislation, so as to be entitled to benefits based on residence (e.g. special non-contributory benefits) in several Member States.[98]

Indeed, as the Court held in Swaddling, pursuant to Article 1 of the Regulation on definitions, the term "residence" has a Community-wide meaning.[99] On that point, it should be noted that, according to the United Kingdom's legislation, as interpreted in the national case-law, the habitual residence test is satisfied where the claimant has the settled intention of residing in the United Kingdom and where, moreover, he has resided there for an appreciable period, the duration of which varies according to the circumstances of each individual case (Swaddling, paragraph 26).It is common ground that in the main proceedings' case, it was the interested party's intention, when he applied for income support, to reside in the United Kingdom. The parties disagree, however, as regards the additional requirement of an appreciable period of residence which, in Mr Swaddling's case, was assessed as being of eight weeks' duration and in respect of which, therefore, he was unable to obtain income support on the basis of the British legislation alone (Swaddling, paragraph 27).

Accordingly, the phrase "the Member State in which they reside" in Article 10a of Regulation No 1408/71 on special non-contributory benefits refers to the State in which the persons concerned habitually reside and where the habitual centre of their interests is to be found. In that context, account should be taken in particular of the employed person's family situations; the reasons which have led him to move; the length and continuity of his residence; the fact (where this is the case) that he is in stable employment and his intention as it appears from all the circumstances[100] (Swaddling, paragraph 29). For the purposes of that assessment, however, the length of residence in the Member State in which payment of the benefit at issue is sought cannot be regarded as an intrinsic element of the concept of residence within the meaning of Article 10a of Regulation No 1408/71 (Swaddling, paragraph 30).

In particular, when, as in the present case, an employed person, on returning to his State of origin after exercising his right to freedom of movement, has made it clear at the time of applying for income support that he intends to remain in his State of origin, where his close relatives live—whilst expressing his readiness, should the need arise in the context of some future employment, to travel from time to time to other Member States—he cannot be deemed not to satisfy the condition concerning residence within the meaning of Article 10a merely because the period of residence completed in his State of origin is too short (Swaddling, paragraph 30). The Court also reiterated the above case-law in the recent Wencel case, adding that since the

---

[98] Coucheir et al. (2008), p. 15.

[99] Judgment of the Court of 25.02.1999, Case C-90/97, Swaddling, European Court Reports 1999 I-01075 ECLI:EU:C:1999:96, paragraph 28.

[100] See mutatis mutandis, regarding Article 71 (1) (b) (ii) of Regulation No 1408/71, judgments of 17.02.1977, 76/76, Di Paolo, European Court Reports 1977, p. 117, paragraphs 17 to 20 and of 08.07.1992, C-102/91, Knoch, European Court Reports 1992, p. I-4341, paragraphs 21 and 23.

system introduced by Regulation No 1408/71 uses the residence of the person concerned for the determination of the legislation applicable, it cannot be accepted, without depriving the provisions referred to in the preceding paragraph of all practical effectiveness, that a person may have, for the purposes of Regulation No 1408/71, a number of habitual residences in different Member States.[101]

Therefore, the concept of residence is not defined at national but at Union level, it is specified in the case-law of the Court of Justice and requires a comprehensive assessment of each person's situation according to a set of criteria that do not need to be cumulative and which by nature concern mainly employees; their application is thus difficult for inactive persons.[102] There are no grounds on the basis of the case-law interpretation for a different concept of residence to determine the applicable legislation or to grant benefits.[103] Thus, regarding the coordination of social security schemes, the concept of residence as defined in the Regulation is considered to be uniform.[104] Besides, the elements for determining residence identified as non-exhaustive in Article 11 of Regulation No 987/09 refer exclusively to actual criteria, i.e. they must be assessed independently from their legality.[105]

Along the same lines, it is noted that an elderly allowance registered in Annex X , Regulation No 883/04 as a special non-contributory benefit, such as for example the Swedish residence-based social security scheme, may be granted to persons solely according to the criterion of habitual residence within the meaning of residence in Regulation No 883/04 in combination with Article 70 of Regulation No 883/04 (and not on the basis of legal residence or the concept of residence in the Swedish legislation).[106]

Furthermore, although many national social security rules provide for the entitlement to benefits to be subject to the condition of legal residence of the interested party in the territory of the relevant state, the coordination social security rules, i.e. Regulations No 1408/71 and 883/04 do not contain such a criterion.[107] It is also noted that the concept of residence in the coordination social security rules is different from the concept of residence in Directive 2004/38, while according to the prevailing view, there are no elements in the EU law that prove that a provision of Directive 2004/38 could impact the application of Regulation No 883/04.[108]

It could be argued that in special non-contributory benefits, residence means the physical presence in the territory of the relevant state, as there is no reciprocity element from the payment of contributions. It is about participating in a community of solidarity, which is manifested through the requirement of physical presence,

---

[101] Judgment of the Court of 16.05.2013, Case C-589/10, Wencel, Digital Reports (Court Reports-general)ECLI:EU:C:2013:303, paragraph 48.

[102] The Greek Ombudsman (2012), p. 839.

[103] Jorens et al. (2010), p. 44.

[104] See in detail Tsetoura (2019).

[105] European Commission (2013a), Employment, Social Affairs and Equal Opportunities, p. 49.

[106] Erhag (2013), pp. 251–252.

[107] Coucheir et al. (2008), p. 2.

[108] Van Overmeiren et al. (2011), p. 46; Jorens et al. (2008), p. 11.

i.e. of residence, in order for a person to also partake in that solidarity. Indeed, the Court has held that in circumstances where acquisition of entitlement to a non-contributory benefit is not subject to conditions as regards contributions, it can be considered to be legitimate for a Member State to award such benefit only after it has been established that there was a genuine link between the claimant and the competent State. The existence of such a link could effectively be established, in particular, by finding that the person in question had been, for a reasonable period, actually present in hat Member State.[109]

Besides, in many countries, eligibility for non-contributory benefits may require a past period of residence and/or a social link between the paying state and the recipient.[110] Of course, as evident in Swaddling, the Court excluded the length of residence as an element of residence, promoting as a result the existence of a genuine social link as a primary element. Therefore, the Member State of residence as the State where the persons concerned habitually reside and where the habitual centre of their interests is to be found,[111] is now understood more as meaning the existence of links with that State. Moreover, the Court had noted that the habitual residence condition adopted by national law can have no bearing whatever on the interpretation of the concept of residence for the purposes of the coordination system on special non-contributory benefits.[112]

As noted in the relevant theory, special non-contributory benefits which were created to guarantee a minimum income in specific categories, such as the elderly, are financed by taxation and that is why Member States had initially argue that they are public welfare benefits excluded from the scope of the Regulation.[113] Besides, as noted, these benefits are intended for economically inactive persons and the financial burden of their payment is solely on the Member State of residence with no involvement of the State in which the recipient may have completed periods of employment or residence; meanwhile, their granting does not require for the recipient of such a benefit to be a taxpayer in the State of payment of the special non-contributory benefit.[114] These benefits therefore are based mainly on solidarity, which, however, is limited within national borders. The maintained limitation of the exportability principle in special non-contributory benefits is based on the view that this kind of benefits are an expression of solidarity within the sphere (smaller group) of a specific Member State, where each State is obliged to carry the responsibility for guaranteeing a minimum subsistence income only for the persons belonging in the specific solidarity community.[115] It could be said however that in this case the welfare-assistance nature is more prominent.

---

[109]Judgment of the Court of 21.07.2011, Case C-503/09, Lucy Stewart, European Court Reports 2011 I-06497 ECLI:EU:C:2011:500, paragraphs 92–93.

[110]Roberts (2004); Cousins (2007), p. 37.

[111]Judgment of the Court of 25.02.1999, Case C-90/97, Swaddling, European Court Reports 1999 p. I-01075, paragraph 29.

[112]Swaddling, paragraph 32.

[113]Pennings (2005), pp. 72–75.

[114]O'Neill (2011), p. 13.

[115]Verschueren (2009), p. 224.

4.5.2 The Underlying Logic of Social Security Benefits

On the contrary, in the case of social security benefits, even those relating to social security and assistance, it is rather usual that they are funded via taxation and the conditions for granting them refer to periods of residence that correspond to periods of insurance as periods of participation in funding the scheme, regardless whether a benefit is granted "in return" for that participation.

In Member States where residence is the criterion for providing social protection (residence-based systems), the sole fact that a person resides in a specific Member State is enough to establish periods of insurance without any economic activity.[116] These systems probably contributed to promoting the social security criterion, i.e. the criterion of the affiliation to a national social security scheme as decisive for the coverage of a migrant person by the Regulation, even if that person had never had an economic activity.[117]

However, in this context, the question is not whether the uniform definition of residence of the Regulation or the national definitions should be applied; the question is, rather, whether participation in the funding of the schemes is established through payment of contributions within the meaning of similar payments[118] (tax levies) in residence-based schemes, known from Scandinavian countries, where social security funding takes place through taxes.[119] The result is a form of implicit reciprocity by participating in a scheme as an indirect condition for these benefits, which is in contrast with non-contributory benefits, which can also require prior completion of residence periods but in itself (i.e. for someone to have been a resident/present) so that a social link between the State and the recipient is established[120] with no requirement of participation or contribution to the funding. Furthermore, for the classification of a benefit, it is crucial for the Court whether the funding for the benefit comes directly or indirectly from social security contributions or from public funding.[121] This second case therefore concerns social security benefits justified on the basis of the participation of the recipient in their funding via tax levies which for the purposes of the Regulation are equivalent to social security contributions.[122] In this case, the insurance nature is more prominent.

---

[116] Spiegel (2007), p. 59; Jorens and Van Overmeiren (2009), p. 54; Sakslin (2000), p. 179; Pennings (2005), p. 77.

[117] Paskalia (2007), p. 169.

[118] Judgment of the Court of 10.05.2001, Case C-389/99, Sulo Rundgren, European Court Reports 2001 I-03731. See also above social security contributions and tax law issues.

[119] Pennings (2005), p. 77.

[120] Roberts (2004); Cousins (2007).

[121] Fuchs (2015), p. 419, invoking judgment of 08.03.2001, Case C-215/99, Jauch, European Court Reports 2001 p. I-01901, paragraphs 30 et seq.

[122] Judgment of the Court of 10.05.2001, Case C-389/99, Rundgren, European Court Reports 2001 I-03731, paragraph 57.

Besides, the fact that a levy is categorised as a tax under national legislation does not mean that, under the Coordination Regulation, that same levy cannot be regarded as falling within the scope of that regulation.[123] The Court has found that it could not agree with the proposition that contributions which are really to be categorised as taxes fall outside the scope of the Regulation,[124] as the decisive criterion is that of the specific allocation of a tax to the funding of a social security scheme of a Member State.[125] It should be noted that one of the social security schemes where contributions are levied under the tax system and where the basis for their calculation is the taxable income is the Finnish scheme.[126]

In addition, it should be noted that although the Regulation does not define the concept of insurance, "period of insurance" means periods of contribution [...] defined or recognised as periods of insurance by the legislation under which they were completed or considered as completed, and all periods treated as such where they are regarded as equivalent to periods of insurance (Article (1) (t) of Regulation No 883/04). Despite the difficulties in determining the limits of social security and in the absence of a generally accepted definition of social insurance and social security,[127] it is generally accepted that the best known techniques of social security is social insurance and social assistance.[128] In the case of social insurance, contributions are generally compulsory (but also optional) for and by the members of solidarity schemes, so that when a member of the solidarity network is affected by a social risk, they are granted a social benefit.[129] Otherwise, by paying social contributions, the insured persons expect to receive the benefits provided where one of the statutory pre-defined standard risks materialises.[130]

[123] Judgment of the Court of 26.02.2015, Case C-623/13, de Ruyter, Digital reports (Court Reports - general), ECLI:EU:C:2015:123, paragraph 24; judgment of the Court of 03.04.2008, Case C-103/06, Philippe Derouin, European Court Reports 2008 I-01853 ECLI:EU:C:2008:185, paragraphs 22; judgment of the Court of 15.02.2000, Case C-34/98, Commission of the European Communities v the French Republic, European Court Reports 2000 I-00995 ECLI:EU:C:2000:84, paragraph 34; and judgment of the Court of 15.02.2000, Case C-169/98, Commission of the European Communities v the French Republic, European Court Reports 2000 I-01049 ECLI:EU:C:2000:85, paragraph 32.

[124] Judgment of the Court of 03.04.2008, Case C-103/06, Derouin, European Court Reports 2008 I-01853 ECLI:EU:C:2008:185, paragraph 22.

[125] To that effect, judgment Commission v France, EU:C:2000:84, paragraphs 39 and 40 as well as Commission v France, EU:C:2000:85, paragraphs 37 and 38.

[126] Judgment of the Court of 10.05.2001, Case C-389/99, Sulo Rundgren, European Court Reports 2001 I-03731.

[127] Stergiou (2014), p. 10; Romanias (2008), p. 29 et seq.; Pieters (2006), p. 1.

[128] Pieters (2006), p. 5.

[129] Pieters (2006), p. 5.

[130] Stergiou (2013), p. 25.

Social security in particular is a combination of insurance methods (conditionality from prior payment of contributions, proportionality of benefits to contributions) with social solidarity.[131] In any event, contributions (or similar payments) are an indispensable part of insurance. Thus, in social security benefits, when referring to "periods of residence" within the meaning of Article 1 (v) of Regulation No 883/04, i.e. to periods so defined or recognised by the legislation under which they were completed or considered as complete, the reference is to periods of insurance in the sense of contributions paid or deemed paid (or equivalent payments).It is thus proven that the definition of periods of residence (Article 1 (v) of Regulation No 883/04) and accordingly the national definitions on periods of residence can be met by reference to Article 1 (t) of Regulation No 883/04 on periods of insurance as periods of contributions. The accession of the Scandinavian countries in the EU is probably at the origins of this confusion.[132] This development in the EU and coordination legal space resulted in the introduction of residence elements in the Coordination Regulation, which, however, were not clearly identified so as to distinguish the precise function of residence as a condition imposed by a scheme.

However, it should also be taken into account the fact that some States may choose for their social security scheme to be funded not exclusively though the taxing system but through a combination of different sources. Once again, if certain taxes are levied for the purpose of funding social security and in particular specific social security benefits, the participation in the funding of a scheme through the tax system follows.

4.5.3 The Finnish Example

To continue with the excellent example of Finland,[133] a requirement for claiming the national pension is that the claimant has lived in Finland for at least three years after turning 16.[134]

However, it is expressly provided that **insurance time accrued in other EU/EEA countries can be taken into consideration for fulfilling the residence period requirement**.[135] It is noted that residence in Finland is not perfectly assimilated with residence in another Member State; rather residence in Finland is assimilated with insurance time.

---

131 Stergiou (2013), pp. 32, 34.

132 Pennings (2005), p. 68; Jorens (2010), p. 170; Paskalia (2007), p. 173.

133 MISSOC 2024 – Finland – 1 January 2024 https://www.missoc.org/missoc-database/comparative-tables/results/.

134 European Commission (2024c) Your rights country by country, Finland-Old-age pension – national pension.

135 European Commission (2024c) Your rights country by country, Finland-Old-age pension – national pension.

However, at least one year of the required period has to have been spent in Finland.[136,137] Given that a national pension may be claimed by those who have not worked and those whose earnings-related pension is small,[138] Finland has stated in Annex XI, Regulation No 883/04 on special provisions for the application of the legislation of the Member States that for the purposes of determining entitlement and of calculating the amount of the Finnish national pension under Articles 52 to 54 of this Regulation, pensions acquired under the legislation of another Member State are treated in the same way as pensions acquired under Finnish legislation (point 1).This is an assimilation of pension income. It should also be noted that the assimilation of a requirement could also have a negative impact for a migrant worker; this could better be understood if the older national Finnish provision is taken into account according to which pensions paid under Regulation No 883/04 that are based on the insurance of the same person and paid by another Member State are not considered as income.[139] It is worth noting that, although the residence requirement is assimilated with the entitlement to the Finnish national pension, according to the relevant provision, its amount depends on the time the interested party lived in Finland between the ages of 16 and 65 taking into account that the general retirement age for the national pension is 65 years.[140] These listings in Annex XI, Regulation No 883/04, as well as the national regulations on social security rights in Finland that make explicit reference to the assimilation initiate a debate as to whether the assimilation applies in every case or in some cases it should be explicitly provided for by national law.

4.6 Granting of a Supplement and Minimum Pension: Member States' Practice

The application of Article 58 of Regulation No 883/04 requires that the retirement law of the State of residence provides a minimum pension.[141] Thus, in Torri,[142] the Court held that Article 50 of Regulation No 1408/71 is applicable only in cases in

[136] European Commission (2024c) Your rights country by country, Finland-Old-age pension – national pension.

[137] The example of the Greek legislation is similar: for the recognition of periods of military service there is a requirement of insurance time. When there are no insurance periods in a Greek insurance body, insurance in another Member State cannot be assimilated with insurance in a Greek insurance body, while a similar approach is applied for the application of optional insurance.

[138] European Commission (2024c) Your rights country by country, Finland-Old-age pension – national pension.

[139] European Commission (2013b), p. 17.

[140] European Commission (2013b), p. 17.

[141] Schuler (2015), p. 367 invoking case C-64-77 Torri, EU: C: 1977:197.

[142] Judgment of the Court of 30.11.1977, Case 64/77, Torri, European Court Reports 1977 02299 ECLI:EU:C:1977:197.

which provision is made in the legislation of the Member State in whose territory the worker resides for a minimum pension.[143] Accordingly, in Browning,[144] the Court held that Article 50 of Regulation No 1408/71 is to be interpreted as meaning that a "minimum benefit" exists only where the legislation of the State of residence includes a specific guarantee, the object of which is to ensure for recipients of social security benefits a minimum income which is in excess of the amount of benefit which they may claim solely on the basis of their period of insurance and their contributions (paragraph 15).

As the Advocate General remarks,[145] the Court in the Browning judgment defines minimum benefit as "a specific guarantee the object of which is to ensure for recipients of social security benefits a minimum income which is in excess of the amount of benefit which they may claim solely on the basis of their periods of insurance and their contributions". In contrast, the Belgian supplement to a miner's pension that was in question in Conti,[146] under strictly defined conditions and by increasing the pension earned to the level of a full benefit, ends up improving the situation of a particular category of persons; precisely this benefit is not related to the actual period of insurance. Consequently the Belgian legislation concerning miners' pensions cannot be regarded as granting a "minimum benefit, while Article 50 of Regulation No does not apply for yet another reason: it necessarily presupposes that benefits are calculated in accordance with the Community rules for retirement benefits within the meaning of Article 46 (2) of the Regulation; according to the wording of Article 50 of Regulation No 1408/71: "...minimum benefit fixed by that legislation for an insurance period equal to all the insurance periods taken into account for the payment".[147] Article 58 of Regulation No 883/04 contains the exact same wording. However, the calculation in the Conti case did not relate to an independent benefit solely on the basis of periods of employment completed under the Belgian system.[148]

Three cases that were presented before the Court regarding supplements are examined below in chronological order; in these cases, the Court examined in particular detail the legal form of the supplements in question. In the first case (Levatino) and following the Frilli[149] judgment, the Court classified the minimum income supplement, i.e. the Belgian guarantee income as a retirement benefit, taking into account that the Regulation also included non-contributory schemes and thus affiliated it to the rules on pensions. In the second case (Stinco and Panfilo), the

---

[143] Torri, paragraph 13.

[144] Judgment of the Court of 17.12.1981, Case 22/81, Regina ex parte Norman Ivor Browning, European Court Reports 1981 03357 ECLI:EU:C:1981:316.

[145] Conti, Opinion of Advocate-General Siegbert Alber of 12th February 1998, paragraph 47.

[146] Judgment of the Court of 22.10.1998, Case C-143/97, Conti, European Court Reports 1998 I-06365 ECLI:EU:C:1998:501.

[147] Conti, Opinion of Advocate-General Siegbert Alber of 12th February 1998, paragraphs 49–50.

[148] Conti, Opinion of Advocate-General Siegbert Alber as above, paragraph 50.

[149] Judgment of 22.06.1972, 1/72, Frilli, European Court Reports Volume 1972–1973, p. 59, paragraph 18.

Court classified the Italian supplement of minimum income as a non-contributory benefit and indeed as affiliated to the special rules on pensions. In the third case (Koschitzki) regarding the same Italian minimum pension income, the Court avoided its classification. The Court noted that the competent institution is not required to take into consideration a supplement intended to bring the pension to the minimum level under national legislation where, on account of the fact that the income limits fixed by the national legislation on that supplement are exceeded, an insured person who has worked exclusively in the Member State concerned cannot lay claim to such a supplement.

More specifically, in Levatino,[150] the question was raised in proceedings between the Office National des Pensions (hereinafter "the ONP"), the competent Belgian authority with regard to the payment of old-age benefits, and Mr Levatino, who has succeeded to the rights of his mother, Mrs Milazzo in the main proceedings. The case regarded both the provision on awarding supplements, Article 50 of Regulation No 1408/71 (currently Article 58 of Regulation No 883/04) and the provision on revalorisation of benefits, Article 51 of Regulation No 1408/71 (currently Article 59 of Regulation No 883/04).

Mrs Milazzo, an Italian national, was resident in Belgium. She had been receiving an employed person's retirement pension in Belgium since 1 October 1967 and a retirement pension in Italy since 1 November 1967.In addition, since 1 January 1973 she had been receiving the guaranteed income for elderly persons provided for by the Belgian Law.

In the question referred for a preliminary ruling, the national court asked whether Article 46 and 51 of the Regulation are applicable to the determination and adjustment of the amount of a benefit such as the guaranteed income which is paid to a worker who has been employed in a Member State, resides in that State and receives a retirement pension from the State and a retirement pension from another Member State, even where the application of those provisions may confer an advantage on a migrant worker in comparison with a non-migrant worker (Levatino, paragraph 17). The provisions of Article 46 of Regulation No 1408/71 (currently Article 52 of Regulation No 883/04) relate to the award of old-age benefits and the provisions of Article 51 of Regulation No 1408/71 on revalorisation of benefits[151] (currently Article 59 of Regulation No 883/04) lay down the circumstances in which benefits "determined under the provisions of Article 46" must be increased on recalculated (Levatino, paragraph 18).

---

[150] Judgment of 22.04.1993, Case C-65/92, Levatino, European Court Reports 1993 I-02005 ECLI: EU:C:1993:149.

[151] Paragraph 19: Article 51 itself is made up of two paragraphs. Article 51 (1) provides that if the benefits of the States concerned are altered by a fixed percentage or amount to take account of an increase in the cost of living or changes in the level of wages or salaries or other reasons for adjustment, such percentage or amount must be applied directly to the amount of the benefits without a need for a recalculation in accordance with the provisions of Article 46. However, Article 51 (2) provides that a recalculation is to be carried out in accordance with Article 46 if the method of determining or the rules for calculating the benefits should be altered.

Invoking its judgment in Frilli,[152] the Court noted that a benefit such as the one at issue in the main proceedings must be regarded as an "old-age benefit" within the meaning of the Regulation. In this case, the beneficiary's rights must, according to Article 44 of the Regulation, be determined in accordance with the provisions of Chapter 3 of Title III of the Regulation, that is to say, in particular, in accordance with the provisions of Articles 46 and 51 (Levatino, paragraph 21).According to the Court (Levatino, paragraph 34):The purpose of a benefit such as the income guaranteed to elderly persons is to offset the inadequacy of the resources of the person concerned so as to enable him to attain the minimum level of resources guaranteed by the Law, at least where he resided in the territory of the State providing the benefit. Entitlement to the benefit is not conditional on the length of insurance cover or, in the case of certain beneficiaries, on the duration of residence. Its amount, which is independent of the length of insurance cover or the duration of residence, is equal to the difference between the minimum income fixed by the national rules, on the one hand, and part of the beneficiary's resources, including the national and foreign pensions which he receives, on the other. In view of its differential nature, the amount of this benefit varies, by its nature, in accordance with the evolution of the amount of the guaranteed income, which is regularly re-assessed, and the resources of the person concerned.

Furthermore, a benefit such as the guaranteed income differs from old-age pensions, since the nature and manner of determination of old-age pensions are—unlike the guaranteed income benefit—not affected by the provisions of Article 51 (1), even if this may put the migrant worker at an advantage (Levatino, paragraph 38).

However, although it is true that the application of the provisions of Article 51 (1) may, regard being had to their purpose, mean that a migrant worker is granted an amount of benefits greater than that to which the worker is entitled under Article 46 of the Regulation, nevertheless it cannot have the effect of jeopardizing the actual purpose of the benefit paid (Levatino, paragraph 39).The Court concluded that the provisions of Articles 46 and 51 (2) of the Regulation are applicable to the determination and adjustment of the amount of a benefit such as the guaranteed income paid to a worker who has been in employment in a Member State, resides in that State and receives a retirement pension from that State and a retirement pension from another Member State Article 51 (1) is not, however, applicable to the adjustment of such a benefit (Levatino, paragraph 51).

It is worth noting that Article 51 (1) of Regulation No 1408/71 corresponds to Article 59 (2) of Regulation No 883/04 and Article 51 (2) of Regulation No 1408/71 to Article 59 (1) of Regulation No 883/04.

[152] Judgment of 22.06.1972, 1/72, Frilli, European Court Reports Volume 1972–1973, p. 59, paragraph 18.

Furthermore, in Stinco and Panfilo,[153] the question was raised in proceedings between Stinco and Panfilo, who are Italian nationals, and the Istituto nazionale della previdenzasociale (INPS) in relation to the refusal by the INPS to take into account the amount necessary to attain the minimum pension set by the INPS when calculating the old-age pension under Italian law. Stinco and Panfilo applied to the INPS for an old-age pension and were each entitled, as from the same date, to an old-age pension from another Member State, namely France and the United Kingdom.[154] The INPS awarded Stinco and Panfilo pro rata pensions in accordance with Article 46 (2) of Regulation No 1408/71 calculated by reference to the notional pensions which they would have received if they had worked in Italy throughout their working life. The amount of the notional pensions was such that, had they in fact been entitled to domestic pensions of the amount, they would have been awarded the statutory Italian pension supplement so as to reach the minimum pension level. The national court states that the pension actually received by them was not, however, supplemented to meet the statutory minimum because the total pension received by each of them after taking into consideration the pensions paid in France and the United Kingdom respectively was above the level triggering payment of the supplement under Italian law.

By its question, the national court was essentially asking whether Article 46 (2) (a) of Regulation No 1408/71 must be interpreted as requiring the competent institution, when determining the theoretical amount of the pension on the basis of which the pro rata pension is calculated, to take into account a supplement intended to bring the pension to the level of the statutory minimum (Stinco and Panfilo, paragraph 12).

The Court initially referred to the previous Levatino case,[155] where it held that the provisions of Article 46 of Regulation No 1408/71 apply to non-contributory old-age benefits such as the income guaranteed to the elderly under Belgian law (Stinco and Panfilo, paragraph 13).In this case, however, the INPS and the Austrian Government argued that, since the supplement provided for under Italian law amounts to a special non-contributory benefit, under Article 4 (2a) of Regulation No 1408/71 as amended by Regulation No 1247/92, it cannot, under Article 10a, be taken into account in the determination of the theoretical amount of an individual's pension under Article 46 (2) (a). In this respect, it should be noted that, under Article 10a of Regulation No

[153] Judgment of the Court of 24.09.1998, Case C-132/96, Stinco and Panfilo, European Court Reports 1998 I-05225 ECLI:EU:C:1998:427.

[154] Paragraph 7: Under Article 8 of Law No 153 of 30 April 1969 *(GURI No* 111 of 30 April 1969), where entitlement to a pension is acquired by aggregating periods of insurance in accordance with international agreements or conventions in the field of social security, that pension must be supplemented to the level of the minimum pensions, taking into account the amount of any pensions paid by other insurance bodies abroad. Under Article 6 of Decree-Law No 463 of 12 September 1983, which became Law No 638 of 11 November 1983, entitlement to the supplement is subject to the recipient's income not exceeding twice the annual amount of the minimum pension.

[155] Judgment of the Court of 22.04.1993, Case C-65/92, Levatino, European Court Reports 1993 I-02005 ECLI:EU:C:1993:149, paragraph 24.

1408/71 as amended by Regulation No 1247/92, the special non-contributory cash benefits set out in Annex IIa of Regulation No 1408/71 are not transferable to Member States other than the Member State in which the worker resides. The possibility of exporting a benefit such as the supplement provided for under Italian law is not in any way connected with the question of determining the theoretical amount of a pension (paragraph 17). It follows that a benefit such as that at issue in the main proceedings cannot be considered to be excluded from the scope of Article 46 of Regulation No 1408/71 by reason of the adoption of Article 10a of the same Regulation (Stinco and Panfilo, paragraph 18).

The Court invoked its judgment in Browning,[156] where the Court pointed out that the method of calculation referred to in Article 46 (2) (a) of Regulation No 1408/71, which relates to the determination of the theoretical amount of a pension, is distinct from the situation referred to in Article 50, which relates to the award of a supplementary payment in excess of the minimum payable in application of the normal rules under a particular national legal system (paragraph 20).It held that it follows that a statutory minimum benefit set by a Member State must be taken into account in calculating the theoretical amount referred to in Article 46 (2) (a) of Regulation No 1408/71 (Stinco and Panfilo, paragraph 21).

Accordingly, the answer to the question referred is that Article 46 (2) (a) of Regulation No 1408/71 must be interpreted as requiring the competent institution, in determining the theoretical amount of the pension on which the calculation of the pro rata pension is based, to take into account a supplement intended to bring the pension to the level of the statutory minimum (Stinco and Panfilo, paragraph 22).

The Court held a different position in the Koschitzki judgment.[157] Ms U. Koschitzki has been the recipient of an old-age pension in Italy since October 1996. She accrued 262 weeks of contributions in Italy and 533 weeks in Germany, that is 795 weeks of contributions in total. In October 1996, Ms U. Koschitzki's family income exceeded the limit provided for in Article 4 of Legislative Decree 503/92. Ms U. Koschitzki and the INPS were in dispute as to whether the supplement intended to bring the pension up to the Italian minimum pension must be taken into account in order to determine the theoretical amount of the pension on which the calculation of the pro rata pension is based. Relying on the judgment in Case C-132/96 Stinco and Panfilo of 24 September 1998 (European Court Reports 1998, p. I-5225), Ms U. Koschitzki takes the view that the answer to that question should be affirmative.[158]

---

[156] Judgment of 17.12.1981, 22/81, Browning, European Court Reports 1981, p. 3357, paragraphs 13 and 14.

[157] Judgment of the Court of 21.07.2005, Case C-30/04, Koschitzki, European Court Reports 2005 I-07389 ECLI:EU:C:2005:492.

[158] She submits that the Italian pro rata pension to which she became entitled on 1 October 1996 must be calculated as follows: minimum pension 1996 (ITL 660 300 = EUR 341.01) × coefficient of the proportional reduction referred to in Article 46 (2) (b) of Regulation No 1408/71 (262 weeks: 795 weeks = 0.32956) = ITL 217 600 (EUR 112.38). The INPS argues that in this case the supplement should not be taken into account in order to determine the theoretical amount. That amount was ITL 36 540 (EUR 18.87), which gave an Italian pro rata pension of ITL 12 042 (EUR 6.21) per month.

The national court asks, essentially, whether, in order to determine the theoretical amount of the pension on which the calculation of the pro rata pension is based pursuant to Article 46 (2) (a) of Regulation No 1408/71, a supplement to bring the pension up to the minimum amount under national legislation must be taken into account where the income limits provided for by the national law relating to the supplement are exceeded (Koschitzki, paragraph 22).

The Court referred to the previous Stinco and Panfilo case and then stressed that, in this case, on account of the fact that the income limits fixed by the national legislation on the supplement intended to bring the pension to minimum pension level are exceeded, an insured person in the position of Ms U. Koschitzki, who worked exclusively in the Member State concerned, cannot claim that supplement (paragraph 25). According to the Court, if the law of the Member State concerned provides that the right to the supplement is subject to the general condition that the recipient does not have an income greater than a specified threshold or an income combined with that of his cohabiting spouse exceeding a higher threshold, that provision must also be taken into account for the calculation of the theoretical amount referred to in Article 46(2) (a) of Regulation No 1408/71 (Koschitzki, paragraph 29).

Thus, the answer to the question referred was that Article 46 (2) (a) of Regulation No 1408/71 must be interpreted as meaning that, in order to determine the theoretical amount of the pension on which the calculation of the pro rata pension is based, the competent institution is not required to take into consideration a supplement intended to bring the pension to the minimum level under national legislation where, on account of the fact that the income limits fixed by the national legislation on that supplement are exceeded, an insured person who has worked exclusively in the Member State concerned cannot lay claim to such a supplement (Koschitzki, paragraph 38).

Further, in Zaniewicz-Dybeck,[159] the Court held that, when the competent institution of a Member State calculates a minimum benefit, such as the Swedish guaranteed pension, it is inappropriate to apply Article 46(2) or Article 47(1)(d) of the Regulation 1408/71. Such a benefit must be calculated in accordance with Article 50 of the regulation, in conjunction with the provisions of national law, without, however, applying national provisions, such as those in the main proceedings, providing for a pro rata calculation.

Mr. Zaniewicz-Dybeck applied for a Swedish guaranteed minimum pension in 2008, which was rejected by the Swedish Pension Service, which had applied the pro rata calculation provided for in Article 46(2) of the Regulation for the periods during which Mr. Zaniewicz-Dybeck had been insured in Poland.[160] The Swedish Pension

[159] Judgement of 7.12.2017, Zaniewicz-Dybeck, case C-189/16, ECLI:EU:C:2017:946.

[160] Stevens and Schoukens (2023), p. 26.

Service concluded that Mr Zaniewicz-Dybeck's earnings-related pension exceeded Sweden's minimum threshold, which meant that he was not entitled to a guaranteed minimum pension, thus, Mr. Zaniewicz-Dybeck brought a claim before the Swedish administrative court, asserting that the free movement of workers was being hampered by the fact that a pro rata calculation was used to determine the amount of pensions, including periods of employment (i.e. insurance) completed in countries where pensions are far lower than in Sweden; as a result, these periods are calculated at a lower rate than if they had been completed in Sweden.[161]

In its arguments, the CJEU claimed that a minimum benefit is provided for in Article 50 of Regulation 1407/71 "where the legislation of the state of residence provides a special guarantee for those who benefit from social security benefits, to ensure a minimum income above the level of benefits to which they would be entitled only on the basis of the periods to which they were insured under a security scheme and their benefits".[162] The guaranteed minimum pension represents such a minimum benefit.[163] Therefore, the Court decided that the Swedish *guarantee pension* should not be calculated according to Articles 52 and 56, i.e. according to the pro-rata calculation method, but according to Article 58 of Regulation 883/2004 (former Articles 46, 47 and 50 of Regulation 1408/71) meaning that the *guarantee pension* is to be classified as a "minimum benefit" in accordance with the Regulation.[164] It furthermore means that the Member State's obligation to pay the difference between the individual's total pension benefit and the amount of the "minimum benefit" is linked to the requirement of *residence* in that country: in relation to the general provision of Art. 7 of the Regulation on the abolition of residence clauses ("export of benefits"), this provision is a lex specialis and therefore takes precedence.[165] Since the Regulation does not require Member States to provide for such a minimum benefit, a method of calculation for Sweden's guaranteed minimum pension based on Articles 46 and 47 was therefore rejected by the Court, but had to be calculated on the basis of Article 50 of the Regulation.[166] Finally, in Zaniewicz-Dybeck, as the Court concluded, Regulation No 1408/71, and in particular Article 50 of that regulation, is to be interpreted as not precluding the legislation of a Member State under which, when calculating a minimum benefit such as the guaranteed pension at issue in the main proceedings, the competent institution must take account of all the retirement pensions which the person concerned actually receives from one or more other Member States.

[161] Ibid.

[162] Stevens and Schoukens (2023), p. 27.

[163] Ibid.

[164] Devetzi (2023), p. 273.

[165] Ibid.

[166] Stevens and Schoukens (2023), p. 27.

Following the Zaniewicz-Dybeck ruling, the Swedish government concluded that a legal basis for continuing to grant and pay the *guarantee pension* to EU citizens residing in another Member State no longer existed; consequently, by 2022, 43,000 pensioners who had previously been entitled to the guarantee pension and were residing in other EU/EEA States lost their right to this benefit.[167] This may generally undermine the principle of free movement.[168] In any case, it would be economically unwise in future to move out of Sweden as a pensioner because it means losing the minimum benefit.[169] The paradoxical effect of this case law is that a provision in a Regulation designed to promote free movement may actually lead to de facto "immobility" in practice.[170]

In a previous analysis on the distinction of social security benefit from social assistance and from the special category of special non-contributory benefits, it was evident that regardless of the difficulties in distinction, a benefit must be a social security one and be subject to the rules on pension of Articles 50 et seq. of Regulation No 883/04. Besides, special non-contributory benefits are expressly excluded from the application of these rules. However, as seen in the cases regarding the distinction of pensions from social assistance, the Court has considered a benefit as relating to both categories of social security and social assistance concluding that it is a non-contributory social security benefit. In cases regarding the distinction of a pension from special non-contributory benefits, the Court has treated a benefit as having a special purpose and not being based on contributions (associated with both social security and social assistance), i.e. as a special non-contributory benefit with no social security character.

It us worth noting that at the moment, the Belgian guaranteed income (Levatino) and the Italian basic pension supplement (Stinco and Panfilo, Koschitzki) are included in Annex X to Regulation No 883/04 on special non-contributory benefits. It can thus be observed that gradually States started expressing reservations regarding non-contributory benefits, which the Court could classify as social security benefits related at the same time to both social security and social assistance categories, listing any non-contributory benefits as special non-contributory benefits. Of course, as previously examined, even the Court itself could not provide a clear picture as to when a benefit may be regarded as associated to both social security and social assistance categories and thus be a social security benefit and when a benefit is regarded as a special non-contributory benefit (although still displaying a connection to both social security and social assistance) and thus not be a social security benefit.

Greece is on the other side, as it awarded said supplement as a retirement benefit to insured residents in Greece, taking into account the supplement during the award of the Greek pension. More specifically, the IKA (Social Security Fund) granted to

[167] Erhag (2023), p. 198.

[168] Devetzi (2023), p. 273.

[169] Wallrabenstein (2018), p. 361.

[170] Devetzi (2023), p. 273.

an insured person with periods of insurance with IKA and other Member States, a supplement up to the ML (minimum limit), increased by the Greek periods; the insured would receive the supplement until they reached the retirement age limit required by the law of another State in which they have completed periods of insurance.[171]

This practice could be compared with the practice of Belgium. In that regard, the relevant Lustig[172] case is interesting where it was held that Article 50 of Regulation No 1408/71 on the supplement was not applicable; the Advocate General's opinion in that case is also interesting.

It seems, however, that benefits, which in principle are more contributory, are regarded as social security benefits and are therefore subject to the rules on pensions. The theory concludes, through the case-law interpretation, that supplementary allowances awarded to pensioners with an income below a specific level are generally regarded as special non-contributory benefits.[173]

The question is whether the minimum benefit in question is a social security benefit, falling under the rules on pensions and therefore regarded as a supplement within the meaning of Article 58 of Regulation No 883/04 (Article 50 of Regulation No 1408/71), which may be taken into account for the award of the retirement benefit of Article 52 of Regulation No 883/04 (Article 46 of Regulation No 1408/71). If a minimum benefit is regarded as a special non-contributory benefit and thus not a social security benefit, it does not fall under the above provisions. This kind of pension exists only if the pension law of the country of residence contains a specific guarantee to ensure that the beneficiaries of social security pensions receive a minimum income (in the form of supplements), which may be higher than the amount of pension that they can claim solely on the basis of the periods of insurance and contributions.[174] Moreover, from the aforementioned conclusions of Advocate General Siegbert Alber as well as the Koschitzki case, it seems to be decisive whether the interested party would be entitled to the benefit in question on the basis of the national legislation of a State if he/she had completed his/her entire career in the State.

---

[171] While in the past, the Greek State provided for pension thresholds taking into account minimum subsistence especially for pensioners, these pensions thresholds have been recently abolished.

[172] Judgment of the Court of 17.12.1998, Case C-244/97, Rijksdienst voor Pensioenen v Gerdina Lustig, European Court Reports 1998 I-08701.

[173] Paskalia (2009), p. 1195.

[174] Schuler (2015), p. 367 invoking case C-22-81 Browning, EU: C: 1981:316.

4.7 Old-Age, Survivors' and Invalidity Pensions[175]

First of all, the provisions of Regulation No 883/04 and of Regulation No 1408/71 on pensions are not particularly divergent; however, since the new Regulation introduced new arrangements, the implementation of Regulation No 883/04 may be set on a new basis. The dominant coordination feature in the field of pensions is the aggregation of periods of insurance completed under the schemes of various Member States. The general aggregation rules in Article 6 of Regulation No 883/04 apply to long-term benefits, but only regarding acquisition, retention or recovery of the right to benefits and not for the calculation of said benefits, otherwise the same periods of insurance would be calculated twice.[176] Thus, aggregation rules allow the completion of qualifying periods (vesting periods) where this is required by the social security legislation of a Member State.[177]

Although it is noted that pensions within the meaning of Article 1 of Regulation No 883/04 are not associated with a specific risk[178] and despite pensions being treated as a whole by both the European Commission[179] and the others provisions of the Regulation—except the special pension provisions—it is accepted that Article 50 et seq. of Regulation No 883/04 applies to old-age, invalidity and survivors' pensions.[180] In case of invalidity the special provisions of Articles 44–49 of Regulation No 883/04 also apply. This rather means that the application of the special rules on pensions excludes pensions for (work accidents or) occupational disease that may constitute benefits within the meaning of Article 38 of Regulation No 883/04 (Article 57 of Regulation No 1408/71) on benefits for occupational disease in case the persons affected by a disease have been exposed to the same risk in several Member States. However, as it will be demonstrated in a next section, the case-law on overlapping of benefits also makes reference to pensions for occupational disease. Furthermore, the question arises whether pensions for a work accident or occupational disease may be subject to said rules as benefits equivalent to invalidity benefits. Indeed, incapacity to work may be the result of a work accident or an occupational disease. Besides, there is no special definition of invalidity in the Regulation, while even the Court approaches the concept in general associating it with the capacity to work.

It should also be highlighted that according to the additional provisions of Article 69 on family benefits for orphans and in particular under Article 69 (2) of Regulation No 883/04, benefits paid in the form of pensions or supplements to pensions shall be provided and calculated in accordance with Chapter 5 of Regulation No 883/04. They are thus paid and calculated in accordance with the rules on old-age and

[175] Articles 50–60 of Regulation No 883/04 in comparison with Articles 44–51a of Regulation No 1408/71.

[176] Pennings (2010), p. 180.

[177] Pennings (2010), p. 180.

[178] Cornelissen (2015), p. 518.

[179] European Commission (2011), Employment, Social Affairs and Inclusion, p. 2.

[180] Pennings (2015), p. 237; Schuler (2015), p. 342.

survivors' pensions (Articles 50–60 of Regulation No 883/04).As noted, to avoid a disadvantage for persons who have lived their professional lives in States that do not provide pensions for orphans, but only special supplements/benefits, Article 69 of Regulation No 883/04 provides that special supplements or benefits for orphans shall be paid by default and in addition to the other family benefits of other Member States.[181] The Administrative Commission shall draw up a list for the additional or special family benefits.[182] Although said benefits are calculated pursuant to the rules on pensions of Regulation No 883/04, they are regarded as additional or special family benefits and not as pensions within the meaning of this analysis.

4.8 Award of Pensions

The transitional provisions of Article 87 (1)-(3) of Regulation No 883/04 are identical with the provisions of Article 95[a] (1)-(3) of Regulation No 1408/71 examined herein. More specifically, as observed in Baldone,[183] the Court prohibits the recalculation by the competent institution, on its own initiative, of a pension that was calculated under Regulation No 1408/71 prior to its amendment, recognising a right of initiative for the review of a pension solely to the person concerned, preventing thus any deterioration of their position.

However, Article 50 of Regulation No 883/04 provides for a recalculation which is conducted automatically not only in case where the interested party requests the award of an old-age benefit which was postponed but also when the conditions to be fulfilled under the other legislations are satisfied. Thus, under Article 50 (4) of Regulation No 883/04, the competent institution of a State may on its own initiative proceed to the recalculation of an old-age pension, which was already calculated solely under its national law, in order to take into account periods completed under other legislations the conditions of which were not previously satisfied (Article 50 (2) of Regulation No 883/04), without however adopting any clause regarding the non deterioration of the concerned party's position.

Such a clause is included for example in Article 94 (2) of implementing Regulation No 987/09 referring solely to old-age, invalidity and survivors' pensions and according to which any claim for invalidity, old-age or survivors' benefits submitted to an institution of a Member State from the date of entry into force of the implementing Regulation in the territory of the Member State concerned shall automatically necessitate the reassessment of the benefits which have been awarded for the same contingency prior to that date by the institution or institutions of one or more Member States, in accordance with Regulation No 883/04; such reassessment,

[181] Marhold (2015), p. 415.

[182] Article 61 of Regulation No 987/09; Marhold (2015), p. 415.

[183] Judgment of the Court of 25.09.1997, Case C-307/96, Baldone, European Court Reports 1997 I-05123 ECLI:EU:C:1997:442.

however, may not result in a reduction in the amount of the benefit awarded. The reference in Article 49 (2) of Regulation No 1408/71 to Article 49 (1) thereof on taking into account periods that would allow the calculation of a higher benefit amount could also be regarded as a similar clause.

The above provisions on automatic reassessment could also be associated with the Court's judgment according to which when a migrant worker has made a claim for invalidity benefits to the institution of the place of his permanent residence and in accordance with the procedure specified by the legislation of the said place, he has no need to make a new claim in another Member State even if at the time of the making of his claim he did not yet satisfy all the fundamental conditions required by the legislation of the second State for the grant of the benefit.[184] Thus, the initial claim of the person concerned, provided it satisfies the formal requirements for its submission, is regarded as continuing to produce legal effects up until the moment where the fundamental conditions for the grant of the benefit are satisfied in all the States where the claimant had completed periods of insurance. If this rationale is accepted, there is no automatic recalculation, but a calculation that is conducted based on the initial claim of the party concerned once the conditions required by the legislation of the State to which the person concerned was subject and under which the periods of insurance were completed are satisfied. However, the aforementioned Court judgment focused on an invalidity benefit, while the provisions of Article 50 (1) and (4) of Regulation No 883/04 refer explicitly to an old-age pension, despite the title of the relevant chapter on old-age and survivors' pensions, as well as the academic remarks according to which Articles 50 et seq. of Regulation No 883/04 apply to old-age and survivors' pensions and by analogy to invalidity pensions.[185]

However, it should also be taken into account that, since the institution in question proceeds with the recalculation pursuant to Article 52 of Regulation No 883/04, it should, in the end, choose the higher benefit between the one established and calculated solely under its national legislation, i.e. an independent benefit and the one established and calculated with aggregation and apportionment, i.e. a pro-rata benefit. In this case, however, any new national rules against overlapping also apply.

In addition as to the interpretation of Article 52(1)(b) of Regulation No 883/2004 the Court has held that for the purposes of determining the limit which non-contribution periods may not exceed in relation to contribution periods, as provided for by the national legislation, the competent institution of the Member State concerned must take into consideration, when calculating the theoretical amount of the benefit referred to in point (i) of that provision, all the periods of insurance, including those periods of insurance completed under the legislation of other Member States, whereas the calculation of the actual amount of the benefit

---

[184] Judgment of the Court of 09.03.1976, Case 108/75, Balsamo, European Court Reports 1976 00375 ECLI:EU:C:1976:38, paragraph 15.

[185] Schuler (2015), p. 342.

referred to in point (ii) of that provision is made having regard solely to the periods of insurance completed under the legislation of the Member State concerned.[186]

The Administrative Commission also seems to follow the new direction of Regulation No 883/04 on calculation (Article 50 of Regulation No 883/04). Thus, according to Decision No P1[187] of the Administrative Commission, point 1: "The institution which pays a benefit shall **automatically make a new calculation when it is informed that the beneficiary satisfies the conditions for the award of a benefit under the legislation of another Member State.** A new calculation shall not be made in the situation where the periods completed under the legislation of the other Member States have already been taken into account for the award of the benefit and no periods have been acquired following the award of the initial benefit. However, where additional conditions apply (other than the fulfilment of insurance periods), such as the attainment of the age required for the award of the benefit or a change in the number of children to be taken into account, this shall automatically require a new calculation to be made".

The institution which makes a new calculation of a benefit which was previously awarded by it shall, for the calculation, take into account all the periods of insurance and/or residence, as well as any other condition which the beneficiary fulfils under its own legislation and under the legislation of the other Member States on the date of the award of the recalculated benefit (Decision P1, point 2).The relevant day shall be the day on which the risk materialised in the Member State where conditions for entitlement were last satisfied (Decision P1, point 3).

In any event, it can be concluded that the legal response to pension claims under Regulation No 883/04 has become more complex. Thus, Regulation No 883/04 establishes the concurrent award of pensions upon submission of a pension claim by the party concerned in a Member State; in order to avoid any adverse effects of an early claim submission, the party concerned has at its disposal the possibility to either withdraw the application regarding the legislation of a State (or more) or the expressly requested deferment of the award of old-age benefits in a State (or more). At the same time, the European legislature intervenes in national social security schemes as well as in national administrative procedures, as it establishes the automated new calculation upon satisfaction of the conditions required by national legislation, not only where the party concerned requests the award that they themselves had expressly deferred, but also, as implicitly inferred, in case where they had chosen to withdraw their application regarding the legislation of a State. The former possibility to withdraw as an expression of the recognised initiative of the claimant is thus automatically lifted and the substantive entitlement results automatically in the formal entitlement without the participation of the claimant (submission of a new application).

---

[186] Judgement of 21.10.2021, Zakład Ubezpieczeń Społecznych I Oddział w Warszawie, case C-869/19, ECLI:EU:C:2021:865.

[187] Decision No P1 of 12 June 2009 on the interpretation of Articles 50 (4), 58 and 87 (5) of Regulation (EC) No 883/2004 of the European Parliament and of the Council for the award of invalidity, old-age and survivors' benefits, EE C 106/21, 24.4.2010.

Further issues arise in case of an automated award as to what is to be considered an application and when a pension claim is to be considered filed, given that a national scheme may consider the filing of a claim to be of decisive importance for the entitlement to pension and the determination of the amount of the pension. It is important therefore for the purposes of establishing entitlement to pension rights if it is the initial claim application of the person concerned (who requested the deferment of award or withdrew their application in respect of a specific Member State) that is considered to be a submission of claim or, rather, it is the date of the automated recalculation. Furthermore, it represents a crucial point in time which may determine pension rights in a different way. Assuming that the initial claim is valid, further problems arise: the retroactive entitlement to a pension right is essentially accepted, where the time of submitting the claim does not coincide with the time of satisfying the national legislation terms. There is thus a paradox where the date of filing a claim with no substantive entitlement (failure to satisfy national terms) is considered as the date of formal entitlement; the consequences of this paradox can become obvious especially if said national legislation is amended in between those dates. In contrast, should the automated recalculation be accepted as a formal entitlement, in situations where national law requires the submission of a claim for the formal entitlement to a right, there will be a formal entitlement without a claim application solely with the substantive entitlement-satisfaction of conditions.

In any event, it is understood that the established system has difficulties and relies to a great extent on compliance with the principle of sound administration on an internal level by the national institutions, which would allow the party concerned to be able to understand at all times the legal information and determine the choice that is the most advantageous for them. Taking account that the information that needs to be disclosed relates to both the Regulation scheme and the national schemes of the various Member States, there are doubts regarding the awareness of the migrant worker regarding their legal interest.

References

Cornelissen R (2015) Regulation (EC) No 883/2004 – Article 87a. In: Fuchs M, Cornelissen R (eds) EU social security law- a commentary on EU Regulations 883/2004 and 987/2009. C.H. BECK-Hart- Nomos, Baden-Baden

Coucheir M (ed), Sakslin M (ed), Giubboni S, Martinsen D, Verschueren H (2008) trESS Think Tank Report 2008, The relationship and interaction between the coordination Regulations and Directive 2004/38/EC

Cousins M (2007) The 'right to reside' and social security entitlements. J Soc Welfare Family Law 29:1. In: Jorens Y (ed), Roberts S (ed), de Cortzar C-G, Spiegel B, Strban G, trESS, Think Tank Report 2010, Analysis of selected concepts of the regulatory framework and practical consequences on the social security coordination, p 37

Devetzi S (2023) Minimum income in old age: comparative aspects and European law issues. In: Devetzi S (ed) Minimum income in old age. Sakkoulas publications, Athens-Thessaloniki, p 273

Erhag T (2013) Changing normative patterns in statutory old-age pensions: reflections on developments due to pension reform and EU citizenship. In: Numhauser-Henning A, Rönnmar M (eds) Normative patterns and legal developments in the social dimension of the EU. Hart Publishing, Oxford, pp 251–252

Erhag T (2023) Guaranteeing a minimum income in old age: the case of Sweden. In: Devetzi S (ed) Minimum income in old age. Sakkoulas Publications, Athens-Thessaloniki, p 198
European Commission (2011) Employment, Social Affairs and Inclusion, Explanatory notes on modernised social security coordination Regulations (EC) No 883/04 & No 987/09, N-Non-Active persons, January 2011, p 2
European Commission (2013a) Employment, Social Affairs and Equal Opportunities, Practical Guide on the applicable legislation in the European Union (EU), the European Economic Area (EEA) and in Switzerland, December 2013, p 49
European Commission (2013b) Your social security rights in Finland, July 2013, p 6. https://ec.europa.eu/employment_social/empl_portal/SSRinEU/Your%20social%20security%20rights%20in%20Finland_en.pdf. Accessed 25 Nov 2024
European Commission (2024a) Your social security rights in Finland, MISSOC, 2024. https://ec.europa.eu/social/BlobServlet?docId=13749&langId=en. Accessed 25 Nov 2024
European Commission (2024b) Annex X, Regulation No 883/04 , CYPRUS, point a) social pension, in comparison with: Your rights country by country, *(updated in 2024)* Cyprus - Social assistance - Social pension. https://ec.europa.eu/social/main.jsp?catId=1105&langId=en. Accessed 25 Nov 2024
European Commission (2024c) Your rights country by country, Finland-Old-age pension – national pension. https://ec.europa.eu/social/main.jsp?catId=1109&langId=en&intPageId=4524. Accessed 25 Nov 2024
Fuchs M (2015) Regulation (EC) No 883/2004 – Article 3. In: Fuchs M, Cornelissen R (eds) EU social security law - a commentary on EU Regulations 883/2004 and 987/2009. C.H. BECK – Hart – Nomos, Baden-Baden, p 419
Jorens Y, Lherhoud J-P (2011) trESS European Report 2011, Organisation and coordination of a network on the co-ordination of social security schemes within the European Union, Lot 1: Expertise in social security coordination, p 13
Jorens Y, Van Overmeiren F (2009) General principles of Coordination in Regulation 883/2004. Eur J Soc Secur 11(1–2):54
Jorens Y (ed), Lhernould J-Ph (ed), Fillon J-C, Roberts S, Spiegel B (2008) trESS Think Tank Report 2008, Towards a new framework for applicable legislation – new forms of mobility, coordination principles and rules of conflict
Jorens Y (ed), Roberts S (ed), de Cortzar C-G, Spiegel B, Strban G (2010) trESS Think Tank Report 2010, Analysis of selected concepts of the regulatory framework and practical consequences on the social security coordination, p 44
Katrougalos G (2006) The impact of Community law on social security law. EDKA (Social Security Law Review):252
Marhold F (2015) Regulation (EC) No 883/2004, Article 69. In: Fuchs F, Cornelissen R (eds) EU social security law – a commentary on EU Regulations 883/2004 and 987/2009. C.H. BECK – Hart - Nomos, Baden-Baden, p 415
Martinsen D (2007) The Social Policy Clash: EU Cross-Border Welfare, Union Citizenship and National Residence Clauses, presented at the European Union Studies Association (EUSA) Biennal Conference 2007, (10th), May 17–19 2007, Montreal
Mavridis P (2004) The freedom of movement of persons, employees and services as a fundamental principle of European integration: their employment and social security. EDKA (Social Security Law Review):810
MISSOC 2024- Finland (1 January 2024). https://www.missoc.org/missoc-database/comparative-tables (last accessed 25 Nov 2024)
O'Neill R (2011) Residence as a condition for social security in the United Kingdom: a critique of the UK right to reside test for accessing benefits and how it is applied in the courts. Eur J Soc Secur 2:13
Paskalia V (2007) Free movement, social security and gender in the EU. Hart Publishing, Oxford
Paskalia V (2009) Coordination of social security in the European Union: an overview of recent case law. Common Mark Law Rev 46:1189
Pennings F (2005) Co-ordination of the social security on the basis of the state-of-employment principle: time for an alternative? Common Mark Law Rev 42:77

Pennings F (2010) European social security law, 5th edn. Intersentia, Antwerp-Oxford-Portland
Pennings (2012) European social security law. Wolters Kluwer Law & Business, Netherlands
Pennings F (2015) EU social security law, 6th edn. Intersentia, Cambridge-Antwerp-Portland
Pennings (2022) European social security law. Wolters Kluwer Law & Business, Netherlands
Pieter Van der Mei A (2003) Free movement of persons within the European Community- cross-border access to public benefits. Hart Publishing Oxford-Portland Oregon
Pieters D (2006) Social security: an introduction to the basic principles. Kluwer Law International, The Netherlands, p 1
Roberts S (2001) Crossing frontiers: migration and social security. In: Ethics, poverty, inequality and reform in social security. Ashgate Publishing. In: Jorens Y (ed), Roberts S (ed), de Cortzar C-G, Spiegel B, Strban G, trESS, Think Tank Report 2010, Analysis of selected concepts of the regulatory framework and practical consequences on the social security coordination, p 2
Roberts S (2004) 'A Strong and Legitimate Link.' The Habitual Residence Test in the United Kingdom. Co-ordinating Work-Based and Residence-Based Social Security. Faculty of Law, University of Helsinki, Helsinki
Roberts S, Bolderson H (1999) Inside out: a cross national study of migrants' disentitlements to social security benefits. In: Clasen J (ed) Comparative social policy. Blackwell
Romanias G (2008) Greek and European myths on social security. Adelfoi Vlassi Publications, Athens, p 29 et seq
Sakslin M (2000) Social security coordination – adapting to change. Eur J Soc Secur:179
Schouckens P, Monserrez L (2011) Introduction to social security coordination in the EU, Reading Material. Master of European Social Security KU Leuven, p 18
Schuler R (2015) Regulation (EC) No 883/2004 – Article 58. In: Fuchs M, Cornelissen R (eds) EU social security law – a commentary on EU Regulations 883/2004 and 987/2009. C.H. BECK – Hart- Nomos, Baden- Baden, p 367
Spiegel B (2007) Die neue europaische Sozialrechtskoordinierung. In: Die Reform des Europäischen koordinierenden Sozialrechts, DRV Schriften 71:59
Stergiou (2013) Social security law, 2nd edn. Zygos, Thesasloniki
Stergiou A (2014) Social security law. Sakkoulas, Athens-Thessaloniki
Stevens Y, Schoukens P (2023) The case of Belgium: plea for a universal income for pensioners? In: Devetzi S (ed) Minimum income in old age. Sakkoulas Publications, Athens-Thessaloniki, p 26
The Greek Ombudsman (2012) Report: residence clauses for granting social security benefits to European citizens. The right of permanent residence of European citizens (non-active persons). EDKA (Social Security Law Review) LIV:844
Tsantilas P (1996) Issues in defining social security in European Community Law (the case-law of the Court of Justice of the European Communities). In: Kremalis K (scientific coordinator) Issues in defining the limits of private and social security, possibilities for private insurance complementing or partially substituting social security. Ant. N. Sakkoulas Publishing, Athens-Komotini, p 35
Tsetoura A (2019) The free movement of persons in the European social model. Papazisis Publications, Athens
Tsetoura A (2023) Guaranteed minimum pensions under the Regulation of Coordination on social security systems: the case of Greece. In: St. Devetzi (ed) Minimum income in old age. Sakkoulas Publications, Athens-Thessaloniki, pp 119–164
Van Overmeiren F (ed), Eichenhofer E, Verschueren H (2011) trESS Analytical Study 2011, Social security coverage of non-active persons moving to another Member State
van Raepenbusch S (2015) Soziales Europa 1992. In: Fuchs M, Regulation No (EC) No 883/2004 – Article 3. In: Fuchs M, Cornelissen R (eds) EU social security law – a commentary in EU Regulations 883/2004 and 987/2009. C.H. BECK- Hart- Nomos, Baden-Baden, pp 18–30, 80
Verschueren H (2007) European (internal) migration law as an instrument for defining the boundaries of national solidarity systems. Eur J Migr Law 9:315
Verschueren H (2009) Special non-contributory benefits in Regulation 1408/71, Regulation 883/2004 and the case law of the ECJ. Eur J Soc Secur 11(1–2):225–226
Wallrabenstein A (2018) Migrationsphänomene im sozialrechtlichen Kontext. ZESAR 9/18:361

Chapter 5
Funded Schemes and the "Mobility of Pension Rights"

5.1 The New Provisions and the Unsuitability of Apportionment for Funded Schemes

As is well known, the coordination rules were originally designed for classic pay-as-you-go pension schemes and their application is not always appropriate for funded schemes, the benefits of which depend solely on the accrued value of the capital built up through contributions.[1] It is thus particularly important to examine the addition of the provisions of Article 52 (5) of Regulation No 883/04. These provisions were added with amending Regulation No 988/09[2] and in particular with Article 1 (13) of Regulation No 988/09.This addition is the result of the academic focus on coordination issues between different pension schemes i.e. pay-as-you-go and funded schemes.

More specifically, Leppik had argued (2006) that the rules of apportionment would benefit some migrant workers where the pro-rata benefit would be higher than the independent benefit. Their application however could distort the substance of funded schemes, raising questions on the funding of "these pay-as-you-go advantages" in favour of the migrant worker in a funded scheme with individual accounts.[3] In Leppik's example, where he attempts to demonstrate the additional benefit of the migrant worker, he makes the following assumption: a person had paid contributions in the Estonian mandatory funded defined-contribution scheme (MFDC) for 5 years, on average EUR 500 per year and these contributions earned an average return of 10% per year. Assume that in the last year before their retirement the person moved to Latvia and paid contributions to the mandatory

[1] Verschueren (2009), p. 160; OSE (2011), p. 19.

[2] Regulation (EC) No 988/2009 of the European Parliament and of the Council of 16 September 2009 amending Regulation (EC) No 883/2004 on the coordination of social security systems and determining the context of its Annexes, OJ L 284/43, 30.10.2009.

[3] Leppik (2006), p. 45, footnote no. 18.

A. Tsetoura, *Pension Rights and Free Movement of Persons*,
https://doi.org/10.1007/978-3-031-91127-9_5

funded defined-contribution scheme of Latvia, while the previously paid contributions remained in the mandatory funded defined-contribution scheme in Estonia. Further assume that the actual rate of return earned on these contributions over the last year declined to 5%.Article 47 (1) (d) of Regulation No 1408/71 requires that when calculating the pro-rata benefit, the Estonian institution shall assume as if also over these two years the person continued to contribute annually pay EUR 500 and the balance of the pension account earned an interest of 10% as these contributions and increases are the average recorded/registered in respect of insurance periods completed under the Estonian legislation.[4] As a result the pro-rata benefit will be higher that the independent benefit.

Depending on the institutional setting of the funded scheme which may vary from country to country, as Leppik observes, these expenses would appear as a cost to the other pension fund participants or as an unfunded liability for the pension fund management company, i.e. a cost for which no premiums have been collected; this further raises the questions whether it is fair to the other members of a pension scheme and who will bear these additional costs.[5] Verschueren has also found the pro-rata temporis calculation to be **unsuitable for funded schemes**, since the **amount of benefits in these schemes is directly linked to the contributions paid in the scheme plus any yield percentage; thus, the time of affiliation to the scheme is not to be directly examined** in the calculation of benefits. During the calculation of the theoretical sum, the question arises as to which contributions and which yield rate should be regarded as corresponding to periods of insurance in other Member States.[6]

Similarly, Spiegel notes that the consistent application of the pro-rata method -which means that the person should always be in the position they would have been if they had completed their entire career in a single State—raises questions on the benefits of capital-funded schemes. For capital-funded systems and pension account systems or notional capitalisation systems the critical factor is the time of contribution payment. Contributions paid early in life have a much higher value (due to interest and compound interest on the capital) within the subsequent pension than the same contributions paid in later on.[7]

In his relevant example, which is an extract from Austria's memorandum to the Administrative Commission (2003) on amending the Regulation taking into account the particularities of capital funded schemes or pension account schemes,[8] Spiegel assumes that a person that has a constant annual contribution income of EUR 1000

---

[4]Leppik (2006), p. 45.

[5]Leppik (2006), p. 45.

[6]Verschueren (2009), p. 148.

[7]Spiegel (2009), p. 207.

[8]He notes that this example is an extract from Austria's memorandum of 14.05.2003 to the Administrative Commission (CA.SS.TM. 156/03) for an amendment of Regulation No 1408/71 (EEC) or Regulation (EC) No 883/04 in order to take into account of the particularities of capital funded schemes or pension account schemes.

and an average annual interest of 6% over a career beginning in 1970 and going on until 2009 (40 years), the result would be EUR 164,948.78 due to interest and compound interest on the capital based on the calculation formula

$$Kn = Ko \times (1 + p/100)n,$$

where "Ko" represents the starting capital, "p" represents the interest rate and "n" represents the period of interest in years.[9]

If, therefore, the person in the example has completed 10 years in the state in question with a capital-funded system, as well as 30 years in another Member State, the classical pro-rata calculation method requires that the monthly benefit be calculated on the basis of 10/40, i.e. 10/40 × 164,948.78 = EUR 41,237.20, of the capital theoretically saved for 40 years. According to the basic philosophy of any capital-funded system, however, payments can only be made on the basis of what saved capital (at least on average) is actually available. This, taking into account the average in capital-funded systems, is based on the consideration that, for the same contributions, one insured party will live longer, while another will not live as long; using the average makes it possible to ensure that the pay-outs made do not exceed the total capital actually available over all cases. When a parameter (most importantly the interest rate or the life expectancy at the fixed pension age) changes, the benefit must be adjusted accordingly.[10]

What is actually available from the 10 years of membership of the system is actually critically dependent on the timing of when the contributions were paid: if these 10 years were at the beginning of the career, thus from 1970 to 1979, the total available is EUR 80,246.03; if, however, those 10 years came at the end of the career, thus between 2000 and 2009, then only EUR 12,655.86 is available (given the much lower amounts of interest).[11] In the first case, the person receives almost twice as much capital as is actually to be granted as a pro-rata benefit calculated above with the pro-rata method (41,237.20), while in the second case the person receives much less, approximately 1/3 of the above pro-rata amount. Thus, the pro-rata calculation method leads to either a much lower benefit (half) than the pension the person is entitled to under a funded scheme according to its operation, i.e. the actual accrued capital or to a much higher benefit (triple) than the pension the person is actually entitled to based on the accrued capital.

Essentially, it can be observed that the decisive factor is the number of years that contributions were saved for: for the 10 years the person was affiliated to the funded scheme, i.e. 1970–1979 the contributions paid were saved for 40 years, until 2009, while for the 10 years between 2000–2009 which were at the end of their career, the contributions were saved only for those 10 years. Thus, in the formula

[9] See Spiegel (2009), p. 207.

[10] Spiegel (2009), p. 207.

[11] Spiegel (2009), p. 207.

Kn = Ko × (1 + p/100)n for the average yield with an average interest rate the only thing that changes is n, the number of years.

It is however noted that these issues are more complicated, as the actual yield rates and consequently the value of future reserves are a random variable[12] and, by analogy, future obligations are also a future variable, especially if life expectancy is uncertain.[13] More specifically, in fully funded schemes, where pensions are based on savings, contributions are invested and returns are credited to the insured persons-scheme participants either individually or collectively.[14] When an insured person retires, the pension fund has at its disposal all their previous contributions, along with the interest rate and earnings acquired on them in the form of dividends, so that this accrued capital can fund the pension of the retiring insured person in the form of an income or in another form.[15]

Furthermore, while occupational and private pension schemes are usually funded, the degree of their funding relative to the pension promises may differ, due to the fact that future pension benefits can be related either to the salary and career length (defined benefit system) or to paid contributions.[16]

As the Commission had noted very early on, in particular for defined contribution funded schemes, returns on a member's slice of the fund will depend on investment choice and ultimate pension benefits will depend on the value of the member's fund at the time of retirement.[17] In addition, the capital and, consequently, pensions further depend on the investment choices of the pension fund in question[18] or the institution or even the insured person themselves.

The case of Sweden is indicative: its system involves many investment funds and the insured person should be adequately informed regarding their function (returns-fees) in order to choose their preferred investment institution.[19] It is noted therefore that the time of contribution payment, highlighted by Spiegel, is not the only important element; the time of retirement from working life is also crucial. In any event, it is stressed that the pro-rata calculation method cannot be used for capital-funded systems or pension account systems.[20]

It is worth noting that Leppik (2006) considered as temporary the solution put forward by Donders (2004) suggesting that states with statutorily mandatory, funded, defined-contribution schemes should make an entry into Annex VI, Regulation No 1408/71 on special procedures for the application of the legislation of

[12] Burtless (2007).

[13] Barr and Diamond (2008), p. 36, footnote no. 2.

[14] Barr and Diamond (2008), p. 36, footnote no. 2.

[15] Barr and Diamond (2008), p. 36, footnote no. 2.

[16] European Commission (2015), Directorate-General for Economic and Financial, p. 55.

[17] Commission of the European Communities (1997), p. 3.

[18] Galazoulas and Tsetoura (2014), p. 140 sub.

[19] Stergiou (2009), pp. 19–20.

[20] See Spiegel (2009), p. 208.

certain Member States.[21] Instead Leppik examined the potential affiliation of such schemes to the Directives on supplementary pensions (then Directive 98/49) or even the simultaneous affiliation to both the Directives on supplementary pensions and Regulation No 1408/71, while he also supported the coordination of these schemes solely on the basis of Regulation No 1408/71, provided it was amended. The amendment proposed therefore is not to apply the pro-rata calculation for mandatory funded defined-contribution schemes. In such cases, only the independent benefit would be calculated, i.e. the amount of benefit would be calculated only under the national legislation of each concerned Member State.[22] Leppik's approach (2006) was supported also by Verschueren (2009) and Spiegel (2009) and is adopted herein by the EU legislature.

Thus, according to Article 52 (5) of Regulation No 883/04, notwithstanding the provisions of paragraphs 1, 2 and 3, **the pro-rata calculation shall not apply to schemes providing benefits in respect of which periods of time are of no relevance to the calculation, provided** that such schemes are listed in **part 2 of Annex VIII.** In such cases, the person concerned shall be entitled to the benefit calculated in accordance with the legislation of the Member State concerned. According to Verschueren, the Commission's proposal in 2006 on waiving the pro-rata calculation in all cases where the pension is based on a defined contribution scheme is reflected in Article 52 (5) of Regulation No 883/04.[23]

More specifically, the States included in part 2 of Annex VIII, Regulation No 883/04 regarding pensions subject to Article 52 (5) of Regulation No 883/04 and thus have a funded system are the following: Bulgaria, Czech Republic, Denmark, Estonia, France, Croatia, Latvia, Hungary, Austria, Poland, Portugal, Slovenia, Slovakia, Sweden, United Kingdom. As it can be noted in the relevant Annex, some of the Member States' pensions refer to supplementary pension schemes, while others refer to the basic pension schemes. Slovenia provides an example of a supplementary pension scheme which falls within the scope of the Regulation: it is a mandatory pension insurance scheme and is considered part of social security in Slovenia.[24] In this context, the position set out above, when examining the pension schemes falling within the scope of the Regulation is reinforced. According to this position, for a scheme to fall under the Regulation, it should be regarded at a national level as social security in the sense of being formalised with the approval of national authorities.

Of course, Article 48 (former Article 42) TFEU which is the legal basis for coordination of all pension schemes, irrespective of their features, prescribes as method of coordination the aggregation of insurance periods to establish the

[21] Donders (2004), p. 44.

[22] Leppik (2006), p. 52.

[23] Verschueren (2009), p. 148.

[24] Jorens and Lhernould (2011), p. 15.

acquisition and retention of the right to benefit as well as the amount of benefit, without however taking into account the diverse types of pension schemes.[25]

5.2 The Time Factor in Funded Schemes

If we were to delve into a critique of the coordination rationale, a fundamental rule of which is aggregation as provided for in Article 48 TFEU, it could be noted that its purpose is to secure a certain proportionality. Thus, the provision of Article 48 on the aggregation "for the purpose of acquiring and retaining the right to benefit and of calculating the amount of benefit of all periods taken into account under the laws of the several countries" aims solely to the provision of a pension that is proportional to the career course lato sensu, in the context of offering protection to the party concerned, i.e. it aims at a fair pension.

This proportionality or correlation was expressed in the Regulation with the pro-rata calculation or the pro-rata benefit in Article 46 (2) of Regulation No 1408/71 and currently Article 52 (1) of Regulation No 883/04.Given that coordination rules were initially intended for classic pay-as-you-go pension schemes,[26] which makes them potentially unsuitable for other types of pension schemes, this proportionality was in principle associated with the duration of the period of insurance. If the various pension schemes operate with parameters other than time periods, this does not mean that the provision of a pro-rata benefit should be ruled out under such schemes as well, in the sense of a broad proportionality (not necessarily a proportionality regarding time).What is important is ensuring a similar (proportional) protection of the migrant worker transferring in these types of schemes. The periods of insurance and the amount may not be proportional in a strict mathematical sense; there is, however, a relative proportionality in the sense that the pension is determined, among other things, by the moment in time where accrued contributions may be released.

Furthermore, it should be noted that, in contrast with the content of provision in Article 52 (5) of Regulation No 883/04, the time periods may be indirectly equally important for both entitlement to a pension right and for the calculation of the amount of the pension even in funded schemes. It should be noted that they are not specifically defined, time periods are calculated in general as time. More specifically, in a number of capital-funded schemes or pension account schemes there are no "qualification periods" and benefit entitlements accrue after very short periods of membership of the schemes. There are also schemes, however, that still have long qualification periods where it is necessary to add periods together in order to trigger a benefit entitlement.[27]

[25] Leppik (2006), p. 53.

[26] Verschueren (2009), p. 148; OSE (2011), p. 19.

[27] Spiegel (2009), p. 208, footnote no. 936.

Undoubtedly, in funded schemes the amount of pension depends primarily on the person's amount of contributions, from the capital accrued by payment of contributions.[28] The link between contributions and benefits is closest in defined contribution schemes which provide benefits dependent solely on the return on assets invested.[29] However, time periods may affect the capital returns in relation to investment choices; the time for starting to paying contributions is, therefore, as crucial as the retirement time. In defined benefit schemes the employer will effectively guarantee a level of benefits relating to the income of the employee at or near retirement.[30] Furthermore, in defined-contribution occupational schemes, after a short vesting period, the worker assumes ownership of their pension account, which ensures the portability of accrued pension rights.[31]

It is also noted that occupational pension plans usually define a vesting period representing the minimum length of service to be completed in order to obtain pension rights' entitlement. Thus, workers leaving the plan before completion of the vesting period forfeit their pension rights.[32] It is also noted that many countries follow tax incentive policies for occupational social security schemes as well as for savings-pension plans (tax deductions known as "tax expenditures").[33] Offering tax advantages to private pensions is justified by their social priority: these pensions are substitutes for the lost wages of the worker.[34] This is why it is prohibited to withdraw accrued contributions prior to retirement.[35] Otherwise, fiscal neutrality no longer works and the amounts are deprived of tax advantages.[36] It is reminded that the Commission itself noted in a relevant communication that, as far as pension schemes are concerned, the words "supplementary" and "occupational" are considered as synonymous,[37] as pensions are normally related to income from work and hence to a professional occupation, while all these schemes have in common that they originated from initiatives of the private sector.[38]

Moreover, it is possible at the time of retirement and calculation of the pension to take into account other factors such as the sustainability factor or other economic

[28] See for example European Commission (2024a), Employment, Social Affairs & Inclusion, Latvia – Old-age pension https://ec.europa.eu/social/main.jsp?catId=1117&langId=en&intPageId=4638.

[29] Commission of the European Communities (1997), p. 3.

[30] Commission of the European Communities (1997), p. 3.

[31] Andrietti (2000), p. 2.

[32] Andrietti (2001), p. 3.

[33] Stergiou (2004), p. 10.

[34] Barthélémy (2002), p. 730.

[35] Stergiou (2004), p. 11.

[36] Barthélémy (2002), p. 731.

[37] Similarly Anagnostou-Dedouli (2005), p. 35.

[38] Economic and Social Committee (1991), p. 1, footnote 1.

indexes or demographic data;[39] thus the time of retirement affects the economic size of that point in time and consequently the amount of the benefit. Indirectly, therefore, time plays a role in establishing entitlement and in calculating the pension in the schemes in question: when someone is allowed to retire and on the basis of which minimum period also determine the pension depending on returns and economic indexes at the time of retirement.

It is also interesting to examine the extent to which the age threshold or the completion of certain periods of insurance for entitlement to a pension right is among the retirement conditions set by States with funded schemes, which have been included in part 2 of Annex VIII, Regulation No 883/04 in accordance with Article 52 (5) of Regulation No 883/04 .Although the aforementioned Annex includes specific categories which are awarded in the context of each State, some conclusions may be drawn from the description of social security rights and the relevant State schemes as provided by the European Commission for the purposes of the Coordination Regulation.[40]

For example, examining the retirement conditions in the Bulgarian scheme, the award of a state old-age pension is possible once the interested party reaches the retirement age set by the State and provided they have attained a given period of social insurance cover.[41] Latvia has similar arrangements and it provides for shared conditions on the retirement age and the social insurance contribution periods for all the pensions of its three-tier pension system.[42] Similarly, Austria's system requires reaching a certain age and completing a minimum insurance period, while at the same times it indicates that where the completion of certain conditions is required for entitlement to a social security right, the authorities shall take into account any periods of insurance completed in other Member States, in Switzerland, in Liechtenstein, in Norway and in Iceland.[43] It can thus be concluded that, for the purposes of establishing entitlement to a retirement benefit, the minimum periods set in funded schemes are completed by the assimilation of periods in other Member States.

In addition, as noted with regards to funded schemes, the Commission proposed waiving the pro-rata calculation (apportionment) in 2006[44] in any case where the pension is based on a defined-contribution pension scheme.[45] Despite waiving the

[39]For example the Greek Single Supplementary Insurance Fund - TEA, with a pay-as-you-go predefined contributions scheme with notional capitalisation (Article 39 (1), Law 4052/2012).

[40]European Commission (2024b) Your rights country by country.

[41]European Commission (2024c) Your rights country by country, Your social security rights in Bulgaria, p. 18.

[42]European Commission (2024a) Your rights country by country, Your social security rights in Latvia.

[43]European Commission (2024d) Your rights country by country, Your social security rights in Austria.

[44]Proposal for a Regulation of the European Parliament and of the Council amending Regulation (EC) No 883/2004 on the coordination of social security systems, and determining the content of Annex XI, COM (2006)7 final, 24 January 2006.

[45]OSE (2011), p. 20.

apportionment under Article 52 (5) of Regulation No 883/04, which was finally introduced with amending Regulation No 988/09,[46] that same amending Regulation introduced a new provision in Article 56 of Regulation No 883/04, i.e. the provision in Article 56 (1) (d) of Regulation No 883/04.

5.3 New Complications

According to Article 56 (1) (d) of Regulation No 883/04, in the event that point (c) is not applicable because the legislation of a Member State provides for the benefit to be calculated on the basis of elements other than periods of insurance or residence which are not linked to time, the competent institution shall take into account, in respect of each period of insurance or residence completed under the legislation of any other Member State, the amount of the capital accrued, the capital which is considered as having been accrued or any other element for the calculation under the legislation it administers, divided by the corresponding units of periods in the pension scheme concerned.

This provision seems to refer indirectly to more specific types of pension systems. The provision on accrued capital refers to funded schemes, the provision on capital which is considered as having been accrued refers to notional contribution or notional capitalisation or notional account schemes while the provision on units of periods is unclear. It could mean the number of periods depending on the unit of measurement used in each system (days/months/years of insurance).

It is worth noting that although academics have examined the provisions on pensions of Article 50 et seq. of Regulation No 883/04 and the provisions on funded schemes in particular, they have not examined in detail the provision in question in Article 56 (1) (d) of Regulation No 883/04. More specifically, Spiegel is the only one to mention this provision stating that prior to its adoption the other Member States that applied apportionment rejected a system of this nature where, in the case of invalidity benefits, for example, apportionment periods were also to have the effect of increasing the benefit in the calculation, as these are periods after all. Thus, for such systems the only remaining option is listing in the relevant Annex as autonomous benefit schemes, the amount of which is independent from the duration of the periods.[47] Indeed, Spiegel argues that in systems where time periods play no role in the calculation, the national benefit amount can always be paid out (so there will no longer be a comparison with a hypothetical pro-rata benefit) whether there is or not need to add insurance periods together for an entitlement to a pension rights (as per Article 52 (5) of Regulation No 883/04) provided that these schemes are registered in

---

[46] Regulation (EC) No 988/2009 of the European Parliament and of the Council of 16 September 2009 amending Regulation (EC) No 883/2004 on the coordination of social security systems and determining the context of its Annexes, OJ L 284/43, 30.10.2009.

[47] Spiegel (2009), p. 208 and footnote 942.

the special Annex VIII, part 2 of Regulation No 883/04.[48] Such a case is Austria that was mentioned above. If, then, in the example described previously, a Member State that has such a scheme has registered in this annex Spiegel argues it is possible for either EUR 80,246.03 or EUR 12,655.86 (depending on the timing of when the contributions were made) to be used for the pension calculation.

However, Spiegel then contradicts himself, as he recognises on the basis of the provision of Article 56 (1) (d) of Regulation No 883/04 the possibility of pro-rata calculation for funded schemes that are not listed in the special annex and this despite the fact that by using the same example he proves the unsuitability of the pro-rata calculation for funded schemes.

He thus uses the amounts that result from the above example, i.e. EUR 80,246.03 and EUR 12,655.86 which he then divides by 120 (the number of months for 10 years) stating that in the pro-rata calculation the result for 480 months (career of 40 years) will be a theoretical sum of EUR 320,984.12 or EUR 50,623.44 respectively, which then on reduction by 10/40 results to the national starting basis again of EUR 80,246.03 and EUR 12,655.86.[49] He basically starts with the actual sums calculated based on the Kn formula with the average return depending on the number of years in order to calculate the theoretical sum and then back to the actual sum. Moreover, he himself proves by using the aforementioned example of the Austrian memorandum to the Administrative Commission that, by applying a pro-rata calculation, the actual sum of the 10/40 pro-rata benefit would be EUR 41,237.20 which does not correspond to reality.

This contradiction is due to the contradictions contained within the actual provisions of the Regulation. In any event, it cannot be accepted that the pro-rata calculation cannot be applied in respect of certain funded schemes, while for others it can depending on whether there is a listing in the Annex, i.e. a formal condition set out in Article 52 (5) of Regulation No 883/04 that does not affect the substance, the operation and the characteristics of said schemes. Thus, although Spiegel considers the provision of Article 56 (1) (d) of Regulation No 883/04 as a good response of the European legislature to the coordination problems in respect of funded schemes,[50]

[48] Spiegel (2009), p. 208 and footnote 942.

[49] Spiegel (2009), pp. 208–209:"Additionally, however, provision was also made for states that were not eligible for inclusion in the said annex whereby, in the pro-rata calculation in systems that take account, in their calculation, of 'other factors not connected to periods', foreign periods were always to be taken to be the average of the appropriate basis of calculation per month. If we apply this arrangement to our example, the Member State in question would, when it comes to the foreign periods, use either EUR 80,246.03 divided by 120 or EUR 12,655.86 divided by 120 for each foreign month in the pro-rata calculation, which would result, for the 480 insured months (40 years) in the two Member States, in a theoretical sum of either EUR 320,984.12 or EUR 50,623.44, which then, on reduction in proportion to the period (120/480), exactly mirrors the national starting basis again".

[50] Spiegel (2009), p. 209.

most experts agree that the Regulation does not take into account the special features of funded schemes.[51]

Indeed, the general observation shared by the European Social Observatory (2011) based on the questionnaires and the interviews carried out and included in the relevant study was that the measures adopted even under amending Regulation No 988/09 are partial and insufficient to take the specificity of funded schemes in due account.[52] In the same context, the European Commission noted that the coordination rules are designed for pay-as-you-go schemes, while hybrid schemes may also be problematic.[53] Although according to the Commission Regulation No 883/04 there is room for improvement, such improvements could be limited taking into account the CJEU case-law and the fact that the chapter dedicated to pensions within the Regulation is one of the most complicated.[54]

Getting into a more in-depth analysis of Article 56 (1) (d) of Regulation No 883/04, let us divide a sum, the capital as a component of a funded scheme by a time period, which is accepted by the Regulation as an element of a pay-as-you-go scheme and not of a funded one. Would the result which is "taken into account by the competent institution" be a sum or time periods? The pro-rata calculation is based on time periods in other States and not on sums in other States.

In our opinion, while Article 52 (5) and in Article 56 (1) (d) of Regulation No 883/04 accept that time periods are of no importance for the calculation of benefits in funded schemes, the Regulation seems to accept the correlation between the time periods in pay-as-you-go schemes and the accrued sum in funded schemes for each one of these periods. It therefore excludes States with funded schemes from the pro-rata calculation, as the periods do not have a direct role in the calculation of the benefit and, at the same time, it provides for the taking into account of the periods during which a person was actually affiliated to other States where time periods play a role in the calculation of a benefit; a contradiction is thus observed. Indeed, the contradiction results in confusion because it does not clarify which is the "benefit" that according to the provision "must be calculated on the basis of elements other than periods of insurance or residence which are not linked to time". Provided this is a national funded-scheme benefit, there can be no reference to a theoretical and pro-rata sum to which Article 56 of Regulation No 883/04 refers to, let alone a division of the capital by time periods, when the periods are not included in the calculation formula of the benefit in a funded scheme. The question thus arises how to reconcile the application of Article 52 (5) of Regulation No 883/04 with Article 56 (1) (d) of Regulation No 883/04, as well as the principles applying in general in the schemes in question.

In other words, the problem lies in the fact that despite the exclusion of the pro-rata calculation for benefits in schemes operating based on the principle of

[51] OSE (2011), p. 20.

[52] OSE (2011), p. 20.

[53] OSE (2011), p. 136.

[54] OSE (2011), p. 136.

capitalisation pursuant Article 52 (5) of Regulation No 883/04, Article 56 (1) of Regulation No 883/04 refers to the calculation of the theoretical and pro-rata sum and then to taking into account the capital from these schemes. On the one hand, States with schemes such as those listed in part 2 of Annex VIII, Regulation No 883/04 calculate the benefit in accordance with their national legislation independently, as per Article 52 (5) of Regulation No 883/04; on the other hand, the provision in Article 56 (1) (d) of Regulation No 883/04 assigns to the States with similar schemes the obligation to take into account the funded elements (capital) and the pay-as-you-go elements (time periods), providing for a division capital/time periods which is not justified; accordingly, the pro-rata calculation procedure for benefits of these schemes is not justified either, pursuant the European coordination at this stage of its development. Indeed, this was the reason for the provision of Article 52 (5) of Regulation No 883/04 which rules out the application of the pro-rata calculation for these schemes. It should be noted that what is taken into account in the pro-rata calculation procedure is the ratio periods/periods.

In addition, it should be noted that the principle of equal treatment between migrant and non-migrant workers as applied by the Court in combination with the principle of free movement, for the purposes of the coordination, cannot apply to migrant workers affiliated to funded schemes. Thus, the classic method of the Court raising in each case the question "what would have happened if the migrant workers have never left the State in question" in order to detect the prohibited disadvantaging of migrant workers[55] faces practical obstacles.

As already seen, in contrast to a defined-benefit scheme (DB), it is the contributions rather than the benefit that is fixed in a defined-contribution (DC) pension plan; the retirement income that will be provided is unknown in advance.[56]

The pension benefit accumulated during the employee's working career will depend on the contributions made while working and the investment returns earned on the plan balances.[57] Therefore, in case where the migrant worker has spent parts of their career in a State with a pension system based on the principle of capitalisation, it is not possible to make a comparison between that migrant worker and a non-migrant worker that spent all their life in that State, even if the starting points for paying contributions and retirement periods are the same. And that is because, in addition to the fact that the time of entry into and exit from such a scheme affects the amount of the benefit (as well as the entitlement to the benefit), there are also many other factors involved that are not objective but subjective. Thus, time is not the only factor as in pay-as-you-go schemes where the insurance time is the prevailing element for entitlement to and calculation of a pension and, at the same time, an objective measure of unit. In funded schemes, subjective factors such as investment choices or unforeseen factors such as the economy status, the life

[55] Spiegel (2009), p. 206, invoking cases C- 1/67 Ciechelski and C-24/75 Petroni.

[56] Broadbent et al. (2006), p. 7.

[57] Broadbent et al. (2006), p. 7.

expectancy, the interest rates, the returns depending on the type of risk of each investment etc. are also important.

Consequently, in the first case there is a dominant constant, while in the second case there are many random variables that would, by definition, make the comparison possible only in the hypothetical situation of finding for every case of a migrant worker a non-migrant reference person with an identical insurance history, with the exact same choices, for each State with a funded scheme to which a person may have been affiliated to.

5.4 Suggestions from Literature

An interesting approach is shown by bilateral social security agreements which generally state that the pensions have to be calculated under national legislation, even if aggregation is needed for entitlement to a pension right.[58] This approach is advisable only if the legislation concerned is based on a linear system where every insurance month (or any other unit used) gives entitlement to the same amount or where the calculation is not based on time elements, like for example, in funded schemes where only the capital accrued is relevant or in pension point schemes where the benefit only depends on the number of pension points collected.[59] Whichever solution is taken for a future European solution should also reflect new developments in pension schemes (which concern not only the Member States but also many Third Countries) and in particular the development of funded schemes or pension account or pension point schemes.[60] Furthermore, certain social security agreements include special provisions for these schemes, which usually aim at safeguarding that the capital available in a fund should be the base for the calculation of the benefit.[61]

The Commission had previously proposed the establishment of pan-European pension institutions, which would be located in one Member State and which would have different sections, each section complying with the requirements for tax approval and the tax regulations of the State where the member is employed and its social law. If in the course of his career with the multinational a person were to change his Member State of employment, he would continue to pay contributions to the same pan-European pension institution, but to a different section. The transfer of accrued benefits between the different sections would not be necessary. After retirement the worker would receive benefits from each national section in

---

[58] Spiegel (2010), p. 45 invoking Article 11 (3) of the Germany-Brazil Agreement or the Agreements concluded by Portugal – e.g. Art. 19 (1) of the Portugal-Australia Agreement.

[59] Spiegel (2010), p. 45.

[60] Spiegel (2010), p. 46.

[61] Ibid.

accordance with the rights acquired under the national rules applicable to these sections.[62] According to the Commission, the proposal for pan-European pension institutions was developed with a single employer and a small group of participating States in mind. However, there seems no reason why it could not provide the basis for more general arrangements for cross-border pension provision within the EU, covering several companies or professions.[63]

This proposal however could, with some modifications, lead to the establishment of a pan-European fund covering the cost for transferring from the pension scheme of one State to the pension scheme of another State that may arise in certain cases, such as those the interviewee from the Netherlands referred to in the above study and which seemed to be an isolated and not a universal phenomenon. However, it has been argued that the reform of Member States' pension systems in view of a coordinated pan-European pension system which would be based on limitless mobility across professions, sectors and regions as well as across life cycles and family structures, on a European concept of solidarity, while at the same time it will allow national preferences of target levels of mandated benefits or contributions and re-distributive allocation of wealth.[64]

In addition, Pieters and Van Steenkiste had previously proposed the creation of the "Thirteenth State", as an alternative to the existing Coordination Regulations, the creation of a European Community social insurance scheme with an inherent dynamic aiming to the harmonization of national social security schemes.[65] Designing such a scheme would initially aim to protect migrant workers, financing it via employee and employer contributions and managing it pursuant European law. In time, non-migrant workers could also choose to be insured via this scheme if they would prefer it over their own national scheme.[66]

Other proposals are based on maintaining national social security schemes as is, making national social security provisions internationally effective preventing double protection or lacunae in protection without modifying the substance of coordination law but by finding a more comprehensible way of expressing its substance.[67] Another suggestion is to reduce the Regulation provisions at the bare minimum and perhaps establish a separate legal instrument that will define the purpose and the operation of coordination; it is argued, however, that it would lead to the replacement of distinct rules for the various social security sectors by a universally applied set of rules and principles (universal coordination system), a development that may not be desirable.[68]

---

[62] Commission of the European Communities (2001), Communication from the Commission to the Council, pp. 18–19.

[63] Commission of the European Communities (2001), Communication from the Commission to the Council, pp. 18–19.

[64] Holzmann (2003).

[65] Pieters and Van Steenkiste (1993), pp. 14–15.

[66] Pieters and Van Steenkiste (1993), p. 10.

[67] Pieters (1997), p. 177; Eichenhofer (1999), p. 411; Eichenhofer (2000), p. 234.

[68] Eichenhofer (2000), p. 234.

Furthermore, the Commission had stressed that to preserve links which may exist between first and second pillar schemes, arrangements could be made to allow employees on temporary secondment to another Member State not to be transferred immediately to the section for that State. Instead they could remain for a certain period within the section for their Member State of origin, as envisaged by Directive 98/49. That period could be determined by reference to the period for which such employees remain subject to that State\s legislation in terms of Regulation No 1408/71. In addition, pan-European pension institutions would comply with the rules on payment and collection of tax applicable in the State of work or residence.[69]

5.5 Our Approach for Guaranteeing Pension Rights

5.5.1 Ideas from Internal Mobility

It is our view that guaranteeing the rights of migrants can be achieved in other ways that are more suitable for these types of schemes. Some of these ways can be found in Member States with funded schemes and in particular in case of internal transfer from one supplementary/occupational scheme or fund to another within the same State. Moreover, pension portability analysis can refer to both portability within the borders of a State as well as cross-border portability.[70] **For example, in the Netherlands** any money transfer from one pension fund to another pension fund is reported to work within the context of a set of legal rules that guarantee no loss of any right of the worker. However, due to issues with the method of liability calculation, the new pension fund may have to pay. It is stressed however, that in defined contribution schemes such transfer is not necessary.[71] Indeed, most occupational funds have lifelong average income schemes, so that workers can leave their pension rights in the old pension fund under the responsibility of their old employer and start working under the new pension fund with new pension rights with no problem.[72]

Beyond the minimum period set as a condition for entitlement which can differ as to the number of years required in each country, the element to consider in portability analysis is the treatment of early leavers' accrued rights. The regulatory framework can generally provide three options in case of within-borders mobility:[73] (a) preserve accrued rights in the leaving scheme; (b) transfer the rights to the new early leaver's pension scheme; (c) cash the rights out to the early leaver. Practice regarding the

[69] Commission of the European Communities (2001), Communication from the Commission to the Council, pp. 18–19.

[70] Andrietti (2000), p. 4.

[71] OSE (2011), p. 125.

[72] OSE (2011), p. 125.

[73] Andrietti (2000), p. 17.

transfer of pension values between countries varies widely from "free transferability" in Ireland, UK and the Netherlands to "transferability upon tax payment" in Denmark to "non-transferability" in Spain.[74]

5.5.2 *Ideas from Supplementary Pension Schemes*

Another issue is whether the provisions included in the Directive for supplementary pensions correspond at the same time to the philosophy of funded schemes and to the protection of migrant workers' rights in correlation with the situations of internal mobility. Before examining these issues however, it should be noted that the Commission had very early on highlighted that an additional issue to the tax obstacles to cross-border participation in pension schemes are the tax obstacles to the cross-border transferability of pension capital. When a worker moves from an employer in one Member State to an employer in another Member State, it may be desirable, both for the employee and the pension institutions that are involved, to transfer the accrued pension capital from the old pension scheme to the new one.[75]

The Commission had then noted that even in cases of mobility within a Member State transfers of accrued pension capital may be difficult or even impossible.[76] Nevertheless in the aforementioned case of the Netherlands that was examined in the relevant study of the European Social Observatory, it was evident that this was not the case given the legal framework of that country which was specifically developed for internal transfers between funded schemes.

As already mentioned, Directive 98/49 on supplementary pensions was replaced by Directive 2014/50.[77] However, there are restrictions as to the choices of the workers who move from one supplementary pension scheme to another across the borders. More specifically, it is recognised that Member States have the right to provide for a minimum vesting period of three years for outgoing workers (Article 4 (1) (a) of Directive 2014/50) or a minimum age for the vesting of pension rights which however cannot exceed 21 years (Article 4 (1) (b) of Directive 2014/50). Nevertheless, where an outgoing worker has not yet acquired vested pension rights when the employment relationship is terminated, the supplementary pension scheme has the possibility to reimburse the contributions paid by the outgoing worker or paid on behalf of the outgoing worker, in accordance with national law or collective agreements or contracts, or, where the outgoing worker bears the investment risk,

[74] Andrietti (2000), p. 17.

[75] Commission of the European Communities (2001), Communication from the Commission to the Council, p. 14.

[76] Commission of the European Communities (2001), Communication from the Commission to the Council, p. 14.

[77] See above for an analysis on this Directive.

either the sum of the contributions made or the investment value arising from these contributions (Article 4 (1) (c) Directive 2014/50).

If, however, the outgoing worker wishes to "leave their pension rights" in the previous pension scheme, they should be able to do so in accordance with Directive 2014/50 but under the above restrictions for vesting rights, i.e. a minimum vesting period and a minimum age. The Directive recognises however that Member States may allow supplementary pension schemes not to retain the vested rights of an outgoing worker but to pay, with the worker's informed consent, including as regards applicable charges, a capital sum equivalent to the value of the vested pension rights to the outgoing worker, as long as the value of the vested pension rights does not exceed a threshold established by the Member State concerned (Article 5 (3) of Directive 2014/50).

Consequently, according to the Directive, the outgoing worker may either "leave their old vested pension rights" in the previous supplementary pension scheme or ask for the reimbursement of the contributions paid by them or on their behalf or to receive a capital sum equivalent to the value of the vested pension rights at the time of their exit. The first option presupposes that States allow the preservation of dormant vested pension rights, which is left to their discretion and also that the national conditions for vesting a pension right on completing a certain period and attaining an age threshold are actually met. Similarly, the third option presupposes the satisfaction of the national terms for vesting a pension right on completing a certain period and attaining an age threshold. The second option seems to be free of any restrictions.

It is noted that, in essence, the Directive on supplementary pension does not guarantee the portability of pension rights trough the transferability of the accrued capital, i.e. the value of the pension. The reimbursement and potential transfer of contributions is one thing; the transfer of the capital sum that is equivalent to the investing and saving value of paid contributions, i.e. the transfer of the pension right as such is another. A funded scheme is associated with savings. Contributions paid during a career are invested and their returns (along with the capital sum) finance pensions.[78] The critical size therefore is the return on capital during the savings' periods (as yesterday's and today's contributions finance the pensions of tomorrow).[79] In contrast, in the aforementioned Netherlands example, it was demonstrated that, for the purposes of avoiding loss of money and rights of the workers moving within a State from one funded supplementary fund to another, the transfer of pension rights is not only protected but formalised in a special legal framework. As highlighted, in defined contribution plans where the annual contribution is placed in the worker's individual account and is then invested on their behalf, the worker assumes ownership of their pension account (after a short vesting period); this ensures full portability of accrued pension rights.[80] Indeed, defined contribution

[78] Spraos and Tinios (1998), p. 2.

[79] Spraos and Tinios (1998), p. 2.

[80] Andrietti (2000), p. 3.

plans are usually fully portable in that they allow vested early leavers to withdraw the actuarially fair value of their accrued pension rights.[81]

Flexible mechanisms should therefore be provided for the transfer of funds within the meaning of actual or notional capital (actual or notional contributions); these mechanisms should also apply to external funded schemes (by assimilation) and not just to funded schemes within a single State for cases where workers move from one employment and one internal funded scheme to another, taking also into account the current trend for flexibility combined with security. This trend is also known as "flexicurity".[82]

5.5.3 *Flexicurity*

The notion of flexicurity has been widely used in the last decade to reconcile the needs of a flexible labour marker with those of a robust social security.[83] Emerging in the Netherlands in the mid 1990s, this concept presupposes a "double bind": high levels of flexibility are required to compete successfully in a globalised market and thus afford high levels of employment security.[84] The European Commission promoted flexicurity to a flagship policy in the mid 2000s. Included in the Lisbon Agenda and reconfirmed in its follow-up, the EU2020 strategy, flexicurity is advocated by guideline 21 of the European Employment Strategy 2007.[85] Member States are then called upon to implement employment policies aimed at achieving full employment, improving quality and productivity at work and strengthening social and territorial cohesion.[86]

Thus, in order to coordinate funded schemes as well as funded schemes with pay-as-you-go schemes, provisions should be made, first, for the transfer of capital representing the value of the pension—in particular in the context of funded schemes, and then a selection of suitable and more complex arrangements combining characteristics of both types of schemes should follow. More specifically, in respect of the methods of transfer of pension rights, the Court held in Casta that Member States may apply the method referred to as "the actuarial equivalent" which

---

[81] Andrietti (2000), p. 4.

[82] European Commission (2024e), Employment, Social Affairs & Inclusion, Flexicurity http://ec.europa.eu/social/main.jsp?catId=102.

[83] European Commission (2024e), Employment, Social Affairs & Inclusion, Flexicurity http://ec.europa.eu/social/main.jsp?catId=102, p. 3.

[84] European Commission (2024e), Employment, Social Affairs & Inclusion, Flexicurity http://ec.europa.eu/social/main.jsp?catId=102, p. 3.

[85] European Commission (2024e), Employment, Social Affairs & Inclusion, Flexicurity http://ec.europa.eu/social/main.jsp?catId=102, p. 3.

[86] European Commission (2024e), Employment, Social Affairs & Inclusion, Flexicurity http://ec.europa.eu/social/main.jsp?catId=102, p. 3.

is used to calculate the current value of a future and contingent pension benefit, the amount of which is normally reduced in order to take account of early payment and the risk of death before the due date, or the method referred to as the "flat-rate redemption value", by which that value is obtained by adding up the contributions paid by the insured person and by his employer, to which interest may be added,[87] or also other methods, in so far as the amount to be transferred actually represents the pension rights acquired by virtue of the previous activities of the worker.[88]

In Casta the Court referred to the principle of the freedom of movement for workers, despite not invoking the Regulation. The Court thus applied the principle of the freedom of movement for workers regardless of the application of the Coordination Regulation. It is worth noting that in this case the Court made reference to the transfer of capital and the aforementioned methods for transferring vested pension rights from one national scheme to the European Union pension scheme, the type of which is not clarified, even though in the national scheme in question the pensions were not necessary proportional to contributions (pay-as-you-go scheme).The Court has thus presented a judgment where it refers to the transfer of pension rights from a scheme where there is no close link between contributions and benefits, creating the need to determine an individual share, the value of the pension corresponding to each insured and ultimately the transfer of that capital even though the principle of capitalisation does not apply.

The question of course arises whether the particularities and options of funded schemes are penetrating pay-as-you-go schemes in order to safeguard at all times the rights of the worker who wishes to leave a scheme and transfer to another. The only conclusion that can be safely drawn is that there is a requirement to ensure some proportionality between contributions and benefits in a national scheme, even if there is no strict reciprocity. Thus, irrespective of the method of distribution of benefits that can operate in solidarity with the weak, fixing inequalities at the expense of vulnerable social groups, the benefit that corresponds to each insured person should be able to be determined, regardless of the method used to this effect. A pension right should thus be clearly identifiable and defined regardless the methods selected for its determination and definition.

Further examining this rationale in reverse, it could be said that a funded scheme that ensures the clearly defined individual share of each insured person due to the close link between contributions and benefits can also use a part of the contributions other than those in the individual pension accounts for the purposes imposed by the principle of solidarity. The fact that some contributions are capitalised and that each insured person acquires ownership of their account or even that current contributions

[87] See concerning those methods of calculation, judgment of 18.03.1982, 212/81, Bodson, European Court Reports 1982, p. 1019, paragraphs 7 and 8.

[88] Judgment of the Court of 05.12.2013, Case C-166/12, Časta, Digital Reports (Court Reports - general)ECLI:EU:C:2013:792, paragraphs 25 and 26.Compare older judgments of 16.12.2004, Case C-293/03, Gregorio My, European Court Reports 2004 I-12013 ECLI:EU:C:2004:821 and of 16.02.2006, Case C-137/04, Amy Rockler, European Court Reports 2006 I-01441 ECLI:EU:C:2006:106.

do not fund current pensions as in a pay-as-you-go scheme, but future pensions, does not mean that serving specific social goals cannot be foreseen. Moreover, as noted, even a fully-funded scheme can shift the balance from high-earners to low-wage earners, i.e. to have redistributive results, while at the same time maintain full capitalisation.[89]

As can be concluded from the Court's judgment therefore, it should be possible **at all times to determine and redeem pension rights in any scheme regardless of its nature.** However, if we were to accept that each scheme should provide for such a transfer of rights, coordination might not be needed for the purposes of pensions or rather not in its current form, as whenever a person would leave a scheme and moved to another scheme in another State, they would also transfer their rights. It would probably have a different form for the simultaneous utilisation of insurance periods and accrued capital. At present, attention should be focused on the issue that, in any event, the transfer of capital should be provided in respect of funded schemes via whichever method is selected by States.

5.5.4 The Cases of Casta, INPS and Repubblica italiana

At this point, it is worth examining in detail the Casta[90] case, despite the fact that no reference was made to the Regulation. The request for a preliminary ruling concerns the interpretation of Article 11 (2) of Annex VIII to Council Regulation (EEC, Euratom, ECSC) No 259/68 of 29 February 1968 laying down the Staff Regulations of officials and the conditions of employment of other servants of the European Communities and instituting special measures temporarily applicable to officials of the Commission (OJ 1968 L 56, p. 1), as amended by Council Regulation (EC, Euratom) No 723/2004 of 22 March 2004 (OJ 2004 L 124, p. 1) ("the Staff Regulations"), and of Article 4(3) TEU.

The request has been made in the context of proceedings between Mr R. Časta and the Česká správa sociálního zabezpečení (social security authorities of the Czech Republic, theČSSZ) **concerning the calculation of the capital value of the pension rights acquired by him in the national pension scheme that may be transferred, on his behalf, into the European Union pension scheme.** The Court initially referred to the legal context, i.e. European Union law and Czech law. Mr R. Časta, an official of the European Commission, was, before taking up his duties for the Commission on 1 December 2006, insured under the Czech old-age insurance scheme. The relevant contributions were paid into that scheme. On 28 November 2008 **Mr R. Časta applied to the Commission to have his pension rights**

[89] Barr and Diamond (2008), p. 36, footnote no. 2.

[90] Judgment of the Court of 05.12.2013, Case C-166/12, Časta, Digital Reports(Court reports - general)ECLI:EU:C:2013:792.

acquired in the Czech Republic transferred, pursuant to Article 11 (2) of Annex VIII to the Staff Regulations.

By its first question, the referring court asks, in essence, whether, on a proper construction of Article 11 (2) of Annex VIII to the Staff Regulations, a Member State may determine the amount of the capital value of the pension rights by means of the actuarial equivalent or of the flat-rate redemption value, provided for by that provision of the Staff Regulations before it was amended by Regulation No 723/2004, or whether it must apply only one of those methods (paragraph 20).Article 11 (2) of Annex VIII to the Staff Regulations, in its version before being amended by Regulation No 723/2004, which resulted from Regulation No 571/92, provided that an official who enters the service of the Communities after leaving the service of a government administration or of a national or international organisation, or after pursuing an activity in an employed or self-employed capacity, was entitled upon establishment to have paid to the Communities either the actuarial equivalent or the flat rate redemption value of retirement pension rights acquired by virtue of such service or activities (paragraph 21).

That provision offered the Member States an alternative with respect to fulfilling their obligation to adopt the national measures necessary in order to ensure that it was possible for officials to have their retirement pension rights transferred into the Community pension scheme. Therefore, since they were not obliged to grant officials the option to choose between the transfer of the actuarial equivalent and the flat-rate redemption value, the Member States were free to use one of those two methods of calculation[91] (paragraph 22).

Indeed, **by now employing the sole concept of "capital value of acquired pension rights", the European Union legislator authorised the Member States to apply the method of their choice in order to determine the amount to transfer into the European Union pension scheme in so far as that amount actually represents the pension rights acquired with respect to the previous activities** of the official concerned (paragraph 24).

Consequently, the Member States may apply the method referred to as the "actuarial equivalent", which is used to calculate the current value of a future and contingent pension benefit, the amount of which is normally reduced in order to take account of early payment and the risk of death before the due date, or the method referred to as the "flat-rate redemption value", by which that value is obtained by adding up the contributions paid by the insured person and by his employer, to which interest may be added,[92] or also other methods (paragraph 25).

In those circumstances, the answer to the first question was that on a proper construction of Article 11 (2) of Annex VIII to the Staff Regulations, a Member State may determine the amount of the capital value of pension rights by means of the

[91] See to that effect, judgment of 17.12.1987, 315/85, Commission v Luxembourg, European Court Reports 1987, p. 5391, paragraphs 20 to 22.

[92] See concerning those methods of calculation, judgment of 18.03.1982, 212/81, Bodson, European Court Reports 1982, p. 1019, paragraphs 7 and 8.

actuarial equivalent, the flat-rate redemption value or by means of other methods, in so far as the amount to be transferred actually represents the pension rights acquired by virtue of the previous activities of the official concerned (paragraph 26).

By its second question, the referring court asks, in essence, whether Article 11 (2) of Annex VIII to the Staff Regulations and Article 4 (3) TEU must be interpreted as precluding application of a method for calculating the capital value of the pension rights acquired in the national pension scheme with respect to earlier activities such as that defined in Czech law, and whether the answer to such a question is affected by the fact that the method results in the amount of capital to be transferred into the European Union pension scheme being set at a level of not even half the amount of the contributions paid by the official and the employer into the national pension scheme (paragraph 27). In order to ensure coordination of the national and European Union pension schemes, it is necessary to carry out two consecutive operations, the second of them consisting in converting the capital value of pension rights acquired in the national system into pensionable years of service to be taken into account in the European Union pension scheme. That conversion is carried out by the institutions of the European Union, in accordance with the general provisions implementing Article 11 determined by those institutions. That operation is governed by European Union law (paragraph 28). On the other hand, the first operation falls within the sole competence of the national authority administering the pension scheme with which the interested person was insured before he entered into the service of the European Union, such an operation determining the capital value of pension rights acquired in the national scheme under the relevant legislation of the Member State concerned[93] (paragraph 29).

It should be noted in respect of the various national arrangements that the European legislature did not intend with Article 11 (2) of Annex VIII to the Staff Regulations to harmonise national provisions in the field of pension, which are characterised by widely differing features and a high degree of complexity.[94] Moreover, as was stated by the Advocate General in point 43 of his Opinion, it follows from Article 48 TFEU and Article 153(4) TFEU that the right of the Member States to define the fundamental principles of their social security systems is recognised by European Union law (paragraph 30).It follows that the Member States enjoy broad discretion in adopting their national legislation implementing Article 11 (2) of Annex VIII to the Staff Regulations (paragraph 31).This is most particularly so in the case of the Member States' method for determining the amount of the capital value of pension rights acquired in the national scheme and intended to be taken into account by the European Union pension scheme. The method must, however, be established in accordance with the nature of the principles and rules governing their pension system (paragraph 32).

---

[93] Judgment of 09.11.1989, 75/88, 146/88 and 147/88, Bonazzi-Bertottilli and others v Commission, European Court Reports, 1989, p. 3599, paragraph 17.

[94] Judgment Commission v Luxembourg, paragraph 21.

In general, the Member States have the option of establishing, in particular, a **funded pension scheme providing old-age pensions proportional to contributions or, on the other hand, a scheme based on a certain degree of solidarity, which envisages that pensions paid in the context of such a scheme are not necessarily proportionate to contributions** (paragraph 33).It is apparent from the order for reference that, in the national pension system at issue in the main proceedings, the amounts of the pensions to which retired persons are entitled are calculated by applying a formula which takes account of the total period of contribution to old-age insurance and the levels of income, although in the latter care in a manner that is markedly degressive. In that system, it is true that a higher income gives the right to a higher pension, but amounts over and above certain income limits are taken into account only on a reduced basis (paragraph 34). In such a pay-as-you-go system which is strongly based on solidarity, it is clear that the capital value of acquired pension rights does not correspond to the total contributions paid by the employer to his employee with respect to the latter's old-age insurance (paragraph 35).

If the calculation of the capital value of pension rights stems logically from the nature, principles and rules of the pension system in force in a Member State, the consistency of that method with European law cannot be called into question. It is only in the case in which the method for calculating that capital significantly diverges, to the advantage or disadvantage of the official, from the nature of the principles and rules of the national pension system **that the legislation of the Member State concerned is likely to constitute a barrier to the free movement of workers guaranteed by Article 45 TFEU or to infringe the obligations provided for in Article 4(3) TEU** (paragraph 36).

It should be noted, first, that according to the Court's settled case-law, an official of the European Union has the status of a migrant worker[95] and, secondly, the Member States' obligation to make it possible to transfer to the European Union pension scheme pension rights acquired by European Union officials with respect to their earlier duties and to establish it in that regard a calculation method falls within the scope of application of Article 4 (3) TEU[96] (paragraph 37).

The national legislation at issue in the main proceedings, as set out in paragraphs 11 and 12 of the present judgment, would appear not to diverge from the nature of the principles and rules of the national pension scheme. Nevertheless, it is for the national court to determine whether that is indeed the case, in particular where an applicant presents serious evidence to the contrary, and to determine, in cases in which national provisions permit the transfer of pension rights into another national scheme or into the scheme of an international organisation, whether the calculation of the sum to be transferred into the European Union pension scheme is not

---

[95] Judgments of 16.02.2006, C-185/04, Öberg, European Court Reports 2006, p. I-1453, paragraph 12 and of 04.07.2013, C-233/12, Gardella, paragraph 25.

[96] See to that effect, judgment of 17.07.1997, C-52/96, Commission v Spain, European Court Reports 1997, p. I-4637, paragraph 9.

performed in a way unfavourable in relation to the calculation of the sum to be transferred into such other schemes (paragraph 38).The mere fact that the calculation method results in a sum to be transferred that is less than half of the contributions paid by the official and his former employer into the national pension scheme does not constitute such evidence. Furthermore, there is nothing in the file submitted to the Court to indicate that the national provisions permit the transfer of pension rights into another national or international scheme (paragraph 38).

In addition, **an official applying for the transfer of his pension rights acquired in a pension scheme of a Member State into the European Union pension scheme cannot usefully rely on unlawful discrimination in relation to officials of the European Union from other Member States arising from the use of a different method for calculating the capital to be transferred. In such a case, the difference in treatment is the consequence of the Member States' power to arrange their pension systems and their discretion in that regard** (paragraph 39).

In those circumstances, the answer to Question 2 was that Article 11 (2) of Annex VIII to the Staff Regulations and Article 4 (3) TEU must be interpreted as not precluding application of the method for calculating the capital value of pension rights acquired earlier, such as that defined in Czech law, even where that method results in the amount of capital to be transferred into the European Union pension scheme being set at a level of not even half the amount of the contributions paid by the official and his former employer into the national pension scheme (paragraph 40).

By its third question, the referring court asks, in essence, whether Article 11 (2) of Annex VIII to the Staff Regulations and Article 4 (3) TEU must be interpreted as meaning that, for the purposes of calculating the amount of the capital value of pension rights acquired earlier and intended to be transferred into the European Union pension scheme, it is necessary to take account of the period during which the official had already participated in that scheme (paragraph 41).The applicant in the main proceedings requests, before the referring court, that the period of employment competed as a Commission official be taken into account in the Member State concerned for the purposes of calculating the amount to be transferred from the national pension scheme into the European Union pension scheme (paragraph 43). It is unequivocally apparent from Article 11 (2) of Annex VIII to the Staff Regulations that the pension rights that an official is entitled to have transferred into the European Union pension scheme from the pension scheme in force in a Member State are those acquired by virtue of only those activities exercised before he entered into the service of the European Union (paragraph 45).

That provision is, moreover, explained in Commission Decision of 28 April 2004 on the general provisions for the implementation of Articles 11 and 12 of Annex VIII to the Staff Regulations, which provides, in the first subparagraph of Article 6, that "[a]ny amount to be transferred, from the servant's pension fund, must be certified as being the updated capital value of pension rights acquired before entering the service of the Communities" (paragraph 46).In view of the foregoing, the answer to Question 3 was that Article 11 (2) of Annex VIII to the Staff Regulations and Article 4 (3) TEU must be interpreted as meaning that, for the purposes of calculating the amount of the capital value of pension rights acquired under the national pension scheme and intended to be transferred into the European Union pension scheme, account is not to be taken of the period during which the official had already participated in that scheme.

Further, in INPS and Repubblica italiana,[97] the request for a preliminary ruling concerns the interpretation of Article 4(3) TEU, Articles 45 and 48 TFEU, Article 11 of Annex VIII to the Staff Regulations of Officials of the European Union ('the Staff Regulations') and Article 8 of Annex IIIa to the Decision of the European Central Bank (ECB) of 9 June 1998 on the adoption of the Conditions of Employment for Staff of the European Central Bank, as amended on 31 March 1999 (OJ 1999 L 125, p. 32). The request has been made in proceedings between, on the one hand, WP and, on the other hand, the Istituto nazionale della previdenza sociale (National Social Security Institute, Italy) ('the INPS') and the Repubblica italiana (Italian Republic) concerning the transfer to the European Central Bank (ECB) pension scheme of the actuarial equivalent corresponding to the pension rights accrued to the applicant in the main proceedings under the INPS Fondo pensioni Lavoratori Dipendenti (Employee Pension Fund). WP has been a member of the staff of the ECB since 1 March 2012. Between 1 August 1982 and 24 February 2012, when he was an employee working in the private sector in Italy, compulsory contributions were paid into the INPS Employee Pension Fund on his behalf. On 12 December 2016, WP applied to the INPS for the transfer, to the ECB pension scheme, of the actuarial equivalent corresponding to the pension rights that he had acquired with the INPS Employee Pension Fund or, in the alternative, the updated capital value resulting from the pension contributions paid to that pension fund, both calculated on the basis of the rules governing pension payments under that fund.

The INPS refused WP's request on the ground that it was not possible to carry out the transfer requested in the absence of a specific legislative measure or of a bilateral agreement between the ECB and the Italian Republic. On 28 November 2017, WP lodged an administrative appeal against the rejection of his application, which was declared inadmissible by decision of 11 April 2018. By application lodged before the Tribunale ordinario di Asti (District Court, Asti, Italy), the referring court, WP essentially sought, primarily, a declaration that the INPS and/or the Italian Republic were required to take all the measures necessary for the purposes of the transfer to the ECB pension scheme of the actuarial equivalent, calculated on the basis of the rules governing pension payments under the INPS employee pension fund, corresponding to the pension entitlements he had acquired as at the date of submission of the request, and an order that the INPS and/or the Italian Republic were to take all the measures necessary for the purposes of that transfer. In the alternative, WP sought a finding and declaration that the INPS and/or the Italian Republic were required to transfer to the ECB pension scheme the actuarial equivalent corresponding to the pension rights he had acquired with the INPS Employee Pension Fund, as compensation for the loss suffered, and that the INPS and/or the Italian Republic should

[97] Judgement of 22.12.2022, INPS and Repubblica italiana, case C-404/21, ECLI:EU:C:2022:1023.

consequently be ordered to transfer to the ECB pension scheme the amount corresponding to that equivalent, as compensation for the loss suffered.

According to the Court (para. 47), the fact that it is not possible to transfer, to the pension scheme of an EU institution, those pension rights acquired under the pension scheme of a Member State might make the recruitment, by that institution, of staff members with a certain length of service from that Member State more difficult, since the movement of the person concerned to the service of that institution could, in the absence of such transfer, entail the loss, for that person, in whole or in part, of the pension rights to which he or she would have been entitled had he or she not accepted employment with an EU institution.[98] Furthermore, as the Advocate General notes in point 63 of his Opinion, almost all Member States of the Economic and Monetary Union have—in some cases, long since—concluded agreements with the ECB to allow the transfer, to the latter's pension scheme, of pension rights acquired by ECB staff members under their national schemes (para. 48). In such a situation, as the Advocate General notes, in essence, in point 58 of his Opinion, ECB staff members who have acquired pension rights under the scheme of a Member State which has not yet entered into such an agreement with the ECB are, without apparent justification, in a less favourable situation than their colleagues who are nationals of Member States which have entered into such an agreement with the ECB, which would be such as to result in unequal treatment and thus to be detrimental to the proper functioning of that institution (para. 49). It should be observed, in the present case, that in so far as concerns the transfer to the ECB pension scheme of pension rights which ECB employees have acquired from a social security institution of a Member State, the ECB has expressed an interest in concluding agreements specifically providing for such transfer (para. 50).

Hence, the Court concluded that Articles 45 and 48 TFEU, Article 11(2) of Annex VIII to the Staff Regulations and Article 8(a) of Annex IIIa to the Decision of the European Central Bank of 9 June 1998 on the adoption of the Conditions of Employment for Staff of the European Central Bank as amended on 31 March 1999, must be interpreted as not precluding, in the absence of an agreement between the European Central Bank (ECB) and the Member State concerned, legislation or an administrative practice of that Member State which does not allow an ECB staff member to transfer, to the ECB pension scheme, an amount corresponding to the pension rights he or she has acquired under the pension scheme of that Member State. However, Article 4(3) TEU requires, in accordance with the principle of sincere cooperation enshrined in that provision, that a Member State to which the conclusion of an agreement is proposed by the ECB, pursuant to Article 8(a) of Annex IIIa, on the transfer, to the ECB pension scheme, of pension rights acquired by its staff members under the pension scheme of that Member State, must

[98] See, to that effect, judgment of 20 October 1981, *Commission* v *Belgium*, 137/80, EU:C:1981:237, paragraph 19, and of 4 February 2021, *Ministre de la Transition écologique et solidaire et Ministre de l'Action et des Comptes publics*, C-903/19, EU:C:2021:95, paragraph 34 and the case-law cited.

participate actively and in good faith in negotiations with the ECB with a view to entering into an agreement with the latter following the opening of negotiations. EU law must be interpreted as not authorising a court of a Member State seised by a European Central Bank (ECB) staff member to order the transfer to the ECB pension scheme of pension rights acquired by the person concerned under the pension scheme of that Member State, in the absence of a provision of national law or an agreement between the Member State concerned and the ECB providing for such a transfer. However, where, owing to the breach, by that Member State, of its obligation, arising from the principle of sincere cooperation enshrined in Article 4(3) TEU, to participate actively and in good faith in negotiations with the ECB with a view to concluding an agreement on the transfer of pension rights, that ECB staff member is unable to have the pension rights which he or she has acquired under the pension scheme of that Member State transferred to the ECB pension scheme, that provision requires that such a national court take all the measures provided by national procedural rules so as to ensure that that obligation is fulfilled by the competent national authority.

5.6 Additional Ideas

As can be concluded, a pension right should be clearly identifiable and defined regardless the methods selected for its determination and definition. Along the same lines, we end up with some proposals regarding how coordination rules can be formed in order to use any "presence" of a migrant worker in each scheme depending on its nature and in combination with the potentially different nature of other schemes.

In case of a cross-border movement and affiliation to several pay-as-you-go schemes and a single funded scheme, the pay-as-you-go schemes may aggregate the periods within the meaning of actual time periods of affiliation of a person to the funded scheme solely for the purposes of vesting a pension right. The funded scheme should provide the pension to which the party concerned is entitled to and when they are entitled to it, in accordance with their national legislation based on the amount of contributions paid for that time period; they will thus receive the pension at a later date. This presupposes recognising the option for early leavers to "leave their rights" in that scheme when moving to another scheme, i.e. what the Directive refers to as preservation of dormant pension rights. In a different case, the funded scheme should recognise the option for transferring pension rights using such methods that the amount to be transferred represents in essence the pension rights acquired with respect to their earlier activities of the migrant worker.

Basically, these methods relate to the withdrawal or the cashing out of pension rights, the value of which may be transferred to the new scheme of the worker. Since the principle of capitalisation is inherent in the ownership of the individual pension account and an individual share is reserved for each insured, each insured may have claims on it. Otherwise, the funded scheme should offer the option of returning the capital at any time during the term of the insurance relation, as well as the option for the insured person to choose to commit their contributions for the purposes of a specific investment program; in this case, however, they should be aware that will not be able to withdraw the capital allocated to them at any time they wish to leave. Funded schemes should therefore be formalised in a similar institutional framework that will offer options to the worker, which will be based on a closer link between contributions and benefits and which will aim to the protection against any loss of their rights. Moreover, as already seen, Member States have the power to organise their social security schemes; however, the consistency of the calculation method with European Union law can be called into question, as the legislation of a specific Member State is likely to constitute a barrier to the free movement of workers guaranteed by Article 45 TFEU.[99] Member States may provide for different methods of transferring capital, the aim being to provide methods for such transfer.

Assuming, however, that the worker transfers from a funded to a pay-as-you-go scheme, the question is whether it would be possible for the pay-as-you-go schemes to provide for the option for the worker to pay this capital value as additional contributions in view of the future increase in their pension at a rate to be determined proportionally by these States according to the conditions prevailing therein (replacement rates, wages) and their own method for calculating the pension. This is the opposite case than the one presented before the Court in Casta, namely not the transfer of capital from a pay-as-you-go, but the transfer of capital to a pay-as-you-go scheme.

Between several funded schemes and a pay-as-you-go scheme, provision should be made for the transfer of the capital-value of the pension between funded schemes, exactly as provided within Member States in their national internal schemes operating on the principle of the capitalisation. Provided that the party concerned transferred each time the capital/value of their pension schemes from the funded scheme they were leaving to the next funded scheme, they should be able to receive a pension from the pension scheme to which they were last affiliated in accordance with its legislation. If the migrant worker chose to "leave their rights" in each of the funded schemes they were leaving, they will receive a pension from each funded scheme in accordance with its legislation as soon as the retirement conditions are met in each of them.

The pay-as-you-go scheme will provide the pension that corresponds to the periods of affiliation to said scheme, in respect to the total duration of the years they were insured in all the schemes. Similarly, the same applies among several funded schemes and several pay-as-you-go schemes, with each of the pay-as-you-go schemes providing the amount corresponding to the periods under that scheme, taking into account the entire career/periods of insurance in all the schemes.

More specifically, emphasis should be put on the cases where a pay-as-you-go scheme is placed between funded schemes: funded—pay-as-you-go—funded scheme. In this case, if the migrant worker chooses to "leave their rights" in the

[99] Časta, paragraph 36.

funded scheme that they are leaving, there is no problem. If they wish to transfer their rights, there is the question, as mentioned before, if a capital transfer can apply to a pay-as-you-go scheme. Subsequently, during the transfer from a pay-as-you-go to a funded scheme, the question is whether the methods of transfer of pension rights from a pay-as-you-go to a funded scheme, such as the actuarial equivalent or the flat-rate redemption value, could be applied (Casta case). Otherwise the explained provision should be made for the transfer of capital from a pay-as-you-go scheme. If, however, this is accepted, the procedure shall include the options recognised under the applicable schemes.

Between funded and notional capitalisation schemes, provision should be made for the transfer of resources or notional resources between these schemes and the party concerned shall receive pension from the scheme to which they were last affiliated to under the principle of capitalisation and the pension shall be calculated under the legislation of such scheme. Otherwise, they should be able to redeem their rights from each scheme they leave. If therefore the principle of capitalisation is applied to a scheme, such scheme should be regarded as a funded scheme.

Between mixed or hybrid schemes, if the principle of capitalisation is identified, then once again provision should be made for the transfer of shares or notional shares in case of a transition from a mixed scheme to another or from a mixed scheme to a funded scheme or notional capitalisation scheme in respect of the funded part of a mixed scheme. However, the methods put forward by the Court in Casta could also prove to be useful for the transfer of pension rights of the pay-as-you-go part of the scheme. If the person concerned also transferred to pay-as-you-go schemes, they follow the usual procedure using the time in the other schemes for the entitlement and calculating their own amount.

What is implicit in each case is the option in the national funded schemes to take into account the accrued capital at any given time, as it may be possible, for example, for this scheme to provide for the blocking and investment of the capital for a certain period of time, which has not lapsed when the party concerned left said scheme. It should be possible therefore to be able to take into account the amount at the time of leaving such a scheme to move to another. Moreover, the time periods may not be important for the calculation of the benefit from a funded scheme, but they may be important for entitlement to a pension right to such a benefit, taking into account that even funded schemes require the completion of a minimum vesting period and a minimum age limit for the accrued pension rights to be considered as vested.

Thus, the critical element that gives rise to the need for coordination is the utilisation of insurance periods in any scheme via the principle of equal treatment and the aggregation for the completion of the minimum period that may be required even in funded schemes for the entitlement to a pension right.

It is understood that the Court cannot continue to question whether there is a restriction of rights solely on the basis of the national legislation in a combined application of the principle of the free movement of workers and equal treatment, through the comparison of the pension amount between migrant and non-migrant workers or national and foreigners; because the various national provisions in the field of pensions are characterised by widely differing features and a high degree of complexity.[100] This cluster of principles should take on a different meaning: to be applied in order to find out whether the same options provided by the national schemes in the context of internal movement or retirement from that scheme are also provided in the context of cross-border movement and retirement from one scheme in order to transfer to another scheme in another State. It is our opinion that the equal or higher status of the migrant[101] or the principle of favour as a general principle should be viewed in light of the provision on methods for securing the pension rights of those wishing to move, even in cases where such methods might not be provided for at a national level.

Furthermore, the cluster of the above combined principles requires taking advantage of the periods of insurance in every Member State by any Member State, regardless of the form of their national social security schemes. Moreover, periods of insurance may not be used for the calculation of the benefit (Article 52 (1) (b) (ii) of Regulation No 883/2004 and Article 52 (4) of Regulation No 883/04) even in type A invalidity schemes where the invalidity benefit amount is independent from the duration of the periods or in pension schemes, where the amount of the benefit is independent from the duration of the insurance periods (Article 44 of Regulation No 883/04) and the independent benefit is greater than the pro-rata benefit, as well as in funded schemes (Article 52 (5) of Regulation No 883/04); they may be used however for the purposes of entitlement to a pension right. Periods may therefore be used in other Member States.

Taking into account the necessity of preserving pension rights in respect of the movement from one funded supplementary defined-contribution scheme of one State to that of another Member State, it is understood that, as per the Directive on supplementary pensions, there is a necessity for regulating basic pension rights, when there is a movement between States where their basic pension schemes operate under the principle of capitalisation; supplementary pension rights also need to be regulated as they constitute a complementary protection to the basic protection. Thus, it is recommended that provisions-options as those suggested above should be introduced in Regulation No 883/04. In view, however, of our analysis in a previous section on the relation between the Regulation and the Directive, the importance of the necessity to adjust the Regulation can be highlighted, taking into account the integration of the French supplementary pension schemes into the scope of the Regulation, which constituted the best way to protect them from the application of European competition law.[102]

---

[100] Commission v Luxembourg, paragraph 21.

[101] Rennuy (2011), p. 316.

[102] OSE (2011), p. 138.

References

Anagnostou-Dedouli A (2005) Social security by legal persons governed by public or private law. Ant. N. Sakkoulas Publishing, Athens-Komotini

Andrietti V (2000) Portability of Supplementary Pension Rights in the European Union, January 28, 2000, research funded by a grant of the European Commission, TMR Programme, Access to Large Scale Facilities, and hosted by IRISS-C/I at CEPS/INSTEAD (Luxembourg), p 2

Andrietti V (2001) Occupational pensions and interim job mobility in the European Union. Evidence from The ECHP Survey May 14, 2001, p 3, https://legacy.iza.org/de/calls_conferences/pensionref_pdf/andrietti.pdf. Accessed 25 Nov 2024

Barr N, Diamond P (2008) Reforming pensions, principles and policy choices. Oxford University Press, Oxford – New York

Barthélémy J (2002) Epargne-retraite ou épargne et retraite. Droit social: 731

Broadbent J, Palumbo M, Woodman E (2006) The shift from defined benefit to defined contribution pension plans -implications for asset allocation and risk management, Prepared for a Working Group on Institutional Investors, Global Savings and Asset Allocation established by the Committee on the Global Financial System, December 2006, p 7. http://www.bis.org. Accessed 25 Nov 2024

Burtless G (2007) Social security privatization and financial market risk. In: Ihori T, Tachibanaki T (eds) Social security reform in advanced countries. Routledge, London and New York

Commission of the European Communities (1997) Supplementary pensions in the Single Market: A Green Paper COM(97)283 final, p 3

Donders P (2004) Implementation of Regulation 1408/71-preparations by new Member States. In Co-ordination of Social Security in an Enlarged Europe- Now and Tomorrow: a Report of the EU Conference on Social Security, Budapest', Hungary 7–8 May 2004, p 44

Economic and Social Committee (1991) Communication from the Commission to the Council, Supplementary social security schemes: the role of occupational pension schemes in the social protection of workers and their implications for freedom of movement. SEC (91) 1332, p 1, footnote 1

Eichenhofer E (1999) Reform des Europäischen Sozialrechts. In: Schulte B, Barwig K (eds) Freizügigkeit und Sozialrecht. Nomos-Verlag, Baden Baden, p 411

Eichenhofer E (2000) How to simplify the co-ordination of social security. Eur J Soc Secur 2/3:234

Commission of the European Communities (2001) Communication from the Commission to the Council, the European Parliament and the Economic and Social Committee, The elimination of tax obstacles to the cross-border provision of occupational pensions, 19.4.2001 COM (2001), pp 18–19

Proposal for a Regulation of the European Parliament and of the Council amending Regulation (EC) No 883/2004 on the coordination of social security systems, and determining the content of Annex XI, COM (2006)7 final, 24 January 2006

Regulation (EC) No 988/2009 of the European Parliament and of the Council of 16 September 2009 amending Regulation (EC) No 883/2004 on the coordination of social security systems and determining the context of its Annexes, OJ L 284/43, 30.10.2009

European Commission (2015) European Commission Directorate-General for Economic and Financial Affairs The 2015 Ageing Report Economic and budgetary projections for the 28 EU Member States (2013-2060), EUROPEAN ECONOMY 3|2015, Luxembourg: Publications Office of the European Union, p 55

European Commission (2024a) Employment, Social Affairs & Inclusion, Your rights country by country, Latvia, Old-age pension https://ec.europa.eu/social/main.jsp?catId=1117&langId=en&intPageId=4638. Accessed 25 Nov 2024

European Commission (2024b) Employment, Social Affairs & Inclusion, Your rights country by country http://ec.europa.eu/social/main.jsp?catId=858. Accessed 25 Nov 2024

European Commission (2024c) European Commission, Employment, Social Affairs & Inclusion, Your rights country by country, Your social security rights in Bulgaria, updated in 2024 https://

ec.europa.eu/social/main.jsp?catId=1103&langId=en Pensions https://ec.europa.eu/social/main.jsp?catId=1103&langId=en&intPageId=4437. Accessed 25 Nov 2024

European Commission (2024d) Employment, Social Affairs & Inclusion, Your rights country by country, Austria, Old-age pension https://ec.europa.eu/social/main.jsp?catId=1101&langId=en&intPageId=4407. Accessed 25 Nov 2024

European Commission (2024e) European Commission, Employment, Social Affairs & Inclusion, Flexicurity http://ec.europa.eu/social/main.jsp?catId=102. Accessed 25 Nov 2024

Galazoulas T, Tsetoura A (2014) Social Security Administration confronting sustainability challenges – the Greek Pension System from a comparative perspective. Eur J Soc Secur 16(2):140 sub

Holzmann R (2003) Toward a coordinated pension system in Europe: rationale and potential structure. Revised study prepared for the joint Watson Wyatt & Deutsches Institut fuer Wirtschaftsforschung (WW-DIW) Lecture on Issues in Pension Reform, Berlin, September 26, 2003, and the NDC Conference in Sandhamm, Sweden, September 28–30, 2003

Jorens Y, Lhernould J-P (2011) trESS European report 2011, Organisation and coordination of a network on the co-ordination of social security schemes within the European Union Lot 1: Expertise in social security coordination Project DG EMPL/E/3 - VC/2010/0436, p 15

Leppik L (2006) Co-ordination of pensions in the European Union: the case of Mandatory Defined-Contribution Schemes in the Central and Eastern European Countries. Eur J Soc Secur 8:45, footnote no 18

OSE (2011) – European Social Observatory deliverable – Authors: Ghailani D, Guardiancich I, Natali D, Ferrera M and Jessula M, Scope of the coordination system in the pension field- Final report, Tender VT/2010/104, p 19

Pieters D (1997) Towards a radical simplification of social security co-ordination. In: Schouckens P (ed) Prospects of social security co-ordination. Acco, Leuven, p 177

Pieters D, Van Steenkiste S (1993) The thirteenth state, towards a European Community social insurance scheme for intra-community migrants. Acco, Leuven

Rennuy N (2011) Assimilation, territoriality and reverse discrimination. Eur J Soc Law 316

Spiegel B (2009) Coordination of new benefits. In: European Commission – responsible editor Jorens Y, 50 years of Social Security Coordination, Past – Present- Future, Report of the conference celebrating the 50th Anniversary of the European Coordination of Social Security, Prague, 7&8 May 2009, p 207

Spiegel B (2010) Section 16 of the Ibero-American Agreement, European Analysis of Member States' Bilateral Agreements on Social Security with Third Countries, Ordered by the European Commission Employment, Social Affairs and Equal Opportunities DG Contract ref. no. VC/2010/0646, December 2010, p 46

Spraos G, Tinios P (1998) Pay-as-you-go and funded schemes: impressions and substance. Economic and Statistical Bulletin of the National Bank of Greece 10:2

Stergiou A (2004) Occupational insurance funds as private social security institutions. In: Amitsis G, Lixouriotis I, Petroglou P (eds) Occupational insurance schemes and labour law issues regarding private group insurance. Ant. N. Sakkoulas Publishing, Athens-Komotini, p 10

Stergiou A (2009) Public Private Partnership in public pension schemes (Market infiltration into the State). Reprinted from the Labour Law Review 68:19–20

Verschueren H (2009) Regulation 883/2004 and invalidity and old-age pensions. Eur J Soc Secur 11(1–2):160

Part III
Pension Loss

Chapter 6
Anti-overlapping and the Case-Law

6.1 Overlapping Through the Case-Law

According to the relevant theory, the Community legislature did not want to grant via the Regulation to the migrant worker an infinitely favourable position compared to national law.[1] Due to differences in the systems, the Coordination Regulation constitutes a compensation for possible loss of entitlement or lack of social security protection that could also result in a protection surplus. The "surplus" may consist of a higher amount of benefits for which the concerned person does not actually satisfy the conditions; such a case is due to a double calculation of the same insurance periods or to an overlapping of benefits when the conditions for various types of benefits are satisfied in more than one Member States. It should also be noted that Member States are laying down national rules against the overlapping of benefits within their territories, which reveals that the constraints imposed by the Coordination Regulation for the purpose of preventing foreign overlapping resulting from its implementation are a continuation of the choices of national social security systems.

Thus, when implementing national clauses against the overlapping of pensions acquired under their law, Member States have the right to take into account any benefits acquired under the law of another Member State.[2] The Court's case-law sometimes refers to national rules against the overlapping of benefits[3] or rules restricting the apportioned benefits,[4] rules against overlapping benefits[5] or

[1] Runft (1991), p. 151.

[2] Cornelissen (1998), p. 697.

[3] Judgment of the Court of 13.10.1977, Case 22/77, Mura, European Court Reports 1977 01699 ECLI:EU:C:1977:154, paragraph 16.

[4] Judgment of the Court of 13.10.1977, Case 22/77, Mura, European Court Reports 1977 01699 ECLI:EU:C:1977:154.

[5] Judgment of the Court of 05.05.1983, Case 238/81, Van der Bunt – Craig, European Court Reports 1983 01385 Spanish 1983/00349 ECLI:EU:C:1983:124, paragraph 15.

A. Tsetoura, *Pension Rights and Free Movement of Persons*,
https://doi.org/10.1007/978-3-031-91127-9_6

provisions for reduction of benefit,[6] while in other instances it refers to an improper plurality of benefits or an unjustified advantage[7] or an unjustified cumulation.[8]

The Court explicitly refers to the so-called **national rules against the overlapping of benefits** in the **Mura** case,[9] while it refers to the so-called **rules against overlapping benefits** in the **Van der Bunt – Craig**[10] case. Thus, a potential advantage that cannot be justified as a result of the combined implementation of a national provision and a provision of the Coordination Regulation is deemed unjustified or the overlapping which results in said advantage is deemed unjustified (or improper).

Already under Regulation No 3, the Court had clarified that Article 11 (2) of Regulation No 3 covers all national legislative provisions for reduction or suspension of benefit intended to prevent overlapping, without distinction as to whether the provisions concern the entitlement to benefit or the provision thereof.[11] According to the Court, a provision of national law intended to prohibit the simultaneous receipt of both sickness benefit and benefit on account of incapacity constitutes a provision for suspension or reduction within the meaning of the above Article; indeed, it is for the national judge to decide whether such a risk of overlapping exists on a case by case basis.[12]

To begin with, already under Regulation No 3, the Court had made reference to **improper plurality,** while also referring to the concept of **unjustified advantage,** which was also reiterated in subsequent judgments. More specifically, in the **de Moor**[13] case, the Court had provided a negative definition on the meaning of improper plurality or unjustified advantage; these concepts appear to be identical in the grounds for the judgment and they are combined with the specific goal of guaranteeing an apportionment of obligations among institutions liable to pay benefits. The question raised by the Supreme Court of Luxembourg in the context of a national system of insurance periods conferring the right to a pension after payment of contributions for a considerable time deals with any effect on the worker's rights of insurance periods completed in three Member States leading first to the acquisition of a right to pension in Luxembourg solely under its national

[6] Judgment of the Court of 04.06.1985, Case 58/84, Romano, European Court Reports 1985 01679 ECLI:EU:C:1985:232.

[7] Judgment of the Court of 05.07.1967, Case 2/67, de Moor, European Court Reports 1967 00255; of 13.12.1967, Case 12/67, Guissart, European Court Reports 1967 00551 ECLI:EU:C:1967:55.

[8] Judgment of the Court of 25.11.1975, Case 50/75, Massonet, European Court Reports 1975 01473 ECLI:EU:C:1975:159.

[9] Judgment of the Court of 13.10.1977, Case 22/77, Mura, European Court Reports 1977 01699 ECLI:EU:C:1977:154, paragraph 16.

[10] Judgment of the Court of 05.05.1983, Case 238/81, Van der Bunt – Craig, European Court Reports 1983 01385 Spanish 1983/00349 ECLI:EU:C:1983:124, paragraph 15.

[11] Judgment of the Court of 15.05.1974, Case 184/73, Kaufmann, European Court Reports 1974 00517ECLI:EU:C:1974:53, paragraph 4.

[12] Cited above, Kaufmann judgment, paragraphs 5–6.

[13] Judgment of the Court of 05.07.1967, Case 2/67, de Moor, European Court Reports 1967 00255.

law, secondly to the acquisition of a right to a pension in Belgium solely under its national law, payable only upon ceasing to be gainfully employed and finally to the acquisition of a right to a pension in Germany as the result of aggregating insurance periods as provided by Article 27 of Regulation No 3. Article 28 (1) of Regulation No 3, which the Court was asked to interpret, provided for the determination by the method of apportionment (subparagraph b) of the "benefits which may be claimed by an insured person covered by Article 27 or his survivors".

Regulation No 3 did not provide for a common system of social security giving the beneficiary a single entitlement based on a simple apportionment of such benefits between national institutions, but allowed separate systems to continue, creating separate claims against separate institutions against which the beneficiary has direct rights either under national law alone or national law supplemented, if necessary, by the system of the aggregation of insurance periods provided for by Article 51 of the Treaty.[14] Indeed, the wording of Article 28 creates doubts whether this legislation piece aims at separating apportionment for which it provides from the aggregation of insurance periods upon which it is based and at making it generally applicable. This doubt cannot be resolved by a liberal interpretation which would moreover be incompatible with the framework and bounds of Article 51 of the Treaty.[15]

It is argued that, with the intention of avoiding **an improper plurality of benefits and guaranteeing an apportionment of pension obligations among institutions liable to pay benefits,** Article 28 might be applied in one state where Article 27 is not applicable, whereas it has to be applied in another State. As, however, cumulation of pensions is not prohibited by any provision but is, on the contrary, expressly provided for by Article 11(1) of Regulation No 3, **it does not of itself necessarily amount to an abuse.**[16]

The acquisition of a right to benefit, conferred solely by virtue of the national law of one state and based on contribution periods completed in that state, in addition to another benefit acquired in another state by means of aggregation in a case where, as required by Article 27, the periods of insurance "do not overlap", **does not constitute an advantage to Community law.**[17] The advantage of aggregation is the acquisition of a right to a pension which would not otherwise arise, the pension acquired in this way being calculated in proportion only to the insurance period completed in the Member State in question, without taking into account in the calculation insurance periods completed in other Member States.[18]

In pension schemes based on insurance periods where a right to a pension is acquired after the completion of a minimum contribution period of a substantial length of time, the addition of this benefit to another benefit directly acquired in another Member State solely under its national law and based on insurance periods

[14] de Moor, p. 207 of the English version of the judgment.

[15] de Moor, p. 207 of the English version of the judgment.

[16] de Moor, p. 207 of the English version of the judgment.

[17] de Moor, p. 207 of the English version of the judgment.

[18] de Moor, p. 207 of the English version of the judgment.

completed in that state alone cannot be regarded as an **improper plurality of benefits.**[19] A different interpretation of the provisions in question might result on the one hand in the exclusion of one of those periods by reason of a rule of national law forbidding the simultaneous receipt of both a pension and remuneration for employment and, on the other hand, in allowing the said period to be taken into account in another state, where the right to a pension has been acquired solely under national law, on the ground that aggregation and apportionment were necessary in a third state.[20]

Following this, the Court referred to **unjustified cumulation** in the **Massonet**[21] case, regarding a special benefit granted for a limited time under Luxembourg law without any direct connection with the insurance period completed and a benefit granted under German law for a notional insurance period. As the Court pointed out, the purpose of Article 12 of Regulation No 3, is to avoid any **plurality** or **purposeless overlapping** of contributions and liabilities which would result from the simultaneous or alternate application of several legislative systems (Massonet, paragraph 15). However, despite the relevant provisions of the Regulation, which is designed to settle conflicts of law both positive and negative, it does not authorize a national insurance institution either expressly or by implication to reduce the benefits which are due to a worker under national legislation alone (Massonet, paragraph 16). It is the same as regards Community law in a case where a Member State, as it is entitled to do even if a right to benefit arises without recourse to the procedure of aggregation, takes measures under its own legislation in order to avoid **unjustified cumulation** resulting from the overlapping of insurance periods (Massonet, paragraph 26).

However, according to the Court, if this interpretation is capable of leading in certain cases other than that of a duplication of insurance periods, to an accumulation of pensions, this consequence follows not from the interpretation of Community law but from the system at present in force, which, in the absence of a common social security scheme, rests on a simple coordination of national legislations which have not yet been harmonized (Massonet, paragraph 27). The Court itself has, of course, specifically stated that the methods of aggregation and apportionment cannot lead to a duplication of benefits for one and the same period.[22] It thus referred to cases where insurance periods completed in the State concerned coincide with insurance periods completed in another Member State.[23]

In that regard, it should be noted that the rule for preventing overlapping contained in Article 46 (3) serves the objective mentioned in the eighth recital of

[19] de Moor, p. 207 of the English version of the judgment.

[20] de Moor, p. 554 of the Greek version of the judgment.

[21] Judgment of the Court of 25.11.1975, Case 50/75, Massonet, European Court Reports 1975 01473 ECLI:EU:C:1975:159.

[22] Judgment of the Court of 21.10.1975, Case 24/75, Petroni, European Court Reports 1975 01149 ECLI:EU:C:1975:129, paragraph 16.

[23] Petroni, paragraph 17.

Regulation No 1408/71, and in particular to avoid unjustified overlapping of benefits which could result in particular from the duplication of insurance periods and other periods treated as such.[24] Such are, in particular, cases in which a Member State recognises for an insured person notional insurance periods for a period during which said person has completed an actual insurance period in another member State or cases where notional[25] insurance periods in two Member States[26] coincide.

A case where actual insurance periods coincide arises, for example, where voluntary contributions are paid in a Member State for a period during which the concerned person is compulsorily insured in another member State, as considered by the Court in the **Niemann**[27] case. The preliminary question was raised in the context of an action relating to the determination of the rights with regard to old-age pensions of a German citizen who, having worked successively in the Federal Republic of Germany and in France, completed 437 months' insurance in the first Member State and 138 in the second, and who, in addition, continued to pay voluntary contributions in Germany during the periods in which he worked in France. The Court noted that aggregation is not applied in cases where insurance periods completed in the State concerned coincide with insurance periods completed in another Member State, adding that if the laws of one Member State allow such a double affiliation there are no grounds based on the objectives of Article 51 which make it permissible to refuse to a worker who does not need to have recourse to the Regulation the advantages of the application *in toto* of the laws of that State (paragraph 7).

A similar case was **Guissart.**[28] In order to take advantage of the transitional provisions of Article 11 (1) of the Belgian Law of 12 July 1957 and of the Royal Decree of 30 July 1957—according to which employees who attain the age at which they acquire a right to a pension before 31 December 1961 and who can show evidence of 12 years' insurance during the 15 years prior to the payment of the pension are deemed to have completed a full period of insurance of 45 years in Belgium—Mr Guissart was obliged to have recourse to Luxembourg insurance periods to supplement the 11 years taken into consideration by the Belgian legislation in order to attain the minimum of 12 years required by the transitional provisions referred to above. In this case, the Court focused on **unjustified advantage**. More specifically, the Court noted that at least under those systems based on insurance periods under which the amount of a retirement pension varies in proportion solely

---

[24] Judgment of the Court of 02.08.1993, Case C-31/92, Marius Larsy, European Court Reports 1993 I-04543, ECLI:EU:C:1993:340, paragraph 18; judgment of 17.12.1987, Case 323/86, Collini, European Court Reports 1987 05489 ECLI:EU:C:1987:574, paragraph 12.

[25] See above "Periods of notional contribution payments or periods of recognition of pensionable service".

[26] Runft (1991), p. 152.

[27] Judgment of the Court of 28.05.1974, Case 191/73, Niemann, European Court Reports 1974 00571ECLI:EU:C:1974:58.

[28] Judgment of the Court of 13.12.1967, Case 12/67, Guissart, European Court Reports 1967 00551 ECLI:EU:C:1967:55.

to the insurance periods which have been completed, these provisions do not apply to a migrant worker who does not have to resort to tie aggregation of insurance periods in order to acquire the right to benefit in any of the Member States in which he has completed insurance periods due to the fact that the objective sought by Article 51 is achieved by virtue of national legislation alone.[29]

However, as per the Court's findings, the complexity of the problems posed by the co-ordination of national legislative systems prevents this interpretation from becoming an absolute principle.[30] In certain circumstances, it might lead to the grant of **unjustified advantages** which the national legislature may wish to avoid. This might be the case where, as in this instance, benefits in respect of insurance periods actually completed in one State are payable in relation to one single period at the same time as benefits in respect of notional periods in another Member State.[31] In these circumstances it must be permissible for a State whose legislation provides for notional periods in favour of the insured person to deduct from such periods the periods actually completed in another Member State, without its being possible to consider this procedure as contrary to Article 51 of the Treaty.[32]

As will be demonstrated below, the Court in the Petroni[33] case referred to the results of the rule contained in Article 46(3) of Regulation No 1408/71[34] that could lead to a diminution of rights, by imposing limitations on the overlapping of a retirement pension, acquired by virtue of the fact that the person concerned fulfils independently all the conditions required by national legislation and for a retirement pension, the latter of which is acquired under Article 46 of Regulation No 1408/71, i.e. with the aggregation of the insurance periods for the entitlement to the pension and the apportionment of the amount of the retirement pension.

6.2 Before Petroni

It is argued that the Regulation No 1408/71 drafters introduced Article 46 (3) in the pension chapter (before its amendment with Regulation No 1248/92) as a Community legislation to prevent overlapping of benefits in order replace the various

[29] Guissart v Belgian State, p. 433 of the English version of the judgment.

[30] Guissart, p. 434 of the English version of the judgment.

[31] Guissart, p. 434 of the English version of the judgment.

[32] Guissart, p. 434 of the English version of the judgment.

[33] Judgment of 21.10.1975, case C-24/75, Petroni, European Court Reports 1975, p. 1149.

[34] Article 46 (3) of Regulation No 1408/71 provided: "The person concerned shall be entitled to the total sum of the benefits calculated in accordance with the provisions of paragraphs 1 and 2, *within the limit* of the highest theoretical amount of benefits calculated according to paragraph 2 (a).Where the amount referred to in the preceding sub-paragraph is exceeded, any institution applying paragraph 1 shall adjust its benefit by an amount corresponding to the proportion which the amount of the benefit concerned bears to the total of the benefits determined in accordance with paragraph 1".

national anti-overlapping provisions.[35] However, in the Petroni judgment, the Court declared that provision invalid as a provision against overlapping that is incompatible with Article 51 EEC, as, making use of the case-law on Regulation 3, the Court considered that the objectives of Articles 48–51 of the Treaty could not be served if, as a result of the exercise of the freedom of movement, the workers were deprived of social security benefits guaranteed in any case by the legislation of a single Member State (Petroni principle).[36] In view of the importance of this decision, which has been, and continues to be, a reference point, the critical parts of the Court's judgment are cited; they are also useful for the fuller understanding of the conclusions set out below.

Thus, regarding the relevant Court judgment, questions have been raised within the framework of proceedings between the Belgian institution responsible for the payment of pensions to employed persons, on the one hand, and the successors of a migrant worker, on the other, in relation to the calculation of the retirement pension to which the latter was entitled until the time of his death. **Said worker, who had completed insurance periods in Belgium and in Italy, fulfilled in the first Member State all the conditions required by the national legislation** for entitlement to benefit, which calculated on the basis of that legislation, amounted to BFR 34 358. On the other hand, in order to establish his right to benefit in the second Member State, he had to invoke the provisions of Article 45 of Regulation No 1408/71, and for the calculation of that benefit the periods actually completed in the two Member States were aggregated and the Italian benefit was apportioned. **Taking advantage of the rule limiting the overlapping of benefits provided in different Member States, laid down by Article 46 (3) of Regulation No 1408/71, the Belgian institution reduced the benefit to BFR 26 427.**

That sum represents the theoretical amount of the Belgian benefit, that is to say, the amount which is arrived at if the periods completed in the two Member States had been completed in Belgium, less the Italian benefit calculated after aggregation and apportionment (Petroni, paragraph 6). This method of calculation by the Belgian institution is intended to put into practice a principle according to which the migrant worker is assured of receiving in total, by virtue of the various pensions granted to him by the various Member States, an amount equal to the highest benefit that he would have obtained if he had spent his whole working life subject to the legislation of one or other of the Member States concerned (Petroni, paragraph 7). According to the same principle that amount represents the maximum that he may receive in total by virtue of those various pensions (Petroni, paragraph 8). The questions referred by the national court ask whether this rule, to the extent to which it constitutes a limitation on overlapping, must be applied in cases such as the present, and, if so, whether it must therefore be regarded as being incompatible with Article 51 of the Treaty (Petroni, paragraph 9).

---

[35] Cornelissen (2009), p. 16.

[36] Ibid.

According to the Court, these questions ask whether Article 46(3) of Regulation No 1408/71 is in conformity with Article 51 of the Treaty and, if so, whether is must be applied to the pension granted to a migrant worker on the basis of insurance periods not duplicated by any of the periods used as the basis for calculating the pension granted in other countries of the Community (Petroni, paragraph 10).

More specifically, it must be noted that **Article 46(3) of Regulation No 1408/71, as in force at the time of the Petroni judgment, had a different form.** More specifically, as mentioned in the Advocate-General's opinion in the context of the Petroni case, **Article 46(3) of Regulation No 1408/71 provided: "The person concerned shall be entitled to the total sum of the benefits calculated in accordance with the provisions of paragraphs 1 and 2, *within the limit* of the highest theoretical amount** of benefits calculated according to paragraph 2(a). **Where the amount referred to in the preceding subparagraph is exceeded, any institution applying paragraph 1 shall adjust its benefit** by an amount corresponding to the proportion which the amount of the benefit concerned bears to the total of the benefits determined in accordance with paragraph 1".[37,38]

In his opinion the Advocate-General also refers to the seventh and eighth recitals of Regulation 1408/71. Thus, according to these recitals: "in order to avoid unjustified overlapping of benefits, which could result in particular from the duplication of insurance periods and other periods treated as such, it is necessary to limit the benefits to the greatest amount which would have been due to a worker from one of these States, if he had spent all his working life there".[39,40] According to the Advocate-General, "the purpose of Article 46(3), or at all events, one of its purposes, is to limit the total amount of old age pension receivable by a person who has been subject to the social security legislation of two or more Member States, to the amount he could have claimed if all the insurance periods completed by him under the legislations of those Member States had been completed in the Member State whose legislation would have afforded him the highest pension".[41]

Additionally, the Advocate-General stressed that in a situation where a person is entitled to a pension under the legislation of a Member State taken alone and can derive no benefit in that State from the application to him of any provision of Community law (which is the situation in which Signor Petroni found himself in Belgium), Article 46 (3) of Regulation No 1408/71 can have no application.[42] In the

---

[37] OJ, English special edition, Series I Volume 1971(II), pp. 416–463.

[38] Opinion of Mr Advocate-General Jean-Pierre Warner of 25 September 1975, Case 24/75, p. 1165 (English version).

[39] Seventh and eight recitals of Regulation 1408/71, OJ, English special edition, Series I Volume 1971(II), pp. 416–463.

[40] Opinion of Mr Advocate-General Jean-Pierre Warner of 25 September 1975, Case 24/75, p. 1165 (English version).

[41] Opinion of Mr Advocate-General Jean-Pierre Warner of 25 September 1975, Case 24/75, p. 1165 (English version).

[42] Opinion of Mr Advocate-General Jean-Pierre Warner of 25 September 1975, Case 24/75, p. 1166 (1) (English version).

situation where a person is entitled to a pension under the legislation of a Member State taken alone, but to an improved pension if the processes of aggregation and apportionment provided for by Community law are applied to his case, Article 46 (3) can be applied quoad the amount by which the improved pension exceeds the amount of the purely national pension.[43] In the situation in which a person is entitled to a pension in a Member State only thanks to the intervention of Community law (which was Signor Petroni's situation in Italy), it was open to the Council to provide that such pension should be reduced in so far as its payment would make that person's total pension rights exceed his highest "theoretical amount of benefit".[44] As a result, the Advocate-General was of the opinion that **Article 46(3) of Regulation No 1408/71 is invalid in so far as it provides for a reduction in the amount of old-age pension to which a person is entitled in a Member State, independently of Community law**.[45]

As the Court stressed, Article 51 of the Treaty (now Article 48 TFEU) deals essentially with the case in which the laws of one Member State do not by themselves allow the person concerned the right to benefits by reason of the insufficient number of periods completed under its laws, or only allow him benefits which are less than the maximum (Petroni, paragraph 14). To remedy this situation, said article provides, in respect of a worker who has been successively or alternately subject to the laws of two or more Member States, for aggregation of the insurance periods completed under the laws of each of such States (Petroni, paragraph 15).

The aggregation and apportionment cannot therefore be carried our if their effect is to diminish the benefits which the person concerned may claim by virtue of the laws of a single Member State, on the basis solely of the insurance periods completed under those laws, always provided that this method cannot lead to a duplication of benefits for one and the same period (Petroni, paragraph 16). **Aggregation is not applied even in cases where insurance periods completed in the State concerned coincide with insurance periods completed in another Member State** (Petroni, paragraph 17).

That interpretation is expressly confirmed by Article 45 of Regulation No 1408/71, according to which an institution of a Member State whose legislation makes the acquisition, retention or recovery of the right to benefits conditional upon the completion of periods of insurance or of residence shall take into account periods of insurance or of residence completed in other Member States only "to the extent necessary" (Petroni, paragraph 18). Thus, a limitation on the overlapping of benefits which would lead to a diminution of the rights which the persons concerned already enjoy in a Member State by virtue of the application of the national legislation alone is incompatible with Article 51 (Petroni, paragraph 21).

---

[43] Opinion of Mr Advocate-General Jean-Pierre Warner of 25 September 1975, Case 24/75, p. 1167 (2) (English version).

[44] Opinion of Mr Advocate-General Jean-Pierre Warner of 25 September 1975, Case 24/75, p. 1167 (3) (English version).

[45] Opinion of Mr Advocate-General Jean-Pierre Warner of 25 September 1975, Case 24/75, p. 1168 (English version).

The Court, therefore, concluded that **Article 46 (3) of Regulation No 1408/71 is incompatible with Article 51 of the Treaty to the extent** to which it imposes a limitation on the overlapping of the two benefits acquired in different Member States by a reduction in the amount of the benefit acquired under national legislation alone (Petroni, paragraph 22).

6.3 After Petroni

6.3.1 General Reaffirmation of the Petroni Judgment

The consequence of the Petroni judgment was that Article 46(3) of Regulation No 1408/71, having been declared invalid, to the extent that it affected rights acquired under national legislation alone, could no longer preclude the application of national rules against overlapping which were aimed at reducing overlapping with foreign benefits of the same nature, as was confirmed in the Greco case.[46,47] The Court referred to the case-law it first established in the Petroni case and other subsequent cases, either expressly invoking that judgment[48] or implicitly (**Manzoni**), reiterating its judgment on the incompatibility of Article 46(3) of Regulation No 1408/71 with Article 51 of the Treaty.[49] In the Manzoni case, of course, the Court referred to the rule in Article 46(3) of Regulation No 1408/71 (before the amendment with Regulation No 1248/1992)[50] setting a ceiling as a rule of restricting the amount of the apportioned benefits.[51]

[46] Judgment of the Court of 13.10.1977, Case 37/77, Greco, European Court Reports 1977 01711 ECLI:EU:C:1977:155.

[47] Pennings (2015b), p. 222.

[48] Judgment of the Court of 13.03.1986, Case 296/84, Sinatra, European Court Reports 1986 01047 ECLI:EU:C:1986:121, paragraph 13. However, the conclusion reached by the Court in the Sinatra case did not relate to the incompatibility of Article 46(3) of Regulation No 1408/71; it rather relied on the judgment to conclude that, notwithstanding Article 46, national legislation shall apply, provided that it is more favourable. On the contrary, the Court has applied, as it will be shown below, the provision on reduction of Article 46(3) of Regulation No 1408/71.

[49] Judgment of the Court of 13.10.1977, Case 112/76, Manzoni, European Court Reports 1977 01647 ECLI:EU:C:1977:152, paragraph 12.

[50] Article 46(3), Regulation 1408/71 provided: "The person concerned shall be entitled to the total sum of the benefits calculated in accordance with the provisions of paragraphs 1 and 2, *within the limit* of the highest theoretical amount of benefits calculated according to paragraph 2 (a).Where the amount referred to in the preceding subparagraph is exceeded, any institution applying paragraph 1 shall adjust its benefit by an amount corresponding to the proportion which the amount of the benefit concerned bears to the total of the benefits determined in accordance with paragraph 1".

[51] Manzoni, paragraph 11.

This case-law principle can be regarded as subsequently reaffirmed in the **Mura** case.[52] More specifically, the question presented before the Court referred to Article 12 of Regulation No 1408/71 authorizing the overlapping of benefits and whether it must take precedence over national rules against overlapping in cases in which the Community provisions result in a migrant worker being placed in a more favourable position than a non-migrant worker (Mura, paragraph 8).

According to the Court, the charge that migrant workers obtain an advantage over workers who have never left their own country cannot be accepted, since no discrimination can arise in legal situations which are not comparable (Mura, paragraph 9). Any differences which may exist to the benefit of migrant workers do not result from the interpretation of Community law but rather from the lack of any common social security system or of any harmonization of the existing national schemes, which cannot be mitigated by the mere co-ordination at present practised (Mura, paragraph 10).

The Court invoked its judgment in the Petroni case, in which it had already accepted that Article 46(3) is incompatible with Article 51 of the Treaty to the extent to which it imposes a limitation on benefits acquired in different Member States by a reduction in the amount of the benefit acquired under national legislation alone (**Mura, paragraph 12**). It follows that the provisions of that paragraph are not applicable where they bring about a reduction in the benefit acquired by virtue of a Member State's legislation alone and that, where is the case, the second sentence of Article 12(2) is inapplicable (Mura, paragraph 13).

The Court therefore concluded that, so long as a worker is receiving a pension by virtue of national legislation alone, the provisions of Regulation No 1408/71 do not prevent the national legislation, including the national rules against the overlapping of benefits, from being applied to him in its entirety, provided that if the application of such national legislation proves less favourable than the application of the rules regarding aggregation and apportionment those rules must, by virtue of Article 46(1) of Regulation No 1408/71, be applied (Mura, paragraph 16). The Court reach the same conclusion in the **Mura II** case.[53] In subsequent judgments, and in particular in the **Schaap**[54] case, the Court held that where, in applying the national rules against the overlapping of benefits, the application in its entirety of such national legislation alone proves less favourable for the worker than the application of the provisions established by the Council with Regulation No 1408/71, the latter provisions must be applied.

It could be argued that the Petroni principle was also reinforced by subsequent case-law findings that did not relate solely to the calculation of pensions.

[52] Judgment of the Court of 13.10.1977, Case 22/77, Mura, European Court Reports 1977 01699 ECLI:EU:C:1977:154, paragraph 12.

[53] Judgment of the Court of 16.05.1979, Case 236/78, Mura, European Court Reports 1979 01819 Greek version 1979:I/00923 Spanish version 1979/00967 ECLI:EU:C:1979:131.

[54] Judgment of the Court of 14.03.1978, Case 98/77, Schaap, European Court Reports 1978 00707 ECLI:EU:C:1978:56.

As the Court clarified in the **Rossi**[55] case, the Community rules could not, in the absence of an express exception consistent with the aims of the Treaty, be applied in such a way as to deprive a migrant worker or his dependents of the benefit of a part of the legislation of a Member State nor as to result in a reduction of benefits acquired under that legislation supplemented by Community law (Rossi, paragraph 14). Additionally, in the **Laterza**[56] case, the Court decided that Regulation No 1408/71, in laying down and developing the rules for coordinating national laws, is in fact guided by the fundamental principle stated in the seventh and eighth recitals of the preamble to the Regulation No 1408/71, that the aforesaid rules must guarantee to workers who move within the Community all the benefits which have accrued to them in the various member States whilst limiting them "to the greatest amount" of such benefits (Laterza, paragraph 8). In accordance with these principles, therefore, the provisions of Regulation No 1408/71 cannot be applied in such a way as to deprive the worker, by substituting the benefits provided by one Member State for the benefits payable by another Member State, of the most favourable benefits.[57]

The guiding principles of Regulation No 1408/71 require, on the other hand, that where, as in the case in question (referring to Article 77(2)(b)(i) of Regulation No 1408/71),the amount of the benefits provided by the Member State in which the worker is residing is less than that of the benefits awarded by the other State responsible for paying them the worker continues to be entitled to the greatest amount and receives from the competent social security institution of this latter Member State a supplement to the benefits equal to the difference between the two amounts.[58]

In that regard, in the **Gravina**[59] case, the Court noted that Regulation No 1408/71, in laying down rules for the co-ordination of the various national laws, is inspired in fact by the fundamental principle that the said rules must guarantee workers moving within the Community the entirety of benefits acquired in the different Member States up to the limit of the greatest amount of those benefits (Gravina, paragraph 7).

[55] Judgment of 06.03.1979, Case 100/78, Rossi, European Court Reports 1979 -00831, p. 844, paragraph 14.

[56] Judgment of 12.06.1980, Case 733/79, Laterza, European Court Reports 1980 01915, p. 1925, paragraph 8.

[57] Cited above, Laterza judgment, paragraph 9.

[58] Laterza, paragraph 9.

[59] Judgment of 09.07.1980, Case 807/79, Gravina, European Court Reports 1980, p. 2218, paragraph 7.

6.3.2 Derogation from the Petroni Judgment: The Universal Principle of Favourability

There have been many pension cases before the Court relating to the overlapping of pension benefits. It must be noted, however, that, **although the case-law following below is subsequent to the Petroni judgment, the Court continues to apply the rule against overlapping in Article 46(3) of Regulation No 1408/71 setting a ceiling (before its amendment)** looking at the same time for the most favourable solution for the migrant worker. Even in the Sinatra case, where the Petroni judgment is expressly invoked, the Court used it to conclude that the application of national legislation is independent from Article 46 of Regulation No 1408/71, provided that it is more favourable to the migrant worker than Article 46 of Regulation No 1408/71. It also stated that the provision on reduction in Article 46(3) of Regulation No 1408/71 had to be applied. The cases cited below are particularly relevant. To sum up the conclusions from the case-law, the application of the principle of favour emerges as a general principle, notwithstanding the approach of the Petroni judgment on the incompatibility of Article 46(3) of Regulation No 1408/71 with the Treaty.

Since the Regulation simply intends to abolish the principle of territoriality in order to ensure that persons crossing national borders will not suffer any disadvantages regarding social security, it is for the Member States to decide whether to take into account facts or circumstances which have occurred in another Member State to avoid the possibility of their national workers suffering disadvantages compared to migrant workers.[60] This is not a task for the Community legislature whose competence is limited by the Regulation's objective, namely to protect migrant workers in terms of social security.[61] On the other hand, the Regulation's objective is to protect migrant workers against the unlimited application of clauses against overlapping of two or more Member States.[62]

In summing up certain conclusions regarding the case-law cited above, the Court initially stressed that, when the worker receives a pension under national legislation alone, the provisions of Regulation No 1408/71 do not preclude the full application of the national legislation, including the national rules prohibiting overlapping.[63]

[60] Cornelissen (1998), p. 697.

[61] Ibid.

[62] Ibid.

[63] Judgments cited above: Judgment of the Court of 2.07.1981, joined cases 116, 117, 119, 120 and 121/80, Celestre, European Court Reports 1981 01737 ECLI:EU:C:1981:159, paragraph 9; Judgment of the Court of 14.03.1978, Case 98/77, Schaap, European Court Reports 1978 00707 ECLI:EU:C:1978:56, paragraph 10; judgment of 05.0.1983, Van der Bunt-Craig, 238/81, European Court Reports 1981, paragraph 15; judgment of 06.10.1987, 197/85, Stefanutti, European Court Reports 1987, p. 3855, paragraph 10; judgment of 13.03.1986, Case 296/84, Sinatra, European Court Reports 1986 01047 ECLI:EU:C:1986:121, paragraph 14; judgment of 13.10.1977, Case 22/77, Mura, European Court Reports 1977 01699 ECLI:EU:C:1977:154, paragraph 16; judgment of 18.04.1989, Case 128/88, Di Felice, European Court Reports 1989 00923 ECLI:EU:C:1989:153,

Otherwise, the **benefit acquired by virtue of national legislation alone and which is more favourable than the benefit acquired by applying Article 46 of Regulation No 1408/71, is due irrespective of that article, by virtue of the national provisions alone.**[64] **If the application of national legislation proves to be less favourable for the worker than the system of Article 46 of Regulation No 1408/71, then the provisions of that article must be applied; that includes Article 46(3)** which aims to limit the overlapping of benefits acquired in accordance with the provisions of paragraphs 1 and 2 of the same article, excluding the rules against overlapping established under national law.[65] Otherwise, Article 46(3) must be applied, excluding the national rules prohibiting overlapping.[66]

It must be pointed out that the **comparison** to be made, for the purposes of Article 46 (1) (2), is between the benefit calculated in accordance with national legislation alone, including the national rules against the overlapping of benefits, and the benefit calculated in accordance with the Community rules laid down in Article 46(2) subject to the application of the rule against overlapping laid down in Article 12 of Regulation No 1408/71 and the rule adopted for putting that provision into effect, namely Article 7 of Regulation No 574/72. If the latter calculation proves to be more f**avourable** to the recipient, that calculation must be applied so that the benefit in question will be determined in accordance with the provisions of Article 46(2) of Regulation No 1408/71.[67]

The competent institution must finally compare the amount of benefits which are due in application of the applicable national law alone, including its anti-overlapping rules, and the amount which would be due in application of Community law in its entirety, including its anti-overlapping rules.[68] If the adjusted amount of the benefit under Article 46(3) sub-paragraph 2 of Regulation No 1408/71 exceeds that resulting from applying only the national legislation in its entirety, including its anti-overlapping rules, the adjusted amount is taken into consideration. On the other hand, if the amount of the benefit due by virtue of the competent institution's national law alone exceeds the adjusted amount, the national amount is taken into consideration.[69]

---

paragraph 9; of 02.08.1993, Case C-31/92, Marius Larsy, European Court Reports 1993 I-04543, ECLI:EU:C:1993:340, paragraph 11; judgment of 11.06.1992, C-90/91 and C-91/91, Di Crescenzo and Casagrande, European Court Reports 1992 I-3851, paragraph 15; Judgement of 18.2.1992, Case C-5/91, Di Prinzio European Court Reports 1992 I-00897 ECLI:EU:C:1992:76, paragraph 16.

[64] Judgments cited above: Sinatra, paragraph 13; Pian, paragraph 8.

[65] Judgments cited above: Celestre, paragraph 9; Schaap, paragraph 10; Mura, paragraph 15; Pian, paragraph 9; Di Felice, paragraph 9; Marius Larsy, paragraph 12; Di Crescenzo and Casagrande, paragraph 16; Di Prinzio, paragraph 17.

[66] Judgments cited above: Van der Bunt-Craig, paragraph 15; Di Felice, 128/88; Pian, paragraph 15; Di Prinzio, paragraph 62.

[67] Cited above, Stefanutti judgment, paragraph 20.

[68] Cited above, Di Prinzio judgment, paragraph 64.

[69] Cited above, Di Prinzio judgment, paragraph 65.

It must also be borne in mind that, according to the eighth recital of Regulation No 1408/71, the ceiling provided for in Article 46(3) is necessary to "avoid unjustified overlapping of benefits which could result in particular from the duplication of insurance periods and other periods treated as such".[70] That recital merely confirms the fact that the rule for preventing the overlapping of benefits contained in Article 46(3) does not apply exclusively to cases in which the ceiling is exceeded because of a duplication of insurance periods.[71] In those circumstances, the anti-overlapping rule in Article 46(3) applies in all cases in which the total sum of the benefits calculated in accordance with Article 46(1) and (2) exceeds the limit of the highest theoretical amount of pension, even if the exceeding of that limit is not due to the duplication of insurance periods.[72]

It is for the national court to give a ruling on the content and interpretation of the provisions of its national legislation on overlapping benefits and to make the necessary comparison in order to determine in each case whether the application of the national rules is less favourable to the worker than the application of the Community provisions as interpreted by the Court. The worker must indeed receive those benefits which are the most favourable.[73] In those circumstances, it must be borne in mind that the Court has held that, where national legislation alone is applied, the classification of the benefits is not governed by Community law.[74] It is therefore for the national court to determine the substance of, and to interpret the provisions of, its national legislation as regards the overlapping of benefits.[75]

More specifically, the Court had applied in combination the old Articles 12 and 46 on pensions, noting that for the application of Community provisions, the following in particular must be taken into account: according to Article **12(2) of Regulation No 1408/71, the provisions of the legislation of a Member State for the reduction, suspension or withdrawal of a benefit in cases of overlapping with other social security benefits acquired in that same Member State or under the legislation of another Member State are not to apply when the person concerned receives benefits of the same kind** in respect of invalidity, old age, death (pensions) or occupational disease which are awarded by the institutions of the different Member States, in accordance in particular with the provisions of Article 46 of said Regulation.[76] An early retirement pension and an invalidity pension are to

[70] Judgments cited above: Collini, paragraph 12; Marius Larsy, paragraph 18.

[71] Cited above, Collini judgment, paragraph 12.

[72] Collini, paragraph 13.

[73] Judgments cited above: Celestre, paragraph 10; Pian, paragraph 10.

[74] Judgments cited above: Stefanutti, paragraphs 16–17; Pian, paragraph 19.

[75] Pian, paragraph 19.

[76] Judgments cited above: Del Grosso, paragraph 21; Pian, paragraphs 11 and 16; Di Felice, paragraph 10; Marius Larsy, paragraph 14.

be regarded as benefits of the same kind within the meaning of Article 12(2) of the Regulation.[77]

Furthermore, as regards the first phrase of that Article 12(2), it is compatible with Article 51 of the Treaty which does not preclude the application of national rules against the overlapping of benefits in case where such benefits are not of the same kind as the benefits in respect of invalidity, old age, death or occupational disease within the meaning of Regulation No 1408/71; where national rules against the overlapping of benefits are applied uniformly to nationals of all Member States without regard to their nationality, there is no discrimination within the meaning of Article 48 of the EEC Treaty.[78] Finally, the amount obtained pursuant to Article 46(1) and (2) of Regulation No 1408/71 must be reduced in accordance with Article 46(3) of that Regulation, which fixes a ceiling for the amount which a worker may receive under Article 46, namely the highest of the theoretical amounts of benefits calculated according to Article 46(2)(a) of the Regulation No 1408/71,to the exclusion of national rules against overlapping.[79]

Following this, it is concluded that the objective of Article 46(3) of Regulation No 1408/71 precludes the application of the anti-overlapping rule of that provision where a person has worked in two Member States during the same period and has had to pay old-age pension contributions in both States during that period.[80] It is therefore for the competent institution to compare the benefits which would be payable solely under national legislation, including its anti-overlapping rules, with those which would be payable under Community law, including the anti-overlapping rule in Article 46(3), and grant the migrant worker the higher of the two amounts.[81]

It should be noted that up to this point, the case-law cited above concerned Regulation No 1408/71 in the form it had before its amendment with Regulation No 1248/92. Thus, Article 46(3) of Regulation No 1408/71 with its clause on a ceiling (before its amendment with Regulation No 1248/1992), did provide to the recipient the sum of benefits they were entitled to from the different Member States in respect of invalidity, old age or death, demonstrating that the overlapping of various retirement pensions, which was possible under the Regulation, is not an unjustified advantage in itself; however, at the same time, it contained a restriction on such an overlapping of benefits, which in principle was allowed the migrant worker could receive from the different Member States in which they were employed benefits, the sum of which could not be higher than the highest theoretical amount, i.e. the sum they would receive had they completed the full insurance period in one of these Member States and indeed in the one where they would receive the highest benefit.[82] For this reason, according to Article 46(3) of Regulation No 1408/71, the

[77] Judgments cited above: Pian, paragraph 16; Di Prinzio, paragraph 19.

[78] Cited above, Valentini judgment, paragraph 22.

[79] Judgments cited above: Pian, paragraph 15; Van der BuntCraig, paragraph 15.

[80] Cited above, Marius Larsy judgment, paragraph 22.

[81] Marius Larsy, paragraph 13; Di Prinzio, paragraph 18.

[82] Runft (1991), pp. 155–156.

retirements pensions that were calculated by virtue of Article 46(1) of Regulation No 1408/71 were proportionally reduced to the amount over the highest theoretical sum.

6.3.3 Critical Remarks

As it can be observed, the Court had been applying a principle that existed before the Petroni principle in case-law and continued to apply it, even after the adoption of the Petroni principle in the titular judgment. It is the principle of choosing the most favourable solution or provision for the migrant, otherwise known as the principle of favour but with a wider content from the Petroni principle and an independent function, as evidenced in the divergent judgments following Petroni. The Court had been applying that principle of favour based, among others, on Article 46(3) of Regulation No 1408/71, which was found to be substantially non-favourable in the Petroni case, and continued to apply this principle in parallel with Article 46(3) of Regulation No 1408/71 even when it was declared invalid, hence the derogation of the relevant case-law cited above from the Petroni judgment. Prima facie, this attitude may raise questions.

However, it seems that up until the amendment of Article 46(3) of Regulation No 1408/70 resulting from the Petroni judgment, the Court held the most favourable position for the migrant. The system under Regulation No 1408/71 ensured the principle of favour for the migrant and at the same time it was operational without the complications of the rules against overlapping introduced in the Regulation with its amendment and the abolition of Article 46(3) of Regulation No 1408/71. Thus, a rule was abolished, the interpretation of which has long been given a consistent interpretation in favour of the migrant, ensuring the simplicity of procedures and balances between the systems of the Member States. Three rules against the overlapping of benefits were put in its stead, resulting in complexity.

It is clear that both in cases before the Court prior to the amendment of Article 46(3) of Regulation No 1408/71 with Regulation No 1248/92 and following that amendment, the comparison takes place between the amount of the independent and the amount of the pro-rata benefit as determined after the application of the rules against overlapping. Such a conclusion, of course, can be drawn more safely from the wording of (amended) Article 46(3) of Regulation No 1408/71, than from the corresponding Article 52(3) of Regulation No 883/04. The application of national rules against the overlapping of benefits is therefore restricted within the limits of Articles 53–55 of Regulation No 883/04 (articles 46a-46c of Regulation No 1408/71).[83]

More specifically, **the amendment of Regulation No 1408/71 with Regulation No 1248/92 resulted in the replacement of Article 46(3) of Regulation No 1408/71 with new rules against the overlapping of pension benefits (articles 46a, 46b,**

[83] Pennings (2015b), p. 223.

46c of Regulation No 1408/71). As noted, articles 46, 46a, 46b, 46c of Regulation No 1408/71, introduced with amending Regulation No 1248/92, are rather complicated.[84] These amendments, however, did not affect the principles of said calculation method.[85] It should be noted, however, that, as results from the case-law cited above, Article 46(3) of Regulation No 1408/71 as interpreted and applied by the Court always resulted in the most favourable approach for the migrant. On the other hand, said provision was declared invalid in the Petroni judgment for the exact opposite reason: because it resulted in a reduction in the pension to which the migrant worker would have been entitled under the national legislation alone; it is from this judgment that the principle bearing the same derives. However, if the details of the Petroni case are examined, while taking into account the way in which the general principle of favour was applied by the Court and in relation to Article 46 (3) of Regulation No 1408/71, it can be concluded that the interpretation of the Court could have been lead to a different direction.

The Advocate-General noted in his opinion regarding the Petroni judgment that a person who has been subject to the social security legislation of two or more Member States may, as regards to his rights to old age pension, find himself, in each of those States, in any of the following four possible situations:[86]

(1) He may be entitled to a pension in that State without recourse to such aggregation as is envisaged by Article 51 and find that he can get no greater benefit by the application to his case of the processes of aggregation and apportionment; or
(2) He may be entitled to a pension in that State without recourse to aggregation, but be entitled to a greater pension there through the processes of aggregation and apportionment; or
(3) He may be entitled to a pension in that State only through the processes of aggregation and apportionment; or
(4) He may be entitled to no pension in that State even if the processes of aggregation and apportionment are applied to his case.

Taking into account the above situation, Mr Petroni was in situation 1 regarding Belgium and in situation 3 regarding Italy. As a result, as he was entitled to a pension by virtue of the national legislation of Belgium, the national institution should not apply in this case Article 46(3) of Regulation No 1408/71. It is clear from the case-law cited above that either the national system or the system of the Regulation should be applied, whichever was favourable; moreover, if the most favourable solution could be found by virtue of national law, Article 46(3) of Regulation No 1408/71 could not be applied. Therefore, the national institution in question should not have reduced the pension under Article 46(3) of Regulation No 1408/71, because Article 46(3) of Regulation No 1408/71 should not apply in this case, as the person

---

[84] Cornelissen (1998), p. 698.

[85] Judgment of 17/12/1998 – Lustig Case C-244/97 European Court Reports 1998 I-08701ECLI: EU:C:1998:619, paragraph 8.

[86] Opinion of Mr– General Jean-Pierre Warner of 25 September 1975, Case 24/75, p. 1164.

concerned could have a more favourable pension by virtue of the national legislation alone. Otherwise, the violation should not have been attributed to the entire content of Article 46(3) of Regulation No 1408/71, but to its application in a case where according to the Regulation and the case-law was not applicable; such was the case in Petroni, where the national provision being more favourable excluded the provision of the Regulation, on the basis of the principle of favour within the meaning of the case-law already presented. It is possible, in terms of the content of that provision, to propose a rewording in order to restrict its application only in the case of pro-rata benefits, expressly excluding its application in case of independent benefits, in line with the case-law interpretation focusing on the principle of favouring the migrant.

6.4 Case-Law Following the Amendment of the Regulation

Regulation No 1408/71 itself contains a provision making reference to its amending Regulation No 1248/92. It is Article 95a of Regulation No 1408/71. The application of Article 95a of Regulation No 1408/71 was examined by the Court in the joined cases **Camarotto and Vignone**.[87] The questions have arisen in proceedings between the Office National des Pensions (ONP, National Pensions Office) and Mr E. Sutto (the proceedings being continued, following his death, by his widow, Mrs G. Camarotto) and between the ONP and Mrs G. Vignone (the widow of Mr Tammaro), concerning the calculation of retirement and survivor's pensions. Mr E. Sutto and Mrs G. Vignone both brought proceedings before the Tribunal du Travail de Namur (Namur Labour Court), Belgium, for an order that their Belgian pensions be recalculated on the basis of their insurance periods being validated at the rates of 42/45 and 30/30 respectively, with no reduction. By judgment delivered on 13 November 1986, the Tribunal du Travail de Namur ruled that Mr E. Sutto should receive a retirement pension calculated on the basis of his insurance period being validated at the rate of 42/45, to be paid by the Belgian social security scheme for employed workers. By judgment delivered on 14 May 1987, the Tribunal du Travail de Namur ruled that Mrs G. Vignone should receive a survivor's pension calculated on the basis of full validation of her insurance period, that is to say, at the rate of 30/30, to be paid by the Belgian social security scheme for employed workers.

Following the amendment of Regulation No 1408/71 with Regulation No 1248/92, and whilst the two cases were still stayed, the ONP sent a letter to the lawyers of the interested parties on 22 September 1994. That letter contained a breakdown of each of the two pensions, calculated on the basis of the rules applicable from 1 June 1992, giving a final amount more favourable to Mrs G. Camarotto and Mrs G. Vignone than that previously calculated. A copy of the letter was addressed to

[87] Judgment of the Court of 22.02.2001, Joined cases C-52/99 and C-53/99, Camarotto (C-52/99) and Vignone (C-53/99), European Court Reports 2001 I-01395 ECLI:EU:C:2001:112.

their trade union representative. However, the ONP did not draw to their attention the fact that, in its view, it was necessary for them to submit to it an application for review within a time-limit of two years from 1 June 1992 in order to benefit from the application of Regulation No 1248/92 and to secure review, with effect from that date, of the calculation of the pensions at issue in the main proceedings. In January 1996, it was decided to resume proceedings in the two main cases before the Cour du Travail de Liège. In order to determine the pension rights relating to the period from 1 June 1992 to 30 November 1997, the Cour du Travail de Liège referred the questions to the Court for a preliminary ruling.

From the outset, the Court noted that in its case-law[88] it held that the worker was entitled to the highest amount of benefits that would be due in application of the national legislation alone and of the benefits that would be due in application of Community law. Where the competent institution determines the benefit due under Community law, it must not take account of the national rules against overlapping pursuant to Article 12(2) of Regulation No 1408/71 but must, if necessary, adjust the amount of the benefit payable, in accordance with the rule limiting overlapping as formerly laid down in Article 46(3) of that regulation. (Camarotto and Vignone, paragraph 4). Following this case-law, Article 46 of Regulation No 1408/71 was amended by Regulation No 1248/92, which entered into force on 1 June 1992, so as to entitle the person concerned to claim from the competent institution of each Member State the highest amount, calculated without prejudice to any application of the provisions concerning reduction, suspension or withdrawal provided for by the national legislation (Camarotto and Vignone, paragraph 5).

The answer to the first question was that Article 95a of Regulation No 1408/71, as amended, laying down transitional provisions for application of Regulation No 1248/92, applies to recipients of pensions who, before the date of entry into force of the amendments introduced by the latter regulation, had already brought proceedings before a national court seeking to obtain the right to the pension by contesting the application of the national rules against overlapping, even if a final decision in those proceedings had not yet been given at the time of the entry into force of the new provisions (Camarotto and Vignone, paragraph 26).

With its second question, the referring Court asked whether, assuming that Article 95a applies to all recipients without distinction, the application referred to in Article 95a(4) must be made to the competent social security institution in accordance with the formalities required by national legislation for the bringing of an application for review, or may it be made to the court before which the dispute has been brought in accordance with the applicable rules of procedure and, in the latter case, must the period of two years referred to in Article 95a(5) and (6) likewise be complied with.

It is apparent both from the terms and the scheme of Article 95a(4) of Regulation No 1408/71, as amended, that application of the provisions of Regulation No 1248/

[88] In particular, judgment of 11.06.1992, C-90/91 and C-91/91, Di Crescenzo and Casagrande, European Court Reports 1992 I-3851.

92 to pension rights acquired before 1 June 1992 is subject to an express application being made by the person concerned (Camarotto and Vignone, paragraph 33). However, although the submission of an application for review is thus made a precondition for the institution of review proceedings, Article 95a of Regulation No 1408/71, as amended, gives no indication as to the form which such an application is to take (paragraph 34).

The Court therefore responded to the second question stating that it is for the referring court to determine, first, whether national law requires an application for review to be made either to the competent social security institution within the period prescribed and in accordance with the relevant formal requirements, or to the court itself according to the applicable rules of procedure. Second, it is for that court to ensure that those requirements are not less favourable than those governing similar situations under domestic law and that they are not such as to render impossible in practice or excessively difficult the exercise of the rights conferred on claimants by Regulation No 1408/71, as amended (Camarotto and Vignone, paragraph 42).

In the **Conti**[89] case, which is discussed below, the Court itself referred to the legal situation created following the amendment of Regulation No 1408/71, allowing for the drawing of safe conclusions. The same judgment is interesting for yet another reason: the Court provided a definition of the concept of a provision on reduction, providing the latter with a Community dimension and highlighting the importance of a uniform interpretation at EU level, excluding any national designations.

The text, thus, reads: Article 12(2) of Regulation No 1408/71, as worded in Regulation No 2001/83, was amended with Regulation No 1248/92, which entered into form on 1 June 1992, which now reads as follows: "Save as otherwise provided in this Regulation, the provisions of the legislation of a Member State governing the reduction, suspension or withdrawal of benefits in cases of overlapping with other social security benefits or any other form of income may be invoked even where such benefits were acquired under the legislation of another Member State or where such income was acquired in the territory of another Member State" (Conti, paragraph 4). **Moreover, following the amendment of Regulation No 1408/71 with Regulation No 1248/92, Article 46(3) provides the following:** "The person concerned shall be entitled to the highest amount calculated in accordance with paragraphs 1 and 2 from the competent institution of each Member State without prejudice to any application of the provisions concerning reduction, suspension or withdrawal provided for by the legislation under which this benefit is due. Where that is the case, the comparison to be carried out shall relate to the amounts determined after the application of the said provisions" (Conti, paragraph 6). **Regulation No 1248/92 also inserted a new provision—Article 46b—in Regulation No 1408/71, as amended by Regulation No 2001/83** (Conti, paragraph 7).

Mr F. Conti, who was born in Italy on 26 October 1934, worked successively in Italy, in Germany, and in Belgium. In Belgium he worked, normally and principally,

---

[89] Judgment of the Court of 22.10.1998, Case C-143/97, Conti, European Court Reports 1998 I-06365 ECLI:EU:C:1998:501.

as an underground mineworker for 26 years between 1965 and 1990. By an administrative decision notified to Mr F. Conti on 23 August 1994, the ONP granted him, with effect from 1 January 1991, a miner's retirement pension of BFR 449 417 per annum indexed at 360.12 on the consumer prices index and calculated on the basis of a 26/30 employment record. That decision also states that Mr Conti is entitled to an annual supplement of BFR 40 591 indexed at the same rate, but adds that "this supplement will be reduced by the amount of the other retirement pensions or benefits taking the place thereof to which [he] could also be entitled under a Belgian or foreign scheme". The supplement was reduced to zero because Mr F. Conti already received two retirement pensions, one in Italy from 1 November 1989 of LIT 101 619 per month, the other in Germany from 1 January 1991 of DM 3 208.80 per annum.

By act of 22 September 1994, Mr F. Conti contested that decision before the Tribunal du Travail (Labour Court), Liège, primarily on the ground that the ONP "disregards the European regulations". His action was upheld on the ground that Article 3(6) of the Law of 20 July 1990 constituted a provision for reduction of benefit within the meaning of Article 12 of Regulation No 1408/71. On 26 April 1996 the ONP lodged an appeal against that decision before the Cour du Travail, Liège. It maintained that, in order for there to be a reduction, suspension or withdrawal of benefit in the case of overlapping with a benefit paid in another Member State, there had first to be a determination of the first benefit in accordance with the Belgian legislation, and that the provisions for reduction of benefit referred to in Article 46b of Regulation No 1408/71, as amended, related to a benefit which had already been granted. Since the Cour du Travail, Liège, had doubts concerning the interpretation of Articles 12(2), 46(3) and 46b of Regulation No 1408/71, as amended, it stayed proceedings in order to refer the following question to the Court of Justice for a preliminary ruling.

The sole purpose of that question is to ascertain whether a national rule which provides that the supplement to a mineworker's retirement pension is to be reduced by the amount of a retirement pension to which the worker concerned is entitled under another Member State's scheme constitutes a provision for reduction of benefit within the meaning of Regulation No 1408/71, as amended (Conti, paragraph 18).

First of all, the meaning of the expression "a provision for reduction of benefit", used in Article 12(2) of Regulation No 1408/71, as amended by Regulation No 2001/83, was not changed by Regulation No 1248/92. Indeed, the amendments made to Article 12(2) by Regulation No 248/92 were concerned with delimiting the application of national rules against overlapping benefits and did not affect the principle of their operation[90] (Conti, paragraph 19).

Consequently, in order to reply to the question referred, there is no need to distinguish between the period before 1 June 1992 and the period thereafter.

[90]To this end, see judgment of the Court of 12.02.1998, Case C-366/96, Cordelle, European Court Reports 1998 I-00583 ECLI:EU:C:1998:57, paragraph 12.

Secondly, the Court referred to the judgment of 4th June 1985, in Case 58/84, Romano (European Court Reports 1985, p. 1679), where it ruled that a national provision which reduces the additional years of notional employment from which a worker may benefit by the number of years in respect of which he may claim a pension in another Member State constitutes a provision for reduction of benefit within the meaning of Article 12(2) of Regulation No 1408/71 (Conti, paragraph 20). It also stressed that **national provisions for reduction of benefits cannot be rendered exempt from the conditions and limits of application laid down in Regulation No 1408/71 by categorising them as rules for calculating the amount payable** (Conti, paragraph 24).

A national rule must be regarded as a provision for reduction of benefit if the calculation which it requires to be made has the effect of reducing the amount of pension which the person concerned may claim because he receives a benefit from another Member State (Conti, paragraph 25).

It should be noted that this definition was also used later in the Insalaca[91] case, in the context of which the Advocate-General noted that, under the terms of this definition, the concept of provision on reduction of benefit contains two main conditions:[92] the first condition concerns the requirement of an extraneous element (the benefits to which the person concerned is entitled must be covered by the legal systems of two or more Member States); the second condition relates to the intention of the national rule on calculation. Its chief consequence must be a reduction in the amount of the pension granted to the recipient.

In that regard, the Court noted that a legislation such as the Belgian legislation governing mineworkers' pensions—both in the version in force at the time of the Romano case cited above and in the version applicable in the Conti case—provides for special advantages for persons employed in that sector. On completion of a minimum period of 25 years' actual employment, the amount of the pension is raised to the level of a pension calculated on the basis of 30 years' employment. The upgraded pension is then reduced by reference to any other pension benefits which the person concerned may claim. (Conti, paragraph 26). Whilst the legislation applicable at the time of Romano provided for periods of actual employment to be supplemented by notional periods, which were then reduced according to the number of years in respect of which the worker could claim another pension, the new legislation provides for payment of a supplement which is also reduced, but by virtue of other pension benefits (Conti, paragraph 27). Thus, both sets of rules lead to the same result: the only difference, as the Advocate-General points out in paragraphs 22 and 23 of his Opinion, lies in the method used for upgrading the pension (Conti, paragraph 28). It follows from the foregoing that legislation such as that at issue in the main proceedings constitutes, as in Romano, a provision for reduction of

[91] Judgment of the Court of 07.03.2002, Case C-107/00, Insalaca, European Court Reports 2002 I-02403 ECLI:EU:C:2002:147.

[92] Insalaca – Opinion of Advocate-General PHILIPPE LÉGER of 25th October 2001, points 27–29.

benefit within the meaning of Regulation No 1408/71 as amended (Conti, paragraph 29).

As such, the Court replied to the question referred that a national rule which provides that the supplement to a mineworker's retirement pension is to be reduced by the amount of a retirement pension which the person concerned may claim under a scheme of another Member State constitutes a provision for reduction of benefit within the meaning of Article 12(2) of Regulation No 1408/71, as amended by Regulation No 2001/83, and within the meaning of Articles 12(2), 46(3) and 46b of that version of Regulation No 1408/71, as amended by Regulation No 1248/92 (Conti, paragraph 30).

On his part, of course, the Advocate-General in his opinion[93] in the Conti case, noted that the relevant provisions of Regulation No 1408/71 were amended with effect on 1 June 1992. Consequently, two different Community provisions apply: the Community provisions for the period from 1 June 1991, the date when the pension was first granted, to 31 May 1992 and the amended provisions which took effect on 1 June 1992. Nevertheless, it is clear that the concept of "provision for reduction of benefit" within the meaning of this legislation has not undergone any change in substance. (Opinion, paragraph 11).

From this observation of the Advocate-General which is also in line with the Court's observations, it can be concluded that the content already adopted in the case-law of the provisions for reduction remains unchanged with a timeless character and independent of any amendments to individual provisions referring to them.

At the same time, it can be concluded that the Attorney-General places the critical point when the Regulation begins to apply to the person in question on the first day of his retirement. The Advocate-General, referring to ***the legal position under the Regulation, as in force from 1 July 1992***, noted that the relevant provisions of the Regulation were amended in order to consolidate it and take into account of and systematise the Court's case-law up to that date[94] (paragraph 27).

It is immediately noted that the second sentence of Article 12(2), which qualified the general principle set out in the first sentence and excluded reduction where the person concerned received benefits of the same kind in respect of invalidity, old age, death or occupational disease which were awarded by the institutions of two or more Member States, *has been deleted; instead, the text contains the phrase* "**save otherwise provided in this Regulation**" (paragraph 28). In these other provisions, e. g. Articles 46a to 46c of the Regulation, the general sense of the passage deleted from Article 12 is repeated and given effect. **Therefore, the special provisions concerning overlapping benefits in Chapter 3 of the Regulation are applicable** (paragraph 28). Thus, Article 46 was completely recast and **the Community-law**

---

[93] Conti – Opinion of Advocate-General SIEGBERT ALBER of 12th February 1998 ECLI:EU: C:1998:501.

[94] Judgments of 04.06.1985, 58/84, Romano (European Court Reports 1985, p. 1679); of 11.06.1992, C-90/91 and C-91/91, Di Crescenzo and Casagrande (European Court Reports 1992, p. I-3851); and of 21.10.1975, 24/75, Petroni (European Court Report 1975, p. 347).

rule against overlapping benefits in the former versions of Article 46(3) was deleted (paragraph 29).

In so far as pension benefits under foreign schemes must be deducted when calculating the pension under national law, this is an external rule against concurrent benefits. In any case, the amendment of Regulation No 1408/71 has not caused the national provision to lose its character as a provision for the reduction of benefit (paragraph 32). Its nature as an external rule against concurrent benefits is likewise not altered by the fact that it forms part of an internal rule against such benefits which, under Article 46(3), may be applied when calculating an independent benefit for the purpose of Article 46(1)(a)(i) of Regulation No 1408/71 and a pro rata pension, based on Community law, for the purpose of Article 46(2) (paragraph 32). It follows that the national provision in question is a provision for the reduction of benefit within the meaning of Regulation No 1408/71 and therefore it is applicable in accordance with the rules laid down in the Regulation (paragraph 33).

Article 12(2) lays down the principle that national, including external, rules against overlapping benefits are applicable "save as otherwise provided in this Regulation". However, such other provisions arise from the special rules in Chapter 3 of the Regulation concerning pensions. The general rules applying *in that context* "relating to reduction, suspension or withdrawal applicable to benefits in respect of invalidity, old age or survivors under the legislations of the Member States" appear in Article 46a of the Regulation[95] (paragraph 34).

The provision applicable in case of overlapping benefits of the same kind due under the legislation of two or more Member States, which shall prevail over the above cited provision, is contained in Article 46b of Regulation No 1408/71[96] (article 54 of Regulation No 883/04). Article 46b(1) excludes the application of Member States' provisions on the reduction of benefits in the case of the pro rata pension calculated in accordance with Article 46(2) (paragraph 36). In the context of that case, however, the Advocate-General noted that an independent benefit should be calculated under Article 46(l)(a)(i) as the 26 years' employment taken into account by the Member State's institution were completed under the Belgian legislation alone. Therefore, Article 46b (2), which provides that provisions on reduction, suspension or withdrawal of benefits are to apply only subject to very precise conditions, would apply (paragraph 38). These conditions are that the amount of the benefit does not depend on the length of the period of insurance or residence *and* that the benefit is referred to in Annex IV, part D, of the Regulation. Neither condition is fulfilled in the case in question, so that the reduction provision in

---

[95] Article 46a(3)(a) reads as follows (opinion, paragraph 35):

> account shall be taken of the benefits acquired under the legislation of another Member State or of other income acquired in another Member State only where the legislation of the first Member State provides for the taking into account of benefits or income acquired abroad.

[96] In the case in question, the pension benefits received from Belgium, Italy and Germany are unquestionably "benefits of the same kind", which are defined by Article 46a(1) as "benefits in respect of invalidity, old age or survivors calculated or provided on the basis of periods of insurance and/or residence completed by one and the same person".

question cannot be applied (paragraph 38), so that it is not necessary in this case to determine whether the main proceedings involve Article 46b (l) or (2) (paragraph 39).

Of course, theoretically, it is possible that a migrant worker whose pension benefit is calculated in accordance with Belgian law would be in a slightly more favourable situation than a worker who has spent his entire working life in the Belgian scheme (paragraph 40). However, this could not be regarded as preferential treatment because a Belgian migrant worker would also, by virtue of the Community rules, avoid the reduction provisions laid down by the legislation of Member States (paragraph 40). Furthermore, the calculation of benefit in accordance with Belgian law is *one* step in the calculation by reference to the Community rules of the benefit to which a migrant worker is entitled, without examining in this case the final result after carrying out all the calculation steps in the complicated system laid down in Chapter 3 of the Regulation (paragraph 40).

There is no doubt that, in revising Regulation No 1408/71 by means of, in particular, Regulation No 1248/92, the purpose of the Community legislature was to create a clearly established framework for the application of national anti-overlapping rules in the calculation of pensions under the Community rules and, with that end in view, Article 46b, which is relevant in the case in question, was added to the Regulation. In this way the consistency of the Court's case-law has been expressly maintained (paragraph 41).

The considerations underlying the amending Regulation No 1408/71 are set out in the recitals of Regulation No 1248/92. The fifteenth recital reads as follows: "in accordance with the consistent case-law of the Court of Justice, the Council is not deemed competent to enact rules imposing a restriction on the overlapping of two or more pensions acquired in different Member States by a reduction of the amount of pension acquired solely under the national legislation [...]; according to the Court of Justice, it is for the national legislator to enact such rules, *bearing in mind that it is for the Community legislator to fix the limits within which the national provisions concerning reduction, suspension or withdrawal are to be applied [...]*"[97](paragraph 42). The above recital of Regulation No 1248/92 was also included in the Preamble of Regulation No 883/04 and in particular in recitals 30 and 31 of Regulation No 883/04.

[97]Opinion, paragraph 42:The sixteenth and seventeenth recitals then state: "To protect migrant workers and their survivors against an excessively stringent application of the national provisions concerning reduction, suspension or withdrawal, it is necessary to include a provision in Regulation [...] laying down *strict rules* for the application of these provisions; [...] for the same reasons, it is necessary to insert a provision [...] stipulating that, in the case of overlapping of benefits of the same kind, these provisions shall be applicable only in the case of certain types of benefits and in certain specific cases". Finally, the eighteenth recital states that "it is necessary to list in Annex IV, D, the types of benefits to which the aforesaid provisions can be applied in the case of overlapping of benefits of the same kind".

The Court referred to the amendment of Regulation No 1408/71 with Regulation No 1248/92 and to the subsequent **Platbrood**[98] case, where it reaffirmed that the amendments made by Regulation No 1248/92 to Regulation No 1408/71 were concerned with delimiting the application of national rules against overlapping benefits and did not affect the principle of their operation (Platbrood, paragraph 5). It should be noted that a similar case was the **van Coile**[99] case.

In continuing the case-law adopted with the Conti case, the Court added that **national provisions cannot be exempt from the conditions and limits of application laid down in Regulation No 1408/71 by categorising them as rules of evidence** (Platbrood, paragraph 27).

The Advocate-General in his opinion in the Platbrood[100] case, after referring to the definition of provision for reduction provided by the Court in the Conti case,[101] stressed that in the case in question it is necessary at first to ascertain how far the person concerned has a "claim". The first step must therefore be to define the conditions for entitlement before proceeding to the second, which involves calculating any reduction in line with this definition (paragraph 27). He also underlined that the structure of the Belgian pension rules at issue in Romano, Di Crescenzo and Casagrande and Conti which the Court defined as provisions on reduction, is essentially different from that of the provisions at issue in the case in question. Each of the above three cases concerned a fixed increase designed—by means of notional years or a supplement—to being the pension paid in respect of periods actually completed up to the level payable in respect of a full employment record in each case (paragraph 36). In the present case, by contrast, the question is how to fill gaps in the record which can be accurately localised in time, whereas the rules in question in the three cases above were intended to "compensate" for factors associated with the person of the beneficiary and the work done (at least 25 years in the mining industry); the judgments cited above do not therefore mean that the national provision at issue in the present case must be held to be a provision on reduction within the meaning of Regulation No 1408/71 (paragraph 36).

In those circumstances, the Court ruled that a national provision which in such a situation provides that the war years presumption is not applicable to periods of

[98] Judgment of the Court of 18th November 1999, Case C-161/98, Platbrood , European Court Reports 1999 I-08195 ECLI:EU:C:1999:564.

[99] Judgment of the Court of 18th November 1999, Case C-442/97, van Coile, European Court Reports 1999 I-08093 ECLI:EU:C:1999:560 on a provision of reduction, suspension or withdrawal by virtue of the legislation of a Member State—national legislation recognising by virtue of a legal presumption ("war years presumption") years of employment, provided that for these periods there is no entitlement to receive a pension payable by another scheme, including foreign schemes.

[100] Opinion of Advocate-General SIEGBERT ALBER of 18th May 1999, Platbrood, ECLI:EU:C:1999:248.

[101] In the Conti case (paragraph 25), the Court defined the provision for reduction as follows: "A national rule must be regarded as a provision for reduction of benefit if the calculation it requires to be made has the effect of reducing the amount of pension which the person concerned may claim because he receives a benefit from another Member State" (Conti, paragraph 25).

employment for which the person concerned receives a pension under a scheme of another State cannot be categorised as a provision on "reduction" within the meaning of Regulation No 1408/71. More specifically, such a provision gives effect to the fact that, for all or part of the periods of employment in respect of which the person concerned is not in a position to prove payment of sufficient social security contributions under the Belgian scheme in question, he is already receiving a pension under another scheme (Platbrood, paragraph 32).

It is worth noting however that in the Cordelle[102] case, which is also referred to below in reviewing the rules against overlapping of benefits of Article 53 of Regulation No 883/04 (Article 46a of Regulation No 1408/71), the Court noted that by virtue of Article 46a which was added to Regulation No 1408/71 and paragraph (3) (d) of which provides, in particular, that where rules against overlapping are applicable under the legislation of only one Member State on account of the fact that the person concerned receives benefits of a different kind payable under the legislation of other Member States, the benefit payable under the legislation of the first Member State may be reduced only within the limit of the amount of the benefits payable under the legislation of other Member States (Cordelle, paragraph 14).

6.5 The Equal Treatment of Migrant and Non-migrant Pensioners

In reviewing the overlapping of pension benefits, the Court has developed the principle of the most favourable treatment of migrants as well as a rich case-law according to which the Community restriction on overlapping benefits (Article 46(3) of Regulation No 1408/71) did not apply to benefits which the insured person already enjoyed under national legislation alone. This principle in combination with the case-law developed, as cited above, was considered to potentially result in the migrant worker receiving a pension amount significantly higher than a worker that was employed only in this country and much higher than the amount deemed justifiable in this country.[103]

This consequence was perceived as an unjustifiably preferential treatment of migrant workers and received strong criticism.[104] It also led various Member States to introduce new provisions against overlapping or to expand the application of pre-existing national provisions against overlapping to foreign benefits or to amend

[102] Judgment of the Court of 12.02.1998, Case C-366/96, Cordelle, European Court Reports 1998 I-00583 ECLI:EU:C:1998:57, paragraph 14.

[103] Runft (1991), p. 157.

[104] Runft (1991), p. 157. See also the footnotes No 847, 849 with references of the author to remarks by national insurance institutions and national courts in relation to the cases before the Court, as well as to the German literature and theory and to literature in other languages, while she also notes that Greek literature rarely mentions this issue.

their legislation, so as the final amount payable to the migrant workers would be considered justified at a national level.[105] Indeed, on the ground that it puts migrant workers on a more favourable position (reverse discrimination due to movement) than the workers employed in a single Member State, the Court initially received criticism by the Commission itself[106] and academics that its case-law referring to Article 46(3) and Article 12 of Regulation No 1408/71 and earlier in relation to the relevant Articles of Regulation No 3/58 was in violation of the principle of equality.[107] It is also argued that Community law precludes, according to case-law, the migrant worker from enjoying an infinitely more favourable position, since the Community law provides not only for the social security "levelling of the disadvantages" but also a certain amount of social security "levelling of the advantages".[108]

As it has already been observed, in its case-law following the Petroni judgment, the Court reaffirmed that Member States have the right, under certain circumstances, when applying provisions of their national rules against overlapping pension benefits acquired under their legislation, to take into account benefits acquired by virtue of the legislation of another Member State.[109] As a result of this case-law, where the person concerned satisfied the conditions for entitlement to a pension under national legislation alone, the process for calculating the pension was more complicated than originally foreseen by the drafters of Regulation No 1408/71.[110] This case-law in a slightly different form is reflected in the text of Regulation No 1408/71 as amended with Regulation No 1248/1992.[111,112] More specifically, the rule of Article 46(3) of Regulation No 1408/71, in the form seen in the Petroni case, which limited the highest possible pension at the highest theoretical amount according to the calculations of each State pursuant to Article 46(2)(a) of Regulation No 1408/71 was repealed with effect from 1 June 1992.[113]

As a result of the Petroni judgment, Article 46(3) of Regulation No 1408/71, which was declared invalid, could no longer prevail and exclude national rules which also had the objective of reducing the overlapping with foreign benefits of the same kind; thus, it was now for national legislations to provide rules against

[105] Runft (1991), pp. 158–159.

[106] Tantaroudas (1976), p. 143 et seq.

[107] Runft (1991), pp. 234–235.

[108] Runft (1991), p. 163. See also Schuler (1985), p. 113; Schuler (1988); Schulte (1988), p. 1195.

[109] Cornelissen (2009), p. 16 and the case-law cited therein including: "37/77 Greco; 296/84 Sinatra II; 197/85; 109/89 Bianchin and 108/89 Pian; 5/91 Di Prinzio".

[110] Cornelissen (2009), p. 16.

[111] Council Regulation (EEC) NO. 1248/92 of 30 April 1992 amending Regulation (EEC) No. 1408/71 on the application of social security schemes to employed persons, to self-employed persons and to members of their families moving within the Community and Regulation (EEC) No. 574/72 laying down the procedure for implementing Regulation (EEC) No. 1408/71, OJ No. LI36, 19.5.92, p. 7.

[112] Cornelissen (2009), p. 16.

[113] White (1999), p. 110.

overlapping.[114] However, as these national rules could have undesirable adverse effects, Regulation No 1248/92 was adopted to determine the application of the national rules against overlapping, amending inter alia Article 46(3) of Regulation No 1408/71.[115]

As a result of the principle of the more favourable national rule, the calculation of pension amounts may vary across Member States where a person has worked, so that coordination in this field becomes complicated.[116] However, this principle clarifies that the national legislature should assess not only the impact of its national legislation, but also look at the European dimension, especially in areas of shared competence, such as social security.[117] The progress of European integration has shown that Member States have obligations and commitments on a European level, even in areas which are in principle within their national jurisdiction.[118] If such a uniform application is not possible, the national court is obliged to apply Community law in its entirety and to protect the rights conferred by Community law on individuals, not applying, if necessary, any provisions that, if applied under the circumstances of a specific case, would lead to a result contrary to Community law.[119]

As evident in the **Van Munster**[120] and **Leyman**[121] judgments, according to the relevant theory, **the principle of most favourable treatment also has an impact when unequal treatment cannot be established, while the coordination rules are applied correctly, but the negative effects from exercising the freedom of movement continue to exist;** in such a case, the Court does not declare the Regulation provisions invalid, but requires from the Member States to find a solution in circumstances of bona fide cooperation.[122]

More specifically, in the Van Munster case, the Court noted that where such a difference in legislation exists, the principle of cooperation in good faith laid down in Article 5 of the EEC Treaty requires the competent authorities in the Member States to use all the means at their disposal to achieve the aim of Article 48 of the Treaty.[123] The above requirement implies that those authorities should ascertain whether their legislation can be applied literally to migrant workers, in exactly the

[114]Pennings (2015b), p. 222.

[115]Pennings (2015b), p. 222.

[116]Schouckens and Monserrez (2011), p. 31.

[117]Zacharis and Tsotsorou (2012), p. 800.

[118]Bokeloh (2012), p. 121 sub.

[119]Judgment of the Court of 26.09.2000, Case C-262/97, Engelbrecht, European Court Reports 2000 p. I-07321, paragraph 40.

[120]Judgment of the Court of 05.10.1994, Case C-165/91, van Munster, European Court Reports 1994 I-04661 ECLI:EU:C:1994:359.

[121]Judgment of the Court of 01.10.2009, Case C-3/08, Leyman, European Court Reports 2009 I-09085 ECLI:EU:C:2009:595.

[122]Pennings (2015a), p. 339.

[123]van Munster, paragraph 32.

same way as to non-migrant workers, without ultimately causing migrant workers to lose a social security advantage and, consequently, discouraging them from actually exercising their right to freedom of movement.[124] In the Van Munster case, the application of national legislation to a migrant worker in the same way as to a non-migrant worker gives rise to unforeseen consequences, hardly compatible with the aim of Articles 48 to 51 of the Treaty and attributable to the very fact that the migrant worker's pension entitlements are governed by two different bodies of legislation.[125]

In the recent ***Crespo Rey***,[126] the Court dealt with the calculation of a pension benefit according to the minimum contribution rate of the Spanish social security institution. As pointed out by the Court, by requiring migrant workers to conclude a special agreement to pay contributions that are based on the minimum contribution rate, the national legislation at issue in the main proceedings gives rise to a difference in treatment, which places migrant workers at a disadvantage compared to non-migrant workers who spent their entire working life in the respective Member State (para. 63). The Court stated that it is for the national court dealing with the dispute to identify the most appropriate means in national law for achieving equal treatment between migrant and non-migrant workers. The Court noted that this objective ought to, in principle, be achieved by granting migrant workers who conclude a special agreement the option to pay social security contributions retroactively based on contribution rates that exceed the minimum rate and to consequently be able to claim their right to a retirement pension based on those higher rates (para. 75). Consequently, the Court concluded that the Agreement on the Free Movement of Persons must be interpreted as precluding the legislation of a Member State, such as the one at issue in the main proceedings, which requires a migrant worker, who concludes a special agreement with the social security institution of the respective Member State, to pay contributions based on the minimum contribution rate, with the result that the competent body of the respective Member State treats the period covered by that agreement in the calculation of the theoretical amount of the worker's retirement pension as a period that has been completed in that same Member State, and will only take the contributions paid under the special agreement into consideration, even though that worker had previously paid social security contributions in the respective Member State that exceeded the minimum before exercising his or her right to free movement, and a non-migrant worker, who did not exercise that right and who also concluded a special agreement, has the option of paying contributions that exceed the minimum contribution rate (para. 76).

Further, in ***Caisse d'assurance retraite et de la santé au travail d'Alsace-Moselle***,[127] the Court reviewed the period during which a mother raised her disabled

---

[124] van Munster, paragraph 33.

[125] van Munster, paragraph 30.

[126] Judgement of the Court of 28 June 2018, Case C-2/17, Crespo Rey, ECLI:EU:C:2018:511.

[127] Judgement of the Court of 12 March 2020, Case C-769/18, Caisse d'assurance retraite et de la santé au travail d'Alsace-Moselle, ECLI:EU:C:2020:203.

child while receiving a carer's allowance for the purpose of calculating her retirement pension. Nonetheless, **in view of the procedure laid down in Article 267 TFEU providing for cooperation between national courts and the Court of Justice**, the Court reformulated the second question referred to it[128] (para. 39). The dispute in the main proceedings concerned the question whether—for the purpose of determining a person's entitlement to a higher pension rate as provided for in French legislation—the circumstances that gave rise to entitlement to 'the German assistance', namely assistance received by that person as a migrant worker in accordance with the legislation of the host Member State, must be taken into account (para. 41). The Court, in line with its case law,[129] held that such an increase in the pension rate can fall within the material scope of Regulation 883/2004 as an old-age benefit within the meaning of Article 3(1)(d) of that Regulation (para. 46). First, an increase in the pension rate is granted to beneficiaries without an individual and discretionary assessment of their personal needs on the basis of a legally defined situation, namely that they raised a child with a disability and were entitled to a carer's allowance for a child with a disability under French legislation (para. 47). Secondly, the benefit at issue intends to offset any disadvantages suffered by the beneficiary in terms of career advancement because he or she had to raise a disabled child, by granting an increase of his or her contribution periods which is proportionate to the period he or she spent raising the disabled child. This is then reflected in the amount of pension he or she receives. Accordingly, this benefit—in so far as it is intended to safeguard the subsistence of persons who, after reaching a certain age, leave their employment and are no longer required to be available for work—is linked to the risk covered by old-age benefits within the meaning of Article 3(1)(d) of Regulation 883/2004[130] (para. 48). Further, the Court noted that the increase in the pension rate is provided on the basis of the occurrence of a fact within the meaning of Article 5(b) of Regulation 883/2004, namely that the child's permanent incapacity must be at least equal to a certain level of disability (para. 50). It follows that the principle of the equal treatment of facts, enshrined in the aforementioned Article 5(b), applies in circumstances such as those at issue in the main proceedings (para. 51).

Accordingly, the competent French authorities must take similar facts that arose in Germany into account, and cannot limit their assessment of the permanent incapacity of the disabled child concerned solely to the criteria laid down to that end by the scale-guide applicable in France under Article R. 541-1 of the French Social Security Code (para. 53). Consequently, to determine whether the level of the child's permanent incapacity as specified in that Code justifies an increase in the

---

[128] Judgement of 13 June 2019, *Moro*, C-646/17, EU:C:2019:489, paragraph 39 and the case law cited.

[129] Judgement of 14 March 2019, *Dreyer*, C-372/18, EU:C:2019:206, paragraph 32 and the case law cited, Judgement of 25 July 2018, *A (Assistance for a disabled person)*, C-679/16, EU:C:2018:601, paragraph 33 to be presented analytically below.

[130] To that effect, see judgement of 16 September 2015, *Commission* v *Slovakia*, C-361/13, EU:C:2015:601, paragraph 55 and the case law cited.

parent's pension rate, the authorities cannot refuse to take similar facts that arose in Germany into account and which can be established by evidence, in particular by medical reports, certificates or prescriptions for treatment or medicines (para. 54). Finally, the Court added that in the context of such checks, the authorities must also observe the principle of proportionality by ensuring, inter alia, that the principle of equal treatment of facts does not give rise to objectively unjustified results in accordance with recital 12 of Regulation 883/2004 (para. 55).

Likewise, in the **Adrien and Others**,[131] the Court had held that Article 45 TFEU must be interpreted as precluding national legislation, such as the French legislation in the main proceedings, which has the effect that a national official seconded to an EU institution or body who chooses to remain affiliated to the national pension scheme for the duration of his secondment loses all or part of the advantages accruing from his affiliation to that scheme if he completes 10 years' service with the European Union entitling him to a pension under the European Union pension scheme. The applicants in the main proceedings were French officials, seconded as legal secretaries to the Court of Justice of the European Union, where they were employed as temporary staff. Since they made mandatory contributions to the EU pension scheme, they were entitled to a pension under that scheme if they completed at least 10 years' service with an EU institution or body. If they should have left the service before having completed 10 years' service, in essence they were entitled, depending on the length of service completed, to either a severance grant equal to three times the sums retained from their basic salary as old-age pension contributions or payment of the actuarial equivalent of the old-age pension rights acquired under the EU scheme to a private insurance scheme or a pension fund of their choice. Under the French rules at issue in the main proceedings, an official seconded to an EU institution or body must choose between two options as regards his pension under the national scheme. The appellants in the main proceedings opted to remain affiliated to the French pension scheme during their secondments and, accordingly, contributed at the same time to that scheme and to the EU pension scheme. They have completed or are likely to complete 10 years' service in an EU institution entitling them to receive a pension under the EU pension scheme. Since the EU pension which the appellants in the main proceedings have acquired or are likely to acquire is greater than the French pension which they would have received had there been no detachment, in accordance with the French rules at issue in the main proceedings, they do not or will not receive any pension under the French pension scheme. According to the Court, EU nationals working for an EU institution or body in a Member State other than their Member State of origin, such as the appellants in the main proceedings, may not be refused the rights and social advantages which Article 45 TFEU affords them.

Further, in the most recent **Rechtsanwaltskammer Wien**,[132] the Court held that Articles 45 and 49 TFEU must be interpreted as precluding national legislation

[131] Judgement of 6.10.2016, Adrien and others, case C-466/16, ECLI:EU:C:2016:749.

[132] Judgement of 15.09.2022, Rechtsanwaltskammer Wien, case C-58/21, ECLI:EU:C:2022:691.

which makes the award of an early retirement pension applied for conditional on the waiver by the person concerned of the right to practise as a lawyer, without taking into account, in particular, the Member State in which the activity concerned is pursued.

FK, born in 1954, has both Polish and German nationality. Since 8 March 1984, he has been entered in the register of the Cologne Bar Association (Germany). In 1996, FK was entered in the register of the Vienna Bar Association in Austria and practised as a lawyer there, in addition to pursuing his activity in Germany. The centre of interest of FK's activities remained in Cologne until 2007, the year from which FK moved his place of residence and the centre of interest of his activities to Switzerland, where he now practises as a lawyer, entered in the list of lawyers who are nationals of a Member State of the European Union or of the European Free Trade Association (EFTA), by virtue of his entry in the register of the Cologne Bar Association. Since 2018, FK has received an early retirement pension in Germany, whilst continuing to practise as a lawyer there. On 16 October 2017, FK submitted to the Vienna Bar Association an application for the award of an early retirement pension from 1 November 2017 in which he stated that he wished to waive the right to practise as a lawyer in Austria, whilst maintaining his entry in the register of the Cologne Bar Association and in the list of lawyers who are nationals of a Member State of the European Union or of the EFTA in Switzerland. By decision of the Committee of the Vienna Bar Association of 29 May 2018, that application was rejected on the basis of Paragraph 26, in conjunction with Paragraph 29, of the 2018 Statute for Part A, under which the award of a retirement pension presupposes that the person concerned has waived the right to practise as a lawyer 'anywhere'.

According to the Court, national legislation which requires that the person concerned waive the right to practice as a lawyer both in the territory of the Member State concerned and abroad in order to protect persons still pursuing that profession from competition from those who have already exercised their right to retirement appears to go beyond what is necessary to attain the objective in question, since that objective can be attained by limiting that waiver of the right to pursue any professional activity to national territory alone or possibly to a limited geographical area in another Member State. Such legislation does not, moreover, take into account the fact that the conditions for acquiring and maintaining the right to a pension are not harmonised between the Member States, but only coordinated by EU law, and that the persons concerned may be obliged to continue to work in other Member States in order to acquire their right to a pension under the national laws concerned (para. 72). Furthermore, the condition that the person concerned waive the right to practise as a lawyer both in national territory and abroad appears to go beyond what is necessary to ensure that income from full-time employment is not added to the early retirement pension thus paid (para. 73).

As regards the objective relating to the financial sustainability of the special scheme concerned, although it is true that the risk of seriously undermining the financial balance of a social security system may constitute an overriding reason in the general interest,[133] it is not, however, clear from the explanations provided by the Austrian Government how the financing system of that special scheme, which is dependent on the contributions paid by the beneficiaries of that special scheme, would be subject to a risk of being seriously undermined by the fact that recipients of early retirement pensions under the special scheme concerned continue to work in other Member States (para. 74). Therefore, although it is ultimately for the referring court to determine whether, and to what extent, the national legislation in question meets the requirement of proportionality as regards the implementation of the objective relating to the financial sustainability of the special scheme concerned, the Court concluded that, in the light of the documents before it, that objective can be attained by less restrictive means (para. 75).

It could be argued that the Petroni principle or in our view the general principle of favour[134] was framed in the case-law also by the principle of equivalence, in combination with the principle of effectiveness regarding pensions. The CJEU case-law is consistent in requiring respect of the principles of equivalence and effectiveness, in the application of national legislation to situations falling within the scope of Community law.[135] Indicatively, in the **Pasquini**[136] case, the Court stressed that although national law is applicable to a situation arising from the overpayment of a pension supplement by reason of the authorised maximum income's having been exceeded, it must however be stated that, with regard to a situation concerning a worker who has exercised his right to freedom of movement under the Treaty, it is a requirement of Community law that the detailed procedural rules governing that situation should observe the principles of equivalence and effectiveness.[137]

In accordance with the principle of equivalence, the procedural rules governing such cases must be no less favourable than those governing purely internal situations (Pasquini, paragraph 57).[138] Otherwise, there would be a breach of the principle of equal treatment for workers who have exercised their right to freedom of movement and those who have spent their entire working life in a single Member State (Pasquini, paragraph 57). In accordance with the principle of effectiveness, those

---

[133] See, inter alia, judgments of 28 April 1998, Kohll, C-158/96, EU:C:1998:171, paragraph 41, and of 11 January 2007, ITC, C-208/05, EU:C:2007:16, paragraph 43.

[134] See above on the critique regarding the Petroni judgment and the conclusions on the principle of favour regardless of the Petroni judgment.

[135] Remarks of P. Petroglou, CJEU Judgment Δ.Ε.Κ. 19.6.2003, Case C-34/02 Pasquini, EDKA (Social Security Law Review) 2003, p. 427.

[136] Judgment of the Court of 19.06.2003, Case C-34/02, Pasquini, European Court Reports 2003 I-06515 ECLI:EU:C:2003:366, paragraph 56.

[137] See relevant judgments of 10.07.1997, C-261/95, Palmisani, European Court Reports 1997, p. I-04025, paragraph 27, and of 15.09.1998, C-231/96, Edis, European Court Reports 1998, p. I-04951, paragraph 34.

[138] See also relevant judgments cited above Palmisani, paragraph 32; Edis, paragraph 34.

procedural rules must not render virtually impossible or excessively difficult the exercise of rights conferred by Community law (Pasquini, paragraph 58).[139]

Moreover, it would be contrary to the principle of equivalence for a situation arising from the exercise of a Community freedom to be classified or treated differently from a purely internal situation when they are similar and comparable, and for the situation of Community origin to be subjected to special rules less favourable to the worker than those applicable to a purely internal situation, the only reason being that difference in classification or treatment (Pasquini, paragraph 59). Article 49 cannot be interpreted as allowing derogation from that principle of equal treatment (Pasquini, paragraph 70). On the contrary, the persons concerned may draw from that article the legitimate expectation that their situation will be treated with due care and attention by the social security institutions of the various Member States in which they have worked, and that they will not be required to satisfy themselves that administrative information concerning them has been communicated by one of those institutions to another (Pasquini, paragraph 71).

Furthermore, EU regulation on the coordination of social security systems cannot be applied in such a way as to deprive the migrant worker or their dependents of benefits granted under the legislation of a single Member State, unless a relevant exception is expressly provided in accordance with such purposes.[140] Thus, on the basis of Article 48 TFEU, the Council adopted as a "necessary measure" the coordination mechanism for social security systems to prevent the emergence of social security disadvantages for workers moving from one Member State to another and, as a result, to create the conditions for ensuring their free movement.[141]

As Pennings argues, the Petroni principle has been part of the Court's case-law, which has given it a wider interpretation over time, but does not constitute a concept which has been sufficiently clarified in the case-law, while its application does not always have the same effects and the latter are not entirely clear, as the solution to the problem is often left to the Member States.[142] It is also argued, however, that the Petroni principle aims to protect the rights that migrant workers have solely by virtue of national legislation alone, rights that they should not be deprived of due to their movement.[143]

It can be observed that the Coordination Regulation and the case-law (as well as the theory) strive to balance between avoiding damage to the migrant and at the same time justifying any additional benefits. Where each state selects, however, the highest amount between the national and Community benefit, any issues regarding damage of the migrant worker that could prevent their movement seem to be resolved. In case of additional benefits, however, it seems they can fall within the scope of the principle of free movement, but they are subject to mitigation under the

[139] See also relevant judgments cited above: Palmisani, paragraphs 28 and 29; Edis, paragraph 34.

[140] Tsotsorou (2013), p. 281.

[141] See Devetzi (2000).

[142] Pennings (2015a), p. 339.

[143] Pennings (2015a), p. 339.

rules against overlapping. **Indeed, it is noted that, as a consequence of the Petroni judgment, the national rules against overlapping have been strengthened.**[144]

In our opinion, in its endeavour not to derogate from preventing any damage to the migrant, the Court ends with a precarious case-law, as it seems to ban the possibility of a "deficit", but in the case of a "surplus", it is up to states to cut such a surplus so as not burden the other insured persons within their systems.

Then, the legislator also tries to limit the application of these national rules against overlapping by establishing parallel Community rules against overlapping. Although in the Petroni judgment, the Court did not rule that it is acceptable for cross-border movement to result in a more favourable position than in case of remaining in a single Member State throughout one's life, it seems to be accepting of this result.[145] In this regard, it should be noted that the recipients to whom the Community rules apply, i.e. the migrants, may very well receive a higher pension than non-migrant workers.[146] According to a different view, free movement can even result in a more favourable treatment of migrant workers than non-migrants.[147]

Taking into account that the coordination has already achieved the deterittorialization of the various systems,[148] it could be said that the new Article 5 of Regulation No 883/04 on equal treatment of facts and events implicitly paved the way for the deterittorialization of national conditions set by the States to the extent it establishes a generalised equal treatment. EU law cannot, therefore, intervene in the establishment of retirement conditions by the States; it has, however, established the principle according to which such conditions may be deemed fulfilled *fictio iuris*. Of course, the European legislature has, within certain limits, room to manoeuvre regarding the establishment and the application of national rules against overlapping.

In any case, in terms of maintaining a proportional approach to social security protection, Regulation No 1408/71 prior to its amendment with Regulation No 1248/92 offered solutions that were simpler, more effective and, ultimately, more accurately fair. It balanced between European law and national legislation, focusing at the same time on the most favourable solution for the migrant. As demonstrated, the ceiling selected was the highest social security protection. This was a solution at EU level, constituting a restriction as a limit to overlapping, but also disabling the adoption of measures against overlapping at the national level by the Member States. In its current form, the Regulation seems to transfer a significant part of such process of calculating pensions to the rules against overlapping of Article 53–55 of Regulation No 883/04, in which it tries to limit the relevant national rules against overlapping.

---

[144] Pennings (2015b), p. 222.

[145] Pennings (2003), p. 191.

[146] White (1999), p. 110.

[147] Tsotsorou and Sklikas (2008), p. 74.

[148] Stergiou (2013), p. 204; Runft (1991), pp. 39–40.

References

Bokeloh A (2012) Das Petroni-Prinzip des Europaischen Gerichtshofes- Inhalt, Entstehungsgeschichte, heutige Bedeutung. Zeitschrift fur europaisches Sozial- und Arbeitsrecht (ZESAR) 03:121 sub

Cornelissen R (1998) The principle of territoriality and the Community regulations on social security. EDKA (Social Security Law Review), p 697

Cornelissen R (2009) 50 years of social security coordination. Eur J Soc Secur 1–2:16

Devetzi S (2000) Die Kollisionsnormen des Europäischen Sozialrechts. Schriften zum Europäischen Recht, Band 64, Berlin

Pennings F (2003) Introduction to European social security law, 4th edn. Intersentia, Antwerp-Oxford-New York

Pennings F (2015a) Principles of EU coordination of social security. In: Pennings F, Vonk G (eds) Research handbook on European social security law, Research handbooks in European law series. EE Elgar Publishing, UK-USA, p 339

Pennings F (2015b) European social security law, 6th edn. Intersentia, Cambridge-Antwerp-Portland

Petroglou P (2003) CJEU Judgment D.E.K. 19.6.2003, Case C-34/02 Pasquini. EDKA (Social Security Law Review), p 427

Runft H (1991) Unification of Europe and Social Security of Repatriates - the limits of community and national social security law. Ant. N. Sakkoulas Publishing, Athens-Komotini

Schouckens P, Monserrez L (2011) Introduction to social security coordination in the EU. Reading Material, Master of European Social Security KU Leuven, p 31

Schuler R (1985) Zwischenstaatliche und gemeinschaftsrechtliche Sozialrechtsintegration im Vergleich. EuR 1985:113

Schuler R (1988) Das international Sozialrecht der Bundesrepublik Deutschland, Baden-Baden

Schulte B (1988) Allgemeine Regeln des internationalen Sozialrechts – supranationales Recht. In: von Maydell/Ruland, Sozialrechtshandbuch (SRH), Neuwied, p 1195

Stergiou A (2013) Social security law. Zygos, Thessaloniki

Tantaroudas C (1976) La protection juridique des travailleurs migrants de la C.E.E. Economica, Paris

Tsotsorou T (2013) Comments on the CJEU judgment of 12.06.2012 on joined cases C-611/10 and C-612/10, Hudzinski and Wawrzyniak. EDKA (Social Security Law Review), p 281

Tsotsorou T, Sklikas N (2008) The modernisation of the coordination mechanism for social security systems - the general principles of equal treatment and aggregation. Ant. N. Sakkoulas Publishing, Athens-Komotini

White R (1999) EC social security law. Longman European Law Series, Pearson Education Limited, UK

Zacharis G, Tsotsorou T (2012) National reforms in the Pension Field under the European Union Coordination of Social Security Systems. EDKA (Social Security Law review) (ND), p 800

Chapter 7
Practical Effects of the Anti-overlapping Rules

7.1 The New Anti-overlapping Rules

The rules of Articles 53, 54, 55 of Regulation No 883/04 replaced the corresponding rules of the complicated[1] Articles 46a, 46b, 46c of Regulation No 1408/71, which were introduced to Regulation No 1408/71 with the amending Regulation No 1248/92. **As noted, these rules have generally remained the same, except for two changes: the addition of Article 53(3)(b) of Regulation No 883/04 and the amendment of Article 46c(1) of Regulation No 1408/71.**[2] The rules against overlapping could schematically be summarised as follows, always taking into account all the provisions of the general article on rules against overlapping, i.e. Article 53 of Regulation No 883/04:

- In case of overlapping benefits of the same kind → application of Article 54 of Regulation No 883/04 (Article 46b of Regulation No 1408/71), in conjunction with Article 53(3)(d) of Regulation No 883/04 (Article 46a(3)(d) of Regulation No 1408/71). It refers to a case of a single independent benefit overlapping with other pro-rata benefits of the same kind, while there is no provision for overlapping of benefits of the same kind, where more independent benefits are involved.
- In case of overlapping of benefits of a different kind → either i) application of Article 55 of Regulation No 883/04 (Article 46c of Regulation No 1408/71) where the legislation against overlapping of several Member States is applicable or ii) application of Article 53(3)(d) of Regulation No 883/04 (Article 46a(3)(d) of Regulation No 1408/71), when the legislation against overlapping of a single Member State is applicable, whose due benefit may be independent or pro-rata, as may be the overlapping benefits.

[1] Cornelissen (1998), p. 698, footnote 35.
[2] Verschueren (2009), p. 155.

A. Tsetoura, *Pension Rights and Free Movement of Persons*,
https://doi.org/10.1007/978-3-031-91127-9_7

- In case of overlapping of a benefit with other income acquired in another State→ application of Article 53(3)(d) of Regulation No 883/04 (Article 46a(3)(d) of Regulation No 1408/71). It refers to the case where the legislation against overlapping of a Member State is applicable. The benefit of the State in question may be independent or pro-rata. The "other income" could be included among others (wages from work) or be a benefit on which the special rules of the Regulation on pensions do not apply.

All the provisions and, of course, in particular Article 54(1) of Regulation No 883/04 (Article 46b(1) of Regulation No 1408/71) demonstrate that the only case where the application of rules to prevent overlapping is excluded is when benefits of the same kind overlap or when a pro-rata benefit overlap with (an) independent(s) benefit(s) of the same kind.

7.2 Rules to Prevent Overlapping

Article 53 of Regulation No 883/04 replaces Article 46a of Regulation No 1408/71, adopted with Regulation No 1248/92, also relating to the amendment of Article 46(3) of Regulation No 1408/71 on a ceiling that was introduced by such amending Regulation No 1248/92. Article 46a of Regulation No 1408/71 was titled "General provisions relating to reduction, suspension or withdrawal applicable to benefits in respect of invalidity, old age or survivors under the legislations of the Member States". It should be reminded that according to consistent case-law, a national rule must be regarded as a provision on reduction, within the meaning of Regulation No 1408/71, if the calculation it requires to be made has the effect of reducing the amount of pension which the person concerned may claim because he receives a benefit from another Member State.[3]

Thus, according to Article 53(1) of Regulation No 883/04, any overlapping of invalidity, old-age and survivors' benefits calculated or provided on the basis of periods of insurance and/or residence completed by the same person shall be considered to be overlapping of benefits of the same kind. This provision corresponds to Article 46a (1) of Regulation No 1408/71. It should be mentioned that Article 46a (1) of amended Regulation No 1408/71 has added a criterion which was already implicit in the case-law cited above in defining the overlapping of benefits of the same kind as the overlapping of benefits in respect of invalidity, old age

[3]Judgments of 22.10.1998, C-143/97, Conti, European Court Reports 1998 I-6365, paragraph 25; of 07.03.2002, C-107/00, Insalaca, European Court Reports 2002 I-2403, paragraph 16; of 21.07.2005, Case C-30/04, Koschitzki, European Court Reports 2005 I-07389 ECLI:EU:C:2005:492, paragraph 35.

survivors "calculated or provided on the basis of periods of insurance and/or residence completed by one and the same person".[4]

However, the Court has consistently held that social security benefits must be regarded, irrespective of the characteristics peculiar to different national legal systems, as being of the same kind when their purpose and object, as well as the basis on which they are calculated and the conditions for granting them are identical.[5]

On the other hand, characteristics which are purely formal must not be considered relevant criteria for the classification of the benefits.[6] In view of the case-law definition regarding which benefits (pensions) are considered to be of the same kind, the question arises whether the pensions granted under a pay-as-you-go pension scheme and the pensions granted under a funded pension scheme are considered of the same kind or not. If return of capital is considered as a primary element for the calculation of the benefit in a funded pension scheme, they should be considered to be of a different kind. If it is accepted that the time periods play an equally important role in the funded pension schemes, so that there is a correlation regarding the method of calculating the benefit with the one in the pay-as-you-go pension schemes, the question arises whether such benefits could be considered of the same kind or not.

Furthermore, according to Article 53(2) of Regulation No 883/04, an overlapping of benefits, which cannot be considered of the same kind within the meaning of paragraph 1, shall be considered as an overlapping of benefits of a different kind. The provision cited above corresponds to the provision of Article 46a (2) of Regulation No 1408/71, offering a negative definition of the overlapping of benefits of a different kind.

It should be noted that Article 53(3)(a) of Regulation No 883/04 corresponds to Article 46a(3)(a) of Regulation No 1408/71; equally, Article 53(3)(c) and (d) of Regulation No 883/04 correspond to Article 46a (3)(c) and (d) of Regulation No 1408/71. From the provision of Article 53(3)(b) of Regulation No 883/04 only the first phrase corresponds to Article 46a(3)(b) of Regulation No 1408/71, while its second phrase is a new addition to Regulation No 883/04. The Court has ruled that in terms of Article 46a(3)(c) of Regulation No 1408/71 (Article 53(3)(c) of Regulation 883/04), having regard to the wording and context of Article 46a(3)(c) of Regulation No 1408/71, and the objective pursued by it, the concept of "voluntary insurance or continued optional insurance" should be interpreted in a broad manner in order not to

[4] Judgment of the Court of 11.08.1995, Case C-98/94, Schmidt, European Court Reports 1995 I-02559 ECLI:EU:C:1995:273, paragraph 27.

[5] Judgments of 05.05.1983, 238/81, Van der Bunt-Craig, European Court Reports 1983, p. 1385, paragraph 13; of 05.07.1983,171/82, Valentini, European Court Reports 1983, p. 2157, paragraph 13; of 06.04.1995, C-325/93, Del Grosso, European Court Reports 1995, p. I-939, paragraph 24; of 11.08.1995, C-98/94, Schmidt, European Court Reports 1995, p. I-2559, paragraph 24; of 12.02.1998, C-366/96, Cordelle, European Court Reports 1998, p. I-583, paragraph 19; judgment of 06.10.1987, 197/85, Stefanutti, European Court Reports 1987, p. 3855, paragraph 12; of 07.03.2002, C-107/00, Insalaca European Court Reports 2002 I-02403, paragraph 47.

[6] Judgment of 05.07.1983,171/82, Valentini, European Court Reports 1983, p. 2157, paragraph 13.

deprive the person concerned of any period of voluntary insurance or continued optional insurance completed under the legislation of another Member State.[7]

In that regard, it should be pointed out that, as the Advocate-General observed at paragraph 43 of his Opinion, the origins of Article 46a(3)(c) of Regulation No 1408/71 also support a broad interpretation of the concept of "voluntary insurance or continued optional insurance".[8] Article 46(2) of Regulation No 574/72, titled "Calculation of benefits in the event of overlapping of insurance periods", provided that, for the purposes of applying the national rules against overlapping in the context of Article 46(3) of Regulation No 1408/71, the amounts of benefits corresponding to periods of voluntary or optional continued insurance shall not be taken into account.

In the Schaap[9] judgment, the Court observed that Article 46(2) of Regulation No 574/72, even if it is included in said title, must be applied in any case falling within the scope of Article 46(3) of Regulation No 1408/71, when, for the purposes of applying this paragraph, the competent institution cannot take into account the amount of benefits corresponding to periods completed under voluntary or optional continued insurance. As can be seen from the proposed amendment to Article 46(2) of Regulation No 574/72 submitted by the Commission of the European Communities, the restriction sought by the insertion of Article 46a(3)(c) of Regulation No 1408/71 was intended to respond to the interpretation made by the Court of the latter provision.[10] According to settled case-law, the concept covers every type of insurance incorporating a voluntary element, whether or not there is any continuance of existing insurance.[11]

Thus, the Court, in the Bouman case, held that[12] the part of the benefit that is based on the period during which Mrs Bouman had the right, in principle, to an

[7] Judgment of the Court of 12.02.2015, Case C-114/13, Bouman, Digital reports (Court Reports - general) ECLI:EU:C:2015:81, paragraph 42.

[8] Bouman, paragraph 43.

[9] Judgment of 05.04.1979, Case 176/78, Max Schaap, European Court Reports 1979 01673 EU:C:1979:112, paragraphs 10 and 11.

[10] Cited above, Bouman judgment, paragraph 46.

[11] Judgment of the Court of 16.03.1977, Case 93/76, Liegeois, European Court Reports 1977 00543 ECLI:EU:C:1977:50, paragraphs 12 to 14; of 18.05.1989, Case 368/87, Troiani, European Court Reports 1989 01333 ECLI:EU:C:1989:206, paragraph 12; of 12.02.2015,Case C-114/13, Bouman, Digital reports (Court Reports - general) ECLI:EU:C:2015:81, paragraph 48.

[12] Mrs Th.-H. Bouman is a Netherlands citizen who lived in the Netherlands until 23 June 1957 and who, after that date lived in Belgium until 3 February 1974. As she was married to a Belgian national who died on 3 August 1968, Mrs Th.-H. Bouman has been receiving a Belgian survivor's pension since 1 September 1969, granted to her on the basis of a decision of the Rijksdienst of 10 July 1969. Since that time, Mrs Th.-H. Bouman has never earned income of her own from any professional activity. After her return to the Netherlands, Mrs Th.-H. Bouman paid contributions to build up a Netherlands old age pension under the AOW ("AOW pension"). In respect of the last four years prior to retirement age, that is, from 1 August 2003, Mrs Th.-H. Bouman requested and obtained, on the basis of Article 22 of the Dutch Decree, an exemption from affiliation under the AOW. She therefore ceased contributing to the Netherlands social security scheme, with the consequence that her pension contributions record under the AOW was not complete. Since 1 June 2007, having reached retirement age, Mrs Bouman has been receiving a partial pension

exemption from affiliation, but did not exercise that option, falls within the concept of "voluntary insurance or continued optional insurance" for the purposes of Article 46a(3)(c) of Regulation No 1408/71, if that continuation of affiliation during the period in question affects the periods of affiliation and, accordingly, the amount of Mrs Bouman's future old age pension.[13]

As noted, foreign pensions (from other Member States) or income acquired in other Member States may be considered as justifying a reduction in their payment under national rules against overlapping if such rules provide for the reduction, allowing for the international application of such reduction (Article 53(1)(a) of Regulation No 883/04).[14] These rules produce unjustified results if they are interpreted strictly as rules against overlapping.[15]

In the Engelbrecht[16] case, where the questions were raised in proceedings between Mr R. Engelbrecht and the Rijksdienst voor Pensioenen (National Pensions Office), the Belgian social security agency, concerning his retirement pension, it was evident that the national rules against overlapping at issue in the main proceedings were specifically devised to deal with the increase in the couple's total income resulting from the receipt of a retirement or survivor's pension by the spouse of the insured person concerned. The Court concluded that in such cases the competent authorities must necessarily know exactly how much both the worker and his spouse receive by way of benefits (Engelbrecht, paragraph 43). In those circumstances, it is contrary to Article 48 of the Treaty for the competent authorities to content themselves with merely reducing the worker's pension without ascertaining whether the pension granted to the spouse actually increases the couple's total income (Engelbrecht, paragraph 44).

In the specific case, once the applicant R. Engelbrecht reached the age of 65, his wife was awarded a Netherlands old age pension. That pension was calculated on the basis of her completed periods of both voluntary and compulsory insurance. As a corollary, the competent national institution withdrew the supplementary pension which it had hitherto paid to Mr R. Engelbrecht. It also notified Mr R. Engelbrecht that, since his wife was receiving in the Netherlands a retirement pension or equivalent benefit within the meaning of the relevant national legislation, the pension which he had been awarded at the household rate would be converted into a pension at the single rate. The Court held that (paragraph 45): "where the competent authorities of a Member State apply a provision of law—which fixes

---

under the AOW. By decision of 4 February 2009, the Rijksdienst informed Mrs Th.-H. Bouman of its decision to deduct, with effect from 1 June 2007, the AOW pension from her Belgian's survivor's pension, and to bring proceedings for recovery of the sum overpaid in respect of the latter pension amounting to EUR 2 271.81.

[13] Judgment of the Court of 12.02.2015, Case C-114/13, Bouman, Digital reports (Court Reports - general) ECLI:EU:C:2015:81, paragraph 54.

[14] Schuler (2015), p. 358 with reference to Case C-279/82 Jerzak, EU:C:1993:228.

[15] Schuler (2015), p. 358.

[16] Judgment of the Court of 26 September 2000, Case C-262/97, Engelbrecht, European Court Reports 2000 I-07321 ECLI:EU:C:2000:492.

the amount of the retirement pension awarded to a married worker;—which provides for that pension to be reduced, by the amount of the pension awarded to his spouse under the scheme of another Member State, but—which provides for the application of a derogating clause in respect of overlapping where the pension paid elsewhere is less than a certain amount, it is contrary to Article 48 of the Treaty for those authorities to reduce the amount of the pension awarded to a migrant worker by the amount of a pension awarded to his spouse under the scheme of another Member State, when the grant of that latter pension does not involve any increase in the couple's total".

Therefore, in order to avoid unjustified overlapping of benefits, it is not allowed to apply provisions on reduction, suspension or withdrawal provided for in the national legislation, subject to the limitation of Article 46a(3)(d) of Regulation No 1408/71 and now of Article 53(3)(d) of Regulation No 883/04.

More specifically, it is worth noting that the CJEU has also applied in the past the provision of Article 46a(3)(d) of Regulation No 1408/71 on overlapping benefits of a different kind. The Court specifically applied said provision on an old-age pension benefit overlapping with a survivor's pension in the Cordelle[17] case. Ms Cordelle had received a survivor's pension, calculated on the basis of her late husband's full working career, paid by the Belgian employees' pension scheme ("the Belgian survivor's pension"), and three pensions in her own right, of which two—an "employee's retirement pension" and a "self-employed person's retirement pension"—are paid by the Belgian scheme and the third—an old-age pension ("the French old-age pension")—is paid by the French scheme.

As the Court noted, **Article 46a was added to Regulation No 1408/71, paragraph (3)(d) of which provides, in particular,** that where rules against overlapping are applicable under the legislation of only one Member State on account of the fact that the person concerned receives benefits of the same or different kind payable under the legislation of other Member States or other incomes acquired in other Member States, **the benefit payable under the legislation of the first Member State may be reduced only within the limit of the amount of the benefits payable under the legislation of other Member States** (Cordelle, paragraph 14). At this point, it should be noted that the Greek version of the judgments refers to a "reduction of the benefit". On the contrary, the English as well as the French version of the judgment refers to a "benefit payable": "the benefit payable under the legislation of the first Member State may be reduced only within the limit of the amount of the benefits payable under the legislation of other Member States"/ "la prestation due en vertu de la législation du premier État membre ne peut être réduite que dans la limite du montant des prestations dues en vertu de la législation des autres États membres".

Pursuant to the rule of Article **46a(3)(d) of Regulation No 1408/71, the Belgian survivor's pension could only be reduced within the limit of the amount of the**

[17] Judgment of the Court of 12.02.1998, Case C-366/96, Cordelle, European Court Reports 1998 I-00583 ECLI:EU:C:1998:57.

French old-age pension/ "En application de cette règle, la pension belge de survie ne pourrait être réduite que dans la limite du montant de la pension française de vieillesse" (Cordelle, paragraph 15). As such, the Court held that Article 12(2) of Regulation No 1408/71 does not preclude a Member State from applying a rule against overlapping under which, when calculating a survivor's pension awarded under its own legislation on the basis of the deceased spouse's career, account is to be taken of benefits to which the survivor is entitled in his or her own right in another Member State where those benefits are to be classified as retirement pension or other equivalent benefits under the legislation of the first Member State. It is for the national court to decide on the classification, for the purpose of applying that rule against overlapping, of the benefits in question (Cordelle, paragraph 25).

It is not clear, however, taking also into account the aforementioned decision, whether the provision of Article 46a(3)(d) of Regulation No 1408/71, now Article 53(3)(d) of Regulation No 883/04 relates to the reduction of a benefit payable or the benefit payable as such. In view of this observation, the questions arising from following one or the other option are discussed in detail below.

Regarding the wording in Article 46a(3) of Regulation No 1408/71, at least in terms of sub-paragraph (d), it read: "where provisions on reduction, suspension or withdrawal are applicable under the legislation of only one Member State on account of the fact that the person concerned receives benefits of a similar or different kind payable under the legislation of other Member States or other income acquired within the territory of other Member States, the benefit payable under the legislation of the first Member State may be reduced only within the limit of the amount of the benefits payable under the legislation or the income acquired within the territory of other Member States". However, both Article 53(3)(d) of Regulation No 883/04 and Article 46a(3)(d) of Regulation No 1408/71 refer to the maximum reduction without excluding smaller amounts of reductions.

As it can be concluded, however, the provision of Article 53(3)(d) of Regulation No 883/04 (Article 46a(3)(d) of Regulation No 1408/71) applies:

- when the legislation against overlapping of a single Member State is applicable, in case of overlapping of a single independent benefit with other pro-rata benefits of the same kind. The State applying legislation against overlapping is the State that is due to pay the independent benefit
- when the legislation against overlapping of a single Member State is applicable, in case of overlapping of benefits of a different kind. The State applying legislation against overlapping may be due to pay an independent or a pro-rata benefit. The other benefits with which the payable benefit overlaps may be independent or pro-rata.
- when the legislation against overlapping of a single Member State is applicable, the benefit payable by it may be independent or pro-rata, in case of its benefit overlapping with another benefit or income acquired in another State. The "other benefit"/"other income" may be a pension on which the special rules of the Regulation on pensions do not apply or wages from work.

Pennings' line of reasoning regarding Article 53(3)(d) of Regulation No 883/04 (Article 43(3)(d) of Regulation No 1408/71) is in combination with Article 54 of Regulation No 883/04. This line of reasoning has also been based on the wording of Regulation No 883/04 in its English version, regarding Article 53 (3)(d) of Regulation No 883/04: "(...)the benefit due may be reduced solely by the amount of such benefits or such income". The wording in the German version of Regulation No 883/04 is also similar: "(...) so kann die geschuldete Leistung nur um den Betrag dieser Leistungen oder Einkünfte gekürzt werden". This line of reasoning is consistent with the interpretation of the Court in its case-law following the amendment of Regulation No 1408/71 with Regulation No 1248/92 and in particular in the Court's judgment cited above in the Cordelle case (Greek version).[18]

However, in the Greek and French versions of the same phrase in Article 53(3)(d) of Regulation No 883/04, the wording is somewhat different than the aforementioned English version. More specifically, the Greek version reads: "[...]the benefit due may be reduced only within the limit of the amount of such benefits or income" (exact translation of the Greek version). Similarly, the French version reads: "[...]la prestation due ne peut être réduite que dans la limite du montant de ces prestations ou de ces revenus". It seems like they are following the former wording of Article 46a (3)(d) of Regulation No 1408/71, which read in its English version: "[...]the benefit payable under the legislation of the first Member State may be reduced only within the limit of the amount of the benefits payable under the legislation or the income acquired within the territory of the other Member States".

The question therefore is raised on what Article 53(3)(d) of Regulation No 883/04 actually provides for: the amount of the reduction or the amount of the benefit payable. It seems likely that it is the latter since it offers a fairer pension protection, as will be demonstrated in the next section.

The confusion, therefore, derives from the definition of the concept of "due benefit" in Article 46a(3)(d) of Regulation No 1408/71 (Article 53(3)(d) of Regulation No 883/04). That is, whether it has the meaning of a pension with or without the supplement of Article 50 of Regulation No 1408/71 (Article 58 of Regulation No 883/04). The CJEU had ruled that the supplement should be taken into account in determining the theoretical amount of the pro-rata pension.[19]

Since the supplement as pension benefit is taken into account in accordance with the case-law when applying the rules for calculating the pension, and in particular when calculating the theoretical amount, we can consider that the "payable benefit" refers to the pro-rata benefit including the supplement. It would be better to calculate the supplement benefit in case of a pro-rata pension at the award stage, during which the rules against overlapping rules apply, without a new retrospective calculation. As already demonstrated, the amounts compared, i.e. the independent and the pro-rata

[18] Judgment of the Court of 12.02.1998, Case C-366/96, Cordelle, European Court Reports 1998 I-00583 ECLI:EU:C:1998:57, paragraph 14.

[19] Judgment of the Court of 24.09.1998, Case C-132/96, Stinco and Panfilo, European Court Reports 1998 I-05225, ECLI:EU:C:1998:427, paragraph 22. See also "Granting of a Supplement".

are compared following the results of the application of the rules against overlapping. Following therefore the application of rules against overlapping, the highest amount is selected and no new calculation of the supplement is required, as the latter has already been taken into account for determining the theoretical amount of the pro-rata benefit at the award stage. Article 50 of Regulation No 1408/71/ Article 58 of Regulation No 883/04 is not therefore applied following the application of Article 46a(3)(d) of Regulation No 1408/71/ Article 53(3)(d) of Regulation No 883/04.

Taking into account that Article 46a(3)(d) of Regulation No 1408/71 (Article 53(3)(d) of Regulation No 883/04) may refer to the overlapping of an independent or pro-rata benefit with another benefit or income, the following distinction can be made:

- If an independent benefit overlaps with another benefit/income, the benefit due is the independent pension calculated under the national legislation. The question is then whether Article 50 of Regulation No 1408/71/Article 58 of Regulation No 883/04, which refers to the calculation of benefits in accordance with the relevant chapter on pensions, can be applied, since it is obvious that said calculation has not taken place neither for the independent, but potentially not for any other benefit/income falling within the scope of that chapter. In this case, we consider the "benefit due" in Article 46a(3)(d) of Regulation No 1408/71 (Article 53(3)(d) of Regulation No 883/04) as having the meaning of an independent benefit without a supplement. The independent benefit is therefore compared only with the other benefit/income, while Article 50 of Regulation No 1408/71/Article 58 of Regulation No 883/04 cannot be applied, due to an independent entitlement to the benefit under the national legislation alone (as more advantageous).
- If another pro-rata benefit overlaps with another benefit/income, the benefit due is the pro-rata pension calculated based on the award under Article 46 of Regulation No 1408/71/ Article 52 of Regulation No 883/04, whose theoretical amount includes the supplement: then, the benefit due is the pro-rata benefit including the supplement, which is compared with the other benefit/income without a new calculation of the supplement after the application of the rules against overlapping. In this case, for the calculation of the supplement, it is obvious that for determining the total of the aggregated pension benefits, the pension benefits that should be aggregated are those under award or according to the wording of Article 50 of Regulation No 1408/71/Article 58 of Regulation No 883/04 in this chapter, i.e. Chapter 3 of Regulation No 1408/71/Chapter 5 of Regulation No 883/04.

In any event, to avoid leading a discussion devoid of purpose, it is important to consider the supplement within a State as a social security pension benefit, so that the relevant provisions can apply to it. States tend not to take into the account the supplement within their territories, which they achieve by treating the supplements of Article 50 of Regulation No 1408/71 (Article 58 of Regulation No 883/04) as special non-contributory benefits, to which the relevant pension rules are not applicable.[20]

However, it seems to remain an issue in all cases, whether other pensions, if not other income, can be taken into account, without falling however within the scope of the special rules of the chapter on pensions (e.g. pension due to a work accident).

Both Article 50 of Regulation No 1408/71 and Article 58 of Regulation No 883/04 refer to the total of benefits due by virtue of the chapter on pensions (Chapter 3 of Regulation No 1408/71/Chapter 5 of Regulation No 883/04). The minimum benefit is the benefit determined in the legislation of the State of residence for a period of insurance or residence equal to the total of the periods taken into account for the purposes of award according to this chapter (of the special rules on pensions) (Article 50 of Regulation No 1408/71/Article 58(1) of Regulation No 883/04). Thus, it should be noted, in that regard, that it is the sum of the pension instalments that should be below the national minimum benefit.[21]

Indeed, according to the aforementioned analysis on benefits due, there is no question of a sum/total of benefit due and of another benefit or other income in the application of the rule against overlapping or following its application. As regards the case of overlapping of a pro-rata benefit with another benefit/income, this is due because the sum/total of the pensions covered by the article on award has been calculated at the award stage. As regards the case of an overlapping of an independent benefit with a pro-rata benefit of the same kind or another benefit/income, there is no issue of a supplement, because the "benefit due" is the independent benefit provided under national legislation alone.

The aforementioned issue also interferes with the issue of pension benefits not covered by Articles 50–60 of Regulation No 883/04 because they are not benefits in respect of invalidity, old age or survivors, which are only covered by such special rules. More specifically, it interferes with cases where the legislation referred to in Article 52 and which by extension affects the application of rules of Articles 53–55 of Regulation No 883/04 is the only legislation on pension in respect of old age, invalidity and death. In this sense, the only insurance periods that may be used are those arising by such legislation alone, excluding insurance periods under, for example, legislation awarding pension for a work accident (in states with a separate insurance scheme for work accidents). Indeed, the Court has already ruled that when it comes to benefits such as the French benefits in the Valentini case that do not fall within the scope of Article 46 of Regulation No 1408/71 (Article 52 of Regulation No 883/04), where such benefits overlap with old-age pensions of other Member States, Community law does not prevent the national rules against overlapping from being applied.[22]

[20] See above "Granting of a supplement".

[21] Zacharis (2014), p. 83.

[22] Judgment of the Court of 05.07.1983, Case 171/82, Valentini, European Court Reports 1983 02157 ECLI:EU:C:1983:189, paragraph 23.

However, pensions for work accidents and occupational disease may be considered as invalidity pensions in their capacity as benefits of the same kind in view of the similarity of their objective and characteristics,[23] a criterion applied in case-law for the determination of benefits of the same kind,[24] while according to case-law characteristics which are purely formal must not be considered relevant criteria for the classification of benefits.[25] In addition, the disability may be related to the incapacity for work resulting from an accident at work or an occupational disease. The Court used to refer to these pensions holding that, calculating these pensions based on Article 46 of Regulation No 1408/71 on award of benefits (according to Article 12(2) of Regulation No 1408/71, the provisions of the legislation of a Member State governing the reduction, suspension or withdrawal of benefits in cases of overlapping [...] do not apply where the beneficiary receives benefits of the same kind in respect of invalidity, old age, death or occupational disease that are awarded by the institution of the various Member States involved, in accordance with the provisions of Article 46 of that regulation[26]).

The unfavourable for the migrant evolution of the rules coordinating the overlapping of benefits was characteristically demonstrated in the van den Booren[27] case, where the Court, in order to mitigate the effects of the application of the rules against overlapping, invoked Article 45 TFEU and applied the principle of free movement, in conjunction with the principles of equal treatment of migrant and non-migrant workers, as well as the principle of proportionality. It held, however, that it is for the national court to assess whether the disadvantage resulting from the application of a national provision against overlapping is justified by objective considerations and is proportionate to the legitimate object pursued by national law.

Mrs A. van den Booren, the appellant in the main proceedings, was born on 18 August 1920 and resides in Maastricht. Her husband, Mr J. Bartels, who died on 1 March 1982, worked as an underground miner in Belgium. By administrative decision of 11 July 1986, the NPO granted Mrs A. van den Booren a Belgian survivor's pension retroactively with effect from 1 August 1985. From that same date, Mrs A. van den Booren also received a Netherlands old-age pension under the

---

[23] See Judgment of the Court of 29.05.1979, Joined cases 173 and 174/78, Villano Barion, European Court Reports 1979 I- 01851 ECLI:EU:C:1979:134 and the Opinion of Advocate-General Francesco Capotorti of 3 May 1979.

[24] See above case-law on overlapping and below case-law on overlapping of benefits of the same kind.

[25] Judgment of the Court of 05.07.1983, Case 171/82, Valentini, European Court Reports 1983 02157 ECLI:EU:C:1983:189, paragraph 13.

[26] Judgment of the Court of 06.04.1995, Case C-325/93, Del Grosso, European Court Reports 1995 I-00939 ECLI:EU:C:1995:103, paragraph 21; judgment of 02.08.1993,Case C-31/92, Marius Larsy, European Court Reports 1993 I-04543, ECLI:EU:C:1993:340, paragraph 14; of 05.04.1990, Case C-108/89, Pian, European Court Reports 1990 I-01599 ECLI:EU:C:1990:167, paragraphs 11, 16; of 18.04.1989,Case 128/88, Di Felice, European Court Reports 1989 00923 ECLI:EU:C:1989:153, paragraph 10.

[27] Judgment of the Court of 07.03.2013, Case C-127/11, van den Booren, Digital reports (Court Reports - general) ECLI:EU:C:2013:140.

Netherlands General Law on Old-Age Insurance, hereinafter: AOW. Mrs A. van den Booren's Netherlands old-age pension was increased to EUR 869.24 per month with retroactive effect from 1 January 2002. That increase resulted from the fact that, at the end of 2002, the Netherlands legislature had filled the legal lacuna affecting certain married women who were resident in the Netherlands and whose spouses had not been insured under the AOW on the ground that they had worked outside the Netherlands during the period from 1 January 1957 to 1 January 1980. By letter of 12 August 2004, the NPO notified Mrs A. van den Booren that the decision of 11 July 1986 had been revised, to the effect that, as a result of the increase in her Netherlands old-age pension, her Belgian survivor's pension was being reduced. By the same letter, the NPO also requested reimbursement by Mrs A. van den Booren of the benefits overpaid in respect of the period from 1 March 2004 to 31 July 2004, an amount totalling EUR 506.45. Mrs A. van den Booren brought an action against the decision revising her survivor's pension and against the reimbursement decision before the arbeidsrechtbank te Tongeren (Labour Court, Tongeren), which declared that action to be unfounded. As regards, more specifically, the argument raised by Mrs A. van den Booren relating to Article 46a of Regulation No 1408/71, that court found that there had been no infringement of that article. As the Netherlands old-age pension had to be considered to be a benefit taking the place of a retirement pension, it was necessary to proceed, in accordance with Article 46a(3)(a) of Regulation No 1408/71, with a reduction of the Belgian survivor's pension.

In the context of said case, the Court held that it is for the national court to assess the compatibility of the rules of national legislation at issue with the requirements of European Union law by determining whether the Belgian rule against overlapping, which admittedly applies without distinction to Belgian nationals and to nationals of other Member States, does not in fact lead, in respect of the person concerned, to an unfavourable situation in comparison with that of a person whose situation has no cross-border element, and, if such a disadvantage is established in the present case, whether the national rule at issue is justified by objective considerations and is proportionate to the legitimate objective pursued by national law (paragraph 46). The answer to the questions referred to the Court is as follows (paragraph 47):

- Article 46a of Regulation No 1408/71 must be interpreted as meaning that it does not preclude the application of legislative rules of a Member State containing a provision under which a survivor's pension received in that Member State is reduced as a result of the increase in an old-age pension received under the legislation of another Member State, provided, in particular, that the conditions set out in Article 46a(3)(d) are observed;
- Article 45 TFEU must be interpreted as meaning that it likewise does not preclude the application of such national legislative rules in so far as they do not lead, in respect of the person concerned, to an unfavourable situation in comparison with that of a person whose situation has no cross-border element, and, if such a disadvantage is established, in so far as it is justified by objective considerations and is proportionate in relation to the objective legitimately pursued by national law, this being a matter for the referring court to ascertain.

The Court upheld the above judgment in the Wencel[28] case. Mrs J. Wencel, a Polish national, has been registered since 1954 as resident in the city of Białystok (Poland). By decision of the ZUS of 24 October 1990, she acquired the right to a Polish retirement pension, by virtue of the insurance periods completed in Poland. Following the death of her husband in 2008, the German insurance institution granted Mrs Wencel a survivor's pension on the basis, inter alia, of her residence in Germany. She is currently living in Poland with her son, daughter-in-law and grandchildren.

By its questions, the referring court asks, in essence, whether EU law must be interpreted as meaning that a social security institution is entitled to withdraw, retroactively, the pension right of an insured person who, for many years, has had two habitual residences simultaneously in two different Member States, and to demand repayment of any pension to which, it is alleged, the person concerned is not entitled, on the ground that the insured person receives a survivor's pension in another Member State in the territory of which he has also been resident (paragraph 42).

Accordingly, the CJEU held that it is for the national court to assess the compatibility of the rules of national legislation at issue with the requirements of European Union law by determining whether the rule requiring the withdrawal of a pension entitlement and the repayment of sums to which, it is claimed, the person concerned was not entitled, which applies without distinction to Polish nationals and to nationals of other Member States, does not in fact lead, in respect of the person concerned, to an unfavourable situation in comparison with that of a person whose situation has no cross-border element, and, if such a disadvantage is established in the present case, whether the national rule at issue is justified by objective considerations and is proportionate to the legitimate objective pursued by national law[29] (paragraph 71). The referring court should also bear in mind that the principle of cooperation in good faith laid down in Article 4 TFEU requires the competent authorities in the Member States to use all the means at their disposal to achieve the aim of Article 45 TFEU[30] (paragraph 72).

The Court reached the same conclusion in both Wencel and van der Booren cases. However, in the Wencel case, the Court also refers to the principle of cooperation in good faith, which should be taken into account by the Court when assessing whether a national measure is based on objective considerations and is proportional so that it can be justified and not deemed contrary to Article 45 TFEU.

---

[28] Judgment of the Court of 16.05.2013, Case C-589/10, Wencel, Digital reports (Court Reports - general)ECLI:EU:C:2013:303.

[29] Cited above, van den Booren judgment, paragraph 46.

[30] Judgment of 05.10.1994, Case C-165/91, van Munster, European Court Reports/ECR 1994 I-04661, paragraph 32; judgment of 01.10.2009, Case C-3/08, Leyman, European Court Reports 2009 I-09085 ECLI:EU:C:2009:595, paragraph 49.

7.3 Overlapping of Benefits of the Same Kind

Article 54 of Regulation No 883/04 replaces Article 46b of Regulation No 1408/71, introduced with amending Regulation No 1248/92. Article 46b of Regulation No 1408/71 includes the special provisions which apply in case of overlapping of benefits of the same kind due by virtue of the legislation of two or more Member States.

The Court has a rich case-law on which benefits can be considered to be of the same kind. According to the Court, Article 46b of the Regulation applies to benefits of the same kind; according to its settled case-law, social security benefits must be considered as being of the same kind when their purpose and basis of calculation are the same.[31] However, the Court has consistently held that social security benefits must be regarded, irrespective of the characteristics peculiar to different national legal systems, as being of the same kind when their purpose and object, as well as the basis on which they are calculated and the conditions for granting them are similar/identical;[32] on the other hand, characteristics which are purely formal must not be considered relevant criteria for the classification of the benefits.[33]

In that regard, according to previous decisions of the Court, where a worker is in receipt of invalidity benefits converted into an old-age pension by virtue of the legislation of a Member State and invalidity benefits not yet converted into an old-age pension under the legislation of another Member State, the old-age pension and the invalidity benefits are to be regarded as being of the same kind.[34] Those decisions also apply in cases in which old-age (retirement due to completion of retirement time) pensions due under the legislation of a Member State do not arise as a result of the conversion of invalidity benefits, provided that the old-age pension, whether or not arising from such a conversion, is of the same kind as an invalidity

[31] Judgments of 05.05.1983, 238/81, Van der Bunt-Craig, European Court Reports 1983, p. 1385, paragraph 13; of 05.07.1983,171/82, Valentini, European Court Reports 1983, p. 2157, paragraph 13; of 06.04.1995, C-325/93, Del Grosso, European Court Reports 1995, p. I-939, paragraph 24; of 11.08.1995, C-98/94, Schmidt, European Court Reports 1995, p. I-2559, paragraph 24; of 12.02.1998, C-366/96, Cordelle, European Court Reports 1998, p. I-583, paragraph 19; of 06.10.1987, 197/85, Stefanutti, European Court Reports 1987, p. 3855, paragraph 12; of 07.03.2002, C-107/00, Insalaca, European Court Reports 2002 I-02403 ECLI:EU:C:2002:147, paragraph 47.

[32] Judgments of 05.07.1983,171/82, Valentini, European Court Reports 1983, p. 2157, paragraph 13; of 06.10.1987, 197/85, Stefanutti, European Court Reports 1987, p. 3855, paragraph 12; of 06.04.1995, Case C-325/93, Del Grosso, European Court Reports 1995 I-00939 ECLI:EU:C:1995: 103, paragraph 24.

[33] Judgment of 05.07.1983,171/82, Valentini, European Court Reports 1983, p. 2157, paragraph 13; of 11.08.1995, C-98/94, Schmidt, European Court Reports 1995, p. I-2559, paragraph 24.

[34] Judgment of the Court of 2.07.1981, joined cases 116, 117, 119, 120 and 121/80, Celestre, European Court Reports 1981 01737 ECLI:EU:C:1981:159; of 05.04.1990, Case C-108/89, Pian, European Court Reports 1990 I-01599 ECLI:EU:C:1990:167, paragraph 12.

pension.[35] Benefits acquired under the legislation of two Member States, which seeks to ensure that an aged person deprived of the income of his or her deceased spouse has sufficient means of subsistence, and the respective amounts of which are determined on the basis of the insurance and social security contributions of that spouse, are benefits of the same kind.[36]

However, for the purpose of applying the legislation of one Member State, an old-age pension calculated in accordance with the legislation of another Member State on the basis of a working career extended by reason of motherhood, the Court clarified that it is to be treated in its entirety as a retirement pension or other equivalent benefit within the meaning of the legislation of the first Member State.[37] Of course, the Court also held that it is for the national court to decide on the classification, for the purpose of applying the rule against overlapping provided in its domestic legislation regarding retirement pensions or equivalent benefits, of an old-age benefit calculated in accordance with the legislation of another Member State on the basis of a working career extended by reason of motherhood.[38] As demonstrated in case-law a personal invalidity pension which is based on the recipient's own employment record in one Member State is not of the same kind as a survivor's pension based on the employment record of the recipient's deceased husband in another Member State;[39] as a result, survivor's pensions could be considered of the same kind as old-age pensions and invalidity pensions, only if the national legislation provided that survivor's pension is awarded based on the insurance record of the survivor and not the deceased person. Additionally, a supplement to a total permanent incapacity pension granted to a worker under the law of a Member State, and a retirement pension acquired by that same worker in a third country must be regarded as being of the same kind within the meaning of Regulation No 1408/71.[40] As the Court concluded in Blanco Marqués,[41] a national rule, pursuant to which the supplement to a total permanent incapacity pension is suspended during the period in which the beneficiary of that pension receives a retirement pension in another Member State or in Switzerland, constitutes a provision on reduction of benefit for the purposes of Article 12(2) of Regulation No 1408/71.

---

[35] Judgment of the Court of 05.04.1990, Case C-108/89, Pian, European Court Reports 1990 I-01599 ECLI:EU:C:1990:167, paragraph 13; of 18.04.1989, Case 128/88, Di Felice, European Court Reports 1989 00923 ECLI:EU:C:1989:153, paragraph 14.

[36] Judgment of the Court of 05.05.1983, Case 238/81, Van der Bunt – Craig, European Court Reports 1983 01385 ECLI:EU:C:1983:124, paragraph 16.

[37] Judgment of the Court of 12.02.1998, Case C-366/96, Cordelle, European Court Reports 1998 I-00583 ECLI:EU:C:1998:57, paragraph 22.

[38] Cordelle, paragraph 24.

[39] Judgment of 06.10.1987, 197/85, Stefanutti, European Court Reports 1987, p. 3855, paragraph 13.

[40] Judgement of 15.3.2018, Blanco Marqués, case C-431/16, ECLI:EU:C:2018:189.

[41] Judgement of 15.3.2018, Blanco Marqués, case C-431/16, ECLI:EU:C:2018:189.

According to Article 54(1) of Regulation No 883/04, where benefits of the same kind due under the legislation of two or more Member States overlap, the rules to prevent overlapping laid down by the legislation of a Member State shall not be applicable to a pro-rata benefit. This provision corresponds to the provision of Article 46b(1) of Regulation No 1408/71. According to the relevant theory, this rule is based on the judgment of the Court in the Pian[42] and Bianchin[43] cases.[44] Its justification is based on the fact that only the total amount of pro-rata pensions from the Member States involved provides full security to the beneficiary, while it makes no difference if there is more than one pro-rata invalidity pension (due to different age limits in the Members States) or for the overlapping of pro-rata invalidity pensions and the pro-rata old age pensions from another Member State.[45]

According to Article 54(2) of Regulation No 883/04, the rules to prevent overlapping shall apply to an independent benefit only if the benefit concerned is:

(a) a benefit the amount of which does not depend on the duration of periods of insurance or residence, or
(b) a benefit the amount of which is determined on the basis of a credited period deemed to have been completed between the date on which the risk materialised and a later date, overlapping with:
   (i) a benefit of the same type, except where an agreement has been concluded between two or more Member States to avoid the same credited period being taken into account more than once, or
   (ii) a benefit referred to in subparagraph (a).

The benefits and agreements referred to in sub-paragraphs (a) and (b) are listed in Annex IX.

The same provisions with the same structure were included in the corresponding Article 46b of Regulation No 1408/71.

It is thus concluded that the "rules to prevent overlapping" referred to in the provision of Article 54(2) of Regulation No 883/04 refer to the rules to prevent overlapping of Article 53 of Regulation No 883/04. Therefore, when benefits of the same kind, i.e. invalidity, old-age and survivor's pension, overlap on the basis of the personal insurance record of a person, according to Article 54 of Regulation No 883/04, the rules to prevent overlapping of Article 53 of Regulation No 883/04 may apply only in the specific cases of independent benefits, as demonstrated in Article 54 of Regulation No 883/04. However, the provision of Article 54 of Regulation No 883/04 in conjunction with Article 53(3)(d) of Regulation No 883/04 ("if a single Member State applies rules to prevent overlapping") applies only where an

[42] Judgment of the Court of 05.04.1990, Case C-108/89, Pian, European Court Reports 1990 I-01599 ECLI:EU:C:1990:167.

[43] Judgment of the Court of 05.04.1990, Case C-109/89, Bianchin, European Court Reports 1990 I-01619.

[44] Schuler (2015), p. 359.

[45] Ibid.

independent benefit overlap with pro-rata benefits of the same kind. It is not clear what happens in the hypothetical case where two independent benefits of the same kind overlap and therefore when more than one Member State apply rules against overlapping. It is possible, however, for one State to not deduct from its pension the amount of the other pension, which constitutes the maximum possible reduction, but less than said amount. It should also be noted that, as the provision of Article 53(3)(d) of Regulation No 883/04 is essentially subject to Article 54 of Regulation No 883/04, the application of the provision in Article 46a(3)(d) of Regulation No 1408/71 was also essentially subject to Article 46b of Regulation No 1408/71.

This means that the provision of Article 46a (3)(d) of Regulation No 1408/71 could not be applied as long as the independent benefit in question was overlapping with another pension of the same kind (and not an income as above), unless it fell under the specific cases of Article 46b of Regulation No 1408/71 (Article 54 of Regulation No 883/04). Thus:

- in case of overlapping of an independent benefit (of the same kind) of the categories listed in Article 54(2) of Regulation No 883/04 with pro-rata benefits of the same kind →, Article 53(3)(d) of Regulation No 883/04 applies in conjunction with Article 54(2) of Regulation No 883/04;
- in case of an independent benefit overlapping with another benefit/income, → Article 53(3)(d) of Regulation No 883/04 applies alone.

When the rules against overlapping of more than one Member States due to pay an independent benefit are applicable, there is no explicit provision as Article 53(3)(d) of Regulation No 883/04 refers expressly to the rules against overlapping of a single Member State; unless we are to consider that in cases where the rules against overlapping of several States due to pay independent benefits are applicable, there are no limitations on the national rules against overlapping.

In terms of Article 54(2)(a) of Regulation No 883/04, in Annex IX, the following countries have registered independent benefits the amount of which is independent of the length of periods of insurance or residence completed: Belgium, Denmark, Ireland, Greece, Spain, France, Latvia, the Netherlands, Finland and Sweden. For the most part, these are invalidity pensions.

However, there are questions raised regarding the registration of Denmark as well as Greece. More specifically, Denmark has included in Annex IX of Regulation No 883/04 the full national old-age pension acquired after 10 years' residence by persons who will have been awarded a pension by 1 October 1989. According to the relevant documents by the European Commission,[46] in principle, the residents of Denmark are entitled to a standard retirement pension (social pension or *folkepension*) when they reach the age of 67 (since 1st January 2023). The following persons are entitled to the social pension: Danish nationals; persons covered by Regulation (EC) No 883/2004 of 29 April 2004 on the coordination of social security systems; other foreign nationals after 10 years' residence in Denmark.

[46] European Commission – MISSOC (2024).

Full entitlement after 40 years of residence between the age of 15 and pensionable age, for people who reach the pensionable age before 1 July 2025. Full entitlement after residence in 9 out of 10 years, between the age of 15 and pensionable age, for people who reach the pensionable age on 1 July 2025 or later.

It is thus observed that the Danish pension in question does not depend on the periods of insurance or residence within the meaning of Article 54(2)(a) of Regulation No 883/04, as it depends on the periods of residence. Taking into account that Danish social security systems are generally financed by taxation based on the former residence in Denmark,[47] it can be concluded that Denmark has a social security system based on residence, which justifies the provision of periods of residence for the entitlement to a pension.

More questions are raised regarding Greece's registration, which has included in Annex IX of Regulation No 883/04, part I, regarding benefits referred to in Article 54(2)(a) of Regulation No 883/04, the benefits under Law No 4169/1961. This registration was not included in the corresponding Annex IV of Regulation No 1408/71, Part D, on benefits referred to in Article 46b(2)(a) of Regulation No 1408/71. Article 4, Law No 4169/1961 reads that in order to establish entitlement to an old-age pension, the insured person must have an insurance record of twenty five years (Article 4(1)(a) Law No 4169/1961) and have paid the insurance contributions corresponding to the insured years (Article 4(1)(c), Law No 4169/1961). It can therefore be concluded that the Greek old-age pension of Law No 4169/1961 depends on periods of insurance. These are, of course, the cases where the entitlement to an agricultural insurance scheme (OGA) old-age pension is created independently, without taking into account periods of insurance in another Member State.

It should also be noted that concerns could arise from the fact that in the funded pension schemes, benefits are independent and not dependent of the length of periods of insurance or residence. However, examining Annex VIII, Part 2 of Regulation No 883/04 on funded schemes and Annex IX of Regulation No 883/04 on independent benefits, the amount of which is not dependent of periods of insurance or residence, it is noted that the content of these two Annexes is not identical and that Annex IX of Regulation No 883/04 refers to other benefits than those of Annex VIII (2) of Regulation No 883/04. Furthermore, Annex IX of Regulation No 883/04 includes mainly invalidity pensions, while Annex VIII (2) of Regulation No 883/04 refers to old-age pensions. In any case, since pension benefits under funded schemes are not included in Annex IX of Regulation No 883/04, they do not fall within the scope of Article 54(2)(a) of Regulation No 883/04. If they were to be included in this Annex, they would match the meaning of Article 54(2)(a) of Regulation No 883/04 for the purposes of applying this Article.

Subsequently, Article 54(2)(b) of Regulation No 883/04 requires the existence of certain specific criteria for the application of rules against overlapping.[48] Thus,

---

[47] European Commission – MISSOC (2024).

[48] Schuler (2015), p. 359.

pensions which may be reduced because of their overlapping with pensions of the same kind (case i) or with pensions the amount of which is calculated based on the periods of insurance or residence of which it is dependent (case ii) are invoked in Annex IX of Regulation No 883/04.

Regarding "benefits referred to in Article 54(2)(b) of the Regulation, the amount of which is determined by reference to a credited period deemed to have been completed between the date on which the risk materialised and a later date" of Annex IX of Regulation No 883/04, the following countries have registered pensions: Germany, Spain, Italy, Latvia, Lithuania, Luxembourg, Slovakia, Finland and Sweden. These registrations also concern mainly invalidity pensions. Finally, the section of Annex IX of Regulation No 883/04 referring to "agreements referred to in Article 54(2)(b)(i) of Regulation intended to prevent the same credited period being taken into account two or more times" includes: the Social Security Agreement of 28 April 1997 between the Republic of Finland and the Federal Republic of Germany, the Social Security Agreement of 10 November 2000 between the Republic of Finland and the Grand Duchy of Luxembourg, the Nordic Convention of 18 August 2003 on social security. However, an issue that may arise is whether the term "of the same type" in Article 54(2)(b)(i) means "of the same kind" or whether the term "of the same type" refers to the same risk or even the same type of legislation regulating the invalidity pensions.

As Pennings highlights in particular, in so far as the rules against overlapping do not apply to a pro-rata benefit, the deduction of a benefit from a pro-rata benefit is not allowed, while a pro-rata benefit may be deducted from an independent benefit, the amount of which is not dependent from the period of insurance.[49] Thus, Pennings points out that if a person receives an independent old-age pension in State w, the amount of which is not dependent on the periods of insurance or residence, while at the same time that person also receives pensions from States x and y, State w may deduct pensions x and y from its pension only up to the amount of the pension benefits of these other States (by virtue also of Article 53(3)(d) of Regulation No 883/04).[50]

7.3.1 *Working Hypothesis 1*

To develop the example according to Pennings' line of reasoning, assuming that a State with an independent benefit will make the biggest possible deduction and placing random values, it can be supposed that:

1. The independent pension of State w (Pension w) is EUR 1000 and the total sum of pensions P(x + y) is EUR 700. Pw=1000, P(x + y)=700 and State w should pay

[49] Pennings (2015), p. 225.

[50] Ibid.

Pwfinal = Pw – P(x + y) = 1000 – 700 = EUR 300. Then, the total sum of pensions or the Total Pension amounts to P(x + y + w) = 700 + 300 = EUR 1000. Note that if Pw > P(x + y) then → TP = P(x + y) + [Pw - P(x + y)] = Pw. That means that when the State w pension is greater than the sum of the other pensions, the final total pension will be the amount of pension w.i.e. if Pw > P(x + y) → TP = Pw. From the initial total pension (TPinitial) 1700, the final total pension received (TPfinal) will be EUR 1000.

The pensioner's "damage" will be: Dpensioner = TPinitial – Tpfinal = 1700 – 1000 = EUR 700. This amount is calculated by a percentile reduction to a percentage of 41.2%. Thus, the pensioner is subject to a damage of 41.2%.

2. If in the above hypothesis, the independent pension of State w (Pw) is EUR 2000 and the sum of pensions P(x + y) = EUR 1500. Given that Pw = 2000 > 1500 [P (x + y)], State w will deduct from its own pension the sum of the other pensions and will have to pay Pw – P(x + y) = 2000 – 1500 = EUR 500. Then, the total pension received by the pensioner will be TPfinal = P(x + y) + [P(x + y) – Pw] = 1500 + 500 = EUR 2000. We see that the total pension that the person concerned will receive will be equal to the amount of the initial Pw pension. From the initial total pension TPinitial 3500, the final total pension received will be TPfinal EUR 2000. "Damage" D = TPinitial – Tpfinal = 3500 – 2000 = EUR 1500. Thus, the pensioner is subject to a damage of 43%.
3. If in the above hypothesis, the independent pension Pw is EUR 1500 and the sum is P(x + y) = EUR 1200. Given that Pw = 1500 > 1200[P(x + y)], State w will deduct from its own pension the sum of the other pensions and will have to pay Pw – P(x + y) = 1500 – 1200 = EUR 300. Then, the total pension received by the pensioner will be TPfinal = P(x + y) + [Pw – P(x + y)] = 1200 + 300 = EUR 1500. From the initial total pension 2700, the final total pension received amounts to EUR 1500 ("Damage" 2700 – 1500 = EUR 1200). Thus, the pensioner is subject to a damage of 44.4%.

We see that the total pension that the person concerned will receive will be equal to the amount of the initial Pw pension. It seems, therefore, that when the independent pension from a state is greater than the sum of the overlapping pro-rata pensions, the total pension is the amount of the independent pension, i.e., when Pw > P(x + y) → TPfinal = P(x + y) + [Pw – P(x + y)] → TPfinal = Pw. Here lies the paradox where the state which owes the highest pension ends up paying a significantly lesser amount of pension, both in relation to its original and in relation to the others.

7.3.2 *Working Hypothesis 2*

If in the above examples, the total amount of P(x + y) was stable, the examples would be:

1A. If the independent pension w (Pw) is EUR 2000 and the total sum of pensions P (x + y) = EUR 1000. Given that Pw = 2000 > 1000 [P(x + y)], State w will deduct from its own pension the total sum of the other pensions and will have to pay Pw − P(x + y) = 2000 − 1000 = EUR 1000. Then, the total pension received by the pensioner will be TPfinal = P(x + y) + [P(x + y) − Pw] = 1000 + 1000 = EUR 2000. The total pension that the person concerned will receive will be equal to the amount of the initial Pw pension. From the initial total pension TPinitial 3000, the final total pension received will be TPfinal EUR 2000. "Damage" D= TPinitial – Tpfinal = 3000 – 2000 = EUR 1000. Thus, the pensioner is subject to a damage of 33%.

2A. If the independent pension Pw is EUR 1500 and the total sum of pensions P (x + y) = EUR 1000. Given that Pw = 1500 > 1000 [P(x + y)], State w will deduct from its own pension the total sum of the other pensions and will have to pay Pw − P(x + y) = 1500 − 1000 = EUR 500. Then, the total pension received by the pensioner will be TPfinal = P(x + y) + [Pw − P (x + y)] = 1000 + 500 = EUR 1500. From the initial total pension of 2500, the final total pension received will be EUR 1500 ("Damage" 2500 − 1500 = EUR 1000). Thus, the pensioner is subject to a damage of 40%.

3A. If the independent pension Pw is EUR 1100 and the total sum of pensions P (x + y) = EUR 1000. Given that Pw = 1100 > 1000 [P(x + y)], State w will deduct from its own pension the total sum of the other pensions and will have to pay Pw − P(x + y) = 1100 − 1000 = EUR 100. Then, the total pension received by the pensioner will be TPfinal = P(x + y) + [Pw − P (x + y)] = 1000 + 100 = EUR 1100. From the initial total pension of 2100, the final total pension received will be EUR 1100 ("Damage" 2100 − 1100 = EUR 2000). Thus, the pensioner is subject to a damage of 95%.

Therefore, with a fixed sum P(x + y), where Pw > P(x + y), the smaller the amount of the independent Pw benefit is, the greater the damage in the total final pension of the person concerned. The values are inversely proportional.

In the hypothetical case where Pw = P(x + y), it will be:

The independent pension of State w (Pension w) is EUR 1000 and the sum of pensions P(x + y) is EUR 1000:Pw = 1000, P(x + y) = 1000, the Total Pension will be EUR 1000. TPfinal = P(x + y) + [Pw - P(x + y)] = 1000 + (1000 − 1000) = 1000 + 0 = 1000. Otherwise, TP = Pw. From the initial total pension (TPinitial) 2000, the final total pension received (TPfinal) will be EUR 1000. The pensioner's "damage" will be: D pensioner = TPinitial − Tpfinal = 2000 − 1000 = EUR 1000. Thus, the pensioner is subject to a damage of 50%.

7.3.3 *Working Hypothesis 3*

Furthermore, if the amount of pensions from States x and y is higher than State's w pension, by constructing personal examples according to the reasoning herein based on Pennings' interpretative approach, choosing some random values, it can be supposed that:

1. Pension Pw is EUR 900 and the sum of pensions P(x + y) is EUR 1100, i.e. Pw < P(x + y). The deduction which State w can normally apply up to the sum of the other pensions will have a negative sign. More specifically, it will be Pw − P(x + y) = 900 − 1100 = −200. Given that State w may reduce its pension (Pw) up to the amount of pensions P(x + y), pension Pw is eliminated. As a result, the beneficiary will receive the sum of the other pensions P(x + y). This happens because there can be no negative sign value in the pension, i.e. a pension deficit. It is simply assumed that pension Pw is set to zero.

   So, when Pw < P(x + y) it will be → TPfinal = P(x + y) + [Pw − P(x + y)] = P (x + y) + 0 = P(x + y). In this case, it will be TPfinal = EUR 1100. Otherwise, the total pension amounts to the sum of pensions of States x and y. Therefore, when Pw < P(x + y) → TPfinal = P(x + y) + [Pw − P(x + y). Damage = 2000 − 1100 = EUR 900. Thus, the pensioner is subject to a damage of 45%.
2. Assuming pension Pw is EUR 500 and the sum of pensions P(x + y) is EUR 1000, i.e. Pw < P(x + y), the deduction that State w could apply up to sum of other pensions will have a negative sign. More specifically, it will be Pw − P (x + y) = 500 − 1000 = −500. Given that State w may reduce its pension (Pw) up to the amount of pensions P(x + y), pension Pw is eliminated. As a result, the beneficiary will receive the sum of the other pensions P(x + y). Otherwise, the total pension amounts to the sum of pensions of States x and y. Therefore, when Pw < P(x + y) → TPfinal = P(x + y). Therefore, since Pw < P(x + y), it will be → TPfinal = EUR 1000. From the initial total pension of 1500, the final total pension received will be EUR 1000 ("Damage" = EUR 500). Thus, the pensioner is subject to a damage of 33.3%.
3. If Pension Pw is EUR 400 and the sum of pensions P(x + y) is EUR 1200, then TPfinal = EUR 1200. Damage = 1600 − 1200 = EUR 400. Thus, the pensioner is subject to a damage of 25%.
4. If Pension Pw is EUR 200 and the sum of pensions P(x + y) is EUR 1500, then TPfinal = EUR 1500. Damage = 1700 − 1500 = EUR 200. Thus, the pensioner is subject to a damage of 11.1%.

7.3.4 Working Hypothesis 4

If in the above examples, the total amount of P(x + y) was stable, it would be:

1A. Pension Pw is EUR 900 and the sum of pensions P(x + y) is EUR 1000, i.e. Pw < P(x + y). The deduction which State w can normally apply up to the sum of the other pensions will have a negative sign. More specifically, it will be Pw − P(x + y) = 900 − 1000 = −100. Given that State w may reduce its pension (Pw) up to the amount of pensions P(x + y), pension Pw is eliminated. As a result, the beneficiary will receive the sum of the other pensions P(x + y). Therefore, since Pw < P(x + y), it will be → TPfinal = EUR 1000. The total pension amounts to the sum of pensions of States x and y. Therefore, when Pw < P(x + y) → TPfinal = P(x + y). If Pension Pw is EUR 900 and the sum of pensions P(x + y) is EUR 1000, then TPfinal = EUR 1000. Damage = 1900 − 1000 = EUR 900. Thus, the pensioner is subject to a damage of 47.4%.

2A. Assuming pension Pw is EUR 500 and the sum of pensions P(x + y) is EUR 1000, i.e. Pw < P(x + y), the deduction that State w could apply up to sum of other pensions will have a negative sign. More specifically, it will be Pw − P (x + y) = 500 − 1000 = −500. Given that State w may reduce its pension (Pw) up to the amount of pensions P(x + y), pension Pw is eliminated. As a result, the beneficiary will receive the sum of the other pensions P(x + y). Therefore, since Pw < P(x + y), it will be → TPfinal =P(x + y) = EUR 1000. From the initial total pension of 1500, the final total pension received will be EUR 1000 ("Damage" = EUR 500). Thus, the pensioner is subject to a damage of 33.3%.

3A. If Pension Pw is EUR 400 and the sum of pensions P(x + y) is EUR 1000, then TPfinal = P(x + y) = EUR 1000. Damage = 1400 − 1000 = EUR 400. Thus, the pensioner is subject to a damage of 28.8%.

4A. If Pension Pw is EUR 200 and the sum of pensions P(x + y) is EUR 1000, then TPfinal = P(x + y) = EUR 1000. Damage = 1200 − 1000 = EUR 200. Thus, the pensioner is subject to a damage of 16.7%.

Therefore, with a fixed sum P(x + y), where Pw < P(x + y), the smaller the amount of the independent Pw benefit is, the less the damage in the total final pension of the person concerned will be. The values are proportional.

As demonstrated above, when pro-rata pensions of the same kind overlap, the pensioner is subject to no damage. On the contrary, when pro-rata pensions overlap with independent benefits, the pensioner is subject to a damage of various percentages, depending on whether the sum of the independent pension is greater or smaller than the total sum of the other pro-rata pensions.

Provided that pro-rata benefits ensure a certain distribution and a fair apportionment of obligations between the states through the application of a time apportionment, the purpose of applying some rules against overlapping of benefits that do not depend on periods of insurance is understood, when the abovementioned time apportionment cannot be applied. However, as already mentioned in relation to Article 52 of Regulation No 883/04, there is an indirect requirement to apply the time apportionment known from benefits the amount of which is dependent on periods of insurance to the benefits, the amount of which is not dependent of periods of insurance. This is because, as a theoretical amount, the national amount may not depend on periods, but in terms of the actual amount, there is no specific provision for distinguishing this category of benefits. Furthermore, priority is given to the possibility of applying rules against overlapping to benefits that are not dependent of the duration of the insurance in comparison with benefits that are dependent of the duration of insurance; as a result, where only pro-rata benefits of the same kind overlap, there is not deduction, while where pro-rata benefits overlap with independent benefits of the same kind, there is a deduction.

7.3.5 Our Interpretative Approach

It should be reminded that the analysis of the above cases was based on Pennings' line of reasoning, according to which the pro-rata pensions may be deducted from the independent pension of the same kind, pursuant to Article 53(3)(d) of Regulation No 883/04 and Article 54 of Regulation No 883/04. In turn, this line of reasoning has also been based on the wording of Regulation No 883/04 in its English version regarding Article 53(3)(d) of Regulation No 883/04: "[...] the benefit due may be reduced solely by the amount of such benefits or such income". The wording in the German version of the Regulation is also similar: "[...] so kann die geschuldete Leistung nur um den Betrag dieser Leistungen oder Einkünfte gekürzt werden".

However, in the Greek and French translation of the same phrase of the same provision the wording is different: More specifically, the Greek version reads: "[...] the benefit due may be reduced only within the limit of the amount of such benefits or incomes". Similarly, the French version reads:"[...]la prestation due ne peut être réduite que dans la limite du montant de ces prestations ou de ces revenus". It seems like they are following the former wording of Article 46a (3) (d) of Regulation No 1408/71, which read in its English version: "[...]the benefit payable under the legislation of the first Member State may be reduced only within the limit of the amount of the benefits payable under the legislation or the income acquired within the territory of the other Member States".

Trying a different interpretative approach, if the latter version is followed, things take a different form, just like in the examples above. More specifically, when the initial pension of State w is higher than the pensions of the other States x + y, the State may reduce its pension to be as low as the sum of the other pensions, and as a result the final pension provided will be P(x + y). Thus, if $Pw > P(x + y)$, then $\rightarrow$ $Pwfinal = P(x + y)$. The final total pension will, therefore, be: $TPfinal = Pwfinal + P(x + y) = P(x + y) + P(x + y) = 2 * P(x + y)$.

On the contrary, when the initial pension of State w is lower than the pensions of the other States x + y, the State cannot reduce it anymore and as a result the final pension provided will be equal to the initial one. Thus, if $Pw < P(x + y)$, then $\rightarrow$ $Pwfinal = Pw$. The final total pension will, therefore, be: $TPfinal = Pwfinal + P(x + y) = Pw + P(x + y)$. It should be noted that there is a big difference in the examples where $Pw < P(x + y)$ depending on how the provision in question is applied. The result is that nothing will change, as the State is allowed to apply a deduction up to P(x + y). Thus, in all the examples above, there would be no reduction in the total pension.

7.3.5.1 Working Hypothesis 1

Based on the different interpretative approach herein, in terms of cases where $Pw > P(x + y)$, then $\rightarrow$ $Pwfinal = P(x + y)$, $TPfinal= Pwfinal + P(x + y) = P(x + y) + P(x + y) = 2 * P(x + y)$, the same examples take the following form:

1. The independent pension of State w (Pension w) is EUR 1000 and the sum of pensions P(x + y) is EUR 700. Pw=1000, P(x + y)=700 and State w should pay Pwfinal = P(x + y) = EUR 700. Then, the total sum of pensions or the final Total Pension will be → TPfinal = Pwfinal + P(x + y) = P(x + y) + P(x + y) = 2 * P (x + y) = 2 * 700 = EUR 1400. From the initial total pension (TPinitial) 1700, the final total pension received (TPfinal) will be EUR 1400. The pensioner's "damage" will be: Dpensioner = TPinitial – Tpfinal = 1700 – 1400 = EUR 300. This amount is calculated by a percentile reduction to a percentage of 17.6%. Thus, the pensioner is subject to a damage of 17.6% (in comparison with 41.2% above in the previous version).
2. If in the above hypothesis, the independent pension of State w (Pw) is EUR 2000 and the sum of pensions P(x + y) = EUR 1500. Pwfinal = P(x + y) = EUR 1500. TPfinal = 2 * 1500 = EUR 3000. From the initial total pension TPinitial 3500, the final total pension received will be TPfinal EUR 3000. "Damage" D = TPinitial – Tpfinal = 3500 – 3000 = EUR 500. Thus, the pensioner is subject to a damage of about 14.3% (in comparison with 43% above).
3. If in the above hypothesis, the independent pension Pw is EUR 1500 and the sum is P(x + y) = EUR 1200. TP = 2 * 1200 = 2400. From the initial total pension of 2700, the final total pension received will be EUR 2400 ("Damage" 2700 – 2400 = EUR 300). Thus, the pensioner is subject to a damage of 11.1% (in comparison with the other version of 44.4%).

7.3.5.2 Working Hypothesis 2

If in the above examples, the total amount of P(x + y) was stable, it would be:

1A. If the independent pension w (Pw) is EUR 2000 and the total sum of pensions P (x + y) = EUR 1000. TP final = 2 * 1000 = 2000. From the initial total pension TPinitial 3000, the final total pension received will be TPfinal EUR 2000. "Damage" D = TPinitial – Tpfinal = 3000 – 2000 = EUR 1000. Thus, the pensioner is subject to a damage of 33%.

2A. If the independent pension Pw is EUR 1500 and the total sum of pensions P (x + y) = EUR 1000. TP final = 2 * 1000 = 2000. From the initial total pension of 2500, the final total pension received will be EUR 2000 ("Damage" 2500 – 2000 = EUR 500). Thus, the pension is subject to a damage of 20% (in comparison with 40% above).

3A. If the independent pension Pw is EUR 1100 and the total sum of pensions P (x + y) = EUR 1000. TPfinal = 2 * 1000 = 2000. From the initial total pension of 2100, the final total pension received will be EUR 2000 ("Damage" 2100 – 2000 = EUR 100). Thus, the pensioner is subject to a damage of 4.8% (in comparison with 95% above).

Therefore, with a fixed sum P(x + y), where Pw > P(x + y), the lower the independent benefit Pw is, the less the total pension damage of the person concerned will be. The values are proportional. This result seems more logical than the one resulting from the English and German version of Regulation 883/04 where the values were inversely proportional.

In the hypothetical case where Pw = P(x + y), it will be:

The independent pension of State w (Pension w) is EUR 1000 and the sum of pensions P(x + y) is EUR 1000: TPfinal = 2 * 1000 = EUR 2000. i.e. TPinitial = TPfinal = EUR 2000. The pensioner's "damage" will be D pensioner = TPinitial – Tpfinal = 0 (in comparison with 50% above).

In any case, regarding Article 54 of Regulation No 883/04, it can be observed that the term "independent benefit" in Article 54 of Regulation No 883/04 is not identical to the independent benefit of Article 52 of Regulation No 883/04 in the sense of an independent entitlement, but it has the particular meaning given to it in case of overlapping of benefits of the same kind. More specifically, it has the meaning of a benefit entitlement to which is created independently and at the same time such entitlement is not dependent on the duration of periods or on a benefit who is dependent on a notional period pursuant to Article 54 of Regulation No 883/04. The ability of State Members to apply rules against overlapping in cases of overlapping of benefits of the same kind is, therefore, significantly restricted. The independent benefits falling under the cases provided are also limited.

However, the general impression is that the current rules of Regulation No 883/04 are extremely complicated; at the same time, their results have not been tested in terms of examining cases to demonstrate that they do not lead in similar or justifiably different results. As already proven, the provision of Article 46(3) of Regulation No 1408/71 alone was more functional and it more in accordance with the rule-of-law, a characteristic that is doubtful whether the current provisions possess.

7.4 Overlapping of Benefits of a Different Kind

According to case-law, benefits that are calculated or provided on the basis of the periods of employment of two different persons cannot be treated as benefits of the same kind within the meaning of Article 46a of the Regulation.[51] Thus, it has been found that a retirement pension granted under the legislation of one Member State, on the basis periods of insurance personally completed in that State by the person concerned, and a retirement pension obtained under the legislation of another Member State by that person as a divorcee, on the basis of periods of insurance completed by that person's former spouse, are not benefits of the same kind.[52] The Court also held that a personal invalidity pension which is based on the recipient's own employment record in one Member State is not of the same kind as a survivor's pension based on the employment record of the recipient's deceased husband in

[51] Judgment of the Court of 11.08.1995, Case C-98/94, Schmidt, European Court Reports 1995 I-02559 ECLI:EU:C:1995:273, paragraph 28.

[52] Schmidt, paragraph 32.

another Member State.[53] It must thus be held that benefits calculated on the basis of periods of insurance completed by different persons cannot be treated as benefits of the same kind.[54]

With its amended content, Article 55 of Regulation No 883/04 corresponds to Article 46c of Regulation No 1408/71, which was also introduced with Regulation No 1248/92. The amendment of Article 55 of Regulation No 883/04 includes mainly the replacement of the provision in Article 46c(1) of Regulation No 1408/71 with the provision of Article 55(1)(a) of Regulation No 883/04. The rule in Article 55 of Regulation No 883/04 which should be applicable to pension payments from the entry into force of Regulation No 883/04 (Article 87(9)) concerns the problem of coordinating the international application of provisions against overlapping of the Member States and the repeated or mutual reduction or withdrawal of pensions.[55] It distinguished pensions depending on whether it is an independent pension, i.e. a purely national pension or a pro-rata pension, i.e. a pension under Community law, without a general assessment as to which of the two coordination methods, i.e. division on the basis of the number of pensions to reduce or pro-rata division, is more favourable.[56]

Thus, while in cases of overlapping of benefits of the same kind, where a Member State applies rules against overlapping, it is a combination of the provisions in Article 53(3)(d) of Regulation No 883/04 (Article 46a(3)(d) of Regulation No 1408/71 respectively) and of Article 54 of Regulation No 883/04 (Article 46b of Regulation No 1408/71 respectively), in cases of overlapping of benefits of a different kind, the legislature invokes in Article 55 of Regulation No 883/04 (Article 46c of Regulation No 1408/71) the simultaneous application of the legislation against overlapping of several Member States. When the legislation against overlapping of a single Member State is applicable, Article 53(3)(d) of Regulation applies, as seen above.

At the same time, contrary to the narrow content of the concept of independent benefit in Article 54 of Regulation No 883/04 (Article 46b of Regulation No 1408/71), in Article 55 of Regulation No 883/04 (Article 46c of Regulation No 1408/71), the "independent benefit" refers to the independent benefit of Article 52(1)(a) of Regulation No 883/04 (Article 46(1)(a) of Regulation No 1408/71 respectively) on an independent entitlement to a pension during the award of benefits. By contrast, Article 53(3)(d) of Regulation No 883/04 applies when there is overlapping of benefits of a different kind and a single State is applying rules against overlapping.

According to Article 55(1) of Regulation No 883/04, if the receipt of benefits of a different kind or other income requires the application of the rules to prevent

---

[53] Judgment of 06.10.1987, 197/85, Stefanutti, European Court Reports 1987, p. 3855, paragraph 13.

[54] Judgment of 12.2.1998, Case C-366/96 Cordelle, European Court Reports 1998 I-00583, paragraph 21.

[55] Schuler (2015), p. 360.

[56] Ibid.

overlapping provided for by the legislation of the Member States concerned regarding:

(a) two or more independent benefits, the competent institutions shall divide the amounts of the benefit or benefits or other income, as they have been taken into account, by the number of benefits subject to the said rules;
 however, the application of this subparagraph cannot deprive the person concerned of his status as a pensioner for the purposes of the other Chapters of this Title under the conditions and the procedures laid down in the Implementing Regulation;
(b) one or more pro-rata benefits, the competent institutions shall take into account the benefit or benefits or other income and all the elements stipulated for applying the rules to prevent overlapping as a function of the ratio between the periods of insurance and/or residence established for the calculation referred to in Article 52(1)(b)(ii);
(c) one or more independent benefits and one or more pro-rata benefits, the competent institutions shall apply mutatis mutandis subparagraph (a) as regards independent benefits and subparagraph (b) as regards pro-rata benefits.

To begin with, the wording of Article 55(1)(a) of Regulation No 883/04 is not clear. It should be noted that in other language versions (English, French) the text reads that "the competent institutions shall divide the amounts of the benefit or benefits or other income". While Article 46c (1) of Regulation No 1408/71 made reference to "amounts which would not be paid", which would then be divided, dividing thus the amount of reduction, Article 55 (1)(a) of Regulation No 883/04 reads that the competent institutions shall divide "the amounts of the benefit or benefits or other income". Of course, the question arises as to which case the division of the "benefit" applies, whether it concerns a single benefit and which benefit would be divided in case of overlapping of two or more independent benefits of a different kind. Moreover, given alternative wording, the question arises as to which is selected and when: the division of a "benefit", of "benefits" or "other income".

The procedure was more clear with the wording of the corresponding Article 46c (1) of Regulation No 1408/71, according to which if the receipt of benefits of a different kind or other income entails the reduction, suspension or withdrawal of two or more benefits referred to in Article 46(1)(a)(i), the amounts which would not be paid in strict application of the provisions concerning reduction, suspension or withdrawal provided for by the legislation of the Member States concerned, shall be divided by the number of benefits subject to reduction, suspension or withdrawal.

Article 46c of Regulation No 1408/71 contains special provisions applicable in the case of overlapping of one or more benefits referred to in Article 46a(1) with one or more benefits of a different kind or with other income, where two or more Member States are concerned. Therefore, if two or more States were to award a benefit pursuant to Article 46(1)(a) of Regulation No 1408/71 and where both or more States could apply their legislation against overlapping due to the granting of benefits of a different kind, then the amounts that would not be paid, would be divided by the number of benefits that would be subject to reduction, suspension or withdrawal (for example, a Greek independent old-age pension and a German independent pension due to death).[57]

Verschueren notes that, pursuant to the provision of Article 46c(1) of Regulation No 1408/71, where a person received an income by two Member States, these States were obliged to divide by two the amount of reduction provided for in their legislation where benefits of a different kind or income overlapped, so that a reduction no more than half could be applied.[58] He also claims that said provision could result in putting a migrant worker receiving retirement benefits from several Member States in a more favourable position than a non-migrant, the benefit of which is calculated solely pursuant the legislation of one Member State, while the non-migrant could also lose their benefit if another benefit of a different kind or the other income amounted to big sums.[59]

This is the reason that, according to Verschueren, Article 55(1)(a) of Regulation No 883/04 introduces a new rule, according to which, where there are two or more independent benefits, the competent institutions should now **divide the amounts of the other benefits or income by the number of the pension benefits subject to these rules and take into account these reduced amounts for the application of the national rules against overlapping.**[60]

Thus, if a person receives income from two Member States, they will first divide by two the amount of benefits of a different kind or of other income and they will take into account only that reduced amount for the purposes of their national provisions against overlapping.[61] Of course, as he acknowledges, this could result in losing a retirement benefit, if half of the other benefit of a different kind or other income is so high that results in the full reduction or withdrawal of the pension, taking into account that the negative effects are balanced out by the second sentence of Article 55(1)(a) of Regulation No883/04.[62]

As Article 55(1)(a) of Regulation No 883/04 (second phrase) provides, even if the application of this rule results in the full reduction of the pension, i.e. the non payment of any pensions, the deprivation of pension cannot deprive the person concerned of his status as a pensioner who is still entitled to the benefits due to disease that pensioners are entitled to. However, the deprivation of a retirement benefit is different from the theoretical capacity of the pensioner, which the person concerned maintains in accordance with the Regulation and the purposes of benefits due to disease.

---

[57] IKA (1996) (Social Security Institution) – Directorate of international social security relations-Department of EEC pensions, Circular No 16/96, Reference No S07/GEN, Athens, 8-2-1996, subject: Reforming and supplementing the guidelines on the application of EEC Regulations No 1408/71 and 574/72, p. 75.

[58] Verschueren (2009), p. 159.

[59] Ibid.

[60] Ibid.

[61] Verschueren (2009), p. 159.

[62] Ibid.

On the other hand, Schuler thinks that it is the **pensions that are aggregated and not the reduced amounts of pensions, which means that the sum of pensions is divided and then the remaining amount is calculated** pursuant to Article 55(3)(c) of Regulation No 883/04.[63] He therefore argues that the Regulation is far from establishing a hierarchy among the Member States' pensions, adopting a numerical criterion in order to achieve an average reduction.[64]

In his example, Schuler notes that where a pension for a work accident pursuant to the legislation of one State can cause the reduction of the national insurance pension pursuant to the legislation of the same State and the pension from another Member State, the total pension shall be divided by 2.[65] He therefore considers that pensions are aggregated (without specifying which pensions are of a different kind and whether the pension due to a work accident is also taken into account) and the total sum is divided by the number of benefits of a different kind.

Furthermore, Schuler's line of reasoning is consistent with Pennings' example, where he seems to believe that it is **the other benefit or income that should be divided by the number of the independent pension benefits,** when two or more independent benefits of a different kind overlap with another benefit or income. More specifically, Pennings makes the hypothesis that a worker is entitled to an old-age pension of EUR 1000 and a survivor's pensions of EUR 500, while the same person starts receiving an unemployment benefit of EUR 800[66] (this is obviously the case of an employed retired person who becomes unemployed). As Pennings notes, in view of the national rules against overlapping, the above retirement benefits cannot overlap with an unemployment benefit; however, pursuant to the Regulation the unemployment benefit shall be divided by the number of the pensions (2) and half (1/2) of the unemployment benefit (400) shall be deducted by each pension, so that the person concerned receives an old-age pension of EUR 600, a survivor's pension of EUR 100 and the unemployment benefit of EUR 800[67] (600 + 100 + 800 = 1500).

At this point, if the above example is modified, assuming that the unemployment benefit or other income was EUR 2000, according to the same example, said benefit or income would be divided and half of 2000/2 should be deducted from each pension, resulting thus in zero old-age pension (1000 − 1000) and zero survivor's pension (500 − 1000 = −500). Assuming that by adding any benefits and income, it would be 1000 + 500 + 2000 = 3500 and then 3500/2 = 1750, then once again the reduction of pension would be problematic. As it can be observed, taking into calculation other benefits or income results to zero pension.

A further question is whether a special rule on overlapping of benefits falling under the rules of the special part of the Regulation on pensions could apply

[63] Schuler (2015), p. 361.

[64] Ibid.

[65] Schuler (2015), p. 361.

[66] Pennings (2015), p. 225.

[67] Ibid.

regarding a benefit that is not in respect of old-age, such as the unemployment benefit that is divided in the example cited above. Thus, however, a non-pension benefit that does not fall within the scope Article 50–60 of Regulation No 883/04 determines the reduction of the pension benefits of these Articles. Another issue could be raised, furthermore, regarding the pension benefits not covered by Articles 50–60 of Regulation No 883/04, as they are not benefits in respect of invalidity, old-age or survivor's pension, which are exclusively covered by said special rules. In this context, pension due to a work accident in Schuler's example, should not be added to the sum that will be divided. Thus, there is a question regarding the justification basis upon which such benefits or other incomes may be taken into account pursuant to national legislation in conjunction with Article 53 of Regulation No 883/04 even if it concerns income not covered by Articles 50–60 of Regulation No 883/04, let alone income taken into account within the context of tax law, upon which the Regulation has no effect. As however was already mentioned during the examination of Article 53 of Regulation No 883/04, pensions due to a work accident or occupational disease may be considered as invalidity pensions and, therefore, as pensions covered by the special rules on pensions.

In addition, it is doubtful that the view that the previous rules could result in a more favourable treatment of the migrant in respect of non-migrant could be a justification reason, in particular in light of the new legislation that, as has already been accepted, may lead to zero pension. In this case, however, a question regarding the less favourable treatment of migrants, which is contrary to the principles of favour and of equal treatment, as well as the principle of free movement itself.

However, the corresponding provision of the previous Article 46c of Regulation No 1408/71 is more appropriate in that it regulates the issues it is authorised to regulate and cannot be considered unfair in view of a more favourable treatment of migrants, as it foresees a reduction based on an objective criterion, the numerical criterion.

Pursuant to the new Article 53(3)(b) of Regulation No 883/04, the benefits and income may also be taken into account sometimes before taxes, contributions and any other individual deductions and sometimes following these deductions of the applicable legislation provides for the application of rules against overlapping following deductions. How, therefore, to take into account the other benefit or income (such as an unemployment benefit or a pension due to a work accident as above or another income), where several Member States are concerned (receipt of pensions from several States), where one State provides for the award of said benefit before deductions, while the other following deductions?

Moreover, in view of the new Article 55(1)(a) of Regulation No 883/04 which focuses on the other benefit or income, it is not clear what happens in case that, among several involved Member States, the legislation of a Member State does not provide for taking into account benefits or income acquired abroad pursuant to Article 53(3)(a) of Regulation No 883/04. In any case, the question on how the withdrawal of the migrant's pension which may be caused by the new Article 55(1)(a) of Regulation No 883/04 can be justified remains unanswered, in particular when the corresponding national legislation does not provide for withdrawal of the pension of the non migrant, and, in any case, in violation of the fundamental principles cited above on the basis of which the Regulation is interpreted. It should also be noted that benefits of a different kind may simply overlap with one another and not with another benefit or income. If, however, they overlap with another income, when is the benefit of another State divided and when is the income?

In this case, it can be considered that each State should divide the overlapping with its own benefit by 2, provided that the overlapping benefit is independent. It is therefore assumed that when Article 55(1)(a) of Regulation No 883/04 refers to "benefit(s) or other income", it refers to independent pensions of a different kind and only the cases where they overlap with one another or with other income.

In the recent case, Service fédéral des Pensions,[68] the Court concluded that Article 55(1)(a) of Regulation No 883/2004 must be interpreted as meaning that, where the receipt of benefits of a different kind or of other income entails the application of national rules against overlapping with regard to independent benefits, it allows each Member State concerned to provide, in its legal system, for the purpose of calculating the amount of benefit to be paid, either that the total amount of income taken into account by those national rules must be divided by the number of benefits concerned or that it is appropriate to divide by that same number the proportion of income which exceeds the ceiling in respect of overlapping laid down by those national rules.

HK's spouse died on 29 November 2016. Since HK had worked and paid contributions in various Member States, namely in Belgium, Spain and Finland, he received, on 1 December 2016, a Belgian retirement pension in the amount of EUR 11 962.55 per annum and a Spanish retirement pension in the amount of EUR 8 276.28 per annum. Since HK's spouse had also worked and paid contributions in the same Member States, HK also received a Spanish survivor's pension, in the amount of EUR 5 123.88 per annum, and a Finnish survivor's pension of EUR 1 281.24 per annum, granted by way of contributions paid by his deceased spouse to those social security schemes. 16 As regards the Belgian survivor's pension, on 22 December 2017 the SFP informed HK that he was not entitled to such a pension, on the ground that the total amount of his retirement pensions was too high. 17 On 26 December 2017, HK lodged a complaint against that refusal. 18 Subsequently, HK and the SFP exchanged numerous emails concerning the manner in which the various pension benefits received by HK were taken into account in order to determine whether and to what extent he was entitled to a Belgian survivor's pension. 19 By decision of 18 September 2019, the SFP changed its initial position by granting HK a survivor's pension under Belgian law in the amount of EUR 1 929.03 per annum, retroactively from 1 December 2016. HK challenged that decision and brought an action before the referring court, the tribunal du travail francophone de Bruxelles (Brussels Labour Court (French-speaking), Belgium), claiming that the annual Belgian survivor's pension should be EUR 6 339.01.

---

[68] Judgement of 12.10.2023, Service fédéral des Pensions, case C- 45/22, ECLI:EU:C:2023:772.

As the Advocate General observed in points 47 and 50 of his Opinion, Article 55(1)(a) of Regulation No 883/2004 is drafted in such a way as to leave it to the Member States to decide whether to divide the amounts, as they result from the application of their national rules against overlapping, by the number of benefits subject to those rules (para. 39). 40 Consequently, it follows from that wording that the competent national institutions may, for the purpose of calculating the amount of the benefit to be paid, divide by the number of benefits concerned, either the total amount of income or the proportion of income exceeding a certain ceiling in respect of overlapping (para. 40); that literal interpretation is confirmed by the context of Article 55(1)(a) of Regulation No 883/2004 (para. 41).

Even though Article 55(1) of Regulation No 883/2004 has been subject to an amendment of its wording, as a result of which it is the amounts of the benefits which are taken into account, and not the amounts not paid as a result of the application of the rules against overlapping, which are divided by the number of benefits subject to the rules against overlapping, the fact remains that both Article 55(1) and Article 46c (1) of Regulation No 1408/71 pursue the same objective, which is to protect migrant workers against the adverse effects of the cumulative application of those rules in the Member States (para. 55). Regulation No 883/2004 modernised and simplified the rules contained in Regulation No 1408/71, while retaining the same objective.[69] Furthermore, as the Advocate General observed in point 61 of his Opinion, both Article 46c(1) of Regulation No 1408/71 and Article 55(1) of Regulation No 883/2004 refer to the provisions concerning reduction, suspension or withdrawal provided for by the respective legislation of the Member States and to the amounts adopted by that legislation, thereby making clear the discretion available to those Member States for the purpose of determining the detailed rules for the application of the rules against overlapping benefits.[70]

7.4.1 Building Our Hypothesis

Let us build our own hypothesis. If, the national legislation of a Member State, Portugal for example, provides for an old-age pension on the basis of the insurance record of a person, the entitlement to which is created independently, i.e. Pp1 and another national legislation, for example Spain's legislation, provides for a survivor's pension based on the insurance record of another person (the spouse of the survivor), the entitlement to which is also created independently, i.e. Ps1, there is an overlapping of independent pension benefits of a different kind. Said benefits may also overlap with other benefits or income that are not pension benefits.

[69] See, to that effect, judgment of 30 September 2021, Raad van bestuur van het Uitvoeringsinstituut werknemersverzekeringen (Uwv), C-285/20, EU:C:2021:785, paragraph 42.

[70] Service fédéral des Pensions, paragraph 57.

A. Supposing that it is accepted that according to Article 55(1)(a) of Regulation No 883/04 the amount that is divided is the total sum of pensions and income. The amount is only divided by the number of the pension benefits of a different kind. Therefore, if the Portuguese old-age pension is for example Pp1 = EUR 1000, the Spanish survivor's pension is Ps1 = EUR 800 and the "other income" taken into account is also EUR 2000, then the total amount is EUR 3800 which will be divided by 2 (two pensions of a different kind), so that the resulting reduction is 3800/2 = EUR 1900. This reduction will be apportioned to each pension and as a result the person concerned may even end up receiving no pension (EUR 50 from one State and 0 from the other) (1000 – 1900/2 = 1000 – 950 = 50 and 800 – 1900/2 = 800 – 950 = 0). TPinitial = Pp1 + Ps1.

It will be TR = (TPinitial + other income)/v, v = the number of pensions

$$\begin{aligned}\text{TPfinal} &= \text{Pp2} + \text{Ps2} = (\text{Pp1} - \text{TR}) + (\text{Ps1} - \text{TR}) = \text{Pp1} - \text{TR} + \text{Ps1} - \text{TR} \\ &= (\text{Pp1} + \text{Ps1}) - 2\text{TR} = \text{Pp1} + \text{Ps1} - 2/v^{*}\ (\text{Pp1} + \text{Ps1} + \text{other income}) \\ &= \text{TPinitial} - 2/v^{*}\ (\text{TPinitial} + \text{other income}).\end{aligned}$$

This means that when any income is added to the sum of the amount of pensions, said income has an effect to the pension reduction by increasing the amount of reduction. The Regulation's scope of application however concerned social security benefits and in particular, Articles 50–60 of Regulation No 883/04 focus on pensions.

B. If it is, therefore, accepted that any income, beyond the independent pension benefits of a different kind should be taken into account, three working hypotheses can be distinguished:

1. Two overlapping independent benefits are aggregated Pp1 + Ps1 and their sum is divided by their number, i.e. 2:1000 + 800 = EUR 1800. The total reduction for each State is Total reduction TR = 1/v * (Pp1 + Ps1) = 1800/2 = EUR 900. The reduction of EUR 900 should be apportioned to and deducted from each pension, i.e. Pp2 = Pp1 – ½ TR = 1000 – 450 = EUR 550 and Ps2 = Ps1 – ½ TR = 800 – 450 = 350. The person concerned will thus received as Final Total Pension half (550 + 350 = 900) of the initial total pension TPinitial (1800). However, the total income is Total Income = TPfinal + Other Income = 900 + 2000 = 2900.

$$\text{TPinitial} = \text{Pp1} + \text{Ps1}.\text{TR} = 1/v^{*}\ (\text{Pp1} + \text{Ps1}) = \tfrac{1}{2}\,(\text{Pp1} + \text{Ps1})$$

Final Total Pension:

$$\begin{aligned}\text{TPfinal} &= \text{Pp2} + \text{Ps2} = (\text{Pp1} - \tfrac{1}{2}\,\text{TR}) + (\text{Ps1} - \tfrac{1}{2}\,\text{TR}) = \text{Pp1} - \tfrac{1}{2}\,\text{TR} + \text{Ps1} \\ &- \tfrac{1}{2}\,\text{TR} = \text{Pp1} + \text{Ps1} - (\tfrac{1}{2}\,\text{TR} + \tfrac{1}{2}\,\text{TR}) = \text{Pp1} + \text{Ps1} - \text{TR} = \text{Pp1} + \text{Ps1} \\ &- \tfrac{1}{2}\,(\text{Pp1} + \text{Ps1}) = \text{TPinitial} - \tfrac{1}{2}\,\text{TPinitial}.\end{aligned}$$

Therefore, TPfinal = TPinitial – 1/v TPinitial.

2. Each independent pension is divided by the number of the overlapping independent pensions of a different kind (2) and each State deducts from its benefit the amount of the other benefit divided by 2. This means Pp2 = Pp1 – Ps1/2 = 1000 – 800/2 = 1000 – 400 = 600. Ps2 = Ps1 – Pp1/2 = 800 – 1000/2 = 800 – 500 = 300. TPfinal = Pp2 + Ps2 = 600 + 300 = 900. The person concerned will thus receive as final total pension half (900) of the initial total pension TPinitial (1800). However, the total income is Total Income = TPfinal + Other Income = 900 + 2000 = 2900.

$$\text{TPinitial} = \text{Pp1} + \text{Ps1}$$

$$\text{TPfinal} = \text{Pp2} + \text{Ps2} = (\text{Pp1} - \text{Ps1}/2) + (\text{Ps1} - \text{Pp1}/2) = \text{Pp1} - \text{Ps1}/2 + \text{Ps1} - \text{Pp1}/2 = \text{Pp1} + \text{Ps1} - [1/2^{*}\ (\text{Pp1} + \text{Ps1})] = \text{TPinital} - \tfrac{1}{2}\text{TPinitial}.$$

Therefore, TPfinal = TPinitial – 1/v TPinitial.

The results of working hypotheses 1 and 2 are identical.

3. Each independent benefit is divided by the number of the overlapping independent pensions of a different kind (2). Thus, Portugal shall divide the overlapping Spanish independent survivor's pension 800/2 and will take into account the amount of EUR 400 (Ps2). In the same way, Spain will divide the Portuguese independent old-age pension 1000/2 and will take into account the amount of EUR 500 (Pp2). So, in this case, each State may consider as another benefit the independent pension of the other State and take it into account during the calculation dividing it by 2. In this example though, it is not possible to determine the final pension.[71]

Taking also into account Article 46c(1) of Regulation No 1408/71 which refers to independent pension benefits expressly invoking Article 46(1)(a)(i) of Regulation

---

[71] See example in IKA (2010), p. 3: "Application for an IKA old-age pension on 1-62010. 4500 days of insurance, Class 13th. The person receives old-age pension from Belgium EUR 200. The person receives old-age pension from Germany EUR 300 - Period of insurance 3000 days. The person also receives pension due to death from Germany EUR 300. Provisions against overlapping are being applied by IKA-ETAM and the German Institution. As the entitlement to the old-age pension and the pension due to death from Germany is created independently, the reduction will be applied on the Germany pension due to death, the amount of which, according to new Article 55(1)(a) of Regulation No 883/04 will be divided by two (2), i.e. by the number of the benefits that must be reduced due to the rules against overlapping applied by the legislations of Greece and Germany. Independent calculation – the calculation of the Greek pension will be as follows:

Basic pension EUR 385.52. German pension due to death 300/2 = EUR 150. Total = EUR 535.52. KO + 25% = 486.84 + 25% = 608.55 – 535.52 = 73.03. Payable amount: 385.52 + 73.03 = 458.55.

No 1408/71 and now Article 52(1)(a) of Regulation No 883/04, it can be concluded that only the pension benefits (in respect of old-age, invalidity or survivor's pension) that are independently calculated as falling within the scope regarding the award of benefits are the benefits to which Articles 53–55 of Regulation No 883/04 also refer to.

According to the above approach, therefore, Pennings' example will be modified as follows: the two independent pension will be added up 1000 + 500 = 1500. Then, that amount would be divided by their number (2), i.e. 1500/2 = 750. The reduction of 750 should be deducted from the total pension so that the person concerned would receive as a total pension 750 (i.e. half of the initial total pension). Each State should deduct from the pension it pays 750/2 = EUR 375. Therefore, the person concerned will now receive as an old-age pension 1000−375 = EUR 625 and as a survivor's pension 500−375 = EUR 125, regardless of the unemployment benefit of EUR 800, since the reduction is calculated only on the basis of the pension benefits to be reduced (total pension 750+ income 800 = 1550).

Furthermore, regarding pro-rata benefits, Article 55(1)(b) of Regulation No 883/04 refers to Article 52(1)(b)(ii) of Regulation No 883/04. Article 55(1)(b) of Regulation No 883/04 corresponds to Article 46c(2) of Regulation No 1408/71.

Pursuant to Article 46c(2) of Regulation No 1408/71where the benefit is calculated in accordance with Article 46(2), the benefit or benefits of a different kind from other Member States or other income and all other elements provided for by the legislation of the member State for the application of the provisions in the respect of reduction, suspension or withdrawal shall be taken into account in proportion to the periods of insurance and/or residence referred to in Article 46(2)(b) and shall be used for the calculation of the said benefit.

In his example, Pennings assumes that a widow who is a German national received a Belgian survivor's pension and a total old-age pension from Germany and Belgium, which is based on 10 years of insurance in Belgium and 15 years of insurance in Germany, based on the total insurance record of 25 years.[72] The pro-rata part that corresponds to Germany is 3/5 (15/25) and the pro-rata part that corresponds to Belgium is 2/5 (10/25); thus, Pennings notes, if the total income of the person concerned is EUR/month 1000, then a reduction of 3/5 will be imposed the German benefits and a reduction of 2/5 on the Belgian benefits.[73] It is noted that the rules against overlapping do not apply on pro-rata benefits of the same kind pursuant to Article 54(1) of Regulation No 883/04. The rules against overlapping may be applied on a the survivor's pension overlapping with the total old-age pension as pro-rata benefits of a different kind.

In respect to the above, it can be concluded that only pro-rata benefits of a different kind should be taken into account in conjunction with the ratio of the

[72] Pennings (2015), p. 226.

[73] Ibid.

periods. However, once again, in our view, three working hypotheses can be distinguished:

1. If the reduction is applied on pro-rata benefits of a different kind, there will be a reduction of both the German old-age pension and the Belgian survivor's pension. If Pennings' example is followed as above, there will be a reduction of the German old-age pension and the Belgian survivor's pension. For Germany: 300 – (3/5 * 300) = 300 – 180 = EUR 120 and for Belgium: 200 – (2/5 * 200) = 200 – 180 = EUR 20. In this case, there is a reduction of the initial total pension (EUR 700) and now the person concerned will receive as a total pension 180 + 20 + 200 = EUR 400. The total income of the person concerned is the total pension + other income = 400 + 300 = EUR 700. This is also demonstrated as follows:

$$\begin{aligned} Pg2 &= Pg1 - (3/5^{*}\ Pg1) \text{ and } Pb2 = Pb1 - (2/5^{*}\ Pb1).TPfinal = Pg2 + Pb2 \\ &= Pg1 - (3/5^{*}\ Pg1) + Pb1 - (2/5^{*}\ Pb1) = Pg1 - 3/5Pg1 + Pb1 - 2/5Pb1 \\ &= Pg1 - 2/5Pb1 + Pb1 - 3/5Pg1 = 5/5Pg1 - 3/5Pg1 + 5/5Pb1 - 2/5Pb1 \\ &= 2/5Pg1 + 3/5Pb1. \end{aligned}$$

From Pg1 – (3/5 * Pg1) + Pb1 – (2/5 * Pb1) the result is → TPfinal = 2/5Pg1 + 3/5Pb1.

It is thus observed that a reverse reduction is applied, i.e. the Belgian benefit is reduced more by the ratio between the periods that corresponds to Germany, where there were more periods of insurance. Similarly, the German benefit's amount depends on the ratio between the periods corresponding to Belgium, where the periods were fewer.

2. If the reduction is applied on pro-rata benefits of a different kind, there will be a reduction of the German old-age pension and the Belgium survivor's pension, but it could be assumed that, pursuant to Article 55 (1)(b), it is the other benefit that each State should take into account in conjunction with its own ratio between periods: in the above example, Belgium will take into account the amount corresponding to 2/5 of the German benefit of a different kind (old-age) and Germany will take into account the amount of 2/5 of the Belgian benefit. Thus, for Germany: 300 – (3/5 * 200) = 300 – 120 = EUR 180 and for Belgium: 200 – (2/5 * 300) = 200 – 120 = EUR 80. In this case, there is a reduction of the initial total pension (EUR 700) and now the person concerned will receive as a total pension 180 + 80 + 200 = EUR 460. The total income of the person concerned is the total pension + other income = 460 + 300 = EUR 760. This is also demonstrated as follows:

$Pg2 = Pg1 - (3/5^{*} Pb1)$ and $Pb2 = Pb1 - (2/5^{*} Pg1)$.$TPfinal = Pg2 + Pb2 = Pg1 - (3/5^{*} Pb1) + Pb1 - (2/5^{*} Pg1) = Pg1 - 3/5Pb1 + Pb1 - 2/5Pg1 = Pg1 - 2/5Pg1 + Pb1 - 3/5Pb1 = 5/5Pg1 - 2/5Pg1 + 5/5Pb1 - 3/5Pb1 = 3/5Pg1 + 2/5Pb1$.

It is noted that the ratio time/ratio between periods is maintained in the final total pension TPfinal = 3/5Pg1 + 2/5Pb1.

If ν = total number of periods of insurance and $\chi\gamma$ = period of insurance in Germany and $\chi\beta$ = time of insurance in Belgium: TPfinal = $\chi\gamma/\nu$ Pg1 + $\chi\beta/\nu$ Pb1.

3. If according to Article 55(1)(b), it is the other benefit that each State should take into account in conjunction with its own ratio between periods. This means that in the above hypothesis, Belgium will take into account the amount that corresponds to the 2/5 of the German benefit of a different kind (old-age). Similarly, Germany will take into account the 3/5 of the Belgian survivor's pension as a benefit of a different kind.[74] This taking into account relates in this case to the sum/total of pension during the award, on the basis of which the supplement will be determined. In this hypothesis, it is not possible to determine the final total pension.

Finally, according to Article 55(1)(c) of Regulation No 883/04, if one or more independent benefits overlap with one or more pro-rata benefits of a different kind, the competent institutions apply mutatis mutandis sub-paragraph (a) for the independent benefits and sub-paragraph (b) for the pro-rata benefits. Thus, the institutions should follow for each overlapping benefit the procedure for reduction depending on whether it is an independent or pro-rata benefit.

Relevant provisions were contained in Article 46c(3) of Regulation No 1408/71 according to which if the receipt of benefits of a different kind or of other income entails the reduction, suspension or withdrawal of one or more benefits referred to in Article 46(1)(a)(i) of Regulation No 1408/71 (on independent benefits) and of one or more benefits referred to in Article 46(2) of Regulation No 1408/71, the following rules shall apply: (a) where in a case of a benefit or benefits referred to in Article 46(1)(a)(i) of Regulation No 1408/71, the amounts which would not be paid in strict application of the provisions concerning reduction, suspension or withdrawal provided for by the legislation of the Member States concerned shall be divided by the number of benefits subject to reduction, suspension or withdrawal; (b) where in a case of a benefit or benefits calculated in accordance with Article 46(2) of Regulation No 1408/71, the reduction, suspension or withdrawal shall be carried out in accordance with paragraph 2.

Assuming always that the rules against overlapping apply only to independent/pro-rata pension benefits and not any other benefits or income and following either

---

[74]Thus, in the hypothesis used in IKA (1996), p. 75a: IKA old-age pension in instalments (2000 Greece + 3000 Germany). Pension due to death from Germany amount A. IKA will take into account A * 2000/5000.

the relevant working hypotheses resulting in the reduction of benefit or those hypotheses resulting simply into taking into account the other benefit, the results are the following:

(i) each State, whether it has to pay an independent or a pro-rata benefit, should take into account the (overlapping with its own benefit) independent benefits divided by the number of the overlapping pension benefits. This is, of course, where a question arises regarding the division by the number of the total pension benefits, including independent and pro-rata and not just the independent ones, as in the case of Article 55(1)(a) of Regulation No 883/04, which applies by analogy to Article 55(1)(c) of Regulation No 883/04 when more than one independent benefits overlap with more than one pro-rata benefits.
(ii) each State, whether it has to pay an independent or pro-rata benefit, should take into account the (overlapping with its own benefit) pro-rata benefits in conjunction with the ratio between the periods resulting from the calculation of Article 52 of Regulation No 883/04. Thus, even if a State has to pay an independent benefit, it should use the ratio between the periods corresponding to it in relation to the sums of periods in all the States from the apportionment during the calculation of Article 52 of Regulation No 883/04. Another question arises here on what happens when a State does not apply the apportionment either because it is subject to Article 52(4) of Regulation No 883/04 or because it is subject to Article 52(5) of Regulation No 883/04 (funded pension scheme). In this case, it may be appropriate to either take into account the pro-rata benefit as an independent one or take into account the pro-rata benefit in conjunction with the ratio between the periods used in the State from which the pro-rata benefits originates.

Furthermore, according to Article 55(2) of Regulation No 883/04, the competent institution shall not apply the division stipulated in respect of independent benefits, if the legislation it applies provides for account to be taken of benefits of a different kind and/or other income and all other elements for calculating part of their amount determined as a function of the ratio between periods of insurance and/or residence referred to in Article 52(1)(b)(ii). The provision of Article 46c(4) of Regulation No 1408/71was similar. Thus, independent pensions shall not be divided if the national applicable legislation provides for a pro-rata reduction, as for example the German Social Code (Section 97(2) sentence 4 SGB VI).[75]

Similarly, according to Article 55(3) of Regulation No 883/04, paragraphs 1 and 2 shall apply mutatis mutandis where the legislation of one or more Member States provides that a right to a benefit cannot be acquired in the case where the person concerned is in receipt of a benefit of a different kind, payable under the legislation of another Member State, or of other income. The relevant article 46c(5) of Regulation No 1408/71 contained the same provision. It is argued that the wording and the content of this rule may in certain cases have the unfortunate consequence that this

[75] Schuler (2015), p. 361.

rule essentially intervenes in the national hierarchy of pensions.[76] However, as Article 87(9) of Regulation No 883/04 stipulates, Article 55 of this Regulation shall apply only to pensions not subject to Article 46c of Regulation No 1408/71 on the date of application of this Regulation.

References

Cornelissen R (1998) The principle of territoriality and the Community regulations on social security. EDKA (Social Security Law Review), p 698, footnote 35

European Commission – MISSOC (2024) Comparative tables, Denmark, 1 January 2024. https://www.missoc.org/missoc-database/comparative-tables. Accessed 25 Nov 2024

IKA (Social Security Institution) (1996) – Directorate of international social security relations-Department of EEC pensions, Circular No 16/96, Reference No S07/GEN, Athens, 8-2-1996, subject: Reforming and supplementing the guidelines on the application of EEC Regulations No 1408/71 and 574/72, p 75

IKA (Social Security Institution) (2010) – Directorate of international social security relations, Circular No 28/2010, Reference Number D-21, Athens, 8-4-2010, subject: Guidelines for the application of Community Regulations No 883/04 and 987/09, p 3

Pennings F (2015) EU social security law, 6th edn. Intersentia, Cambridge- Antwerp-Portland

Schuler R (2015) Regulation (EC) No 883/2004 – Article 53. In: Fuchs M, Cornelissen R (eds) EU social security law – a commentary on EU Regulations 883/2004 and 987/2009. C.H. BECK – Hart- Nomos, Baden- Baden, p 358

Verschueren H (2009) Regulation 883/2004 and invalidity and old-age pensions. Eur J Soc Secur 155

Zacharis G (2014) Minimum social security protection benefits and coordination: challenges and problems. EDKA (Social Security Law Review), p 83

[76] Ibid.

Chapter 8
Conclusion

Taking a look back at the main findings, we could generally observe that there are divergent views in academic legal writing as to the evolution of the coordination rules, as well as the interpretation provided by the case-law.

As already mentioned, the Regulation 883/2004 on coordination of social security systems does not provide a definition of the term 'social security systems' despite the title of this legal instrument and despite the fact it entails a large number of definitions of the concepts used therein. This lack of definitions has an impact on the application of Coordination Regulation trying to answer the question which pension schemes fall under its scope. In parallel, the social role of supplementary pension rights is highlighted. Coordination Regulation tends to provide a broad protection of pension rights including both main and supplementary pension schemes. However, it is the member states that will decide if they bring their supplementary pension schemes under Coordination Regulation utilizing the possibility provided i.e. the right to declarations.

In the discussion regarding the pension schemes falling within the scope of the Regulation, we reached the conclusion that the Regulation adopts the formal criterion with the intermediate requirement of a public investiture of the schemes. In order to protect their social function, supplementary pension schemes could be placed under the scope of the Regulation. The application of the Regulation to these schemes can better protect the pension rights of the migrant workers as well as the actual operation of these schemes compared to the relative Directives. Further, the CJEU proceeds to elements such as solidarity, mandatory or optional affiliation to a scheme, but there are many cases where contradictory judgments are observed. In light of the complexity of the pension systems, the author concludes that Coordination Regulation sets out the simplest criteria that could be selected and be fulfilled. Hence, it includes any pension scheme that a member state is willing to place under the coordination mechanism putting forward the social function of pension rights.

Pension benefits are a key aspect of social protection in the European Union. We presented which benefits are considered pension benefits for the purposes of

A. Tsetoura, *Pension Rights and Free Movement of Persons*,
https://doi.org/10.1007/978-3-031-91127-9_8

Coordination Regulation, namely, social security benefits to be distinguished from social assistance and special non-contributory cash benefits. In principle, social assistance is excluded from the scope of Coordination Regulation. However, the Court interprets the social security benefit in the broad sense accepting certain characteristics traditionally pertaining to social assistance. The need of clarification is greater regarding the special non-contributory benefits, on which the coordination pension rules do not apply. In general, it could be observed that there is a persistent tension between contributory and non-contributory benefits reflecting the perceptions of the various Member States regarding the principle of solidarity.

Further, we examined the issues arising from the coordination of pay-as-you-go and funded systems. The problematic implementation of Coordination Regulation concerning the new provisions was pointed out. For this purpose, we have advanced our reasoning and referred to the necessity of a clear definition of the pension right in order to enable it to be 'portable'.

Analyzing the new provisions on funded systems and concluding that they are not appropriate, we have put forward more specific proposals. In our opinion, the Coordination Regulation could "borrow" certain techniques from the national legal context of member states with funded schemes where the national legislator provides for options promoting the internal mobility of the insured persons. Additionally, we conclude to our own suggestions of revision of the Coordination Regulation taking into account the Directive on supplementary pensions as well.

More specifically, the question is how to coordinate funded systems but also how to coordinate these systems with pay-as-you-go systems. The transfer of the capital representing the value of the pension should be provided for, especially in the context of funded systems, and then the appropriate more complex arrangements should be selected, combining the characteristics of both categories of systems. In particular, the methods of transferring pension rights may include the so-called 'statistical insurance equivalent' method (Casta case). The latter consists in calculating the real value of a future and contingent pension benefit, the amount of which is generally reduced to take account of the early nature of the payment and the risk of the beneficiary before the date on which the benefit becomes due, or the so-called 'lump sum redemption' method, under which that amount is obtained from the sum of the contributions paid by the insured person and his employer, to which interest may be added. However, there may also be other methods, in so far as the amount to be transferred essentially represents the pension rights acquired on the basis of the worker's previous activities. The question is, in view of the consideration of the pension right as a clearly definable right, whether it is possible to provide capital transfer options from each system.

The conclusion drawn is that the pension right should be clearly identifiable and defined regardless the methods selected for its determination and definition. The principle of favour as a general principle should, in our opinion, be viewed in light of the provision on methods for securing the pension rights of those wishing to move, even in cases where such methods might not be provided for at a national level.

As already seen, the funded system, which ensures the clearly defined individual portion of each insured person due to the close connection of contributions and benefits, cannot be ruled out from the principle of solidarity. The fact that some contributions are capitalized and each insured person acquires ownership of the account or that even today's contributions do not finance today's pensions as in the pay-as-you-go system, but tomorrow's pensions, does not mean that the service of specific social goals cannot be envisaged. Indeed, as highlighted, even a fully-funded system can shift the balance from high-wage earners to low-wage earners, i.e. have redistributive effects, while at the same time maintaining full funding.[1]

The coordination of pay-as-you-go and funded schemes (as well as mixed schemes) remains a field that requires further improvement aiming at a better social protection of pension rights. Because of the complexity characterising the pension schemes, there is the necessity of new descriptive provisions giving certain options of "mobility of pension rights".

In the same vein, the Court has to consider if it will continue to compare the amount of the pension between migrants and non-migrants or nationals and foreigners in the context of free movement and equal treatment. This might be the case because the various national provisions in the field of pensions are particularly diverse and complex. This set of principles might take on a different meaning, namely to be applied with the aim of finding out whether the same options are provided. The options provided by national systems in cases of internal movement or withdrawal from a system could be compared with the options provided by the coordination system in cases of cross-border movement and withdrawal from a system for the transition to another system of another state.

The equal or higher status of the migrant[2] or the principle of favourability as a more general principle, according to our view, should be seen in the light of the provision of methods for ensuring the pension rights of those who wish to move even in cases where such methods are not provided for at national level. As a possible proposal, we also mentioned the creation of a common European fund for the compensation of states that may be burdened with additional costs of covering potential losses from movements in order to prevent migrants from suffering losses.

Similarly, the creation of a new European solidarity fund for the reimbursement of healthcare costs has been proposed by introducing solidarity elements into reimbursement procedures, which would be financed by all Member States taking into account various parameters (the number of insured persons, but also the general economic situation of a particular Member State).[3] Regardless of the type of benefits, the coordination regulations are argued to not adequately address the sharing of burdens between the Member States concerned in a given situation, although certain economic challenges or the new mobility of pensioners or other inactive persons lead to the search for a more realistic and fair sharing of the burdens resulting from coordination.[4] However, other options that are administratively much more

[1] Barr and Diamond (2008), p. 36, footnote no. 2.

[2] Rennuy (2011), p. 316.

[3] Jorens et al. (2013), p. 52.

[4] Ibid.

manageable could be considered to deal with a situation that proves to be very disadvantageous for one of the States concerned: instead of fixing each refund individually, the amount to be refunded could be determined on the basis of average costs and general statistics on the persons concerned.[5]

Moreover, a series of cases was presented in order to show the interpretative approach of the Court and its impact on the anti-overlapping rules and thus pension rights. It is shown that the principle of favourability has been applied as a general and autonomous principle regardless Petroni principle from the namesake judgement which established the principle at issue. In fact, we criticised the reasoning of the Petroni judgment, as the Court did not apply its line of reasoning established in respect of Article 46 of the previous Coordination Regulation 1408/71. As we argue, the evolution of the anti-overlapping rules would be different if there had been a different direction in this crucial judgment. In the cases following Petroni, the Court sometimes reaffirmed and sometimes derogated from Petroni applying the (universal) principle of favourability independently from Petroni. Furthermore, the amendment of Article 46 of Regulation 1408/71 was presented in order to enlighten the different legal positions before and after Petroni which had as a consequence a strengthening of the anti-overlapping rules. As we argue, in its endeavour not to derogate from preventing any damage to the migrant, the Court ends with a precarious case-law. In the same context, the equal treatment of migrant and non-migrant pensioners was analysed.

Hence, as a primarily important finding, we highlight the emergence of the principle of favourability of the migrant as a more general principle that exceeds or absorbs or in some way overturns the Petroni decision. Deviating from the broader jurisprudential principle of favourability that had already been formed and continued to be applied after the Petroni decision, the Court's interpretation led to the replacement of one Community anti-overlapping provision by several provisions. Consequently, the application of national anti-overlapping rules and their complex interaction with the anti-overlapping rules of the Regulation has become challenging. As we have seen, the general principle of favourability as the choice of the most favourable solution each time between the national and European system and the application of the respective principles offered functional solutions. On the contrary, after the Petroni decision, the national anti-overlapping rules were strengthened.[6]

The benefits of the same kind and the benefits of the different kind were presented through the case-law. On the one hand, the practical effects of the anti-overlapping rules were examined in view of the existing interpretative approach; there is a significant pension loss due to the application of the anti-overlapping rules following a certain direction. On the other hand, the practical effects of the anti-overlapping rules were presented in view of our approach following a different direction. Therefore, we proposed a specific interpretative approach for the anti-overlapping rules that does not result in a drastic decrease of pension, which, however, we proved

[5] Ibid.

[6] Pennings (2015), p. 222.

it can happen by applying the current academic approach. Making mathematic calculations to prove that pension loss would be limited following our suggestion, we insist on the importance of this application of anti-overlapping rules for ensuring the pension rights of the European citizens.

Undoubtedly, the content given by the CJEU to the concept of the principle of free movement goes beyond the text of the relevant provisions of the Treaty, as with a series of its decisions, the Court gave from the first Regulations a much more favourable content for migrants than what the letter of the provisions allowed.[7] The role of the CJEU is therefore considered to be catalytic in interpreting the initially de facto restrictive texts that referred primarily to homo economicus, so that with its telological method of interpretation it contributed to the shaping of a European social policy that places man at the centre of European construction.[8]

However, the lack of clarity, the descriptive wording, the case-by-case and fragmentary nature of the provisions of the Regulation are elements that make its interpretation and application in practice complicated.[9] At the same time, part of the theory leans towards harmonisation to address practical problems that may arise from the application of the Regulation. Thus, sometimes proposals are made for harmonisation and sometimes for simplification based on the difficulties of dealing with certain overlaps of national legislation or gaps in protection. In particular, Pieters and Van Steenkiste have proposed in the past the creation of the 'Thirteenth State', as an alternative to the existing Coordination Regulations, the creation of a European social security system with an inherent dynamic aimed at harmonising national social security systems.[10] The design of such a system would initially aim to protect migrants, financed by contributions from employees and employers and administered in accordance with European law, while over time non-migrants could also choose to be insured in it if they prefer it compared to their own national system.[11]

Other proposals are based on maintaining national social security systems as they are, making national social security provisions internationally effective, preventing double protection or gaps in protection without changing the substance of the coordination law.[12] It is, thus, proposed to reduce the provisions of the Regulation to a minimum and perhaps create a separate legal instrument with a universally applicable set of rules and principles (unified coordination system), a development that is questionable whether it is desirable.[13]

However, the reform of the pension systems of the Member States has also been supported with a view to a coordinated Pan-European pension system which will be

[7] Runft (1991), p. 130.

[8] Mavridis (2004), p. 834.

[9] Tsampasi (2000), p. 2.

[10] Pieters and Van Steenkiste (1993), pp. 14–15.

[11] Pieters and Van Steenkiste (1993), p. 10.

[12] Pieters (1997), p. 177; Eichenhofer (1999), p. 411; Eichenhofer (2000), p. 234.

[13] Eichenhofer (2000), p. 234.

based on unlimited mobility between professions, sectors and regions, but also between stages of the life cycle and family structures, in a European concept of solidarity, while at the same time allowing for national preferences in targeted levels of mandatory benefits or contributions and the redistribution of wealth.[14]

On the other side, there is the view that brevity does not always imply simplicity.[15] It is argued that the Commission could elaborate specific chapters to be added to Regulation 883/2004 for each of the types of benefits, as it is stressed that for a truly effective modernisation, more coordination rules are required in the Regulation, not fewer.[16] We tend to agree with this view, because as our research has shown, the descriptive nature of the previous Regulation, even its lengthy provisions, contributed to a clearer understanding of their meaning. Ultimately, simplification means reducing problems and this sometimes requires even more rules.[17]

As is well known, EU law, and therefore the Coordination Regulation, is at the same time national law, that is to say, the Regulation has direct effect in the domestic legal order, is directly applied by the Administration and the National Courts and is required to coexist with the national social security system in force in each country.[18] This further implies that the position of the national judge is of strategic importance.[19] If a judge considers that it is impossible to interpret his/her domestic legislation in accordance with EU law, he/she is obliged not to apply it and even to apply the provisions of EU law instead of the provisions of domestic legislation, unless this results in a deterioration of the legal situation of citizens.[20] The importance of the obligation to directly protect the rights which individuals derive from the EU legal order is by no means negligible, since the Court of Justice entrusts the national judge with a particularly crucial task.[21]

In conclusion, we should note that the coordination system constitutes a system of legal settlement of cross-border social security situations that has been in operation for more than 50 years. It can therefore only be based on a coherent set of rules that will promote unification but at the same time respect the perception of the concepts of social security and solidarity in each national system separately. Otherwise, there is a risk of losing the consensus on which this system is based, as is social security itself, which is identified with participation in a community. The possible expansion of the broader community of solidarity that the EU constitutes can only take place with the corresponding consensus and with the time it requires. Under this spectrum, the value of case law and the role of the Court are not to be underestimated in any manner.

[14] Holzmann (2003), pp. 28–30.

[15] Sakslin (2000), p. 171; Pennings (2005), p. 260.

[16] Pennings (2005), p. 260.

[17] Ibid.

[18] Tsampasi (2000), p. 2.

[19] Mavridis (2004), p. 828.

[20] Mavridis (2004), p. 830.

[21] Ibid.

In any case, a more careful approach is encouraged which will be coherent and, if we may be allowed to use the phrase, will not seem haunted by the fear of not reaching a favourable outcome for the migrant. In our opinion, such an approach led in the Petroni case to the incompatibility of the provision of Article 46, paragraph 3 of Regulation 1408/71. This resulted in a decisive change in the rules of coordination, not necessarily for the better; in the end, the general principle of favourability that had inspired the coordination system for the benefit of migrants was overturned.

It is therefore one thing to protect the social security rights of migrants from potential losses, and another to develop a contradictory case law that negates legal certainty itself, just to reach a favourable outcome, at the given moment and at any price. Let us seek more, but following the pace that ensures good cooperation and legal certainty at all times.

References

Barr N, Diamond P (2008) Reforming pensions, principles and policy choices. Oxford University Press, Oxford – New York

Eichenhofer E (1999) Reform des Europäischen Sozialrechts. In: Schulte B, Barwig K (eds) Freizügigkeit und Sozialrecht. Nomos-Verlag, Baden-Baden

Eichenhofer E (2000) How to simplify the co-ordination of social security. Eur J Soc Secur 2/3

Holzmann R (2003) Toward a Coordinated Pension System in Europe: Rationale and Potential Structure, revised study prepared for the joint Watson Wyatt & Deutsches Institut fuer Wirtschaftsforschung (WW-DIW) Lecture on Issues in Pension Reform, Berlin, September 26, 2003, and the NDC Conference in Sandhamm, Sweden, September 28–30, 2003. https://www.worldbank.org/ext/en/home. Accessed 28 Dec 2024

Jorens Y (ed), Spiegel B (ed), Fillon J-C, Strban G (2013) trESS Think Tank report - Key challenges for the social security coordination, Regulations in the perspective of 2020, Training and Reporting on European Social Security Project DG EMPL/B/4 - VC/2012/1110

Mavridis P (2004) Free movement of persons, workers and services, as a basic principle of European integration. Their employment and social security, Social Security Review (EDKA)

Pennings F (2005) Inclusion and exclusion of persons and benefits in the new coordination regulation. In: Dougan M, Spaventa E (eds) Social welfare and EU law. Hart Publishing, Oxford

Pennings F (2015) European social security law. Intersentia, Cambridge – Antwerp – Portland

Pieters D (1997) Towards a radical simplification of social security co-ordination. In: Schouckes P (ed) Prospects of social security co-ordination. Acco, Leuven

Pieters D, Van Steenkiste S (1993) The thirteenth state, towards a European Community social insurance scheme for intra-community migrants. Acco, Leuven

Rennuy N (2011) Assimilation, territoriality and reverse discrimination. Eur J Soc Law

Runft H (1991) European integration and social security of returnees, delimitation of community and national social security law. Ant. N. Sakkoulas, Athens-Komotini

Sakslin M (2000) Social security co-ordination - adapting to change. Eur J Soc Secur 2

Tsampasi A (2000) Thoughts and observations on issues of community social security law. Social Security Review (EDKA) January

The manufacturer's authorised representative in the EU is Springer Nature Customer Service Centre GmbH, Europaplatz 3, 69115 Heidelberg, Germany. If you have any concerns regarding our products, please contact ProductSafety@springernature.com

Printed and bound by CPI Group (UK) Ltd, Croydon, CR0 4YY
30/09/2026
02225599-0005